By Courtesy of Colonel Creighton Webb

JEAN DE RESZKE

JEAN DE RESZKE

AND THE GREAT DAYS
OF OPERA

BY CLARA LEISER

WITH A FOREWORD BY
AMHERST WEBBER

GREENWOOD PRESS, PUBLISHERS
WESTPORT, CONNECTICUT

REVERENTLY DEDICATED
TO THE MEMORY OF MY MOTHER
AND TO ALL OTHER
LOVERS OF SONG
C. L.

122925

Originally published in 1934
by Minton, Balch & Company, New York

First Greenwood Reprinting 1970

Library of Congress Catalogue Card Number 74-109766

SBN 8371-4256-3

Printed in the United States of America

PREFACE

A CRITICAL DISCUSSION of David Garrick as an actor which appeared in the *Theatrical Review*, or *Annals of the Drama*, of 1763, ended thus: "Upon a review of the whole, we will venture to affirm, that impartial Justice must pronounce Mr. Garrick as the First of his Profession: and that the amazing Blaze of his Excellencies greatly obscures, if not totally eclipses, his Defects."

When one considers that in the case of Jean de Reszke a like valuation is placed, almost unanimously, not only upon his abilities as an operatic artist but also upon his qualities as a man, it is interesting to speculate on how a truthful book about him would have been received a few years ago, during the vogue for biographies which seemed less concerned about presenting "the whole man" than about smashing idols. Almost any writer who had set out to "debunk" the great Polish tenor would, I feel sure, have given up the task in despair, for want of supporting materials.

My own anxiety (quite apart from a disinclination to trample upon the sensibilities of living relatives of the de Reszkes) was of a somewhat different nature. The more I read about Jean, the more I discussed him with his friends, his fellow artists and his pupils, the more I realized that not only might it prove very difficult to secure belief in the truly "amazing Blaze of his Excellencies," but that so much goodness might make pretty dull reading. For any defects Jean may have had were certainly greatly obscured if not totally eclipsed. To illustrate: One of the first people I interviewed was Mrs. Anton Seidl. She dwelt on his lovable nature, on his simplicity and generosity, and then added that "Tony" and she considered him a perfect artist. I agreed that as an artist Jean must have been almost perfect: but I ventured to add that there were probably some natural frailties; that as a

v

human being he could hardly have been perfect. Her answer
was: "There *were* no faults! and if anybody tries to tell you
otherwise—well, it simply isn't true!"

Mrs. Seidl's comment represents the attitude of almost
every one with whom I discussed my subject by letter or in
person. Occasionally, after careful questioning and a suggestion that I did not want to be charged with whitewashing my
subject, some one might admit that perhaps there was just a
hint of selfishness in Jean, but he would quickly add: "You
mustn't write that, though. It wasn't a selfishness that harmed
anybody. It just helped him to concentrate on his work, so
that he would be a better artist."

The response to the announcement of my undertaking
was in itself a clear indication of the place Jean and his
brother Edouard held, and still hold, in the esteem and affections of the men and women whose lives were touched by
theirs, whether directly or through the medium of their art.
It also silenced any doubt I may have had whether, even if
the difficulties of treating one art in the terms of another could
be overcome, Jean de Reszke was of sufficient importance as
the subject of a book to warrant the labor necessary to secure
even a fairly satisfactory result.

Within a few weeks following my request for certain
kinds of information, more than a hundred people wrote to
me, from places as far apart as Portugal and Alaska, and
the stream of letters still continues; friendly letters, offering
various kinds of help, giving useful information, and almost
invariably expressing pleasure that some one had undertaken
the task. I wish it were possible to specify in just what manner all these people, many of whom I have since come to
know personally, have contributed to this book, but lack of
space forbids even a list of their names. I can only hope that
if they read the book they will be pleased to realize that they
helped to make it.

Let me cite just one of the many spontaneous acts of
generosity for which I am grateful. When Mrs. Henry T.
Finck, widow of the New York music critic, learned of my
proposed book, she informed me that she had written her
reminiscences of Grand Opera in the de Reszke period, and
suggested that as they had not been published the chapter on
"the boys," as she and her husband called Jean and Edouard,
might be useful. She read it to me, and asked: "Is there anything there that you could use?" When I replied, "Indeed—

much!" she turned the entire chapter over to me, to use in any way I might choose.

I want to express my deep gratitude to Mlle. Minia de Reszke, and to Baron Leopold de Kronenberg and his son, for the hospitality and help accorded me during my stay in Poland. They did everything possible to assist me in my work, granting me free access to family records, and giving me many photographs and information which, I need hardly say, could not have been secured from any other source. I would specially thank Dr. M. Marchlewski, Polish Consul-General in New York, and the Foreign Office at Warsaw, for doing everything in their power to facilitate my researches. I also received generous help from other people in Warsaw, chiefly from Mr. Leopold Kotnowski, President of the Polish-American Chamber of Commerce, and Mr. Clayton Lane, U. S. Commercial Attaché.

Mr. Amherst Webber, Jean's friend and associate for many years, and now of the Webber-Douglas School of Singing and Dramatic Art, in London, has shown me much kindness. Generously he gave me counsel, paved the way for certain essential interviews, and then took time out of a busy life to go over the manuscript and read the whole book in proof, making valuable suggestions. In addition to all this, Mr. Webber consented to write a Foreword. I welcome the opportunity to thank him publicly.

Mr. Bernard Shaw very generously allowed me to reproduce a letter of reminiscence concerning the de Reszkes, and to quote freely from his books of music criticism.

I wish also to thank Mr. Walter Johnstone-Douglas for helpful information, and in particular for permitting me to reprint his article entitled "Jean de Reszke's Principles of Singing"; and the Editor of *Music and Letters*, in which journal it first appeared.

I am likewise deeply indebted to my publishers, and particularly to Mr. Garfield Howe, for criticism, encouragement and patience, and for making the Index. For assistance of various kinds I thank the Polish Institute of Arts and Letters and its gracious Director, Mrs. E. B. Cullis; Mr. Reynaldo Hahn; M. Louis Vachet, Jean's secretary; my own singing teacher, Miss Anita Loew, of New York, and Professor Max Klein of Vienna; Philip King, of the editorial staff of *Musical America*; Selma B. Waterman, Florence Fehrer Wilson, Bronislaus Gliwa, Miecislaus Haiman, Mrs. Clinton P. Farrell, Alfred J. Blackman, D. H. Silvius, Jr., Carol Hubbard, Avis Bliven Charbonnel, and the Honorable Cornelius F. Collins. Among Jean's pupils I owe special thanks to Rachel Morton, Mrs. S. F. Low (the Florence Stevens mentioned in the book), and Charlotte Lund. I have also to thank many authors and publishers for allowing me to quote from the books of which particulars are given in the Appendix. I am indebted to many friends for helping me to collect the illustrations and for loaning originals for reproduction. Last, but very far indeed from least, I am grateful for the understanding and various help of Mr. F. Buckley Hargreaves.

Any errors on my part have been committed in good faith, and I take all responsibility for them.

It is a commonplace that the written word bears inadequate testimony to the achievements of a great actor, and I am well aware that, lacking the aids of gesture, facial expression, and, above all, voice, written language is a poor medium through which to attempt to portray the greatness of Jean de Reszke, from whose art thousands received, as some one said he had received from Thomas Betterton the actor, "more strong impressions of what is great and noble in human nature than from the arguments of the most solid philosophers, or the descriptions of the most charming poets." But no other medium exists. If, therefore, a few readers can recapture even a part of the thrill of a "De Reszke Night" at the Opera, if here and there a student of the lyrical drama finds something to help him in working towards an artistic ideal, I shall feel proud and happy.

CLARA LEISER

NEW YORK, February 1934

CONTENTS

ILLUSTRATIONS

REPRODUCTIONS IN FACSIMILE

FOREWORD

BY AMHERST WEBBER

SOME thirty years have passed since Jean de Reszke made his last appearance on the stage, and although books have been written about many of those who sang with him, no attempt has yet been made to set down a record of his career. Miss Leiser has valiantly stepped into the breach and has accomplished her task in the face of very great difficulties.

Jean never kept a diary; he was not a great writer of letters, and he kept very few of those he received. The only available records of his life had therefore to be gleaned from short articles and from conversations with his surviving relatives and friends. Miss Leiser has been indefatigable in collecting such material and has succeeded in piecing it together into a consecutive and interesting narrative. Her book will be especially welcome to those of us who can still remember how this singer "gave to every word the fullness of its meaning and to every note the perfection of sound." *

But it cannot fail to have a far wider appeal as well; for Jean de Reszke will always remain a great figure in the annals of Grand Opera. The remarkable operatic revival which began towards the close of the last century both in England and America was in a large measure due to the peculiar prestige which he enjoyed at that time in both countries. He was the first to show how rôles such as Tristan and Siegfried could be beautifully sung and not merely declaimed in the manner which, *faute de mieux,* had been accepted up to his time. His reading of these parts was full of exquisite poetry and tenderness. Incisive declamation was not wanting whenever the music called for it, but never at the sacrifice of beauty of tone, for his singing always had the quality which one of his French critics described as "le charme dans la force." These moving interpretations of his came as a revelation to many and proved

* Camille Bellaigue: obituary notice in the *Revue des Deux Mondes.*

triumphantly that *bel canto* was not only possible, in the later Wagner works, but essential to a complete understanding of them.

In the early days of my long friendship with Jean it was my privilege to spend two months with him every year at his home in Poland and to assist him and his brother Edouard in studying the later Wagner rôles. This was his only holiday in the year, but it was not spent in resting his voice. His energy was inexhaustible. Every day he was up at cock-crow to see his yearlings exercise; after that he worked at his new roles continuously throughout the morning and for an hour or more in the afternoon as well. Then in the evenings he would sing away into the small hours, trying the effect of various kinds of voice production and tone color on any phrases with which he had not been satisfied during his previous season.

He never lost his affection for the operas that had thrilled him in his younger days, and many of their hackneyed melodies, which I, in my ignorance, had hitherto branded as trivial and antiquated, seemed suddenly to be alive and full of meaning when he sang them. No idiom of musical expression came amiss to him; but singing always appealed to him more strongly than other forms of music, because to him the expressiveness of words meant almost as much as that of the music which accompanied them. That is why it is almost impossible to recall any musical phrase one has heard him sing without also remembering its words and the peculiar charm he gave them.

In his teaching days he constantly urged his pupils to cultivate "l'amour de la parole." The learning of the music of a new rôle gave Jean very little trouble, but he spent no end of time and care in getting exactly the right color into every phrase. He would not be satisfied until he had succeeded in expressing the whole of the beauty which he felt to be inherent in both words and music. He was always a very severe critic of his own work and never ceased to be a student up to the end.

During his last years he was as completely absorbed in his pupils as he had been in his own career. He was in full possession of his voice and of his wonderful energy right up to his last short illness; so he died in harness, a very great artist and a most beloved friend.

JEAN DE RESZKE

THE PARENTS (JAN AND EMILJA RESZKE)

OVERTURE

EVEN the most sensitive music critic, even one who can command that eloquent language which comes closest to the flow of beautiful musical sounds, finds it strangely difficult to set down in words what he has felt in listening to a truly great artist; and of all the arts, that of the singer is at once the most personal and the most fugitive. When a singer dies, what remains—of even the greatest—especially if he lived before the day of phonograph records? The dead poet has life in his published work, the composer in the symphony which outlives him; but what of him whose art consists in portraying human emotions, through so perishable a medium as the human voice?

Yet, mention the name of Jean de Reszke, and you evoke at once memories of experiences in beauty that seem peculiarly alive, many years after; experiences of which practical men say: "The seats seemed costly to a young struggling business man, but they represented one of my best investments, for to hear Jean whenever I could, kept a high mark always before me"; or, "Now, my musical interests, though keen, are extremely narrow, and do *not* include singing, but my prejudices against vocal music disappeared when I heard Jean de Reszke sing that Prize Song." In 1933, thirty-three years after the great tenor had last sung at the Covent Garden Opera House in London, a critic ended his review of a performance of T r i s t a n u n d I s o l d e with the cry: "Wanted, a Jean de Reszke!"

Around this artist's name is the aura of the great Victorian age—an age rich in artists; but although there are differing evaluations of his eminent contemporaries in the other arts, he stands alone as the supreme interpreter of the musical drama. "Where words leave off, music begins," wrote Heine, and, one may add, where the art of other singers left off, Jean de Reszke's began. It was the glory of this Polish artist so to

3

use the human voice that his singing flooded the hearts of his listeners with a dreamy consciousness of beauty, quickening their souls, and reaffirming for them the eternal verities of courage and loyalty and love; for it was out of that domain that he spoke to them most directly and poignantly, helping them to a vicarious expression of thoughts and feelings that lie too deep for ordinary speech. Like another and gentler Prometheus, he reached into the celestial regions where music dwells, seized some of the supernal splendor, and brought it down to beauty-hungry, love-hungry mortals.

When other singers are discussed, some personal eccentricity is usually mentioned, some astonishing high note or particularly crashing effect; but always, when two or three are gathered together and the talk turns to a "De Reszke night," you will hear of the beauty with which Jean clothed the *words* he sang; of the comforting, winning, glowing, and, sometimes, the utterly sad and despairing tones with which he sang words of love. For music comes from and reaches to the heart; this Jean understood deeply. Once, while practicing an amorous phrase, another artist asked him, "Where should one lean the voice in singing this?" and the laconic reply was: "On the heart." Musset must have been lamenting the loss of such a voice as Jean's when he wrote:

> C'est cette voix du cœur qui seule au cœur arrive,
> Que nul autre que toi ne nous rendra jamais.

"But," you may say, "the man has been dead for some years, and he had not sung for a quarter of a century before his death. His voice is gone. There is nothing left." When Sarah Bernhardt died, the late C. E. Montague wrote: "As long as any two persons who saw Bernhardt, live, and can communicate, the world retains some sort of corporate sense of the nature of her greatness: after that it may be that her death, now unfinished, will become complete." Her death, *now unfinished*—what a glorious implication that is! In this rich sense Jean de Reszke lives abundantly; and will, even after the death of the last two persons who heard him sing on the stage; for those who did hear him considered it so rare a privilege that they tried to share it in some small way with their children and their children's children. Shortly before Jean the man died, at the Villa Vergemère in Nice, in 1925, a friend asked the celebrated tenor to sing a few notes for his little daughter, so that she might treasure the memory of having heard the incomparable Jean de Reszke. Pressing the pretty blonde head to his heart, Jean sang, out of the plenitude of his power and his memories, Romeo's words of loving adjuration: "Ah! reste, reste encore en mes bras enlacée!" Then he said to the child: "Once, at least, in your life, you have been Juliet!" And that is how, through the mists of bequeathed memories, "the centuries kiss and commingle."

What, then, was this art? Whence came its power, and how did it communicate itself? The immortal Jean's hold on the imagination and affections of the public was attributable to his art and his personality. He inspired affection as well as admiration. (It is significant that almost every one spoke of him simply as Jean; nor was it merely to distinguish him from his likewise famous brother.) In him were met an imposing physique, intelligence, musicianship, a lovely voice, a generous heart, and charm—a peculiar magnetism which grew out of a profound understanding of the mysterious relationship between the forces of beautiful sound and the forces of soul. Socrates must have had such a human being in mind when he said: "The soul which has seen most of truth shall come to the birth as a philosopher, or artist, or some musical and loving nature."

Jean's outward life was singularly free from the exciting events and affairs which so often determine the biographer's choice of subject. His career played havoc with the tradition according to which a musical director strolling along may suddenly become aware of a wonderful voice arising from a ditch, and looking down, discover—a full-fledged tenor! (While such tenors may succeed in singing airs which are drilled into them, they are also frequently destined to earn the witticism of Berlioz, "performers on the larynx.") De Reszke was never "discovered" in that sense at all. To Jean himself it seemed that a career as a singing artist was almost unescapable; something to which he had been born and towards which all his youth tended. At the height of his fame he wrote to a fellow artist: "It seems to me that today I have more experience, more style and personality, but fundamentally I sing the way I sang as a child." Difficulties he did encounter, of course, but the struggles with poverty and misunderstanding that lend impetus to so many careers, he was fortunately spared. The sympathetic insight which some other artists acquire through the jolts of misfortune was his by the heritage of exquisite artistic sensibility and poetic imagination.

He was perhaps the most imaginative operatic singer the world has known; certainly the greatest operatic lover. He became—utterly—the character he was portraying. It was peculiarly in his power, even in bodying forth virile, powerful emotions, to endow them with overtones of wistful charm. "I recall," writes the composer Reynaldo Hahn, "that in L e P r o p h è t e, when he cried, '*Roi du ciel et des anges*,' there was in his voice not only the exaltation of the warrior who hurls himself into battle, but also the affectionate humility of the young Saint John who rests his weakness on the breast of the Saviour."

As Romeo he was romantic, tender, pathetic; but what manliness and superb virility in the duel scene! "Hear his Romeo," wrote one critic, "and then, so far as that opera is concerned, go off into the wilderness and die. You will never hear it again without regret and pain!" As Lohengrin he was warmly human, and yet, true to his character as a transcendent being from another world, true also to the knightly element in his own character, he enveloped the rôle with a mystical effect that held his listeners spellbound. And when, having surpassed the Italians in their own operas, the French in theirs, he turned his talents to German opera, he proved anew the truth of Wagner's assertion that the human voice is the most beautiful organ of music. When it is used by an artist who can command the infinite variety of tone coloring of which the voice is capable, it makes even the most manifold combination of orchestral tints seem less wonderful. Jean served a twenty years' apprenticeship to Grand Opera before he sang Tristan and Siegfried, and then he astounded the musical world by the wealth of mingled emotion which he proved that a greatly endowed artist could convey in one single word of a language that had been called unsingable. No other artist has ever equaled the thrilling effect produced by Jean de Reszke when, in the delirium of the dying Tristan, he cried out, for the last time, "*Isolde!*" The critic of the London *World* best succeeded in describing it:

> Nothing struck me more than his singing of the phrase "Isolde" as he dies. It was most wonderful; not merely affecting as the despairing and adoring cry of a dying man thinking of the woman he worships, but far more than that. In it one hears not only love but death. It is the mysterious, whispering utterance of a spirit al-

ready far away; as if the soul, having started on its dark
journey, were compelled by its old and beautiful earthly
passion to pause, and to look back down the shadowy vista
to the garden of the world that it had left, to the woman
that it had left, perhaps forever, and to send down the
distance one last cry of farewell, one last dim murmur of
love, spectral, magical already with the wonder of another
world. Such an effect as this is utterly beyond the reach
of any one who is not a great artist. It is thrilling in its
imaginative beauty. It opens the gates as poetry does
sometimes and shows us a faint vision of a far-away
eternity.

Is it possible to crowd such a weight of significance into
one word of three short syllables? Jean de Reszke did, again
and again; and it requires no effort on the part of those who
heard him to recall the thrill. Down the arches of the years it
comes rushing upon them. For the art and the greatness of de
Reszke were never dismantled. He did not linger on the scene
to make a younger generation ask whether he had really been
so wonderful as their elders insisted. He had the wisdom and
the good taste to leave the stage while people could still ask
in dismay: "But why does he leave us now?" instead of saying
regretfully: "He should have retired some years ago."

FIRST ACT

THE BARITONE

1850-1883

A CERTAIN eighteenth century regiment of Prussian guards included a young man by the name of Jan Wilhelm Reszke.* He and his captain were courting the same girl, and as the situation developed it became doubly distasteful to the captain; for though interference in a love affair was irritating enough, to have his place in the lady's affections usurped by a mere *chorazy* (the lowest and now extinct grade of Prussian officer) was utterly intolerable, and the captain vowed to avenge the slight. One day when he encountered his successful rival during a military parade he hurled a remark at him, in the hearing of all the troops, which stung Chorazy Reszke so suddenly and so sharply that he dealt a blow to his superior officer's cheek before the captain's lips could close on the insult.

Gone the dream of a military career! For, notwithstanding bitter provocation, such an offense carried with it the death penalty, and Jan Wilhelm was sent to prison to bide the time of his execution. But he had endeared himself to Count Kalbreuth, General in charge of the regiment, and the Count, perhaps applauding the discrimination shown by the young woman, and sharing her preference for this high-spirited youth, decided that the penalty was out of proportion to the crime, and helped his friend Reszke to escape. The latter fled to Saxony, where he found refuge with his mother's uncle, Major von Zwicker, Commandant of Dresden. Here life was pleasant and easy, and Jan Wilhelm was popular in Dresden society. He married a daughter of the wealthy house of von Runckel, but the following year the birth of a son cost her her life, and before long the youthful father became enmeshed in financial difficulties which precipitated a succession of quarrels with the von Runckel family. He was not equipped to earn a living, could find no employment in Saxony, and on the advice of a friend went to Poland, hoping to join the Polish army.

* Jan is pronounced Yahn: Reszke, Reshke (both e's short).

In Poland he might have found his place and been happy. There where, between the Baltic Sea and the Carpathian Mountains, Slavonic tribes had for hundreds of s roamed over the vast plain cut by the Elbe and Vistula Rivers, the Reszke tribe had also made their home. As far back as the thirteenth century they had inhabited that part of Poland called the Mazowsze, the site of present-day Warsaw. From there they had migrated to various neighboring regions, to Prussia and to Saxony. The name was sometimes changed to Reschke, Reschker, or Reszkowski, but all branches of the family bore the Pruss arms.

Jan Wilhelm was well received in the land of his fathers, and secured an appointment as "captain instructor" in a Poznanian division of the army, but before he could assume his new duties he succumbed to an infectious disease raging in Warsaw. His five-year-old son, Jan Bogumił, had been taken into the home of Commandant von Zwicker, but he was not destined to live the gay life his father had enjoyed in Dresden, for the Commandant's days were also numbered, and upon his death the child was sent to Warsaw, where Baron von Runckel, a relative who held a high public office, befriended him. The generous plans of this good man were frustrated by his sudden death, and Jan Bogumił, fourteen years old, was left in a strange city, without relatives or friends and with very little money. Four times in this boy's short life had Death struck at his benefactors. He was sturdy, however, and though he left school reluctantly, for he had been making good progress, he lost no time in finding work to support himself. A talent for overcoming difficulties and a reputation for honesty and forthright dealing helped to make him, at twenty-nine, the head of an important business, and by 1830 one of the richest men in Warsaw, where he was highly esteemed as a citizen and loved for his liberality to the poor. His wife, Josefa, was a lateral descendant of King John III Sobieski.

As he grew older, Jan Bogumił longed to go back to Germany, once more to see his father's and his mother's people. His physician had prescribed a rest, suggesting a trip, and in the summer of 1835 Reszke set out, hoping to combine the quest for health with the search for relatives. Neither objective was attained, for he died on the way. His son Jan, born in 1818, was heir to the father's good qualities as a man and as a business man. The property bequeathed to him was made to pay profits, and he built the Hotel Saski, still standing in the heart of Warsaw. In 1843 he married the Countess Emilja Ufniarska, a Galician. These were the parents of the famous singers, Jean and Edouard de Reszke.

When for some reason it became necessary, in pre-Soviet times, for a Russian subject to reëstablish his right to be listed as a nobleman, certain requirements of the Department of Heraldry of the Russian Senate had to be satisfied, as provided by the Acts of March 14 1845 and December 12 1857. In the case of the Reszkes that need arose through the migration of some members of the family to Germany. The foregoing account is based on documents which Jean de Reszke's father submitted, in accordance with the requirements, to support his application for listing in the books of noblemen of the Gubernia (County) of Grodno. That right was finally sanctioned by Tsar Alexander III in 1890.

Various legendary backgrounds have been assigned to Jean de Reszke. He himself was by no means indifferent to social rank, but even if he could not, like Pooh-Bah, trace his ancestry to "a protoplasmal primordial atomic globule," Jean would have scorned to make answer to questions or assertions concerning his parentage, though he could not have been entirely unaware of the charge of arrogated nobility or of the whispers as to the identity of his father. He might indeed, had it seemed worth the trouble, have referred to a certain performance of H é r o d i a d e in 1884 and replied in the spirit of Napoleon, who said to a genealogist, "Friend, my patent of nobility comes from Montenotte," Montenotte having been his first great victory.

One of the most persistent rumors is that of the Hebraic strain in the de Reszkes. "Did you know that his father was a Jew?" some one will ask, and then, by way of confirmation, add: "Why, of course; he was a cantor in the synagogue at Warsaw." Jean did not lack some of the enviable qualities of the Hebrew, but it happens that his father was not a Jew. He and his forefathers were Protestants, and he lies buried in the Reszke plot in the Evangelical Cemetery of Warsaw; but his wife, the mother of Jean and Edouard, was a Roman Catholic, and the children were reared in that faith.

And of course the father was not a cantor, though he was deeply musical. He played the violin fairly well. He was the first, it is said, to advocate giving Wagnerian operas in Warsaw. Occasionally he composed simple songs for his pretty wife, an amateur singer of ability who lent her talents—frequently and entirely—to the relief of the needy. Years later Jean liked to speak of the time when he heard Trebelli sing the duet from S e m i r a m i d e with his mother. A biographical dictionary [1] records this concerning her:

> Reszke (Emilie née Ufniarska), cantatrice amateur à Warsovie, possède une voix puissante et dramatique, chante souvent pour les bonnes œuvres avec un véritable succès. Ayant voyagé en Italie, elle eut l'occasion d'entendre les chefs-d'œuvre des grands maîtres et les opéras des compositeurs à la mode. Dans un concert donné à Warsovie par la Société de bienfaisance elle chanta le rôle de Desdemona dans l'opéra d'Otello de Rossini au Grande théâtre et fut très applaudie.*

A similar notice appears in *Slownik Muszków Polskich Dawnych I Nowoczesnych* for the same year.[2]

Jan was an enterprising, respected citizen. He was appointed an honorary judge and a Chevalier of the Order of St. Stanislaus. Under his management and with the help of his energetic wife the Hotel Saski prospered. Warsaw was at that time a convenient stopping place for artists going to and from Paris, Berlin, and Moscow, and most of them stayed at the Saski. They were also cordially received in the adjoining home of the proprietor, where rehearsals of forthcoming operas frequently took place, as did many an impromptu concert in which Madame Reszke took part.

One day in January 1850 she was extremely uneasy. She was expecting the birth of her second child. Unlike many of her compatriots, she was not very superstitious; yet—if her baby came into the world on the thirteenth, would life be kind to it? "Go and sing a little," suggested the doctor, thinking that might ease her mind. In the joy of singing her anxiety disappeared, and a few hours later a son was born.

Some of those who stayed in the hotel that night may have read, years later, of a Polish artist whose audiences were bewitched by the beauty of his singing, and smiled to remember that early in the morning of January 14 1850 annoyance had been their only emotion upon being awakened by the

* "Reszke (Emilie née Ufniarska), amateur singer of Warsaw, possesses a powerful and dramatic voice, sings frequently for charity, with true success. Having traveled in Italy, she had the opportunity of hearing the chief works of the great masters and the operas of contemporary composers of fashion. In a concert given at Warsaw by the Benevolent Society she sang the rôle of Desdemona in the opera O t e l l o by Rossini at the Grand theater and was heartily applauded.

wailing of a newborn child; for Jean de Reszke's first whimperings could have been no more mellifluous than any other youngster's. His sister Emilia probably eyed him with curiosity no different from that which any first-born child bestows upon a newcomer who may deflect attention from himself.

In Weimar, that year, the white-haired Franz Liszt was conducting the very first performance of L o h e n g r i n—an opera this squirming bundle of new life was destined to enhance beyond the dearest dream of its composer. And thousands of miles away audiences marveled at the voice of a girl so little (she was only seven) that she had to stand on a table in order to be seen as well as heard. One day her voice was to blend with that of Jean de Reszke's and give new radiance to old operas. Adelina Patti made her first public appearance in the year of Jean's birth.

On March 17 1850 "at half past four in the afternoon, arrived [at the Registry Office] Jan Reszke, 32 years old, residing in Warsaw at the Kozia No. 62, in the presence of Władysław Ufniarski, Lieutenant of Artillery of the Troops of the Tsar of Russia, and another witness, and he presented a child of masculine sex, born in Warsaw in his residence on the day of January 14 of the current year at the hour of twelve and a half after midnight, of his wife Emilja, *née* Ufniarska, 23 years old. At the holy christening which took place this day, this child was given names Jan Mieczysław and his god-parents were Jan Władysław Kurc and Laura Trzcinska. The above act, after having been read aloud, was signed by us, together with the father and witnesses.

> Father Jan Bogdan, Head of the Parish
> Jan Reszke, Father
> Władysław Ufniarski, Godfather
> Jan Szepan Kulescha, witness." * [3]

This should end the speculation about Jean de Reszke's age at the height of his career. On December 22 1853 a brother was born to Emilia and Jan Mieczysław, and was named Edouard August.[4] On June 4 1855 a daughter, Josefa, was added to the family, and on June 12 1859 another son, Viktor, was born.

These five Reszke children grew up in a musical atmosphere. When Jan was eight years old he heard Liszt play, and

* Literal translation from the Polish.

the vision of the great man sitting at the piano, the sun gleaming on his silvery hair, was a lifelong memory. The children heard most of the famous artists of the day, and very early their mother taught them how to sing. All but Emilia responded quickly and pleasingly. She, however, learned to play the piano, and accompanied that first de Reszke quartet, composed of her brothers and sister. Viktor's natural voice, it is said, was even better than Jan's and Edouard's, but he never inclined toward an artistic career. Hard work of any kind held no appeal, and from childhood on he devoted himself to a masterly inactivity. Jan was always the leader, and at least a part of the reason for Edouard's enthusiasm lay in his adoration of his older brother. From his earliest years he regarded Jan as one in whom the elements had been so mixed that they had formed a being far superior to other mortals, and in his brother's career Edouard later sank some of the possibilities of his own, gladly and without a thought of sacrifice.

At the age of twelve Jan was choirboy and solo singer in the Carmelite Church of Warsaw. His earnestness and the sweetness of his voice alike impressed the congregation and soon he was their favorite. Once, on the occasion of a festival for which special music had been prepared, Jan failed to appear. When a messenger arrived to ask the reason, the youthful soloist sent back word that his throat was sore; he could not sing. Another messenger came, saying that every one was waiting; Jan simply must sing. The boy was not to be persuaded. Finally the priest himself came to plead with the youngster.

"I can't sing, Father. I couldn't sing *well*."

"But you *must* sing," replied the divine.

"No, I will not come."

"Jan, nobody else can sing the part as you do. If you will only come and try I will give you anything you want."

Silence for a moment, and then, his grave eyes half tearful, the sensitive mouth quivering, Jan said shyly: "Father, I get very poor marks in religion. If you will help me to get better marks in religion—I will sing."

Another priest was, however, compelled to make quite a different kind of appeal. The Reszkes used to spend the summer months at Wilanow, where the children sang in the village church. One Sunday a ripple of amusement passed through the less pious section of the congregation, while their

more devout brethren looked at the priest in outraged amazement. That dignitary could ill conceal his consternation, but
he was also amused. At the close of the service he called the
five children, even Emilia having been allowed to join in the
singing that day, and said: "Children, children! How can I
keep my mind on the mass when you sing such songs! You
make me want to think of other things." Instead of singing
a sacred song, the youngsters had rendered, and with gusto, a
rollicking operatic air.

Of operatic airs they had a larger store than even their
mother dreamed. "Those boys are never quiet unless they are
at the opera," she said one day to a caller who inquired about
Jan and Edouard. They were there more often than she
knew; for though they frequently attended *con permisio,* on
many an evening when she and her husband were enjoying
an opera from their *loge,* their two music-loving sons occupied
the gallery. On such nights the boys could enjoy the first two
acts of the opera to the full, but after the second intermission
they had to take turns in shooting frequent if hasty glances
at one particular *loge*; for the instant papa and mamma made
a move to leave, the children had to rush home, no matter how
absorbing the music or exciting the plot. In a trice they were
in bed. Had their mother turned back the bedclothes, she
must have been surprised to find her two sons lying there fully
dressed, boots and all, feigning sleep. As teacher she should
have been pleased at such breath control, even though as
housewife she might have viewed the scene in dismay.

But although music was of absorbing importance to this
entire family, it was not the only interest of the father. He was
intensely patriotic and zealous for the welfare of his fellow
Poles. Since he was also outspoken, he incurred the wrath of
the Russian government, and for being one of the leaders in
the unsuccessful uprising of 1863 he was sentenced to five
years' exile in Siberia. Warsaw mourned the fate of one of its
best loved citizens. On the eve of his departure the Polish
painter Joseph Simmler made a hurried sketch of the family
group, under the watchful eye of Russian guards.

Mother and children met the cruel blow courageously.
A portrait of Mme. Jan Reszke which hangs in the living-
room at "Skrzydlow" * reveals the qualities which helped her
to bear the responsibilities of both fatherhood and mother-

* Jean de Reszke's residential estate in Poland, where, thanks to the hospitality
of Edouard's daughter Minia, who now occupies it, a part of this book was written.

hood. Intelligence, energy, and determination mark that countenance in unusual degree. Her children were not to be deprived of their proper training. She managed the hotel and them too, and she was very stern. Edouard used to tell his own children that even when he was a grown man it seemed wonderful to him to reach up and discover that his ears were still there, so frequently and vigorously had they been boxed and pulled in his youth.

The softer influences also remained, however, and the mother continued to give her children singing lessons, though she did not intend singing to be their life work. Edouard was sent to an agricultural school. Jan was to become a lawyer, and he took his degree. But the love of singing, the memories of those evenings when he had heard his beloved compatriot Dobski and the Italian baritone, Antonio Cotogni, interfered with the pursuit of the law. Besides, he was frequently the soloist on special college occasions, and he took vocal lessons from Ciaffei, a retired Italian singer then teaching in Warsaw. It was Ciaffei who made the original error in training as a baritone a voice that was really tenor. It may be that he wanted to avoid overstraining a vocal apparatus which had just undergone a fundamental change, or he may have been deceived by the richness of the low tones. At any rate, Jan's voice was developed as a baritone. Several years later, Ciaffei, knowing of his pupil's admiration for Cotogni, wrote to that singer and asked him to take Reszke as a pupil. Cotogni was at Turin, learning a new rôle, and replied that he was too busy to give any one lessons, especially as Ciaffei had informed him that the youth in question, though talented, seemed to be "a little wild."

Nothing daunted by the refusal, Jan proceeded to Turin and presented himself to the popular baritone. Cotogni recognized the newcomer's genius, and, delighted at finding in one individual so many of the qualities necessary to a true operatic artist, he changed his mind and decided to give him all the help he could. Many years later he told other pupils of the boy's astounding capacity for learning; of how, if he heard an operatic rôle sung on the stage once, he knew the part almost entirely the next day. Whenever a new opera was being prepared, Jan learned his own part, and the parts of the other artists as well. For five years he worked and traveled with Cotogni, hearing and seeing—and above all studying—artists, operas, orchestras and their conductors, from both sides of the

THE EXILE

Painted by Joseph Simmler on the eve of the departure of Jan Reszke
for Siberia. Edouard's concern for Jean is apparent

curtain. But Cotogni, like Ciaffei, trained his talented pupil as a baritone.

During these years Edouard was courageously trying to become a good farmer, though he found it difficult to visualize himself as "the man with the hoe." When he returned to Warsaw for a vacation at the end of a two years' course, he was met at the station by his elder brother, whom he had not seen since he departed for the agricultural college in Germany. It was a joyful reunion, but Edouard noticed that when he spoke, his brother looked at him searchingly.

"Do you see anything wrong about me?" he asked.

"No-o, but where did you get that deep voice? You didn't talk like that when I saw you last."

"Don't you like it?"

"I can't tell yet. Let's hurry home. I must hear you sing, Edouard. Come along. Don't bother about your luggage. Hurry!"

Off they rushed, Jan dragging Edouard straight to the piano and making him sing scales and arpeggios over and over again.

"Splendid! splendid!" he exclaimed. "Let me hear that deep note. Once more! That's it! Magnificent!"

The mother and father, the latter now returned from exile, heard these strange bass notes and tiptoed in to learn what new singer had arrived in Warsaw. They had not seen Edouard for two years, and felt hurt because he had not sought them out at once, but Jan, excited with his discovery, waved aside the parental reproaches and protested: "You shan't make a farmer out of Edouard! Not with a voice like that! He must come to Italy with me. I know he can make a name for himself as a singer."

To Italy Edouard went, and studied with Steller. Some time later his father wrote to Cotogni, asking him to accept Edouard as a pupil too, but this the famous singer could not do. He sent Edouard, instead, to his friend Coletti, a retired operatic baritone.

IN THE MEANTIME the instruction Josephine received from her mother had been supplemented by lessons from Warsaw singing teachers, and for a year she had studied at the Conservatory of St. Petersburg with Mme. Nissen-Salomon, pupil of the celebrated Manuel Garcia the elder. In 1874, before she had reached her twentieth year, she was singing leading rôles at the Theatre Malibran in Venice. Many years earlier the English diarist Evelyn had had a taste of Venetian opera, with its "variety of sceanes," its "machines flying in the aire, and other wonderful motions," and thought it "taken altogether . . . one of the most magnificent and expensive diversions the wit of man can invent." Had he been there in January 1874 he might have attended the début, at the Theatre Fenice, of one called Giovanni di Reschi, who sang the part of Alfonso in L a F a v o r i t a; but he would probably not have recorded the event in the famous diary, for the new baritone, while achieving moderate success, caused no furor. Some of the critics noted that his voice had a tenor quality. He had, indeed, finished up the *cabaletta* with a ringing A natural!

A letter sent to the *Musical World* by one Michael Williams, and published on January 31 1874, describes the event thus:

> M. di Reschi who has studied under Signor Cotoni [*sic*] of our Covent Garden, is by birth a Pole. He is only twenty-three; and, it being his first appearance on any stage, perfection was hardly to be anticipated. But if inexperienced as an actor, he is seldom awkward, and possesses a high baritone, if not remarkable for volume or power, sufficient to fill such an area as that of the Fenice, and of the purest and most sympathetic quality. M. di Reschi forces his voice; but—clear proof of sound training—every note tells. Despite the nervousness inevitable upon a first night, his tones, his charm, his finished method found their way at once to the hearts of his auditors and ensured success. It is, indeed, a hopeful sign, in these days of exaggeration and incompetence, to find a young singer so well prepared. The experience of subsequent performances will give increased firmness to Di Reschi's singing, and it rests with himself to become one of the recognized baritones of Europe.

Had Evelyn wandered over to the Theatre Malibran on August the first of that same year, he might once more have been "held by the eyes and eares," though perhaps not "till two in the morning," as he had been that night when opera was in its infancy even in Italy. For on August 1 1874 the Theatre Malibran of Venice opened with a performance of F a u s t, and the rôles of Marguerite and her brother Valentine were portrayed by Guiseppina di Reschi and her brother Giovanni. The great success of the evening was for the blonde soprano of imposing presence. Her unusual voice and convincing interpretation so impressed M. Halanzier, Director of the Paris Opera, then in Venice seeking new talent, that he promptly secured her for his company.

Ambroise Thomas's H a m l e t was chosen for her Paris début on June 22 1875 at the Académie Nationale de Musique. Critics agreed that a brilliant career was possible for this Ophelia, but regretted that she had not spent more time in preparation. Her physical appearance caused as much comment as her singing and acting. Small wonder, for the snub-nosed lady was almost six feet tall. She had curly blonde hair, and her large dark eyes, arched by the blackest of brows, looked out of a large, almost square face. Her neck, according to one observer, was "set so far down into her shoulders that she just escaped deformity." (This last was, however, written by a hypercritical contemporary prima donna, and must be accepted *cum grano salis*.)

Such a physique, accompanied by a powerful, energetic voice, would hardly seem the ideal equipment to convey the delicate nuances of Ophelia's lyrical utterances; to portray the fragile Ophelia whose father chides her because she speaks "like a green girl." The voice also was too vigorous for the calm passages M. Thomas wrote for this girl who, strewing rosemary for remembrance the while, complains that she is "of ladies most dejected." Still, its superb timbre and unusual range brought warm applause, especially after the trio in the third act. The consensus of opinion was that, when she had studied more and when she had herself been emotionally stirred, Josephine de Reszke would be impressive in more forcefully dramatic rôles. One writer mentioned her imperturbable sang-froid, commenting that one could hardly drown oneself more methodically. The "millionaire Polish Ophelia," as she was frequently spoken of, would, he said, be a better singer when time had softened the inner organism.

Though her début and the major part of the voluminous criticism concerning it made Josephine de Reszke the subject of enthusiastic musical talk after this performance, she herself was not at all sure how she ought to report the event to her father. She asked the composer about it, and he replied:

June 24

DEAR MADEMOISELLE:

Prompted by a feeling of modesty which I find charming, but which seems to me exaggerated, you ask my testimony to your father. I can do no better than to repeat to you here what I was happy to express to you last night.

Yes, it is a fine and a real success to have obtained the warm and sincere applause of our public *in this rôle,* so admirably created, which was even very recently one of the most splendid triumphs of our great French singer.

The agreeable recollection of the applause you received and your delightful letter are really necessary to help me endure the din of trumpets which deafens me while I hurriedly write these few words.

I am touched by your kind thought for me. I thank you with all my heart, my beautiful Ophelia, and send you my affectionate regards.

AMBROISE THOMAS

It was said that Josephine sang the difficult rôle of Ophelia without a single orchestral rehearsal. Whether that was true or not, she did appear in direct succession to Mme. Miolan-Carvalho, the great virtuoso of the French school, and was bound to suffer prejudiced comparisons. Though she lacked the poetic insight to give a moving portrayal of Ophelia, and although, as one observer regretted, she had had only success when she might have secured a triumph, her technical mastery of the part was eminently satisfactory.

Later performances of this and other rôles fulfilled the promise of Josephine's Paris début. What was called her "second début" took place a few months later, when she first sang the slight part of Mathilde in G u i l l a u m e T e l l. Soon thereafter she sang Marguerite in F a u s t, and then the brilliant and dramatic passages, particularly the "Jewel Song," called out special praise. Concurrent with the reports of success ran stories of fabulous sums offered by M. Strakosch for

MADAME JAN RESZKE AND FAMILY
(Taken during the father's exile in Siberia)

Jean   Emilia   Edouard   Josephine   Mother   Viktor

an American tour, but Josephine de Reszke did not go to America that year or any other. The following spring found her still in Paris, winning commendation for her new rôle of Valentine in Les Huguenots, a part for which she was thought well suited physically, though in spite of her intelligence and intensity she seemed to be somewhat lacking in authority. She was too inexperienced to personify the heroine of this drama; but she improved rapidly in the part, and a few months later we find the critic of Le Ménestrel exclaiming: [5]

> What homogeneity and evenness in this fine vocal *clavier*! and in addition, what transcendent execution! As soon as Mlle. de Reszke perfects herself in the art of enunciating the French text, as soon as she learns to sing in the *style noble,* simple but elevated, we shall quickly number her among our great dramatic stars.

Rachel in La Juive followed soon and was considered an improvement over the representations of earlier interpreters, as were her portrayals of Isabella and Alice in Robert le Diable.

It was about this time (June 1876) that Josephine's baritone brother joined Edouard and her in Paris. After a dozen or so performances in Italy in the early part of 1874, Jean had gone to London to sing at Drury Lane, then called Her Majesty's Opera. As in Venice, his first appearance, on July 7, was in La Favorita, and as in Venice, comment was made on his high range. "Saturday's performance of La Favorita included the début of Signor de Reschi as Alfonso. This new baritone singer has a voice of beautiful and even quality with an exceptionally high range (reaching to G), he phrases well, especially in cantabile passages, and adds to his vocal qualifications the possession of a good stage presence. Although we believe somewhat under the influence of indisposition, he obtained a more than ordinary success, having been encored in the closing movement of his aria in the first act and greatly applauded in several other instances." So ran the account in the *Illustrated London News,* April 18 1874. The rôle of Alfonso was followed by that of De Nevers (Les Huguenots) and Count Almaviva (Le Nozze di Figaro). Critics and public meted out high praise to the youthful baritone, calling him "a prize" and "a decided acquisition." Later he sang Valentine in Faust and the title rôle in Don Gio-

v a n n i. Concerning his Valentine the musical critic of the
Athenæum wrote: [6] "Signor di Reschi re-asserted his claims as
a vocalist with a rare organ, and ... gave much promise of a
bright and distinguished future." The trio in the duel scene,
"*Che grati qui, Signor*," contains an exceptionally high part
for the baritone, and this was magnificently rendered by "di
Reschi." It was suggested, however, that with the personal ad-
vantages this singer possessed he ought to be a better actor.
The same criticism was made of his Don Giovanni. "This is
essentially an acting part, and at present Signor de Reschi is
not qualified for it, being ill at ease on the stage, awkward in
his movements, and unable to represent dramatic emotion.
He has a 'pretty' voice, more of second tenor than baritone
quality; but he is deficient in power, and the concerted music
suffered accordingly." [7]

The *Musical Times* verdict was that "Signor de Reschi,
although singing much of the music extremely well, lacked
the vitality inseparable from Mozart's D o n G i o v a n n i."
Another commentator remarked: "Signor di Reschi is very
young and inexperienced to undertake such a trying part
as that of the Don, but he has some natural qualifications
and his success, so far as it went, encouraged a hope that his
chief faults are those which time will cure." [8]

Certainly the audience must have agreed that the new
baritone had "some natural qualifications" in addition to a
sympathetic voice. Even as a very young man Jean had, both
on and off the stage, an air of distinction enhanced less by his
lithe physique than by the almost defiant way he held his head
and the somewhat stern and melancholy aspect of his face.
When the lips opened in a smile one forgot that his mouth
was full and sensuous, that on each side of it there were deep
lines; one was conscious only that the whole face became
luminous as the smile suffused cheeks and eyes and seemed
to blend into the rippling brown hair.

At the end of the season, which began on the 17th of
March and closed on the 20th of July, the *Athenæum* critic
had this to say:

> The sympathetic voice of the Polish baritone, Signor
> de Reschi, may, with stage experience, be turned to the
> best account. . . . There is infinite charm in the quality
> of the organ, which is, perhaps, more of the robust tenor
> timbre than of the baritone.

That season Jean also sang at the New Philharmonic Society concerts under the conductorship of Wilhelm Ganz, and in September and October 1874 "an Italian company" was singing in Dublin, with "Signor di Reschi" in the rôles of Valentine, Don Giovanni, and Richard Cœur de Lion in I l T a l i s m a n o. Among his fellow artists were Italo Campanini, who had made his London début in 1872, and Christine Nilsson. No contemporary criticism is available, but when Campanini died a writer for the *Musical Age* [9] said of these appearances in Dublin, "The young baritone got rather better 'notices' than he had received in London."

In 1875 we find him back in England, singing with emphatic success. That year London saw its first performance of L o h e n g r i n. Little did one dream that the young man who sang the baritone rôles of Don Giovanni, de Nevers, Valentine and Almaviva so delightfully, would return as a tenor and be hailed as the ideal Knight of the Grail. And yet the more discerning might have predicted something of the kind had they known what happened during a certain performance of F a u s t. Campanini, singing the title rôle, complained of hoarseness. Much of the success of the male trio of the duel scene depends upon the climactic B flats, and these Campanini said he would be unable to sing. "Leave it to me," baritone di Reschi is said to have suggested, and he sang the notes with ease and tremendous effect. So even then he had the range and the urge toward high notes. "A pushed-down tenor" they might have observed who later hurled "pushed-up baritone" at Jean as though it would have been most reprehensible to have the double endowment.

The next year, 1876, the three de Reszkes (the French form of their names was now used by all of them) were in Paris together: Josephine singing the rôles in which she already excelled and learning the one that was to transport her into the very firmament of operatic stars; Jean to meet with great discouragement and retire from the stage; Edouard to make his first appearance on any stage and thenceforth to develop into one of the most imposing personalities in the history of opera.

Edouard had left his studies in Italy and joined his mother and Josephine in Paris for the latter's début, while Jean was singing in London. He attended all the rehearsals and heard all the old operas. A very agreeable young man, he was welcomed to the musical circles of Paris. The popular

Josephine and her tall, very thin brother were frequently invited to fashionable dinners, and Josephine was usually expected to sing, which was distasteful to her, as it is to most artists. It was even a little difficult, for she enjoyed eating. So Josephine would whisper to Edouard: "Come, be a good fellow. You haven't eaten half as much as I have. Save me." Then she would say to her hostess: "If you will excuse me, I will get my brother to sing for you instead."

Those who knew Edouard in later years may exclaim incredulously: "What? Edouard thin? *Edouard* abstemious at table?" But it is true. As a young man his great height was accentuated by extreme thinness.

Thus Edouard gained recognition as an amateur, having no thought of singing in opera. M. Escudier, director of the Paris Opera, had heard him sing in private, however, and when Verdi despaired of finding a suitable King for the first Paris performance of A ï d a, which was to take place in April 1876, Escudier said to him, "Perhaps that big fellow, Edouard de Reszke, could do it."

Edouard was summoned, he knew not why. Verdi greeted him cordially, looking him over from head to foot, from foot to head. With a smile he turned to Escudier.

"He has the physique," was his comment. Edouard was mystified.

"So I thought," replied Escudier. Then Verdi said to Edouard:

"Do you know the music of A ï d a, M. de Reszke?"

"Most certainly," was the prompt response.

"You are quite familiar with the score?"

"I think I know it from beginning to end."

"Good! Won't you do me the favor of letting me hear you sing—say—the music of the King?"

In recounting the incident years later Edouard laughingly remarked: "I think I even tried some of Aïda's and Amneris's arias. Every now and then Verdi would look up at me, nod his head and say, 'Good! Good!'

"When we were through with the score he closed the book, rose from the piano, put his hand on my shoulder and said: 'I am quite satisfied. You shall take the part of the King. Come to rehearsal tomorrow.' "

At the rehearsal Edouard almost collapsed from stage fright. Verdi laughed and told him he had better be frightened at the rehearsal than at the performance which was to take place only a few days later. Edouard made his début on April 22 1876 without mishap, however, though in the entr'acte Verdi said to him: "Nom de Dieu! But you look more like the son than the father of Amneris!" The press said some kind things about the juvenile basso, but advised him to get a beard which would make him look more like a venerable Egyptian monarch than a Russian droshky driver. Soon thereafter he was engaged for two seasons at the Théâtre des Italiens, and thenceforth all was plain sailing for him.

Not so with Jean, who had also made his Paris début in 1876, on October 31, at the Salle Ventadour, as Fra Melitone in La Forza del Destino. While Josephine and Edouard were gathering laurels along the way, their elder brother, the first to appear in opera, seemed to make little progress. To his old roles—Don Giovanni, Valentine, de Nevers, Figaro—he added the part of Severo in Donizetti's Poliuto. He was well received in all these operas, of course, but he caused no stir. At the end of a performance he usually complained of feeling tired. In vain Edouard tried to convince Jean that he was a tenor. Then he appealed for aid to Sbriglia, a Paris teacher of reputation with whom he had studied a little, hoping that the advice of an outsider would carry more weight than that of a member of the family; but there is no record of how Sbriglia's suggestion was received at that time.

On December 19 1876 Jean sang Figaro in Il Barbiere. In London he had been very popular in this opera, it being felt that it gave him a good opportunity to display his best qualifications, and that he sang the music with animation and humor. His father had come to Paris from Warsaw to hear him. Jean sang with success, some critics believing, as in London, that the role was better suited than any other to show his verve and artistic intelligence. Le Figaro held, however:

"The voice of M. de Reszke (a tenor who does not go up) lacks amplitude and 'relief' in the part of Figaro, but the actor is not without intelligence and vivacity."

Jean himself enjoyed this particular performance, spreading himself especially upon the high notes and taking his cadenzas up to B flat.

"Well, how do you like it?" he asked when his father came to his dressing-room after the first act.

"It's very good, very good," replied the father in a non-committal tone.

"Tell me the truth, father. You are disappointed?"

"Yes, I am," came the honest reply.

"But why?"

"You know as well as I do that you are a tenor, and that this baritone singing is a mistake."

"If father thinks that way about it," said Jean to brother Edouard after the performance, "I'm afraid he must be right."

And that was the end of baritone rôles for Jean de Reszke. That same year the first Bayreuth Festival took place. Little could the disappointed baritone realize that two who played a prominent part in that first production of the entire R i n g were to be associated with him twenty years later in Wagnerian performances which made those at Bayreuth slide into second place. Lilli Lehmann was one of those first Festival singers, and Wagner had appointed Anton Seidl one of the executive officers in charge of the production.

Jean began his studies with Sbriglia. There has been a great deal of discussion, verbal and printed, about who changed Jean's voice to tenor. Every one knows that he studied with Sbriglia between the time of his singing baritone roles and his first appearances as a tenor. Friends and pupils of the teacher assert belligerently, "He can take *all* the credit for making Jean a tenor!" Friends and admirers of Jean, especially those best acquainted with his equipment and habits, are inclined to think that, once he himself was convinced that he was a tenor and not a baritone, he would have directed all his efforts toward achieving excellence in tenor roles, teacher or no teacher. As a matter of fact, Jean had studied some such rôles, but one night not long before he began his professional career, he heard the famous Cotogni sing the part of the Marquis di Posa in Verdi's D o n C a r l o s, with the likewise famous Mariani directing. Young de Reszke was swept off his feet by the splendor of the role and its magnificent interpretation by Cotogni; nothing would do but he must become a baritone, so that he might sing it.

Most people know of Jean's talent for mimicry. Almost everybody knows that he studied with Cotogni, and there is no doubt about his having imitated that baritone. His natural and acquired vocal and intellectual resources would have enabled him to sing—and sing well—any baritone role that did not descend too far into the bass, or any tenor role worthy of his intelligence. Those who noticed a tenor quality during his baritone days made no great fuss about it. Charles Santley, a singer whom Jean admired very much, complimented him on his performance in London one evening, and then added, "But mark my word, my boy, you're no baritone!"

In later years various critics, professional and otherwise, could not forget that de Reszke had once been a baritone, and they called him a "screwed up," "pushed up," "manufactured" tenor. As though, in those later years, it would have made a particle of difference to his audiences if he had been a coloratura soprano or a basso profundo in the earlier! As though contemplation of the other-worldly splendor of Jean's Lohengrin did not banish all else! As though to feel the emotional power and the grandeur of his Tristan left room for wondering who had been his teacher at a certain period of his life! If Jean de Reszke was not a true tenor, then it was simply so much the worse for tenors in general.

One would think Jean had denied having gone to Sbriglia or that he had cried "Forgery!" at the mention of his photograph which later pupils saw on that teacher's piano, inscribed "À mon cher Maître." Why shouldn't Jean have given Sbriglia such a photograph so inscribed? (Though accounts of what appeared on the photograph differ widely.) Sbriglia himself probably knew how much of any great artist's success may be claimed by his teachers, and how much of Jean's achievement he had guided. There was another who claimed he had first discovered that de Reszke might be a tenor. This was a Pole who taught singing in New York, a compatriot whom Jean wanted to befriend. He allowed him to come to his rooms occasionally to play accompaniments because that made it possible to pay him a generous fee. He was never in any sense of the word a teacher of Jean de Reszke, and that is also true of various other singing teachers who have been mentioned in like connection. One hesitates to suggest the obvious consideration that an operatic artist may frequently require the services of such people as accompanists and vocal teachers, not necessarily to "take lessons" from them but, in the one case, as accompanists, and in the other as, say, consultants. Doctors and engineers are not likely to fall into the error of thinking themselves the teachers of those who ask their opinions; why should not a singer discuss vocal technique with a number of other specialists in his field, without having them assume responsibility for his success? The facts are that Jean did sing his last baritone rôle in December 1876 and that he did study with Sbriglia intermittently for several years thereafter. But he did not by any means adopt all of Sbriglia's suggestions. He refused, for instance, to try to settle his head down into his shoulders in order to shorten the vocal column, because to do so would have interfered with his natural ease. Whenever Sbriglia suggested something that Jean could adapt to his needs he lost no time in doing so, just as he made use of hints from other sources; Jean de Reszke was a student of singing to the end of his days.

When he felt he had mastered a tenor rôle (and it was not very long after he had deserted baritone parts) Jean decided to send up his *ballon d'essai* in some small city. He secured an engagement at Como in Italy, and thought his chance had arrived when the leading tenor became ill on the day of a performance; but, all in keeping with operatic tradition, when the gentleman learned that he was to be replaced his health quickly improved, and Jean's hopes were routed. He stayed in Como, however, and worked alone for some time. Then he joined Josephine and Edouard, both of whom were becoming very popular.

Massenet asked Josephine to be the original Sita in his new opera Le Roi de Lahore, and with its first performance on April 27 1877 her reputation made a substantial advance. The rôle requires a voice of exceptional compass and force, and critics were at one in giving the highest praise to both singing and acting. With a single bound the Polish soprano had mounted several rungs on the ladder which leads to the heaven of lyrical stars. She was urged, however, to make war on increasing *embonpoint*. *"Pour les escalades il ne faut pas de surcharge."*

A week later Josephine received word of her father's sudden death in Warsaw. In her carefully kept book of cuttings this written entry appears in Polish:

> On Friday the fourth of May 1877 at 3:15 in the afternoon, died my dear father Jan Reszke in Warsaw, after living fifty-nine years, buried there in the Evangelic Cemetery, in the family tomb of the Reszkes. Peace to his beloved soul. These words on this sad occasion are dedicated to the never to be solaced memory of dear father by his forever grateful daughter

JOSEFA RESZKE

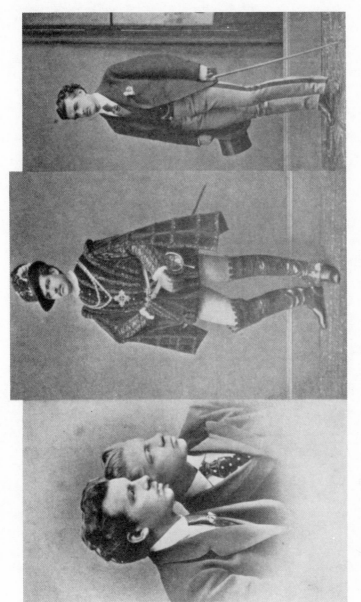

JEAN AND EDOUARD
As young men

JEAN AS DON GIOVANNI
(baritone period)

JEAN DE RESZKE
Aged about 21

AT THE END of each operatic season all three de Reszkes went home to Warsaw. Josephine seemed never to require any rest. Following her mother's example, she lent her talents unsparingly to charitable purposes. Throughout her life she made it a rule to give to philanthropic organizations all the proceeds of any performances in the homeland. There she was counted truly great. It would seem that her singing of songs was even more impressive than her operatic work, and the welcome she received on the occasion of a concert was more than once the subject of editorial comment. Songs and dance music and poems were dedicated to her by well-known poets and composers, flowers literally covered the stage whenever she sang, and in Kraków grateful citizens ordered her portrait to be painted by the Polish artist Adjukiewicz, to be hung in the National Museum.* As she left the stage on the last evening of her stay in Poland the entire audience sang the national anthem—"Jescze Polska nie zgineła" ("Poland is Not Yet Lost"). In Poland the singing of the national anthem is an honor reserved for some one who has done a really significant thing for the nation, and some of those who clung to ancient traditions resented these demonstrations.

Artistically Josephine was considered the equal of Patti by her compatriots, though one could hardly compare the respective endowments and achievements of the two singers, the Polish woman's being in almost every way a more heroic equipment. And yet, though she was a most dramatic soprano, she sang light songs with ease and understanding. Polish critics described her as being lavishly endowed with a beautiful natural voice and artistic sensitiveness, with dramatic insight and good taste, and thought her the embodiment of all that the art of singing could mean. Native sympathy helped her to communicate that art to her own people. Once, according to newspaper records, when she sang Gounod's "Ave Maria" her strange face seemed transfigured and as she poured out the soaring melody the whole audience was so deeply moved that in tacit accord they yielded to an inner need and knelt to pray with her. But the entire scope of her voice and her talents showed best in H a l k a, the Polish national opera. Hers was considered the finest portrayal of the rôle that

* Only a few months before this writing was Baron Leopold de Kronenberg, her husband, able to effect an exchange of paintings and secure this life-size portrait of Josephine for the Kronenberg palace in Warsaw.

had ever been given. Her hearers actually shuddered with her own pain and despair as she sang the trying part of the wretched girl in this intense opera. In a way that Jean and Edouard never were, Josephine de Reszke was Poland's own.

While the prima donna of the family was still engaged in giving concerts for the benefit of the Polish needy, Jean and Edouard had returned to Paris. When Josephine passed through the French capital on her way to Madrid, where she was to sing, she persuaded Jean to go with her. Her sensational success as Valentine in L e s H u g u e n o t s on the open-ing night was followed by almost equally great success in L ' A f r i c a i n e, L a F a v o r i t a, and D o n G i o v a n n i. Patti was in the company, and was especially well received in L u c r e z i a, but a contemporary report insisted that her great success did not lessen the effect produced by the Polish diva, and that the patrons of the Theatre Royal were "abso-lutely enthusiastic" about the superb voice of Mlle. de Reszke. An admirer of Josephine's still living in Lisbon writes: "I knew one very serious household where they almost came to blows in discussing the relative merits of 'La Reszke' and an Italian prima donna who was also of the troupe. The de Reszke was a beautiful woman, but colder than the Italian." Two parties were formed, one of the De Reszkistes, the other the Pasquistes, and each party had a "chief."

It was doubtless through Josephine's influence that Jean was engaged at the Theatre Royal. On November 9 1879 he made his début as a tenor, singing Robert in Meyerbeer's R o b e r t l e D i a b l e, with Josephine as Alice. According to some reports he was successful, but newspaper accounts ignored his performance almost entirely. He appeared in L a F a v o r i t a too, with his sister and Gayarre, but was scarcely mentioned. The de Reszke name was writ large in Spanish and Portuguese operatic annals of this period, but it was the vigorous, sometimes almost savage Josephine who was responsible for that, and not her brother. Jean himself wandered far into the valley of doubt during those uncertain days. To his friend and counsellor, Jean Styka, he wrote a letter sorrowfully admitting that he had been "whistled at," and that he thought he would leave the stage entirely and not disgrace his father's name. Music lovers—Grand Opera itself—must give thanks to whatever, whoever, made him decide to retire, not permanently, but merely to study, to try to perfect the art he still felt sure he could command. But this studying, this searching for the way to achieve his artistic ideals, was done with very little help from teachers. He traveled from city to city with Edouard and Josephine. He watched and listened to all the artists, learning what to avoid, appropriating—perhaps, in his perplexity, for only imaginary use—everything that was worth emulating. Graziani was one of those he studied carefully, as was his old teacher Cotogni.

His brother was advancing steadily. Massenet had asked him to sing the part of Indra in Le Roi de Lahore when that opera was given in Milan in 1879. The same year he also sang, at the Scala, in Maria Tudor, and in 1881 he appeared in The Prodigal Son, Simon Boccanegra, and Ernani. In alleged interviews Edouard was quoted as having said that he went to Milan in 1879 to attend the début of his brother, but a letter from the Teatro Scala informs me that Jean never sang there, though Josephine did.

Turin, Trieste, Lisbon, and other southern cities were visited by the de Reszke basso, and he made a notable success in two new parts—the King in Catalani's Elda and Charles V in Marchetti's Don Giovanni d' Austria.

In 1880, while Josephine continued her triumphant way on the continent, Edouard secured an engagement at Covent Garden, his initial appearance (on April 13) being as Indra, with Gayarre, Lassalle, and Albani also in the cast. London audiences found the newcomer a valuable member of the company. A contemporary critic expressed amazement that although Edouard played the part of Count Rodolfo in La Sonnambula without the slightest regard to the conventional "business" which audiences expected, he scored a great success. He returned the following year and added the rôles of Giorgo in I Puritani, Frère Laurent, Walter (William Tell), and St. Bris. As St. Bris he eclipsed the smaller parts in which he first appeared.

Josephine made her London début, in Aïda, on April 19, the opening night of the 1881 season. Opinions differed. Certainly she was not so popular here as she had been on the Continent, though the following critique, while not unstinted praise, shows a sympathetic attitude:

> Her vocalization was that of a well-trained artist, and she sang and acted with considerable dramatic power. Her voice is rich and sympathetic in the medium register, but is weak in the lower, and appears to be a mezzo-

soprano which has been injuriously affected by undue
exertion of power on the higher notes belonging to the
compass of the legitimate soprano.

When she sings above F (fifth line) her voice is apt to
become reedy and harsh in quality, while ineffective in
ensemble passages. It is not improbable that her vocal
powers were last night unfavorably affected by atmos-
pheric influences, combined with nervousness. That she
is a genuine artist cannot be doubted, and we may hope
hereafter to hear her under more advantageous conditions.[10]

But this critic was almost alone in his opinion. His colleagues admitted that the Polish diva had set herself a severe
task in selecting Aïda for her début before an English audience (for Covent Garden had grown accustomed to the performance of Madame Patti), but agreed that her voice had
been forced out of its natural register and had suffered
through her adoption of the French style of vocalization. They
felt that her intelligence and dramatic feeling compensated
only partly for these defects of style, and one of them insisted
that she manifested no special histrionic ability, adding: "In
brief, we cannot regard her as an acquisition, chiefly because
nothing can atone for the fatal defects in her system of vocalization." Whether this devastating criticism aggravated the
indisposition which prevented Josephine from singing Valentine in Les Huguenots, as scheduled for an early date
thereafter, one cannot say, but she did not sing. Before the
end of May it was announced that she had secured a release
from her contract because she had been unable wholly to
recover from an attack of laryngitis. The next autumn found
her back in Madrid, where she was happier.

Jean and Edouard remained in London, however, and
the de Reszke bass was in favor, his "pure voice and high
intelligence" rendering him "acceptable" in everything he
undertook. He returned to Covent Garden in 1882, adding to
his rôles Senon in Lenepveu's Velléda, and proving an
"efficient" Prince Gudal in Rubinstein's Il Demonio. The
latter, being the first of Rubinstein's operas ever given in
England, was conducted by the composer himself, with "fairly
sensational" success.

The Polish actress Helena Modjeska was playing in London at this time, and almost every Sunday evening her artistic

THE SHAH OF PERSIA AT COVENT GARDEN
(From The Graphic, July 13, 1889)

compatriots gathered at her home, the de Reszke brothers
included. Many a time an impromptu concert lasted until the
early hours of morning. Late one night came a sharp rap at
the door, and every one thought the important-looking police
officer standing there was going to demand that the untimely
singing be stopped, but he merely inquired who had sung the
last air.

"Jean de Reszke," was the reply. "Why do you ask?"

"A man in the next house wanted to know. Go on. Good
night."

But though Jean's singing kept neighbors listening at
their windows and passers-by standing in the street, he could
not be persuaded to sing in the theater. "I am afraid to appear
on the stage," was his response to urgent pleas, "and my fear
is greater than my desire for fame." He was seemingly content
to let his brother and sister maintain the family prestige.[11]

In 1882-83 we find Josephine and Edouard singing together again in Spain and Portugal, she the idol of music
lovers and society alike, and Edouard steadily increasing in
artistic stature. In Lisbon each leading operatic artist was
given a "Festa Artistica," and on that occasion all receipts were
turned over to him. On the night of Edouard's "Festa Artistica" every box in the theater was decorated with flowers and
beribboned wreaths, and draped with the richly colored, gor-
geously embroidered *colxas* found in most of the old Portuguese homes. Josephine had sung with him, and after the
performance the two were taken to their hotel in a very
sumptuous carriage drawn by four horses, accompanied by
a *marche aux flambeaux* and all the élite on horseback. All
along the way bands played and huzzas rent the night air.
Jean and young Viktor now joined their brother and sister.
Good-natured, handsome, a lover of racing and of society,
Viktor became very popular. The King and Queen of Portugal were fond of the de Reszkes and entertained them
frequently. All four of them received royal decorations.

When next Josephine returned to Poland, the Warsaw
Musical Society presented her with a Diploma of Honor, previously bestowed only upon Anton and Nicholas Rubinstein.
That summer the poor profited more than ever through the
devotion of this artist whose charities were never limited by
considerations of class or creed. She offered to sing twelve
concerts, without a fee, for the benefit of the Warsaw Opera,
on the condition that she should receive five hundred roubles

each for a second series for the benefit of philanthropic insti-
tutions. This generous offer was quickly accepted, with the
result that the Opera earned about 40,000 roubles and the
poor benefited by about 20,000. When, a little later, the Russian Government organized a gala concert in honor of the
coronation of the Tsar, they asked Josephine under what conditions she would take part. She asked 800 roubles. They
were quickly paid; and an hour later were in the treasury of
a charitable institution—needless to say, a Polish organization.
Her fairy godmother activities extended to other cities as
well, and grateful citizens of Posen gave her a large diamond,
saying: "It is the tear of the unfortunate. You have dried it;
it is right that you should carry it away."

It is interesting to note, in view of how much has been
written and said in praise of Jean de Reszke's diction, that
in commenting on the development of Josephine's art and
expressing surprise that a mezzo-soprano should conquer the
difficulties of coloratura singing with such ease and precision,
some one wrote on one occasion:

"The rendering of the intricate aria from Gounod was,
from the standpoint of diction, so plastic that of itself it almost
begged for action."

In the meantime Edouard had added to his repertory the
rôles of Alvise in Ponchielli's La Gioconda, in which he
"created as much effect as could fairly be expected in the
part," Ramfis in Aïda, and Daland in Der Fliegende
Holländer, which was considered "one of the finest realiza-
tions" theretofore seen. In London he was now considered one
of the most valuable members of the company. In all the old
rôles he was eminently successful, with the possible exception
of his Plunket in Marta, in which he was accused of both
heaviness and stickiness. In 1884 he sang Assur in Semira-
mide for the first time, and his voice and manner excited
admiration anew. Since the days of Tamburini, with whom he
was favorably compared, no one, it was said, had filled the part
so satisfactorily. He was also well liked as Pietro in
L'Africaine and as the Prefect in Donizetti's Linda di
Chamounix. In the latter he was the only member of the
cast who did score a real success, singing with so much beauty
of tone, purity of phrasing, and spontaneous power of expression that he invested the part with new importance. "In the
duet with Signor Cotogni (Antonio) he shone conspicuously,
the latter holding back the time, bar after bar, in the most

irritating manner, the former following the indications given by Donizetti." [12]

The principal event of the 1884 London season was the production of Reyer's S i g u r d, and "perhaps the best played part was the Hagen of Signor de Reszke." The next season he created Le Duc de Santa Fé in Theodore Dubois's A b e n - H a m e t in Paris (December 16 1885), on which occasion Emma Calvé sang there for the very first time. During the same season he sang Silva in Verdi's E r n a n i, and he also won especially high praise for his Basilio, it being remarked that such a representation of that character had perhaps never before been seen in Paris.

In later years Edouard was often accused of laziness. There was, to be sure, some difference in the care with which he and Jean studied details, and it took Edouard longer to learn a part, but no one could read the mere list of his rôles without reflecting that to sing so many even fairly well would be no small feat. And for the most part Edouard's singing was not only "fairly good" but truly excellent. He was seldom ill and he was seldom allowed very much time to rest between performances. Besides, he had a family to support, and basses do not receive the high fees paid to tenors; he felt compelled to sing more often than his brother. During the last season when Edouard and Pol Plançon, the great French basso, were both members of the Metropolitan Opera House company, Edouard sang at almost every performance. Plançon sang less than half as often, and marveled at the way de Reszke could stand the work. One night they were both singing in R o m e o. Plançon, arrayed in the magnificent robes of Capulet, strode into de Reszke's dressing-room, gazed at him in lofty disdain, and said: "You, my friend—you are not a singer; you are a horse." *"Le Cheval"* remained Edouard's nickname.

SECOND ACT

THE TENOR

1884-1901

JULES MASSENET had written Hérodiade, for which it was extremely difficult to find a leading tenor. In fact, its Paris *première* had to be postponed a year because no one suitable could be found. It had seemed to Edouard de Reszke, however, and to the composer, that the former's brother was ideally suited to the part, but apparently Jean had given up all thought of resuming an operatic career. Rumor said that he had been on the point of contracting a *mariage d'inclination*, a condition to which was renunciation of the theater. It is impossible to say whether the tale was true, though it may have been then that Jean's hope to marry Natalie Potocka, daughter of one of the oldest noble families in Poland, was finally crushed. From boyhood he had loved her and she him. He was well liked by her family, and Natalie's brother was one of Jean's best friends, but when it became a question of marriage between his sister and a young man connected with the stage, especially a young man of limited means, old prejudices crystallized into unsurmountable barriers, and the boy and girl gave up their dream. It may have been, too, that the brother was aware of a closer relationship, or the possibility of a closer relationship, between Jean and Natalie than that of friendship. It is forever impossible to prove as truth or legend the story that Jean de Reszke was the son, not of the proprietor of the Hotel Saski, but of the latter's wife and a Count Potocki; though whether the father of Natalie was the Count Potocki referred to, no one seems to know even by the report of gossip.

Jean loved Natalie always. She never married, and she died not long after that melancholy day in the spring of 1925 when the world had to realize that henceforth the voice—the voice and the magnificent art—of Jean de Reszke had life only in memory. It may be that this youthful love affair had something to do with the delay in Jean's reappearance on the stage. Or perhaps the cool reception he received in his first tenor rôle did actually make him decide, temporarily, that he could not be so successful an artist as he had thought. It may be, too, that the memory of that Madrid performance in November 1879, and the cruelty of an audience ignorant of or callous to the sensitive nature of the young tenor it hissed (without sufficient cause), was never entirely forgotten and was in part responsible for Jean's trying nervousness throughout his career; though in after years he attributed his fears to the condition of his bronchial tubes. Had a sane psycho-analyst brought his skill to de Reszke's aid at the right time, the great singer might possibly have been freed from a nervous condition which caused him great agony and his fellow artists some discomfort. This would seem even more plausible if it were true, as Madame Modjeska relates, that once during a performance in the baritone days, Jean drank a glass of ice-water and lost his voice, suffering a paralysis of the vocal cords; but this tale sounds a trifle far-fetched.

Although Jean had not been singing in the theater, he had kept on traveling with Edouard and Josephine, helping them and learning from them and their associates, and he sometimes sang in private concerts. Edouard, sure of the talents of his beloved brother, was distressed at his persistent refusal to resume his career. One day they were both in a music store in Paris, going over some scores in a little back room. Massenet also came into the store. The singing he heard sent him hurriedly to that back room, and when the cast for the first performance of H é r o d i a d e was finally announced, Jean de Reszke's name appeared opposite John the Baptist. Years later he wrote to Lilli Lehmann of this period in his life: "Then I spent the best years of my life, that is to say, from 1876 to 1884, traveling with my sister and my brother, who had engagements at Madrid, Lisbon, Milan, Turin, London and so on. I helped them with my counsel, I heard all the great singers of the period, I compared, I worked at home, without letting myself be seduced by the brilliant propositions which impresarios made me. I should perhaps have continued not to sing in the theater, if Massenet and Maurel had not taken me by force to create H é r o d i a d e at Paris in 1884. There began my career as a tenor." *

When it was first announced, in the autumn of 1883, that Jean was to sing in H é r o d i a d e, a writer observed: "It will

* A translation of the complete letter appears in the Appendix. All letters written by Jean de Reszke, or extracts from such letters, which appear in this book, have been translated from the French.

be interesting to see the transformation into a tenor of the young baritone, Jean de Reszke. He was, we remember, a charming gentleman, well-bred, distinguished, with a quick intelligence, and was, in addition, a good musician and a lively comedian. If he has really been able to tenorize [*ténoriser*] his voice, one can predict he will appear as an accomplished artist." That prediction was richly fulfilled, though at the last minute it seemed the whole venture might come to naught. Everything had gone well through the preparatory stages, even through the final rehearsal. Then, on the night of the performance, half an hour before the curtain was to go up, the new tenor balked. He simply announced that he refused to sing. The case was desperate. Words made no impression. Edouard and Maurel then locked Jean in his dressing-room, somehow managed to dress him, and at the right moment pushed him on to the stage. With what an aftermath the world knows.

Jean's triumph was complete. Other members of the cast on that memorable date, March 1 1884, were Victor Maurel, Hérode; Edouard de Reszke, Phanuel; Mme. Fides-Devries, Salomé; and Mme. Tremelli, Hérodiade—all popular artists; but it was the new tenor who received the warmest ovation. Listeners nodded assent when they heard Salomé sing, "Il est doux, Sa parole est sereine." After the prison scene, which Jean ended with a high C, there was lusty and prolonged applause. M. Chapelle, critic of *Sport,* said that no tenor could ever surpass him in this aria; but another critic, though he found the voice of pleasing timbre and sufficient power, the acting restrained but sufficiently warm, thought that a slightly faulty emission resulted in high notes that were sometimes hollow. Gaston Serpette, writing in the *Clairon,* said: "The more I hear this artist, the more I am impressed with the charm and freshness of his voice, his profound understanding and his diction. I was still under the dazzling influence of the vocal prowess of M. Gayarre, and I must say that, in spite of his immense ability, the Spanish tenor has never given me the delicious sensation which I experienced last night in listening to M. Jean de Reszke; I do not think I am mistaken in predicting a magnificent future for him."

Only those who themselves have studied the art of singing can fully appreciate Jean's achievement. To alter the placing of a voice is a task that calls for great intelligence, great understanding, great patience, and great skill. Jean had not

only to learn how to produce the high notes which he knew
he *could* produce even though they had never been brought
out; he had to learn, also, how to use his low notes so that
their baritone quality would not interfere with the brilliancy
of the upper notes. These difficulties he conquered through
his own efforts. No teacher could finally achieve what he
achieved through his own intelligent perseverance. Once when
a pupil of Cotogni's asked him whether he had changed Jean's
voice to tenor, Cotogni replied: "A year after leaving me he
wrote that he had new notes at the top of his voice—what
ought he to do about them? I wrote him that I had taught him
enough for him to know what to do about it as well as I myself did. So if anybody changed him, he changed himself. But
he never became a tenor. He was only a baritone with a high
enough range to sing tenor notes."

In spite of the brilliant success of this occasion, Jean again
became panicky just before the second performance, and
threatened to throw himself under a street car. But he caused
an even greater furor than the first time, astonishing his
audience by the freshness and firmness of his voice, and
charming them by a style of singing and acting which was a
felicitous combination of the precision of the French lyric
artist and the warmth of the Italian.

In this same performance Edouard was excellent as
Phanuel, but the general feeling was that the part was too
insignificant for his talents. That made no difference to him,
however. He enjoyed the rôle and he gloried in his brother's
success. Perhaps the leading prima donna rejoiced just as
wholeheartedly in the popularity of the new tenor, but one
cannot be sure; for after eight or nine performances Mme.
Fides-Devries decided, according to report, "to prove her
musical tendencies by executing the *fugue* of which one
knows." Massenet, who had taken her side in the difficulty
which precipitated this situation, did not feel that he could
authorize any one else to sing the rôle of Salomé without her
consent. But Josephine de Reszke had been the original Sita
in Le Roi de Lahore and Massenet had been pleased with
her interpretation; Edouard had been an eminently satisfactory Indra; Jean had been his special choice for the first Paris
production of Hérodiade; and when it was suggested that
Josephine should sing Salomé, Massenet gladly assented.

For the first time, all the de Reszkes were singing together. The public was delighted, for these three had endeared

themselves no less by their winning personalities than by their singing. The three were delighted as well, for they were great friends, and they thoroughly enjoyed each other's art. "The omnibus is complete," they laughed. "For," it was said, "a certain baron, well known for his music-mania, who appreciates their talent, always recommends them *en bloc* to his friends. Out of gratitude they have given him the degree of 'Conductor of the Omnibus.'" This was undoubtedly Baron Leopold de Kronenberg, who later became Josephine's husband.

Josephine, who had not sung in Paris for several years, triumphed as Salomé. Her voice had reached its full development and she was complete mistress of it. Passionate and brilliant when the situation required it, she now also commanded the understanding and the action necessary to lyrical tragedy. The incomparable de Reszke trio singing in one opera called out many a "Vive la Pologne!" They playfully suggested that if the chorus needed augmenting they could send home for relatives. They enjoyed singing together at the Opera, and they had, naturally, a unique private repertoire of operatic trios. For Josephine there was a special satisfaction in singing with her brothers. Too often she had as operatic lover a singer over whom she towered head and shoulders, a situation which could easily make a scene seem comic when it was designed to be romantic or tragic. Indeed, they might now have had a magnificent quartet, for brother Viktor, possessor of a splendid tenor voice, was frequently with them. He refused to study, however, quietly remarking that the family contained enough crazy ones.

One of these joint performances always meant a trying day for the de Reszke cook. Jean dined at three o'clock, Edouard at four, and Josephine at five. As they finished each of them stretched out on an enormous sofa and quietly stayed there, without whispering a word, until it was time to go to the theater. In spite of their artistic desires, this must have been a difficult feat, for they were a jolly trio. Energetic, handsome, even-tempered, gifted linguists, free from the customary eccentricities of the "star," they were social favorites. The imitative faculties which Jean and Edouard had shown since childhood were generously exercised to aid a host. Colleagues and friends were hilariously entertained by "take-offs" of friends and colleagues, but though the brothers enjoyed caricaturing to amuse, they never did so to wound. They were always gentlemen: "fram'd in the prodigality of nature," they never experienced the need some lesser human beings feel, to be unkind. They loved practical jokes, but their jokes were never cruel. They liked to tell about the time when they and Mierzwinski, another Polish singer, were walking home from the opera in Milan. Mierzwinski wasn't quite sure of the carrying power of his tones, and as they were just then passing a building which surrounded a large courtyard where everything was quiet, Edouard suggested that they should turn to account the acoustical properties of the large space. Mierzwinski stood in one corner and sang pianissimo, while Jean went to an opposite corner to judge the effect. Edouard was to stand outside to guard against interference by passers-by. "Let's see how the louder tones go," said Jean. Soon Mierzwinski was singing into the stillness of the night at the top of his voice, when suddenly Edouard appeared with a policeman, and the singer was arrested for disturbing the peace. Outraged, Mierzwinski followed, and not until he was about to enter the jail did Jean and Edouard let him and the astonished policeman know that their fellow artist had been "framed."

If Jean's star was now in the ascendant, Josephine's was sinking on the operatic horizon, not because she ceased to be popular with continental audiences, but because she married Baron Leopold de Kronenberg, and thenceforth, though she continued to sing for charity in Warsaw, where they lived, she gave up all professional singing. In February 1891 her second child, Jan, was born. Twelve days later, just as she took the baby into her arms, she suffered a heart attack, and fell back dead. Josephine died young, at thirty-six.

And Edouard? Edouard was studying hard. He was soon to sing for the first time in Paris the rôle in which he became most famous—Mephistopheles in Gounod's Faust. No qualms assailed him when the day came round, even though it was the thirteenth and he had some lingering superstitions. He and Jean, for instance, never walked under a ladder, though there was probably no conscious decision not to do so each time they encountered one; and they disliked being photographed, for they were just a little afraid that it brought bad luck. One of Edouard's private fears dated back to a painful childhood adventure. A gypsy fortune teller had told him he must never ride a white horse on a holy day. Once, on a day devoted to the Virgin Mary, he not only rode a white horse, but rode straight through a square which was no thor-

oughfare. He fell and broke his leg. His common sense might
have suggested that the fury with which he tried to get out
of that forbidden territory had something to do with his fall,
but he never rode a white horse again. The gypsy's warning
was handed on to his children, with this added reason for
heeding it.

On April 13 1885 Edouard received many notes of encouragement and good wishes, most of them in dainty pen-
manship and some of them saying, "I am going to burn a
candle for you," which was most gratifying to his religious
sympathies. But no superstitious or religious urge was allowed
to deprive his stomach of its customary generous treatment.
That would have been too much to expect of a de Reszke.
They were all enormous eaters. One of the acts Edouard used
to supply for private entertainment was an imitation of Jean's
timidity when, the first time they were alone in Paris, they
went to an expensive restaurant, and Jean was afraid to refuse
anything the eager waiters suggested. The boys were well supplied with money and were accustomed to spending it liberally, but their bill was something to make even them shudder.
Practical Edouard soon found a cheaper place to eat, where
his tremendous appetite could be appeased with less danger
of depleting the parental exchequer. But that time was in the
dim past.

Not that Edouard ate simply for the sake of eating, or that
he was especially anxious to heed Dr Johnson's dictum that
"he who does not mind his belly will hardly mind anything
else," but simply that his huge body required prodigious
quantities of food to sustain it. Jean's appetite was not canary-
like either, and sometimes after a magnificent dinner the
brothers would go elsewhere to continue the feast. A friend
who was with them on one such occasion describes how they
ordered, "to begin with," a dozen large beef sandwiches and
four half-bottles of wine. This was followed by a second dozen
of equally huge sandwiches, and four more bottles of wine.
"And," said the friend, "it was actual hunger, and not the
jaded palates of two gourmets, being satisfied by the meal."

Now there seems to be in the minds of prima donnas
who write their memoirs—and they all do—a charm about the
condescension of confessing their embarrassment in coping
with foreign customs at table. Mesdames Melba and Schumann-Heink tell identical stories about their confusion on
discovering, at a great house in Russia, that they had made a

meal of hors d'œuvres. This seems to have befallen both of
them in St. Petersburg when they and the de Reszkes were
entertained in the same house. Jean and Edouard must have
looked at them pityingly to think that such a slight error
could interfere with their enjoyment of the rest of the meal.

"Why should I fill up on soup?" Edouard would ask. "A
dinner should begin with a *pasta!*" James Huneker, who
sometimes watched the brothers eat their midnight meal
after a performance at the Metropolitan, writes: "It was a
spectacle that would have driven a dyspeptic frantic. The
spaghetti was literally wheeled into the room and disappeared
like snow under the rays of the sun." But the de Reszkes
feared not dyspepsia. Still, though they relied on their
stomachs to manage anything they chose to give them, and to
do so without protest, their singing careers might have been
longer had they indulged their appetites a little less. During
the last years when Jean sang at Covent Garden at least one
man worried about the welfare of the swan which drew him
in the magic boat along the waters of the Scheldt. He felt
that although Jean was still graceful, there were indications
that the time would certainly come when the Royal S.P.C.A.
would have to insist on a team instead of a single bird.

However, all these considerations were in the far future.
On the evening of Edouard's début in F a u s t he ate a good
dinner, in which he was joined by Jean and their boon companion Jean Lassalle, lighted a large cigar, and casually
strolled across the rue Scribe to don the scarlet doublet of
Mephisto.

"À la grace de Dieu!" he said to Jean, and then, just
before emerging from the wings: "If they only don't hiss me!
That's all I ask!"

Hiss him! "They" took him to their hearts. Mere critics
might—and did—object to the open Italian method of tone
emission; they felt that the big basso sang the serenade in the
third act in the lulling love-tones of the serenade from D o n
G i o v a n n i instead of in a bantering, piercing, tormenting
voice to the accompaniment of a guitar whose strings cracked
and twisted under the fingers of Satan. But the public did
not mind these little inconsistencies. They loved this Her-
culean Mephisto, constructed not at all along the angular pat-
tern of the traditional Evil One. The ladies rejoiced at the
sight of the magnificent figure revealed to their lorgnettes. It
was good to have a Mephisto whose physique could dominate

even the huge stage of the Paris Opera, and whose voice could
fill the immense auditorium with rich sounds that made the
very rafters ring. They were delighted to hear this giant Pole
enunciate French better, so they thought, than most of their
own singers. Even the sophisticated and taciturn *habitués* of
the orchestra applauded generously after the "Calf of Gold"
song and joined in the storm of approval that followed the
garden scene. But the church scene eclipsed all. Marguerite
was swallowed up in the voluminous folds of Mephisto's cloak.
Mephisto's domination was complete. Every sound uttered,
every posture, whether he stood with defiant head held high
or cringed before the solemn tones of the organ, was in turn
triumphant. From that scene on, Edouard de Reszke was
crowned a true artist by all Paris. He and his brother were
becoming very important to the directors of the Paris Grand
Opera.

Jean had so delighted Massenet with his interpretation of
John the Baptist that the composer begged him to create
Rodrigue in L e C i d, on which he was then working; and
upon Jean's consenting, Massenet finished the opera with him
in mind for the part. Printed accounts of this episode invariably say that the entire opera was written for Jean, but the
fact is that Massenet was already at work upon it when he met
de Reszke, and simply finished it with the latter in mind. Jean
began to study the rôle at once, as did Edouard that of Don
Diègue. Pol Plançon was to be the Comte de Gormas.

Jean had been much encouraged by his success in H é r o-
d i a d e, and determined to excel that performance. He devoted himself to the new rôle assiduously, consulting Edouard
and Massenet frequently. "How many times did I climb the
stairs of the Hotel Scribe, where they lived!" wrote Massenet
in *Mes Souvenirs*. Jean's artist friend, Jean Styka, was called
on for aid as well. Styka himself had a beautiful tenor voice
and de Reszke never ceased urging him to forsake his painting
and sing. Styka was adamantine to that suggestion, but out of
his knowledge as a painter he helped Jean a great deal with
problems of make-up, and, unlike some other singers, de
Reszke was always ready to listen when any one had a thoughtful suggestion to make. For instance, the sleeves of one of the
costumes were of metal cloth. "This," explained Styka, "will
catch all the light and people's eyes will follow its gleam instead of watching your face. Besides, your gestures will be lost
because of the scintillation." Promptly black satin sleeves were

substituted. "If you colored the under part of your nose a little darker, it would give your face a more luminous look." The hint was acted upon at once. Today of course all such details are watched very carefully, the exigencies of the film having helped to emphasize their importance, but forty or fifty years ago such niceties were rare. These are but isolated instances of the care with which Jean studied one phase of a single part. Voice production, phrasing, action, all were studied just as carefully, for every rôle. Baron de Kronenberg knew intimately how de Reszke worked. "Jean," he told me, "was never satisfied with studying just the music and the text. He read every book he could find which would throw any light on the manners and habits of dress of the period he was portraying, and he remembered everything he read, just as he remembered everything he had ever seen any other artist do."

Le Cid was first produced on November 30 1885 at the Paris Opera. Even long after he had outgrown the heroics of this rôle Jean was fond of playing Rodrigue. It gave him little scope for subtle nuances of singing and acting, but a great many opportunities for flourishing a sword and posing as a grand chevalier. And he was a "grand sight." If there was by no means unanimity among the critics as to the quality of singing, neither was there disagreement as to his acting and his personal magnificence. His admirers began to hope he would sing Faust, for they felt as if they heard again Capoul, who had excelled in that rôle, and that Jean's imitative faculties had been put to good use in observing him. Once more his pronunciation was called perfect, a virtue that commends itself especially to the French.

If critical opinions differed with respect to de Reszke's singing, that of the public was unanimously favorable. He was wildly acclaimed. Hérodiade had meant success; Le Cid meant fame. It was at this time that Amherst Webber, then a young composer studying in Germany, first heard of Jean de Reszke. Like every one else, he was thrilled by the descriptions of the art of this new tenor, but how could he dream that he was to become so important to Jean's life and career over a period of many years!

Massenet was delighted. He wrote Jean a letter saying:

DEAR FRIEND,

  I must tell you the profound satisfaction I experienced last night in listening to you. You are unique in

JEAN DE RESZKE
As Raoul in Les Huguenots

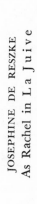

JOSEPHINE DE RESZKE
As Rachel in La Juive

the rôle of Rodrigue and you have a sincerity of emotion which no other will equal—it seems that you are really Rodrigue and Jean de Reszke at the same time. It is Rodrigue whom one sees and it is your heart which sings—and, I add, with a voice of such charm, such power, such extraordinary virtuosity! Thank you, thank you.

No one could doubt any longer that Jean was in truth a tenor, for the rôle is peppered with B flats, B's and high C's, and they were by no means timidly sung. Jean himself was so gratified with his success that he vowed then and there not to be satisfied with anything less than the highest achievement possible in the world of Grand Opera. From that time on he steadily improved, until he stood the greatest of operatic artists. Not that he had the greatest voice. He himself knew this; in fact, he underestimated the quality of his voice, late in life he said, regretfully, "au fond j'avais une sale voix." He marveled at the limpid beauty of Caruso's. But he could not, of course, be ignorant of his own success. He knew, not in the manner of the egotist, that his audiences thrilled to the intellectuality and emotion with which he suffused a composer's thought. And his was, indeed, a lovely voice. To say that Jean de Reszke did not have a "great" voice, means no more than that in his throat there was not that accidental structure, found once or twice in a century, which forms a voice that without much training, without intellectual endowment or dramatic insight, carries its listeners to heights one cannot reach by any other vehicle than human song. Jean's voice was excellent, but it was always susceptible to slight bronchial irritations. He had to be constantly watchful, especially after he had established his unique reputation. He could not afford to appear when he could not sing his best. In the first place, the public expected too much. In the second place, there is the cruelty of some critics, fellow artists, and sections of any audience, always half waiting for the opportunity to say, "Well, *he's* done for!"

De Reszke's supremacy did not come by chance. It was a steady growth, the result of artistic insight and perseverance, not of luck. He knew what he wanted to do, and he knew how to go about doing it. There are enough "artists" who have a fairly definite or even a fixed idea of what they want to do but who never strike upon the exact way to achieve it. Jean was not of these. I do not mean to imply that when his creation of

Rodrigue met with high favor he said to himself: "I shall not stop until I have sung Tristan and Siegfried as no other has ever sung them"; I mean that there was nothing meteoric about his rise. Quietly, unceasingly, he worked and studied and absorbed—and gave forth again. He became the idol of the Parisians and was the principal tenor of the Paris Grand Opera for several years following his great success in Hérodiade and Le Cid. He sang Radames, Vasco di Gama, Jean de Leyde, Faust, and Don Ottavio (in Don Giovanni) with equal artistry. His fame spread through the operatic world.

In London impresarios had suffered reverses. Mr. Augustus Harris, however, energetic, courageous in launching new artistic enterprises, was undaunted. He had, in fact, been dreaming of doing "something big" in Grand Opera, though it was a new field for him. One day early in the spring of 1887 he said to Herman Klein, the London critic: "What I am going to do is to give a month of Italian opera on a large scale at Drury Lane, at the height of the London season!" Klein did not respond with the expected enthusiasm. On the contrary, he asked, did not Harris feel that enough English impresarios had been wrecked on the shoals of Italian opera? But Harris saw no reason why he should suffer the same fate. If opera were well done, he insisted, it should pay. Society—the capital S kind—had to be interested. Signor Lago had not failed at Covent Garden the previous year, even though his company had been far from excellent. Well, Lago might have "the old fogies and *habitués*" at Covent Garden; Harris would draw "the real aristocracy" to Drury Lane. Klein agreed that the thing might be possible with a strong company. "There," said Harris, "is where you can be of service to me, if you care to." They decided to go abroad at Easter. Harris had already engaged Luigi Mancinelli as conductor. Suddenly Klein said: "I know of a splendid tenor for you, if you can get him." Harris had heard about Jean de Reszke, but had made no decision concerning him. His companion urged him not to hesitate.

The de Reszkes had had a busy season in Paris, singing their accustomed rôles with their now wonted success. There was hardly a season when Edouard did not acquire at least one new rôle. In December 1886 it had been the Duc D'Albe in Patrie. It was a very high part, and he sang it only once. Several years later the opera was produced again with Plançon in this rôle, and even Paris, which loved Edouard and admired almost everything he did, felt that the change was well made. But in his other parts he continued to be a great favorite, and Jean's place in the affections of Paris music lovers was also secure. The brothers were of course much interested in what Harris had to say, both of them having enjoyed their popularity with London audiences in other years. Mr. Klein's impression of Jean at this time was of a man "wholly free from affectation or conceit; in a word, a delightful man and a thorough gentleman. His conversation was marked by ease

53

and freedom, and it offered a fascinating combination of
humor and intellectuality." [13]

Arrangements were quickly settled. Jean was to receive
£100 a night, Edouard £320 a month, fees they were well
satisfied to accept. In later times, when there was much discussion, some of it most acrimonious, about the size of Jean's
salary, one read, every now and then, that in 1886 Signor Lago
had been offered his services for the paltry sum of $100 a night
and had refused them. Herman Klein comments in a footnote on this report:

> It is possible, of course, that some musical agent in
> London or Paris did offer to try to secure the new tenor
> for Signor Lago; but if so, it was not done at M. de
> Reszke's instigation. And in any case the "refusal" would
> not have come so much from the impresario as from
> Signor Gayarre, who was at the back of the concern, and
> would assuredly have objected to the engagement of an
> artist who might prove a formidable rival to himself.

Mr. Klein also writes:

> Little did I then dream that the mission...was to
> have results of far-reaching magnitude; that it was to
> affect the whole future of opera in England, and also in
> an appreciable degree the nature and methods of operatic
> enterprise in the United States. Still less did I imagine
> that the words which turned the balance in favor of the
> engagement of Jean de Reszke were also to mark the turn-
> ing point in the singular career of that illustrious artist—
> to lift him from the sluggish waters of the stream of
> Parisian operatic life; to pave the way for his brilliant
> rise to fame in the two great English-speaking lands; and
> to lay the foundation of a friendship that should enable
> me materially to aid in kindling those Wagnerian aspira-
> tions which have borne such precious and universally
> cherished fruit. [13]

Is Mr. Klein correct in assuming that Jean de Reszke,
with his equipment and his popularity, would have stayed in
Paris for the rest of his days except for the critic's suggestion to
Augustus Harris in the spring of 1887? Whether or no, the
thirteenth of June saw the tenor's London début, at Drury

Lane, in Aïda. Stage and cast were resplendent with scenery and costumes specially imported from Italy. The great triumph of the evening was, however, most markedly that of the baritone become tenor. There was no hesitancy on the part of the audience, no quibbling on the part of the critics. Here, at last, was a more than worthy successor to the much talked-of Mario! "Gifted with fine presence and liberal allowances of every artistic quality, both as actor and singer, Mr. de Reszke easily excited the enthusiasm of the house, which recognized that no such tenor had recently appealed to an English audience." So declared the *Musical Times.* "M. Jean de Reszke is now a magnificent *tenore robusto,* and his impersonation of Radames is one of the finest we have witnessed in London for many years." So ran the critique in the *Athenæum.* And the *Magazine of Music* recorded: "The prominent success of the evening, however, was M. de Reszke.... His voice is now a robust tenor of very fine quality, his singing, full of power, is never merely boisterous, and his acting, manly and unaffected, exactly suited the part."

All in all, it was one of the most brilliant opening nights London had ever known, and was a fitting contribution to the splendor of the Jubilee year. There was really no need for the following letter, which was sent to a London critic the day before Jean's London début:

Sunday
12 June 1887

Dear Sir and Friend,

For four days we have intended to go to see you, but, to our great regret, Harris has not left us a moment of liberty; morning and night we have had rehearsals of Aïda, Lohengrin, Don Giovanni, etc. As an artist of the French Opera and on the basis of our friendly relations for two years, I wish, dear sir, to recommend to you my brother who makes his début tomorrow in Aïda. In Paris he had a great success in this opera, and if it is the same here (as I hope), I should be infinitely grateful, dear sir, if you would mention it in your London letter.

You know how much we think of the *Figaro,* and in what esteem it is held in Warsaw, our native city.

Would you be so kind also, dear sir, to tell me whether one could find you at home around five o'clock? I should like to present Jean to Madame Johnson, and combine a little dinner where we four could talk quietly.

As I am afraid that Harris has no press service, I take the liberty of sending you two cuttings, hoping that you might find some interest in listening to my brother and judging him with your usual ability.

Hoping for a word of reply concerning the hour when Madame can receive us, I ask you, dear sir and friend, to accept my most cordial greetings.

Your devoted
EDOUARD DE RESZKE

Hotel Continental
Regent St.

When I showed this letter to Minia, Edouard's daughter, in order to determine its authenticity, a puzzled look came over her face. Then she laughed, and said: "This letter was written by my Uncle Jean, and signed by my Uncle Jean, with my father's name. It is just another example of my uncle's nervousness and of his modesty."

On June 22 the brothers both sang in Lohengrin for the first time on any stage. This was, of course, in Italian. Edouard demonstrated by his portrayal of Henry the Fowler how much a real artist can make of comparatively small opportunities, and Jean was voted the best Lohengrin London had seen. Minnie Hauk, the Elsa on that occasion, throws a ray of light on one of his means of moral support.[14] When Lohengrin takes leave of Elsa in the last scene of the opera, he gives her his ring and his sword. In her grief Madame Hauk handed the ring to one of her attendants. The next morning a messenger brought the following urgent appeal:

DEAR MADAME,

I would be very grateful to you if you could remember what you did with my ring last night. This ring is my fetish, my *porte-bonheur,* and I tremble at the thought that you may have thrown it away somewhere, thinking that it might only be a theatrical accessory. If you have given the ring to somebody, please let me know to whom.

I beg your pardon for importuning you, but I must be reassured, as soon as possible, as to what has become of my poor ring.

A thousand respectful greetings from your devoted

JEAN DE RESZKE

Dimanche
12 Juin 81.

Cher Monsieur et Ami

Depuis quatre jours nous nous faisons un pouvoir d'aller vous voir, mais a notre grand regret. Nous ne sommes pas un moment de liberté; matin et soir nous avons des répétitions d'Aida. Stranger. J'ai été en qualité d'artiste de l'Opéra français et ma travaux sur nos relations et amicale. S'il y a deux ans. j'étais chez Monsieur

Notre compositeur habituelle. Déjeunons un petit mot de réponse pour en qui concerne l'heure a laquelle Madame et vous prie. Vous prie. Cher Monsieur et Ami. d'agréer mes salutation le plus cordiales.

Votre d'une

Edouard de Reszke

Hotel Continental
Respire - P. 2.

After a long search the ring was found in an obscure corner of the property room.

Three nights later, there was still another triumph, this time in Faust. Jean, Edouard, and Victor Maurel played the principal parts, and the verdict was that no such Faust, Mephistopheles, and Valentine had appeared together within the recollection of London opera-goers. Jean's *"Salve dimora"* then, as for years later without exception, called out highest praise.

Musical London was awake. The Prince and Princess of Wales were enthusiastic admirers of Jean from the start, and society followed the royal example in going to hear him. To hear him once was to go again. But in spite of good operas carefully staged and sung by superb artists, the crowds did not flock to Drury Lane, and the impresario's financial loss was heavy.

Gradually, however, this situation was to mend. On July 11 there was a revival of Les Huguenots. Critics began to complain about having exhausted their supply of superlatives in describing the singing and acting of the de Reszkes, especially when the rest of the cast was excellent as well. Here was the grandest performance of the season. Even the restrained *Musical Times* said: [15] "No words of praise are too strong for the acting and singing of Miss Nordica and Mr. Jean de Reszke in the great duet. They rose fully to the occasion and evoked a storm of applause." Many years later Herman Klein recalled the event thus: [16]

> Imagine Jean de Reszke at this time as Raoul! Always remarkable for its refinement, distinction, and passionate warmth, his impersonation was just then peculiarly imbued with the spirit of the true Meyerbeer school. Alike in a vocal and a histrionic sense, it was supremely great. His "velvety" tones, fresh, clear, and mellow as a bell, were emitted with an unsparing freedom that would thrill the listener not once, but twenty times, in the course of a single scene. There was no "saving up" for the last act then; it was *"laissez-aller"* throughout, with plenty to spare at the finish. And what tenderness, withal, in that famous grand duet of the fourth act! Not Mario himself had phrased the *"Tu m'ami, tu m'ami!"* (this was still an Italian performance) with a greater wealth of delicious surprise and pent-up adoration. Little

wonder that Nordica nearly lost her head through nervousness and emotion.

That this should have been considered, as it was, the most notable performance of the season is eloquent testimony to the artists, for the opera lasted until nearly one o'clock in the morning, partly because the fifth act, ordinarily suppressed in England, was given, and partly because the performance was half an hour late in getting under way. But for the resourcefulness of Mr. Harris it might not have got started at all. Some time after the curtain was supposed to rise, he found the leading baritone in the throes of one of those paroxysms politely called a display of temperament. There stood the singer, raging, wasting his expensive voice and using up quantities of nervous energy in wild gesticulations, while the de Reszkes watched in amusement. Some one asked the reason. What could be the matter? "Matter!" roared the indignant baritone, and invited his questioner to look at the "specimen of an English-made costume" and tell him whether he had ever seen such a disgraceful fit. Would a fastidious gentleman like Nevers wear a doublet that his valet would have sneered at? "Look at this right sleeve!" he shouted. Except for a rip in the seam under the arm, it was as elegant a habit as purse could buy, but the Comte de Nevers of the evening refused to sing in it. Finally Harris threatened to tell the audience the reason for the delay, whereupon a few pins speedily closed the rent in the garment, and the incident; and the de Reszkes too were allowed to proceed in their triumphs before the English public.[17]

Well pleased with their first season together in London, Jean and Edouard returned to Paris, where opera-goers awaited them eagerly. Both sang in the centenary performance of Don Giovanni on October 26, but although in some places the event was described as "brilliant," according to a correspondent of the *New York Times* none of the artists was in good form.

Lassalle, in spite of his remarkable voice and method, made very little out of the title rôle.... Edouard de Reszke also is too big for Leporello, but his voice did good work in the solos. His brother Jean was satisfactory as Don Ottavio, but his singing could be taxed with heaviness. Every one of them seemed to be impressed with the idea that they were singing in a large building and must make all possible noise. Moreover, no one seemed to like Mozart or to understand him.[18]

These charges must seem strange to those who heard the de Reszkes in other times, places, and rôles. But when, on November 4, the five-hundredth performance of Gounod's Faust took place, and both Jean and Edouard outdid themselves, that same correspondent probably transmitted quite a different report.

Magnet and Salvayre's opera La Dame de Montsoreau, based on Dumas' novel, had its *première* on January 30 1888. It was reported that with the exception of Jean de Reszke, who sang the part of Bussy, and one other singer, "the cast was heart-rending." Strangely enough, the ballet was a failure because it was excessively naughty even for Paris. Less than two weeks later a cable announced: "The failure of the Dame de Montsoreau at the Opera is stupendous and final." Paris was beginning to feel that the same might have to be said of the entire opera season if anything happened to the de Reszkes. There was some fear that they might not return the following season, even though it had been announced that Jean would sing Eleazar (La Juive) in October. At least one musical journalist felt that Messrs. Ritt and Gailhard, directors of the Opera, had not given the brothers sufficient consideration. He complained that they had to sing every note called for by their contract, but were allowed no extra performances, because that would have meant an additional fee.

London was impatiently awaiting their return. Augustus Harris had been very busy since his "flyer" had proved successful. He enlisted the aid of Lady de Grey and Lady Charles Beresford, both of whom were devotees of opera and warm admirers of the de Reszkes, particularly Lady de Grey. They were friends of the popular singers as well, especially Lady de Grey. With the help of these two valiant supporters—and workers—a sufficient number of subscribers was secured to warrant not only the leasing of Covent Garden Theatre, but also renovation of the theatre and its accoutrements. In fact it was the largest subscription secured for many a year.

The season opened on May 14, without the de Reszkes. Harris had good artists in good operas, and a spick and span house and stage. The de Reszkes were missed, but at the beginning of the season the new conditions were enough to insure good audiences even without them. The Prince and Princess of Wales attended the opening performance, and this set the pace for Society. There was, also, the début of Nellie Melba, which, though not an overwhelming success, was of sufficient importance to help stay the operatic appetite while it awaited the popular Poles. It was announced that the "French Trio," meaning the de Reszkes and Lassalle, would be first heard in a revival of L'Africaine. Had Jean not yet been considered an artist deserving the people's excited admiration, the night of June 4 alone would have achieved his renown; for he was voted a magnificent Vasco di Gama, "the only tenor who has a fine voice and who can both sing well and act intelligently." It was a night of triumph for Augustus Harris and for the "French Trio" (two-thirds of which was Polish). The packed house, led by the Prince and Princess, broke into torrential applause at the end of Jean's impassioned singing of the air "O Paradiso." Only Nicolini, who had been unrivaled in the part nearly a quarter of a century before, could be mentioned in comparison. Like Nicolini, Jean invested a scarcely agreeable rôle with grace and dignity and charm. Lassalle's Nelusko was likewise superb, and Edouard's Don Pedro, a rôle not bristling with opportunities, was masterly. He was hailed as the best operatic basso the English stage had known since the days of Bagagiolo.

But in other parts the big basso was not lavishly praised that season. In Il Barbiere, for instance, he was censured, with Signor Ciampi, for pantomimic extravagances, and although Mr. Klein holds that he "made a notable hit" in Boito's Mefistofele, other critics, one of whom felt that histrionically Edouard was "weak and commonplace," did not agree with him. Nor did Jean escape rebuke. On June 16 there was a noteworthy performance of Lohengrin, but it was Mme. Albani's Elsa that received most eulogy. Seldom did it happen, throughout his career, that when Jean de Reszke was in the cast a prima donna received the higher praise, and still more rarely was Jean de Reszke accused of even a single inartistic detail. On this occasion, however, although the *Athenæum* recorded that the Polish tenor's performance was "only just short of perfection, the one weak point being the notice he takes of the audience when emphasizing a point," the critic of *The Times* rebuked him severely as follows: [19]

This singer was in many respects an ideal Knight of the Grail, and when he fell short of that ideal it was not from want of ability, but from want of artistic conscience. His farewell to the Swan and the duet with Elsa in the bridal chamber were simply perfection. Here M. de Reszke seemed to forget himself and the public, and float on the waves of beautiful sound. Unfortunately, this self-surrender to the spirit of the hour was only momentary. At the climax of the opera, where Lohengrin reveals his nature and his mission, he turned his back upon Elsa and the King, stepped to the footlights, and made an absolutely vulgar appeal to the gods, eliciting a short burst of applause, which, however, as it always is in Wagner's operas, was immediately checked by the more intelligent part of the audience. In his calmer moments, M. de Reszke will no doubt feel ashamed of this kind of success, of which so great an artist as himself does surely not stand in need. If operatic singers ever read books, we should advise M. de Reszke, by way of penance, to peruse the letter in Wagner's recently published correspondence with Liszt, where that master speaks of the abomination of what he calls the "harangue."

Jean may have deserved this scolding; but he usually had a good reason for every gesture he made on the stage. It may be that he turned too far away from his fellow artists on this particular occasion; but when Lohengrin says farewell to Elsa he also says farewell to the world she represents, and always in this scene Jean deliberately walked to that part of the stage from which he could take leave of the greatest part of it, thus indicating the severance of all earthly ties. (To be sure, if such a motive is not clear to the beholder without explanation the gesture is artistically incorrect.) Jean, moreover, may not have been the most comfortable man in the world during that performance. For more than a week he had been suffering from blood-poisoning. An iron armlet which he wore in Aïda inflamed a wound left by the bite of a cat, and a surgical operation became necessary. Lohengrin's armor scarcely resembles a soft bandage. The public seldom knows, and the critics not much more often, what difficulties an artist may be laboring under on a given evening.

Jean played Riccardo (Un Ballo in Maschera) for the first time that season, and Guillaume Tell was put

on for Edouard and Lassalle. The season as a whole was eminently satisfactory both financially and artistically, and from
it, according to Grove's *Dictionary of Music and Musicians,*
dates the revival of opera as a fashionable amusement. The
cable which a correspondent sent to America,[20] saying that
Madame Albani was the only artist in the company who could
be numbered as great, though nearly all had been "good,"
scarcely reflects the contribution of the de Reszkes to this
success, and certainly would not have given rise to reports that
both Harris and Colonel Mapleson had contracted to take
them to America the following winter. Paris especially was
alarmed at this prospect, for in that capital it was felt that no
satisfactory substitute for the de Reszkes could be found. Still,
it was known that Jean had accepted the principal part in
Saint-Saëns's new opera A s c a n i o, scheduled for the next
spring, and he was also pledged to Harris at the Royal Italian
Opera for June 1 following. Finally the *Sunday Times* declared, on December 9:

> We are in a position to state that MM. Jean and
> Edouard de Reszke and M. Lassalle consider themselves
> no longer under an obligation to place in Mr. Mapleson's
> hands the management of their projected American tour.
> The period within which the stipulated "guarantees"
> were to be forthcoming elapsed some time ago, and Mr.
> Mapleson's chance is now at an end. Whoever may step
> in to undertake the business, we can warn him that there
> is among the Parisian friends of the great trio a tre-
> mendous opposition to their going to America at all.
> The latest idea is to get up a petition, signed by all the
> prominent musicians and *dilettanti* of Paris, begging
> those favorites not to abandon the Opera next year—at
> any rate not to sing further away than London. Their
> desire, nevertheless, is to pay a visit to the New World,
> if they can do so under satisfactory conditions.

It was true that Mapleson had been negotiating with the
famous trio for a visit to America in the spring of 1889. The
matter dragged on, however, and in November (1888) Mr.
Klein received the following letter:

PARIS, Wednesday

MY DEAR FRIEND:
    At last Lassalle has returned from Lyons, and I am
able to give you an answer on the subject of Mapleson.

With Lassalle nothing has been signed. Mapleson has verbally settled the clauses of the contract, but no signatures have been exchanged; and it is even very disagreeable, because Lassalle, as a matter of delicacy, will accept no other engagement while Mapleson shows a sign of life. My brother and I have arranged the bases of our contracts, the salary, the repertory, the number of representations, etc.; but we are waiting in vain for the contracts. Mapleson was to have given us certain guarantees that we asked for, and for our part we also, as a matter of delicacy, are waiting until he decides to come and sign these clauses. There you have the truth: as in London, so at Ems, we talked over with Mapleson the whole of the project for America, discussed figures, and separated good friends; but in words only—in writing not so much as a shadow! This is very annoying for us, for we are refusing quite a quantity of business for this "unsigned" America. I hope that Mapleson will end by arranging the whole affair, for just now he is counting a little too much on our patience. My dear friend, I shall be delighted to see you at the *première* of R o m e o. A place will be reserved for you. Bayreuth was superb! I cherish the memory of it among my most poetic souvenirs. A thousand friendly greetings and a shake of the hand from

Your devoted
JEAN DE RESZKE [21]

The London season had, as related, been very successful, but Harris realized that the repertory needed freshening. In Germany a giant genius had written wonderful operas, and yet in London, one of the world's great cities, only a few of his earlier works had been given, and those in Italian. The "great German invasion" which had startled operatic London in 1882 was not yet to be repeated, but Italian opera was certainly falling into disrepute. Harris decided to go to Bayreuth with Mancinelli in July. Herman Klein arrived there three weeks later, just as they were leaving. Harris was full of the spectacles he had seen and the music he had heard in P a r s i f a l, T r i s t a n u n d I s o l d e, and D i e M e i s t e r s i n g e r. In his heart a hope had been born that he might produce D i e M e i s t e r s i n g e r, even if it were necessary to have the text specially translated into Italian. "If only Jean de Reszke would sing Walther!" he mused. "See poor old Gudehus in the part here, and then imagine what a perfect Walther Jean would make!"

The de Reszkes, Lassalle and Lillian Nordica were at Ems that summer, and Klein went there too. He gave them a full account of the Bayreuth performances, dwelling on D i e M e i s t e r s i n g e r, describing eloquently the artful and musical wooing of the Franconian knight and taking care to point out the importance to Walther of Hans Sachs. The three artists proceeded to Bayreuth, with the result that Jean and Lassalle determined to study the opera for the following season. Immediately upon learning of their decision Augustus Harris commissioned Giannandrea Mazzucato to translate the text into Italian.[22]

"AT THE PARIS OPERA things are 'going to the dogs' generally. De Reszke has been ill for some time, and appeared in P r o-p h è t e under unfavorable conditions.... A ï d a was announced subsequently, but at the eleventh hour MM. de Reszke and Muratet sent word that they were unable to appear." Thus ran the Foreign Notes in the *American Musician* on December 1 1888.

If it had seemed, when this correspondent was preparing his note in the early part of that season, that "things were going to the dogs," and on account of Jean de Reszke, they had, even while the note was in transit, improved so much that events at the Paris Opera "set the wild echoes flying" round the whole musical world. And on account of Jean de Reszke.

Suddenly it was announced that Paris was to hear Patti and Jean in a *reprise* of Gounod's R o m e o e t J u l i e t t e. This opera, which had fallen into disrepute because it was "sticky," and because the composer had "preferred to make concessions to the doctrine of the music of the future, while discarding the exigencies of taste and ear, and making of it a realistic drama," [23] was first produced in Paris in 1867, at the Théâtre-Lyrique, with Madame Miolan-Carvalho, the original Marguerite of the same composer's F a u s t, singing Juliette. That same year Adelina Patti created the part at the Royal Italian Opera in London. Mario was the Romeo. In 1873 the work was produced at the Opéra-Comique, the Théâtre-Lyrique having ceased to be, and Patti was still singing Juliette at Covent Garden; but the opera never captured the affections of London or Paris audiences. In a decade, however, opinion had begun to change. Gounod consequently arranged to have his work transferred to the Paris Opera, and to satisfy the requirements of that institution furnished the music for a ballet. He himself was to conduct the initial performance. Mme. Darclée, a French soprano, was to be the Juliette. After a few rehearsals she developed "nerves." There was no other suitable Juliette available, and consternation reigned. Then Gailhard, the Director, had an inspiration. He betook himself post-haste to Craig-y-Nos Castle, and thanks to great diplomacy was able, forty-eight hours after his return to Paris, to wave before the rehearsing *ensemble* a telegram saying in part: "You invite me to assist in the performance of an artistic

66

ROMEO ET JULIETTE

Edouard as Frère Laurent   Jean as Romeo

masterpiece conducted by the Maître himself. My reply is, Yes. PATTI." Gounod, who had been kept in ignorance of the trip across the Channel, was ecstatic. "He embraced every member of the company within reach, and dispatched a message to his *chère Adelina* thanking her with all his heart for the promise of her 'gracious and inestimable help.'" [24]

Here was indeed an event! The great diva had never sung at the Paris Opera, and she had never sung an opera in French in Paris or anywhere else. For several years she had been dividing her time and her talents between the opera and the concert platform, but it was fifteen years since she had sung on any Paris stage. Paris loved Jean de Reszke, the most popular tenor in the starry firmament of opera. Gounod himself had asked Jean de Reszke to sing Romeo, and expressly for Jean he had composed a new finale to the third act—the air *"O jour de deuil."* But even the beloved personality and the art of Jean de Reszke took second place when it was announced that the divine Adelina was to sing Juliette. That was before the event.

A few private rehearsals for Jean and Patti, with Gounod at the piano, then one stage rehearsal and the *répétition générale,* all within about six days after Patti's arrival in Paris, and the evening of November 28 had arrived. Hundreds of would-be purchasers of seats—at any price—were turned away disappointed. Side boxes on the second tier were gratefully accepted by princesses. Dressmakers had been besieged for weeks by women who foresaw that the event would offer most gratifying opportunities for display. Nellie Melba, not yet famous, was then singing in Brussels, and when she read of the performance-to-be she sprang to her feet and exclaimed: "I am going to Paris, whatever happens. I don't care if I have to postpone performances. I don't care if I never sing again. To hear Patti and Jean de Reszke would make up for anything, any sacrifice." And she was there.

It was fashionable to arrive at the Opera late. That evening, however, as by universal agreement, the great hall was full fifteen minutes before the curtain went up. Aristocracy and officialdom were there in dazzling numbers and splendor. Jewels flashed. Haughty lorgnettes found objects worthy of generous admiration. Great was the curiosity. How would Patti now look as the love-awakened young Juliette? How would the shimmering voice sound to ears that had not heard it for years? How would she act?

To Jean de Reszke little thought was given.

Gounod made his way into the orchestra amid thundering acclaim, wondering how his beloved opera would be received by this critical audience and by the hypercritical gentlemen of the press. Of the genial white-haired composer's uneasiness there was no outward sign. With Patti it was different. The state of her nerves was apparent. She had, in opera and concert, sung the waltz air hundreds of times, and yet—"She jumped four measures," said Gounod later; but so skillful a singer was she, so level-headed a conductor he, that few noticed the blunder. The air had to be repeated, amidst great applause. She looked, according to Klein, "positively more youthful than when she had last sung the part at Covent Garden a dozen years before," and he adds: "Not a word was uttered or written save in unstinted admiration," [25] which is, of course, the rather natural superlative of a biographer lost in admiration of his glamorous subject. Audience and critics were indeed lavish with admiring applause, but the written accounts were not quite so untinged by adverse comment as Mr. Klein would have us believe. "The runs toward the end were rather labored; it was also noticed that her high notes from G up are veiled and wavering." Then there was, also, the inevitable "transposed-down-a-tone" charge, this time made in connection with Patti's singing of the famous waltz.

Unstinted admiration, yes; but the greater, deeper admiration was for this new Romeo. He captured the eye immediately upon entering the scene, clad in tights of dark blue and steel-gray, embroidered in silver blue, and a doublet of deep blue velvet under a cape of dull blue silk, wearing his rich costume with the elegant ease of a patrician. As had happened before, as happened so many, many times thereafter, Jean de Reszke's conquest began simultaneously with his appearance on the stage, before he had uttered a sound.

And then he sang. Jean's name on the program had indicated, as a matter of course, that there would be good singing; but even his admirers had been so carried away by the excitement of Patti that the charm and beauty of his Romeo was as surprising to them as to those unfamiliar with his work. From one corner of the house came an audible "A-ah"—then from another corner, then from all parts of the great auditorium. What style! and what a voice! Such youthfulness, and such maturity too! Here was a Romeo—why here was a Romeo Shakespeare himself might have dreamed of.

"Shakespeare has expressed," wrote Émile Montégut,[26] "all that the sentiment of love contains, and all that which it is capable of pouring forth upon that human soul of which it takes possession. The love of these two hearts is the exaction of the absolute; it seizes upon the entire being, body and soul —ideal and real. Thus has Shakespeare bound in one sheaf the different elements which make perfect love; his *Romeo and Juliet* is more than a great drama, it is the living metaphysics of love."

Here, then, was an artist who seemed to know, and know deeply, that ultimate nature of love. Triumphantly he revealed to those thousands of spellbound listeners the full range of his artistic insight. He sang *"Ah! lève-toi, soleil!"* and received an ovation. He was called back. Modestly he slipped away. Behind a pillar, old Duprez, singer of an earlier day, furtively dried a tear. Then he took a notebook from his pocket, tore out a leaf, and wrote. His neighbor leaned over and read:

> Si je chantais encore, que je serais jaloux,
> Bien qu'on ait tant vanté de mes accents la flamme!
> De Reszke, quand j'entends ceux qu'émettent votre âme,
> Mort depuis si longtemps, je crois revivre en vous!

Never had this tenor, who combined the grace of Mario, the strength of Duprez and the passion of Nourrit, seemed so admirable. "Jean de Reszke seems to us the best interpreter of the rôle of Romeo that we have heard," concluded the critic of *Le Journal Illustré*. "He realizes, by his person, his elegance and his acting, the ideal of the poetic, amorous personage created by Shakespeare. His voice has all the accents of tenderness and emotion, his diction is clean and exact, and his singing is full of grace and charm." The following critique embodies the general opinion:

> The satisfaction with Madame Patti which the public manifested did not cause any one to lose sight of the admirable talent of Jean de Reszke, and we are not certain that the applause was not more hearty, more spontaneous in any case, when it was addressed to the valiant tenor who has reaped the large following of Talazac.
> M. Jean de Reszke was what one expected, a Romeo who was elegant, passionate, full of excitement and flame, but full also of gentleness and charm: refined but bitter

in the first scenes; tender, entranced and entrancing in the love duet of the second act, and at the close of the opera terrifying.

It is impossible to sing with more fire and persuasion, with more soul and more taste, to show oneself, above all, a better actor. It is a well merited success which the sympathetic artist has just won.[27]

It was Madame Patti on whom the management had counted; it was Jean de Reszke who took the honors. At the end of a scene it was plain that Romeo was more popular than Juliette. The moment he reappeared on the stage applause broke out anew, and between acts his dressing-room was so crowded that it was difficult for him to change costumes. Once when, after eight recalls, he finally managed to get into at least half of his costume for the next scene, the clamoring continued so persistently that he had to change back to the other costume and return for another ovation. All Paris, it seemed, had gone mad.

One solitary critic felt that Jean played the part a bit too vigorously. The real Romeo, he thought, had less assurance; he even showed some timidity, and certainly more gentleness. He was submissive to Juliette; afraid of being scolded (the word was Shakespeare's) at once by his beloved and by Frère Laurent.

Poor Frère Laurent! Though his physique was overpowering and his voice torrential, on this occasion Edouard de Reszke went almost unnoticed. One was sorry that his part was so short, since he portrayed it so admirably; one applauded him in the air of the benediction and in the beautiful scene with Juliette; one felt that a little unctuousness might not have been out of place; one thought he lent to the friar a little of the bearing of a Russian pope and sang more or less like a choir; but that he was a fine artist, conscientious and sincere. That evening the giant Edouard was dwarfed. It is no wonder, for almost the whole of R o m e o is in four love duets; quite naturally the lovers who sing them are of most importance.

Gounod was not surprised at the sensation Jean created. He had been deeply gratified by what he had seen and heard during the rehearsals. Once the producer had interrupted Jean with a suggestion, and the composer called out, "Laissez-le! Je ne veux pas qu'on touche à ce garçon." During the performance that first night he frequently laid down his baton to applaud his talented interpreter, and afterwards he said: "This is my ideal Romeo, even as Patti is my ideal Juliette!" Nor was Jean himself greatly surprised at his success. He had studied his part, and the whole opera, very carefully. He felt certain that his interpretation was correct; but he doubted whether the audience would have sufficient poetic intelligence to recognize its truth.

Subsequent performances only enhanced the magnificence and popularity of his impersonation. "Mario's Romeo was now completely forgotten; Nicolini's gently brushed aside." Patti sang in a few more performances and was of course enthusiastically applauded, though, as on the first night, not all the critiques gave superlative praise. It was suggested that she should study the artistry of her partner in conveying nuances of emotion. The great Patti was probably not too elated at these criticisms, or at being eclipsed by this Romeo, whom she had known as an extremely youthful baritone when she was already a star. Those few joint appearances in Paris marked the only time in their careers when they sang together, except informally, many years later, for friends in Jean's private theater. Various writers have insisted that there was a slight coolness between them after this performance, though nobody seems to know just why. Mme. Jean de Reszke denies this emphatically and maintains that they were good friends always.

Patti told some one, however, that before she sang with Jean when she created Juliette at the Paris Opera, nobody had known anything about him, which was, of course, an absurd statement. He did certainly owe something to the advance publicity given to the occasion because of her, but the publicity he received afterwards was based on sheer merit. He had thrilled Paris with a masterly interpretation, and Paris was not slow to show where its preference lay. One disgruntled opera-goer voiced his feeling in an open letter to Patti, of which I found an undated cutting in Jean's scrap-book. It runs in part as follows:

Out of sympathy for the directors of the Opera, the press has carried you to the clouds, not wishing that the cost of your cooing should be their ruination. It has done so much that I wish all Paris had gone to hear you. That would have filled their treasury, and all the world would

be able to judge, that, as a singer, you would do well
henceforth to stay out of the limelight. You could stay
at home, contenting yourself with your past—and
formerly merited—glory.

Briefly, the contract made with you has been kept
and you have had the number of performances agreed
upon. It is time to say that the enormous success of
R o m e o et J u l i e t t e was first for the composer, and
then for M. de Reszke. But for the latter alone as a singer;
you know that better than anybody.

But the preponderance of critical opinion was that Patti
was exquisite and that Jean was exquisite. That the occasion
assumed historic significance was, nevertheless, due to Jean
de Reszke's fresh, individual interpretation, which lifted what
had until then been considered a cloying, monotonous opera
into the ranks of the most popular lyrical dramas, and kept it
there until his retirement. Moreover, the movement to have
all operas sung in their original languages owed its main
impetus to Jean de Reszke's superb singing in R o m e o. This
Polish artist had excelled Italian singers in Italian opera, and
he now entered the period of his supremacy in French opera,
a supremacy acknowledged by the French themselves.

Augustus Harris, now (because of the death of Carl Rosa)
managing director of the Carl Rosa Company, lessee and
manager of Drury Lane, and impresario of the Royal Italian
Opera, was not one to ignore this Paris success, and he made
arrangements to produce R o m e o at Covent Garden during
the season of 1889. And in French. The announcement of
Jean's return was hailed with delight, as it had been alleged
that instead of singing in London he was to help dedicate the
new Chicago Auditorium with a series of concerts. Speculation
was rife as to who would be the Juliette in London. Several
ladies were in the running, or rather, since the rôle is not an
athletic one, five prima donnas, it was said, aspired to sit on
the balcony with Jean. Mme. Melba was finally chosen. "I date
my success in London quite distinctly from the great night of
June 15 1889 when I appeared as Juliet to Jean de Reszke's
Romeo," she wrote in her memoirs.

It was the first time that a French performance of
R o m e o had been given in London. Even the chorus sang
French. Jean, Melba, Edouard, all won fresh laurels, though
it was realized that "that painstaking but entirely non-French

soprano, Mrs. Melba Armstrong," could hardly be compared
with Patti. As for Jean, though one critic felt he did not excel
the impersonation of Nicolini, another said that even Mario,
the original Romeo in London, in 1867, was then not the
equal of the new Romeo, and added:

> Although the Polish tenor was at the outset flustered,
> and in the serenade in the garden scene for once in a
> way dropped unconsciously into the vibrato, he soon
> picked up, and gave such a rendering of his part in the
> garden duet, the duel scene, and the love duo of the
> "Lark" in the sleeping-room of Juliette, as we have cer-
> tainly not hitherto heard in England.[28]

Mr. Fuller Maitland, then the new critic for *The Times*,
said in part:

> Mr. Harris's bold experiment of producing R o m e o
> e t J u l i e t t e in its original language was crowned, on
> Saturday night, with complete success.... In singing and
> acting alike, M. Jean de Reszke is an ideal Romeo; the
> tenor has comparatively little to do, beyond the four
> duets with the soprano, but these were sung by both
> artists in exquisite style. M. de Reszke's facial expression
> as he received his sentence from the duke's lips proved
> that he knows his Shakespeare as well as his Gounod; and
> that he remembered the lines
>
> > For exile hath more terror in his look,
> > Much more than death; do not say—banishment.

The *Standard* made the following comment:

> The power and passion of M. Jean de Reszke's
> Romeo were as evidently recognized and acknowledged
> in London as in Paris. His voice is even better than it has
> been in former years, and, in addition to the beauty of
> its tone, it is a special treat to hear his perfect enuncia-
> tion of the words. That some few of the characters, and
> particularly the chorus, not being French, should not
> have a perfect accent is a matter for no surprise, but M.
> Jean de Reszke's delivery was all the more welcome....
> The scene in Juliette's chamber was equally remarkable,
> Madame Melba sharing the honors, though perhaps the

most impressive episode was Romeo's rapturous cry, "Ah, vienne donc la mort, je reste!" The magnificent voice of M. Edouard de Reszke lent peculiar dignity to the music of Frère Laurent....

The one entirely new opera of that season was the Italian version of Die Meistersinger. De Reszke and Lassalle had been studying their rôles all through the winter and spring. In this they were helped by a certain Herr Saar, a thoroughgoing student of Wagner. Saar was ecstatic about the bright future for Wagnerian singing implicit in Jean's work on this opera. Walther's opportunity in Die Meistersinger lies mainly in the "Probelieder" and the "Preislied," but Jean, with his capacity for delving straight into the heart of a rôle, with his deep understanding of the poetry of every line, invested the part with new meaning, gave it new charm. And when on July 13 he sang it for the first time on any stage, the hopes of London opera-goers were completely fulfilled. Though all artistically possible cuts had been made, the performance lasted from half-past seven until midnight, and not every one remained for the final Prize Song; consequently Jean's success depended chiefly upon his singing of the Trial Songs and his part in the love duets in the second act. The public had been curious; and it was enraptured by the revelation of beauty which it experienced in seeing and hearing Jean de Reszke. As the villagers of Nürnberg declared that Walther von Stolzing had won the prize, so the music lovers of London, when they awoke from the dreamy beauty of this singing, pronounced this other Walther victor once more. Fifteen years after the event one of them still remembered how "the entire embodiment presented features of originality that surprised by their freshness no less than by their truthful adherence to the Wagnerian conception; and, as with his Lohengrin, so with his Walther, the vocal rendering of the part constituted a veritable revelation. The final rendering of the "Preislied" on that hot July night was something that never before had been approached, and has not since been surpassed." [29]

Jean loved the rôle, and his impersonation of the Franconian knight was eloquent with the distinction of his own personality; but he was not satisfied. The visit to Bayreuth had worked a deeper desire than merely to sing Wagnerian rôles. He remembered the singers there, and though he thought well of Mazzucato's adaptation, he was beginning to rebel against trying to convey the crispness and ruggedness of Wagner's original text through the medium of the soft Italian language. What the idolized tenor's dissatisfaction was to result in, however, not even his warmest enthusiasts could guess.

The de Reszkes contributed not only to the success of opera; they enhanced the social season as well. That year they participated in a gala operatic performance in honor of the Shah of Persia, the first such celebration at Covent Garden since the visit of the Emperor· and Empress of France many years before. The brothers' popularity with members of the Royal Family had not waned, and the reports of the latter had aroused the curiosity of Queen Victoria. The Queen had indulged in few social or musical activities in the twenty-five years following the death of the Prince Consort, but now she issued a command for the appearance of Jean and Edouard at Windsor Castle. What heartburning there must have been among some of the other high-priced prima donnas, when they learned that Mme. Albani alone had been chosen to sing duets with Jean in the presence of the Sovereign! It was the de Reszkes' first visit to Windsor, and Jean described the event thus: [80]

MY DEAR FRIEND:

The concert began with the air from "L'Étoile du Nord," which Edouard sang wonderfully. Then Madame Albani and I sang the duet from Lohengrin, after which the Queen expressed a desire to hear me in "Salve dimora" from F a u s t. This I gave, and she appeared delighted. Next Madame Albani sang an air by Handel, with the accompaniment for flute obbligato—I think "Sweet Bird" was the title, but you will know better than I the particular piece in question; and she sang it like a true *virtuose*. I accompanied Edouard in Denza's romance "À un portrait," with which the Queen was much pleased; then Edouard and I thundered out the unaccompanied duet from C a r m e n, arranged by ourselves—a great success! At her Majesty's request, the concert ended with the duet from the T r a v i a t a, sung by Madame Albani and myself. The Queen, smiling and full of kindness, approached us and paid us many compliments. Among them she told me that I reminded her

of Mario, only that my voice had more power. She refused
to believe that I was the elder brother, and this discussion, in which Madame Albani was called upon to arbi-
trate, greatly amused the Queen. Then, after the
customary courtesies, the Queen retired. I found her
extremely well, charming in manner, speaking French
like a Parisian, and a genuine lover of music—as one
could easily see by her eyes and in the movements of
the head with which she emphasized the chief passages.
In a word, this musical pilgrimage was anything but the
solemn function which we at first feared it might be.
Thanks to the amiability of the sovereign, there was not
a vestige of fog at Windsor! Mancinelli accompanied. A
thousand greetings.

JEAN DE RESZKE

This marked the beginning of a real friendship between
Her Majesty and the de Reszkes. The Queen, who thoroughly
enjoyed their singing, wrote in her journal, after one occasion when they sang at Windsor: "Edouard's voice is marvelous, so powerful and deep. . . . They are most gentleman-like
fine men, and their voices (though Jean's is tenor) have a great
likeness. Tosti played the accompaniments. It was indeed an
immense treat. I told them I hoped I might some day have
the pleasure of seeing them act." She was especially fond of
Jean. One day she brought out a little volume whose pages
were yellowed with age. This book, explained Her Majesty,
had been used during her childhood to receive the autographs
of celebrated people; M. de Reszke must write in it. He did
so, and his name will remain among the relics of the Royal
Family. At Sandringham, among a group of trees planted only
by European monarchs, is one placed there by Jean at the
Queen's request. These friendly relations endured until the
death of the great sovereign. Friends of Jean love to describe
how, during one of the last of the royal processions in which
Queen Victoria was the observed of all observers, she turned
her head coyly when she passed the hotel where she knew
Jean was staying, to see whether he was at the window. The
Queen's death affected Jean deeply.
During the subsequent coronation procession of King
Edward VII, the new sovereign was astounded, on passing a
certain hotel, to see a man in kingly robes step out on the
balcony and make a deep bow. In consternation he sent a

messenger to find out what fellow monarch this could be of
whose presence in London he was unaware. He was convulsed
with laughter when he was informed that the magnificent
vision which had met his eyes was merely Edouard de Reszke
in his costume as König Marke.

The de Reszkes were received by the Royal Family as
personal guests, they partook of the family cup of tea, and
were made entirely at home. Indeed, they felt at home wherever they happened to be. Their attitude toward the aristocracy was hardly that of the French woman who, though she
lamented the shortcomings of a certain nobleman and had
misgivings about how he would fare in the hereafter, announced with confidence: "But the Almighty will think twice
before damning a gentleman of his quality!" They enjoyed
taking part in occasions when uniforms jostled against coro-
nets, but they were unawed.

Once when the King of Greece was visiting the Prince of
Wales (later King Edward VII), the de Reszkes were also
guests of His Royal Highness.

"Well," said the King of Greece to Edouard, "you have a
very fine voice, and I can't sing, but I'm fairly sure you can't
do what I can do." Whereupon he turned a handspring.
Edouard, not to be outdone by the royal caperings, promptly
retorted, "Oh, I don't know," and sent his well nourished
six-feet-two hurtling through the august chamber in a cart-
wheel.

But it was the home of Lady de Grey that the de Reszkes
visited most often in England. This handsome lady, six feet
tall and tremendously energetic, had been an important factor
in the rejuvenation of Grand Opera in London. She knew
nothing about music technically, it is said, nor was hers a
musical nature; but she had few interests and she chafed at
inactivity. Grand Opera needed attention; it received it when
that fact was brought home to her, and a year of her indus-
trious interest left its mark on the fortunes of Covent Garden.
Nothing that could contribute to improvement escaped her
eyes.

"It was not," relates E. F. Benson in *As We Were,* "that
Lady de Grey made sure for herself that the swan's neck in
L o h e n g r i n was robustly joined to its body, or that she
swung in the Rhine maiden's trapezes, or tried Jean de Reszke's
voice." She had a house not far from London, and it always
seemed a coincidence that on evenings when the Princess of

Wales dined with her a few of the most luminous operatic
stars shed their radiance over the gathering. The private reports of how marvelously Nellie Melba, say, or Jean de Reszke,
had sung, traveled far and were the politest kind of advertising for Covent Garden. All this Lady de Grey managed quite
privately. "She completely evaded the limelight, and though
she immensely enjoyed entertaining her royal guests, and
having the evening stars to sing to them, she had not the
faintest desire to let the public know about it." [31]

This cloak of privacy was not less of a consideration for
the de Reszkes than for members of the Royal Family, and
secure in the knowledge that their "goings-on" would not be
noised abroad, they enjoyed the hospitality of Lady de Grey
and her genial informality, and "cut up" freely. Edouard, to
be sure, had no objection to indulging in antics wherever he
was, and even Jean, always more reserved, always the *grand
seigneur*—though with great sincerity and simplicity—seldom
failed to contribute his share to an evening's fooling. Mr. Benson describes one such evening at Lady de Grey's home, when
the assemblage tried to rouse the Duke of Cambridge from an
unaristocratic snooze into which he had fallen.

Then Alick Yorke came tripping in, with a little
rouge and an eyebrow and a stupendous carnation in his
buttonhole, not much more than five feet tall. He looked
up at his hostess, who had done her hair in some amazing
manner, piling it on the top of her head, while somewhere near the summit was a diamond crescent; indeed
for once she looked almost too tall. Alick Yorke surveyed
her critically, blinked at the crescent, and with a little
lisp he said, "Dear Gladys, I like the way you've done
your hair tonight. It gives you what you've always wanted.
Height." Oscar Wilde came drifting largely along, and
caught sight of some new arrival. "Oh, I'm so glad you've
come," he said. "There are a hundred things I want not
to say to you." Then Réjane recited "La Poupée," and
after a few trifles of that kind, all rather informally bestowed, Lady de Grey, purely for a joke, said to Edouard
de Reszke: "Won't you sing something?" He, instead of
answering her according to her folly and saying he hadn't
brought his music, said, "But certainly I will, though I
have never sung in so small a room. I will sing you *Le
Veau d'Or* from F a u s t." He had a prodigious volume

of voice when he chose to open it out, and now he sang
Le Veau d'Or as loud as he possibly could, and the windows rattled, and the crystal festoons of the chandelier
quivered. He sang it with extravagant operatic gestures,
parodying himself, with an eye all the time on the Duke
of Cambridge, but he never disturbed the light trance.
And then Jean de Reszke, fired by this noble exhibition,
and slightly jealous, said, "But I want to sing too. I will
show you how I sing the 'Preislied!'" So he found two
footstools and placed them in the middle of the room, and
insecurely perched on them proceeded also to parody
himself. He sang it as he always sang it, but with some
absurd exaggeration of gesture and caricature of the way
he took his high notes. Never was anything quite so
ludicrous, and before he had finished his singing there
was not, quite in the Victorian manner, a dry eye in the
room except those of the Duke of Cambridge.... Bohemia in excelsis: Bohemia in tiaras.

Now possibly Réjane might have recited at a party
of the Duchess of Devonshire's or of Lady Londonderry's
for some colossal fee and, just possibly, the de Reszkes
might have consented to sing there, but there was no
one but Lady de Grey for whom they would have rol-
licked like this, just for the fun of it. They were not
stars at this remarkable party, they were merely her
guests in the milieu which they all loved.[32]

Another time at Lady de Grey's home in the country, the
fun was so absorbing that Jean and Edouard were almost late
for a Covent Garden performance. They missed the last train
to London, and opera that night seemed very uncertain. Fortunately a resourceful member of the gathering recalled that
he was honorary president of the local fire brigade, and in a
trice the precious operatic cargo was borne on its way to
Covent Garden on the town's best engine hitched to the fastest
local horses. That evening Jean could not have been so
leisurely about preparing his make-up as was his wont. For
he used to stroll down to the Opera about two hours ahead
of the rising of the curtain, so that he might see to every detail
of make-up, costume, and properties, and might get himself
imbued all over again with the spirit of the rôle of the evening. It was not by chance that his every performance was
perfection.

The same attention was paid to details after the performance as well. The de Reszkes and Lassalle lived at the Continental Hotel in Regent Street when they were in London. They occupied adjoining apartments, took their meals together, worked out together their individual and joint ideas for improving their art. After each opera they would discuss everything that each of them had done, seeking for betterment. The furniture moved aside, they would go through a scene with full stage action. Jean might show how a tenor should manage his tones so as to form the perfectly equal scale. Then Lassalle would demonstrate the "one and only" method which he designated *"la grande ligne."* Edouard would strip to the waist to show how he controlled his abdominal muscles. With ribs expanded and lungs completely filled, "he seemed to raise the lower half of his figure until, like one barrel sliding inside another, it had concealed itself in the vast cavity of his chest."

Herman Klein describes one of these sessions when Tamagno joined the party. The latter had a cold on the chest, but insisted that that did not affect his head tones. It was not as though he were suffering from catarrh in the nose, he said.

> Upon this, Lassalle offered to wager that he could sing higher with his falsetto than Tamagno with his *voce di petto*. The challenge was accepted, and forthwith the two began a vocal duet the like of which I am certain I shall never hear again. Out came Tamagno's A's and B flats, as quickly responded to with the falsetto equivalents from Lassalle's sturdy throat. Then the Italian "went one better"; and the Frenchman, in order, as he said, to help himself up the scale, mounted his chair and emitted the B natural; whereupon Tamagno also stood upon his chair and brought out not only a high C, but a ringing D flat. Lassalle was now for mounting the table, but, this being "ruled out" as an unfair advantage over a less athletic opponent, he proceeded to get the necessary notes from the eminence of his chair, amid terrific applause from the rest of the company. Tamagno now made a bold dash for a D natural but did not quite succeed; and as Lassalle fared no better, we pronounced the result a "dead heat." [33]

Such discussions and helpful suggestions were not confined to fellow artists. The de Reszkes were always ready to give advice and actual instruction to beginners. One day a man, a stranger to them, who had heard of their kindness, took a boy tenor to see them after the opera. "They listened to the boy's singing," he said, "gave him suggestions about placing his tones, how to change the ending of his piece to suit his voice, and so on. The tenor then played on the piano for us and the big basso gave the boy some instructions in breathing. To illustrate this he invited us to hit him in the diaphragm while he explained his ideas. He was surely solid. You would have thought he was an old, intimate friend."

There were a few young men to whom Jean gave lessons quite regularly during these years. One of them, himself a fairly well known tenor, tells a story which shows how conscientiously de Reszke regarded teaching even then. Once this young man sang over a phrase from L o h e n g r i n eighteen times during a lesson, but couldn't produce it to Jean's satisfaction. Wearily the pupil complained, "I can't sing it again," to which Jean replied: "Sing it until you are black in the face and till you get the idea and the expression you need." Finally he said, "Come to the Opera tomorrow evening and stand in the wings." Mr. B. did so, and when Jean reached the phrase, instead of singing it to the audience he turned and sang it to the artist student. Who knows, this may have been the time he was so roundly criticized for turning his back to his fellow artists.

Jean knew that his words were as easily understood in the last row of the theater as in the first, and he said it was because he sang as he spoke. Once he was explaining this to a group of pupils in his dressing-room. "Suppose," he said, "some one came into the room and left the door open. You say, 'Shut the door.' He does not hear you, so you take an easy breath and say, '*Shut the door!*' Still he doesn't hear, so, taking a very deep expansion of the lower ribs, and holding by the expansion of these lower ribs, you put the full force of this air on to the larynx, and pitching the voice into the head with a forward attack, you say, 'SHUT—THE—DOOR!'" He gave this in a singing voice which was heard all over the theater. The cleaners began to scurry around, looking for the imaginary door, for Jean's voice always carried the note of authority; and the pupils had a conclusive demonstration that their teacher really did know what he was talking about.

If the brothers thought a young singer had little chance in a company of famous artists, they not only said so, but helped him or her to secure an engagement in a different company. Or if such a young singer seemed not to be getting a fair deal from a manager they did not hesitate to make their opinion known. When a young woman at the beginning of her career became ill during a season in Boston, and the management sent word that she would have to sing or her contract would be broken, she promptly sent for Jean and Edouard, secure in the knowledge that they would befriend her. Jean went straight to the manager and insisted on his according this young artist the same consideration shown more famous singers.

Even the choristers were protected by the de Reszke kindness. The Covent Garden stage manager was given to using rather strong language. One day at rehearsal, when the ballet girls failed to respond to his directions as quickly as he would have liked, he flew into a rage and swore roundly at them. The sympathetic de Reszkes endured it for a few moments and then called the manager aside and remonstrated with him, saying that the girls had to work very hard, for very poor pay, that they were worthy of respect, that they objected to hearing them so roughly spoken to, adding that it might be to the gentleman's advantage to remember these things. And a humble charwoman still recalls with a thrill the time when, just as she reached the entrance of the Metropolitan, she noticed the elegant M. Jean de Reszke a few steps behind her and held the door open for him, well pleased to serve him. To her surprise he removed his hat with a sweep, held the door himself and begged her to precede him. "There wasn't anybody there to watch him either," she explained, "so it shows he really wanted to treat me like a lady." Nor was Jean less liberal with more practical help. Whenever he learned of a needy case among the staff he promptly supplied money. Once when he was in the manager's office, word came up that a workman had been injured in moving a piece of scenery. Promptly Jean went down to see for himself what had happened. He had the man removed to a hospital, paid his expenses and gave him enough money to relieve him from worry during his enforced idleness. He never forgot that at the end of the season all the less luminous employees of the Metropolitan had a party, and always he insisted on supplying the champagne and contributing money too.

Sometimes men achieve a reputation for generosity because they have given a large sum of money to a single cause,

Photo Dupont, N. Y.

THE BROTHERS
Jean and Edouard de Reszke

From a portrait by Adjukiewicz

JOSEPHINE DE RESZKE
Aged about 30

and sometimes they are considered gentlemen because they happen to have been born into "good" families; but when from all sides and from people in all walks of life comes the spontaneous exclamation, "The de Reszkes were such gentlemen!" followed by specific instances of that largeness of spirit, that gentleness in strength, that practical kindness, all of which one likes to associate with the older meaning of the term, the conviction is borne in that here were two men who did indeed adorn humanity. Dear old Mrs. Malaprop—one can hear her asking either of them: "You are not like Cerberus, three gentlemen at once, are you?"

THE WINTER OF 1889-90 Jean and Edouard sang in Warsaw and St. Petersburg. For Jean this meant two fresh ordeals. He was a Russian subject, and he was to sing before the Tsar. His nervousness was painful, and even Edouard's steadying presence and reassurance were of small avail. But all went well, and the Tsar conceived a great affection for both de Reszkes. Jean, it is said, was the only professional artist who ever dined with him at his own table. He commanded the brothers to sing for him whenever that would not interfere with their regular engagements; for of course a "command" from their sovereign could not well be ignored. On one of these occasions the Tsar, knowing that Jean had received many rich gifts, and knowing too that he had no need of money, asked what he might give him to show his appreciation. It was then that Jean said he would be grateful if the Reszke patent of nobility were confirmed, and the suggestion was promptly acted upon. For years caustic journalists had asked, "Whence the *de?*" Now they said: "But if our friends were *de* Reszke all the while, why does the Tsar need to ennoble them now?" Even Warsaw smiled at what it thought an amusing aspect of Jean's snobbishness.

But all Warsaw turned out to hear its choirboy grown world-famous tenor. How, Jean asked himself, would the "home folks" receive his art? Elsewhere he had been thunderingly applauded, but how would it be here in the homeland? That moment, just before he came upon the Warsaw stage, was one of the most difficult in his entire career. And then a shower of roses, such as had perhaps been received only by his sister Josephine, singing to the Polish audiences who loved her, rained upon him. Before him were not the strange faces of a London or a Paris audience, but those of friends, of men and women he had played with as a child, of schoolmates. He gripped his throat and could hardly keep from sobbing. It required an almost superhuman effort to begin; but having begun, he lost all nervousness, and Warsaw also echoed, "This is the ideal Romeo."

The Tsar invited Jean to return to St. Petersburg the following season, but this he could not do. When his retirement from the Paris Opera was announced at the same time, some Paris newspapers laid the blame, for blameworthy the loss was considered, on the management, who were accused of

84

being niggardly. Jean's fee at this time was, however, 15,000 francs ($3,000) a month, more than any other artist had ever received at the Opera, under any management. The following letter, sent to him by the Director, attests the place the famous tenor held in both public and managerial esteem.

PARIS, 30 May 1890

MY DEAR JEAN,

You must have seen the article which appeared yesterday in *Le Figaro*. Your departure is, you see, the pretext for a campaign against us, and I am sure you will be pained by it.

It is said we did not wish to renew your engagement. You know there is nothing in that; that the Opera is your home, that the directors are your friends, that no question of importance has ever divided us, that you have always been treated, as much by us as by the public, like a spoiled child, and that your leaving us depends only on you.

I cannot believe that you have, as one hears, renounced for the coming winter the Parisian public which loves you so much. In its interest, in ours, and even in your own, let us hope that you have not spoken the final word on this subject and that you will arrive at an arrangement which will permit you to give us a few months.

If you have important reasons for going to St. Petersburg and elsewhere for a season, could you not make at least one *rentrée* at the Opera, even if only for a month or two, say in October? You could sing what you wished, you could earn some money, and that would not prevent your having a season in Russia following this, after which you could still give us several months before your departure for London.

It is of course understood that if you decide not to sing elsewhere we beseech you to grant us eight months in Paris and we shall be happy to have you.

Finally, give us something, even if it must be only a little, and the more the better. I appeal to your old affection and I count on a favorable response.

My kindest regards

P. GAILHARD

The London impresario and public did not have these worries. Operatic prognosticators there whetted the Wagnerian appetite in 1890 by announcing that Jean had agreed to play Siegmund in Die Walküre. Of course that particular hope was never realized, though within a lustrum the Wagnerites were to be more than satisfied. The production of Romeo in French had started a craze for giving all operas in their original languages, and Jean's exquisite diction had played no small part in creating this desire. During the 1890 season Le Prophète, La Favorita, Hamlet, and Carmen were all sung in French for the first time.

Many years earlier Joseph Addison had set down an account of the progress of Italian opera on the English stage, because he was sure that the great-grandchildren of the operagoers of 1710 would be "very curious to know the reason why their forefathers used to sit together like an audience of foreigners in their own country, and hear whole plays acted before them in a tongue which they did not understand." When English poetasters began to translate Italian operas the result brought Addison new and strange delights. "I have known the word 'and' pursued through the whole gamut; have been entertained with many a melodious 'the'; and have heard the most beautiful graces, quavers, and divisions bestowed upon 'them,' 'for,' and 'from,' to the eternal honor of our English particles."

"At length," he goes on, "the audience grew tired of understanding half the opera; and therefore, to ease themselves entirely of the fatigue of thinking, have so ordered it at present, that the whole opera is performed in an unknown tongue.... I have often been afraid, when I have seen our Italian performers chattering in the vehemence of action, that they have been calling us names, and abusing us among themselves; but I hope, since we put such an entire confidence in them, they will not talk against us before our faces, though they may do it with the same safety as if it were behind our backs. In the meantime, I cannot forbear thinking how naturally a historian who writes two or three hundred years hence, and does not know the taste of his wise forefathers, will make the following reflection: 'In the beginning of the eighteenth century, the Italian tongue was so well understood in England, that operas were acted on the public stage in that language.'"

What indignation poor Addison would have felt had he

known that even 180 years later the grandchildren of those great-grandchildren were content, not only to listen to opera in a foreign tongue, but to sit through operas written in English and then translated into a foreign tongue! For that is what happened in 1890 (though not for the first time). E s m e r a l d a, an opera by Goring Thomas, an Englishman, had been produced in English seven years before, without success. Its French *reprise* was, however, played to a house in which every seat and every inch of standing-room were occupied; but the part of Phœbus, sung by Jean de Reszke, was the only conspicuous success. Addison was answered (not by name) by a commentator who inquired whether anything could have induced the composer to allow E s m e r a l d a to be played in English when to do so would have meant depriving himself of the services of the de Reszkes and Lassalle.

The early eighteenth century had its Addison and Steele to satirize some of the absurdities of the stage. For a few years in the late nineteenth that particular function of theirs was assumed by Bernard Shaw, who went threshing around among London's musical doings with his satirical flail. In 1890, to be exact, he became the music critic of *The World,* and for four years thereafter his lucid, biting comments were applied to matters which lay somewhat outside the scope of the rationalizing which was his strength. Fortunately he amused himself in this way for only a few years, so that his cyclonic, stimulating assaults did not reach that stage when satire too persistently indulged becomes subversive of the end it seeks. Both the de Reszkes came well within reach of his attacks, though a gentleman who signed himself "Sforzando" was quite wrong when he wrote, after admitting that even he was beginning, in 1902, to speak of Jean de Reszke as the one great tenor he had heard: "And yet (to be quite truthful) I quite remember the day when amateurs and critics, with G.B.S. at their head, used to object to Jean's singing in the Wagner roles." [34]

This Mr. Shaw denies, in a letter with which he has favored me, and which is here printed in full:

Malvern Hotel
Malvern
5th September 1932

DEAR MISS LEISER:

Never mind what Sforzando—Heaven forgive him! —wrote in 1902. It is the exact contrary of the truth. You

will find in my three volumes of Music in London, covering three years of the heyday of the de Reszkes, that I
never ceased to urge them to give up their eternal repeti-
tions of Lohengrin and Gounod's Faust, and bring themselves up to date by tackling the mature Wagner. At
last, when some officious hanger-on tried to get up a
testimonial to Jean, I contemptuously refused to sign it
or to take Jean seriously until he had qualified himself
as a modern first rank tenor by playing Siegfried and
Tristan.

My taunts had their effect; for he presently appeared
as Siegfried and sang the part as it had never been sung
before, in beautifully uttered German, with Edouard as
Wotan. It was such an astonishing new departure for a
man who was then finishing his career that I then believed what I had been told about his having been long
familiar with the Ring and Tristan in private.

When I was a youth in Dublin I heard Jean play
Don Giovanni and Valentine in Faust. He was a godlike
juvenile, and was easily the best I had heard in both
parts. And I have not since heard him surpassed. Some
years later, in London, I went to a performance of Le
Nozze di Figaro expressly to hear this wonderful baritone
as Almaviva. To my astonishment he had grown fat and
genially stupid, and his fine high baritone had become a
basso cantante, rather weak in the bass.

Of course this was Edouard, of whom I had never
heard; and Jean had become a tenore robusto.

When Poles are not cretins they are sometimes very
beautiful creatures; and Jean was decidedly one of the
beautiful ones. And he never had a rival who was anything but a foil to him except Vandyk [sic], who soon
shouted a fine voice away, and Alvary, a remarkable
Siegfried, who, though a fine actor and diseur, had no
voice at all in the De Reszke sense, and seemed to be
making the best of a cracked clarinet. The rest were
Carusos without Caruso's voice, and seemed to have
developed their larynxes by calling newspapers and
announcing the names of railway stations. Jean's difficulty
was his range. He could sing a ringing B natural when
he was in good form; but he could only touch C, and
was afraid of it. He could barely get through the duel
scene in Les Huguenots, transposed half a tone down.

Both Lohengrin and Die Meistersinger suited him exactly; but he was not a high note stunter, and, as far as I know, never touched the Verdi operas of the Trovatore phase.

His nearest predecessor must have been Mario; but when, as a smallish boy, I heard Mario at a concert, he was a toneless baritone with a falsetto C. He had smoked all the quality out of his voice.

I wrote quite a good deal about the De Reszkes, not, I hope, inappreciatively; and I shall read your book with lively interest when it appears.

Faithfully
G. BERNARD SHAW

A perusal of Mr. Shaw's collected musical criticism bears out parts of this letter, though what he says about Jean's high notes is refuted by other observers.

The 1890 season opened with Faust. Mr Shaw fully appreciated the good qualities of both de Reszkes, who sang "like dignified men, not like male viragoes" (and that other singers didn't take the hint exasperated him), but he felt that Jean, though his voice was better than the year before, was "still vaguely romantic rather than intelligent in his acting." However, "the chance of hearing such a Walther as Jean de Reszke with such a Sachs as Lassalle ... ought to set on foot a Wagnerian pilgrimage to London from the ends of Europe." Still, Jean was guilty of "exasperating unpunctuality and ir-resolution." Edouard escaped with the stricture that he ought never to have relinquished the part of St. Bris, which fitted him to a semitone, in favor of that of Marcel, which was too low for him.

Bernard Shaw might make shrewd thrusts with his critical rapier and find here a soft spot, there a weak one, in the de Reszke equipment, but the non-critical public, who went to the opera to watch the beautiful acting, to lose themselves in enjoyment of rich sounds, found Jean perfect in his romantic, Edouard in his robust, way. When Le Prophète was given in French for the first time, it was also Jean's first London appearance as Jean de Leyde. The loveliness of his portrayal was startling. He invested every word with its fullest meaning, every note with perfection of sound. And when the King appeared, there in the vaults of the Cathedral of Münster, and de Reszke sang: "Jean, tu regneras ... C'est donc vrai! ...

Je suis l'élu, le fils de Dieu," he murmured the words as one
in a dream; in an ecstasy which illuminated eyes, face, the
very voice itself. His whole being seemed transfigured. After
the "Hymne de Triomphe" he was thrice recalled. Then when
he sang Walther again Londoners thought it an even more
beautiful impersonation than the year before. They loved the
earnestness of his appeal for the chance to join the contest,
they admired the dignity he preserved in remonstrating
against the restrictions enforced by the pedantic Meistersinger. They felt it proper that his love scene with Eva should
combine respect with passion, they were touched by his
modesty in the triumph over Beckmesser in the final scene,
and they thrilled to the beauty of his "Preislied" as though
they themselves were lover or beloved.

Whether Edouard appeared in his resplendent Mephisto
costume, or whether, as once in S o n n a m b u l a, his top-
boots stubbornly refused to go over his breeches, and he had
to wear checked trousers of the latest cut while the top half of
him was garbed in the mode of the early nineteenth century,
the people loved this human pipe-organ, for his voice, for his
never-failing good humor, for his own enjoyment of his rôles.

On the last night of the season a gala performance of
C a r m e n was given as a benefit for Augustus Harris. The
chief interest centered in Jean de Reszke and Jean Lassalle,
as Don Jose and Escamillo, both of whom sang these parts
for the first time. Don Jose is one of the de Reszke rôles about
which opinion has been divided, but that first performance
was joyously received. Jose is a character that calls for vigorous
acting besides good singing, and admirers of the Polish tenor
had for some time wished to see him in it. Jean had read
Merimée's story carefully, and had thought out its histrionic
details without particular regard to the views of his predeces-
sors, who had indulged freely in melodramatic exaggeration.
There was much that was new in his stage business, notably
in the second act, when Jose is tempted by the wily enchantress
to make the plunge that lands him among vagabonds and
outcasts. He showed effectively the growth of Carmen's influence over the susceptible soldier, and his bearing and expression were marked by genuine tragic intensity at the close of
the third act when Jose recognizes that the heartless girl who
has led him from the path of duty is anxious to throw herself
into the arms of the sturdy bullfighter, Escamillo. Immediately
after he had plunged the dagger in her heart a look of

unutterable remorse and love came into his eyes. That was a true de Reszke touch.

The *Daily Telegraph* [35] dealt out superlative praise:

> The great feature of the performance was undoubtedly the Don Jose of Mr. Jean de Reszke. Many artists have played the ill-fated dragoon in English opera-houses, but none so as to give the fullness of satisfaction easily imparted by the Polish tenor. To say that he sang the music with as much vocal art as beauty of tone and truth of expression, is to repeat words applicable to his every effort. It was in the embodiment of the character that Mr. de Reszke strikingly surpassed his predecessors. Jose is not seldom a dull sort of personage, blazing up in the last act, to the astonishment of onlookers, who wonder where he has got the fire from. The Jose of last evening was not in any sense wooden. From the moment of his coming under the spell of Carmen the possibility of a great revenge became obvious. He loved passionately, with his whole being absorbed into one overmastering feeling, which shone in his eyes, vibrated in his tones, and spoke eloquently in every gesture. This was the fiery Southern adorer, whose hand is never far from his knife. The last act, therefore, seemed the inevitable end, and very grandly it was played out. Here, then, is an ideal Jose, with memories of whom all who follow him in the part will have to reckon.

The critic for *Truth* [36] was less favorably impressed, feeling that Jean was not at his ease, although certain points in his impersonation showed "a touch of the true artist. He was at his worst in the second, and at his best in the last act, where the scene of Carmen's murder was very finely rendered."

Herman Klein evaluated the performance in these words:

> M. de Reszke did not make himself up like a starved ghost [in the last act], neither did he rush about like a savage animal in a cage. He looked the picture of despair, and he made his piteous appeal to Carmen with the tone of a man who is yearning for love, not for an excuse to commit murder. When at last driven to extremities, he did not gloat over his revenge nor chase his victim from corner to corner as a cat might chase a mouse. He simply

stood at the entrance to the bull-ring, and when Carmen
made her attempt to escape, he seized his dagger as by
a sudden impulse and stabbed her as she was endeavoring
to pass him. An instant later he was leaning over her
lifeless body in tears, horror-stricken at the deed he had
committed. This surely was the true reading of the
episode. Nor was it the only scene upon which M. Jean
de Reszke, with rare artistic insight, contrived to throw a
new and consistent light. . . . Fierce and absorbing passion
revealed itself in his facial expression, his gestures, and,
above all, the thrilling tones of his voice. Never before
has the beautiful passage where Jose brings forth the
flower that Carmen gave him and tells her how it cheered
his lonely prison hours, been invested with such charm
of voice and such tenderness and warmth of delivery.[37]

Paris agreed with the praising contingent. It had an opportunity to judge for itself when a gala performance was
given on the eleventh of December 1890 to raise funds for a
statue to the composer of C a r m e n, Georges Bizet. How vital
Jean's assistance was to the success of the undertaking may be
judged from the following telegram:

                                         November 17
JEAN DE RESZKE, near Vienna,
        The Bizet Committee, presided over by Thomas,
Gounod and Reyer, composed of all the big artists and
journalists of all parties, has decided to give a gala performance of C a r m e n at the Opéra Comique. I come
in their name to ask you to give to this single performance the prestige of your participation. We should then
be certain of large receipts for the statue and could cele-
brate gloriously the glorious memory [of Bizet]. I shall
be happy to receive and communicate your favorable
response. We shall accept your date. Our best wishes.
                         ARTHUR MEYER, Director
                                 Le Gaulois

The splendor of this occasion, to which Jean gladly contributed his art, and which was attended by tout Paris, caused
great excitement. Even in the highest galleries, the Parisian
lorgnette, astonished at being pointed so high, revealed
Parisian "somebodies." Almost $10,000 was raised, and the

evening was no less an artistic than a financial success. "The ideal tenor, M. Jean de Reszke, is really the perfect Don José whom we have awaited in order positively to determine the type we have so long dreamed of," was the verdict.

The Covent Garden season of 1891 confirmed this opinion, the *Illustrated Sporting and Dramatic News* reporting that "every possible effect was made with apparent spontaneity, and the pathos and dramatic power of his acting in the fearful scene with which the opera closes, held the audience spell-bound."

"In every sense M. de Reszke's embodiment of the unfortunate dragoon transcends that of any other artist who has yet appeared," concluded the critic of the *Athenæum*. Some time thereafter Henry Finck, the critic for the *New York Evening Post*, said: "His Don José is certainly his best rôle, with the exception of that of Walther." (More recently Zélie de Lussan, one of the most famous Carmens, announced that she had sung the rôle seven hundred and eighty-nine times, to forty-nine different Don Josés, and that "the thirteenth and most satisfactory was Jean de Reszke.") Later Chicago also added its testimony of approval, admitting some surprise at the ardor which Jean added, in his Don José, to the poise and manliness of his more dignified characters.

Before Chicago had a chance to hear the de Reszkes they had another season to fill in London, where there was some complaint that, although the prima donna had been deposed as the be-all and the end-all of an operatic season, a new idol had been set up in her place. Yet there was some comfort in knowing that the affections of the English public had at least centered on a worthy object. Jean de Reszke was a consummate artist; his impersonations were considered flawless by most of the public, and they worshiped where they pleased. There was a feeling, nevertheless, that opera ought not to depend on one man, as it had, for one or two seasons, depended on de Reszke. He had filled the opera house. He had, through his superb art, given thousands of people some understanding of Carlyle's description of music as a kind of unfathomable speech which "leads us to the edge of the Infinite, and lets us gaze for moments into that." For this and for his lovable personality London was, of course, grateful, but all the same, this singer had become too important. His salary, which later became such a burning question in New York, was never much discussed in Paris or London. Opera was bigger than any single artist; but nobody would have sacrificed this particular single artist.

The 1891 Covent Garden season offered fewer new things than enterprising journalists promised and recorded. Jean, it was said, was going to sing Siegfried or Siegmund; it was hoped he would learn the chief rôle in Mascagni's C a v a l-l e r i a R u s t i c a n a; and it was not only said he would sing in T a n n h ä u s e r, but it was reported, of course inaccurately, that both he and his brother *had* appeared in it with Madame Albani. One would hardly think the rawest reporter would have the temerity to dismiss artists of the standing of these two—these three, for Albani was not to be sneezed at— without so much as attending the opera.

The critic of *The World* had a good deal to say about the de Reszkes that season, and his vigorous comments were certainly based on a lively presence at the performances. Van Dyck made his début, and in him, said Shaw, Edouard had met his match. He played Mephistopheles, owing to the new-comer's presence, "with fratricidal relish and vigor," and he resorted to unnecessary foolery. One evening his eye lighted on a huge sunflower in Marguerite's flower-bed, and he very nearly queered the pitch of the quartet by plucking it and depositing it in the dress of Fräulein Bauermeister, "before whose diminutive figure it flourished like an umbrella during the rest of the scene." Mr. Shaw was not alone in hoping that this jape would not become traditional, nor was he the only one who thought Edouard's singing that season not up to his usual form, but his were, as one need hardly remark, the most pungent comments.

Edouard himself knew that his Mephisto was not like any other. When any one suggested that he did not create a very convincing illusion of the Evil One, he replied complacently: "Je suis un *bon* diable"; and, he might have added, "the prince of darkness is a gentleman." He tried his best not to look too kind a devil, but his jolly blue eyes, his generally comfortable aspect, and his face made that difficult. The care of his beard, an embellishment he would have been glad to dispense with, was a great trial to him. It irked him to spend so much time getting every hair into place, but he felt that if left unadorned his round face would look positively cherubic. He was sure, moreover, that it was quite in keeping with the Devil's nature to be very genial and attractive when he first made his suggestions to Faust. He did try to look more

satanic as the opera progressed, but though every one delighted in his own enjoyment of his antics, not every one
thought that his was a true interpretation. The following
Shavian dissertation expresses the views of the dissenting
minority, and since it adds observations on Jean which no one
else would have dared to make concerning that idol, it is
quoted at length:

> His [Edouard's] firm conviction that he is curdling
> the blood of the audience with demonstrations of satanic
> malignity when he is in fact infecting them with his
> mountainous good humor; his faith in the diabolic
> mockery of a smile that would make the most timid child
> climb straight up on his lap and demand to be shown
> how a watch opens when blown on; the exuberant agility
> with which he persuades himself that his solid two hun-
> dred and forty pounds of generously nourished flesh and
> blood are a mere vapor from the mists of the bottomless
> pit—all these sights are dear to the hearts of stalls and
> gallery alike.
>
> And then his singing! Singing is not the word for it:
> he no longer sings: he bawls, reveling in the stunning
> sound with a prodigality which comes of knowing that
> he has so much voice to draw on that no extravagance
> can exhaust it. It is magnificent; but it is not Mephistoph-
> eles. The price we have to pay for it is the destruction
> of all dramatic illusion whilst he is on the stage; that is
> to say, during about three-quarters of the whole perform-
> ance. To say the least, it is not cheap. It would be out of
> all reason if the singing were like the acting. Fortunately,
> it is not; for the separation between the musical and the
> intellectual is uncommonly marked in the de Reszke
> family. In Edouard's case there is more than separation:
> there is divorce. Not that I would imply for a moment
> that our pet baritone has no intelligence. I have not the
> slightest doubt that if he had to live by his brains, as I
> have, he would find plenty of them—in an extremely
> rusty condition, no doubt, but still of sufficient quantity
> and quality. What I do say is that he has found his voice
> and his musical instinct so entirely adequate to his
> modest needs, that he never thinks about his work, and
> never makes any point that is not a purely musical one.

The intellectual vacuity of his king in Lohengrin

baffles description; a deaf man would mistake the opera for Donizetti's Anna Bolena, so unlike anybody except Henry VIII does he look as he stands there making the chandelier buzz with "*O sommo Dio.*" ... Even in the not exactly super-subtle part of Friar Lawrence, of which, especially in the exquisite potion scene, he shows the most perfect musical comprehension, he cannot divest himself of a puzzle-head air, as if he were far from sure what was going to come of it all, and were depending rather doubtfully on Brother Jack to see it safely through. Only as Mephistopheles does he wake up, not to the dramatic requirements of the character, but to the opening for a rare piece of sport as the devil in a red dress, with a serenade full of laughs (in which, by the by, it must be admitted that he sings his rivals' heads off). Jean, whom it is hard to conceive as the big brother, may be presumed to have his mind kept active by domestic cares; for if the two brothers and Lassalle still live together, it is evident that Jean must think for the three. And yet it cannot be said that he overtasks his brain on the stage. Except in a character like Romeo, which proceeds on the simplest romantic lines, he creates very little dramatic illusion.

...Now whether Jean, in his anxiety to prove himself a real tenor after he had compromised himself by starting as a baritone, resolved to dissemble the intelligence which made him such a memorable Valentine, is more than I care to decide; but it is certain that he has not fulfilled his early promise as an actor. He is an enchanting Lohengrin; and his Walther von Stolzing, though the very vaguest Franconian knight ever outlined on the stage, makes Covent Garden better than Bayreuth on Meistersinger evenings. But Wagner would have urged Jean somewhat vehemently to make these heroes a little more vivid, alert, and willful, even at the cost of some of their present nebulous grace.[38]

Edouard's Plunket in M a r t a escaped serious strictures for a change; was even praised by some critics. His Leporello, which many still consider his best rôle, was mercilessly flayed in some quarters, whereas Mr. Shaw not only approved, but had been peevish at his delay in assuming the rôle. In Leporello, he insisted, Edouard would have an ideal part, exactly right for his range, "and full of points which his musical intelligence would seize instinctively without unaccustomed mental exertion." Edouard sang the part in the centenary performance of D o n G i o v a n n i in Paris on November 4 1887, as Mr. Shaw would have known had he kept in touch with affairs operatic in the French capital. Others felt that Edouard had a wrong conception of the character. "Some of the mistakes he makes as Leporello," was one adverse opinion, "he might surely avoid without distressing himself; for instance, when he talks about the unearthly quality of the eyes of the Commendatore, it is not according to the fitness of things that he should stand at the back of the figure, where the terror-stricken eyes could not possibly be seen." [39] However, Edouard might have been comforted, if indeed, criticism ever discomfited him, had he read that in Chicago only a few months later Lilli Lehmann was thought "very absurd" as Donna Anna, and his Leporello the only feature which saved the performance from utter inanity.

Maurel's Don Giovanni suffered in comparison with that of Jean. Shaw had seen Jean in this part when he had less than a tenth of Maurel's skill and experience; and yet, he thought, Mozart would have found the younger man the more sympathetic interpreter. The older man's Valentine suffered similarly. Gounod, Mr. Shaw said, had made Valentine a saint, a martyr, and "a dreamy and pathetically beautiful youth with a pure young voice" was the ideal actor for the part:

"Jean de Reszke, when he sang baritone parts, and was eighteen years younger and some thirty odd pounds lighter than today, was far more moving and memorable as Valentine than Maurel is now, though Maurel acts with great power... or than Lassalle, who, conscious of his merits as a singer, avoids invidious comparisons by the quick-witted expedient of not acting at all." [40]

It was a season, this of 1891, that offered only one novelty —Verdi's O t e l l o, given on August 15 with Jean in the title rôle. The event was awaited with curiosity like that evoked in earlier years by the announcement that he would sing Don Jose. Tamagno, who had seemed the physical ideal for the rôle, lacked refinement and intelligence, but had a voice considered better than de Reszke's. There were those who warned Jean, in print, against attempting this declamatory music, taking the opportunity to remark that he was "no longer a

chicken," and was probably a year or two older than some
journalists "made out."

According to some reports Jean finally agreed to learn the
part only because he was alarmed by the sudden success of
Van Dyck, and "fell first morally and then physically ill, until
at last (not merely in the American sense of the word) he was
sick, and in his convulsions broke a small blood vessel in his
throat. This was bad enough; but to make matters worse, Mr.
Harris, after many postponements of what he knew would be
the great artistic success of the season, resolved . . . to engage
another tenor. . . . Not until the very day of the performance
was it known whether M. de Reszke or his newly-imported
substitute would play." [41] It is true that Jean hesitated a long
time before agreeing to sing the rôle. In the first place, though
he loved the music, he disliked playing a murderer; it did
not suit his temperament. In the second place, he thought
Tamagno's interpretation excellent; but it was a conception
entirely different from his own. He knew of the reasons assigned for his failure to sing Otello, and wanted to prove
gossips in the wrong, but it seemed to him that, feeling as
he did about the interpretation of the rôle, it would not be
wise to undertake it. Moreover, he had been ill frequently
during that season, so ill that Queen Victoria asked her personal physician to make inquiries; and even after he agreed
to study the opera and it was definitely scheduled, it had to be
postponed again and again. On July 15 it was finally performed, and the consensus of opinion was that he gave an admirable performance after he had overcome the nervousness
apparent at the start. Comparison with Tamagno's interpretation were inevitable, but for the most part Jean came off
the better. The *Figaro* correspondent sent home word that
Tamagno had been outdistanced by a hundred cubits, and
that the Milanese, who had borne him on their shoulders in
triumph when he first sang the part, had they heard de Reszke,
would have wanted to march around carrying the very walls
of Covent Garden.

Jean made O t e l l o a thing of beauty. He lacked, to be
sure, the animal fury of his predecessor in the title rôle, but he
also spared his listeners the latter's high tones, which were
often "like the scream of a brass nine-pounder." He endowed
the rôle with the chivalric and romantic elements which had
been lost in Tamagno's almost hysterical savagery. If there
were not so many ringing, startling notes, there was more ele-

gance, more humanity, more truth; and in the last scene his impersonation was charged with an intensity of love and remorse and pity quite beyond the power of Tamagno to portray. There were some, however, who felt that Jean's smooth voice was ill suited to the ferocity and bursts of passion of a Moor and a murderer—as such are popularly conceived—and that for excelling in these respects Tamagno might be forgiven many a fault of vocal style.

The evening was an exciting one from more points of view than that of a new de Reszke rôle. Victor Maurel's interpretation of Iago was especially fine. He sang to the galleries once in a while, he was guilty of some exaggerations of gesture and facial expression, but he gave an inspired performance. Bernard Shaw got really excited about this Otello affair, and admitted having witnessed with a certain satisfaction the curious demonstrations which enlivened it. As usual, he gave at once the most exhaustive and the sprightliest account, part of which follows:

> The first sign of tumult was a disposition to insist on applauding Maurel in season and out of season, even to the extent of causing ridiculous interruptions to the performance. The second was an almost equally strong disposition to disparage—I had almost said to hoot—Jean de Reszke, who was defended by vehement counterdemonstrations, in leading which Lassalle...was the most conspicuous figure. Partial as the demonstration was, it was far too general to be the work of a claque; and I recommend it to the most serious consideration of Brother Jean.
>
> His acting as Otello was about equally remarkable for its amateurish ineptitudes and for its manifestations of the natural histrionic powers which he has so studiously neglected for the last fifteen years.... His reluctance to determined physical action came out chiefly in his onslaught on Iago, which he managed in such a way as to make the audience feel how extremely obliging it was of Maurel to fall. And at the end of the third act, in simulating the epileptic fit in which Otello's fury culminates, he moved the gods to laughter by lying down with a much too obvious solicitude for his own comfort.
>
> ...Throughout the first two acts his diffidence and irresolution again and again got the better of his more

vigorous and passionate impulses. This was intensified no doubt by nervousness; but it was partly due also to his halting between a half-hearted attempt at the savage style of Tamagno and the quieter, more refined manner natural to himself. In the third act, when the atmosphere of the house had become friendly, he began to treat the part more in his own fashion, and at last got really into it, playing for the first time with sustained conviction instead of merely with fitful bursts of self-assertion. Indeed, but for that gingerly fall at the end, this third act would have been an unqualified success for him. As it was, it showed, like his Don Jose and other post-Van Dyck performances, that when the rivalry of younger men and the decay of his old superficial charm with advancing years force him to make the most of all his powers, he may yet gain more as an actor than he will lose as a singer.[42]

Bernard Shaw's chiding of Jean was like that of the Lord, who chasteneth whom He loveth. Jean should have been swinging the sledge-hammer and making the sparks fly in Mime's stithy, or waking Brünnhilde on the fiery mountain, rather than "shouting that detestable and dishonorable drinking song in the last act of the most conventional of the historical impostures of Scribe and Meyerbeer." (The reference is to L e P r o p h è t e.) He might at least have played T a n n- h ä u s e r once before the end of the season. He had played Don Jose only once. But for the success of Van Dyck, so thought Shaw, he would have shirked Raoul; as it was, "had Van Dyck been dressed at the wing, ready to go on and take his place at the slightest sign of indifference, he could not have worked harder at his part. The very attitudes of fifteen years ago came back to him: there was no more irresolute mooning about the stage and thinking better of each languid impulse to do something: he acted with passion and sang with his utmost eloquence and tenderness. Any great brilliancy of vocal effect was put out of the question by the audacious transpositions to which he resorted in order to bring the highest notes of the part within his range; but he was all the better able to handle his music sympathetically."[43]

Mr. Shaw's impatience was partially justified, though at the time it might have seemed that he was expecting more of Jean than one expects of the proverbial leopard. Jean's public gave no thought to whether he ought to be playing more heroic rôles. Less critical than impressible, they simply loved him as he was and for what he did, and Edouard shared in this affection. Sir (as he was by that time) Augustus Harris knew the strength of that affection, and, aware of the high salaries paid in America, took the precaution to have several of his contracts settled before his artists visited that country, from whose bourne not all singers returned. The de Reszkes might have journeyed to the United States sooner but for the astuteness of the directors of the Paris Grand Opera. During the preparations for the *reprise* of R o m e o at Paris in 1888, those gentlemen had been profoundly impressed with the significance of Jean's interpretation, and two months before the first performance they persuaded both Jean and Edouard to sign a new two-year contract.

IN NEW YORK Grand Opera had known vicissitudes sometimes amusing, sometimes disheartening. The battle between Italian and German opera had been heated even if not sanguinary. In 1825-26 Manuel Garcia had given America its very first Italian opera. New York having decided that the Park Theatre, where that event occurred, was no longer sumptuous enough to house the exotic luxury, built its first opera house in 1833, and called it the Italian Opera House. This endured only two years, and was not succeeded by another institution built especially for opera (or, rather, remodeled for that purpose) until eleven years later, when Palmo's Opera House came into existence.

Ferdinand Palmo owned a popular restaurant called "Café des Milles Colonnes," near Duane Street in Broadway. His reason for deciding to serve opera instead of plaice and chips is shrouded in mystery. He bought a building for his new venture, but "Stoppani's Arcade Baths" remodeled into a theater made little appeal to that portion of the public which considered an opera house the ideal place for lavish display. In the first place, there were no boxes at all, and secondly, the neighborhood was so unsavory that the impresario felt called upon to issue an announcement that for the accommodation of his patrons a large car would be run uptown as far as Forty-Second Street after the performances, and that police protection would be provided. For four years these baths become opera house served their owner's ambitions. Then, even though opera devotees had the privilege of upholstering the hard benches, which had slats across the back shoulder-high and from which they could see and hear the orchestra composed of "thirty-two professors," the institution was no more, and Signor Palmo retired to the pots and kettles he had deserted.

New York's third opera house, called the Astor Place Opera House, was built in 1847. After five years, according to H. E. Krehbiel,[44] it was killed by the competition of Italian opera with Italian opera, and was succeeded, in 1854, by the Academy of Music, which housed Grand Opera continuously from then until 1886 (and unrivaled until 1883), when it ceased to function because it could no longer accommodate both the old Society, which had always considered Grand Opera its particular show, and the *nouveaux riches* who had

begun to invade the ancient stronghold.* The Metropolitan
Opera House, built in 1883, supplied the need for maintain-
ing nice distinctions of social prestige. Krehbiel calls it "the
last illustration of the creative impulse which springs from
the growth of wealth and social position."

Whether any one had the temerity to violate the sacro-
sanctity of the new Metropolitan's box region as boldly as
one man assaulted the crumbling dignity of the Academy of
Music, one cannot say, but concerning the latter there is an
amusing story.

> It was told of a man who had suddenly risen to what
> was then great wealth, that, having taken a lady to the
> opera, he was met by the disappointing assurance that
> there were no seats to be had.
>
> "What, nowhere?"
>
> "Nowhere, sir; every seat in the house is taken, ex-
> cept, indeed, one of the private boxes that was not sub-
> scribed for."
>
> "I'll have that."
>
> "Impossible, sir. The boxes can only be occupied by
> subscribers and owners."
>
> "What is the price of your box?"
>
> "Six thousand dollars, sir."
>
> "I'll take it."
>
> And drawing out his pocketbook he filled up a check
> for six thousand dollars and escorted his lady to her
> seat, to the surprise and, indeed, to the consternation of
> the elegant circle, which saw itself completed in this
> unexpected manner.[45]

Neither Mr. Henry E. Abbey, manager of the new Metropolitan, nor Colonel James H. Mapleson, manager of the
Academy of Music, was successful in the exceedingly costly
rivalry which ensued. Colonel Mapleson had among his artists
Mesdames Patti and Gerster, and Madame Nordica made her
début under his auspices, but none of them sang to full houses.
At the Metropolitan, where things had gone no better, even
though Mesdames Nilsson and Sembrich were among the
artists, the financial losses were very great. Negotiations were
begun to transfer the house to Ernest Gye, then manager of

* See Amram C. Dayton: *Last Days of Knickerbocker Life in New York*, for
what Krehbiel calls the "social decay" of this period.

Covent Garden, London, but they were not concluded. Mr. Gye had, in the meantime, been experimenting not only with some of Wagner's lyric dramas in German, but with an English opera (Charles Villiers Stanford's S a v o n a r o l a) in German translation. The year 1883 saw the performance of five new operas by English composers, two of which (Mackenzie's C o l o m b a, in addition to S a v o n a r o l a) were performed in German, C o l o m b a being given in Hamburg. French operas were being sung in French, German in German. New York, however, had thus far followed the prevailing practice in London and clung to the traditional Italian opera.

The next year Dr. Leopold Damrosch presented a plan for giving opera in German at the Metropolitan, which was accepted by the directors. He abandoned the star system and worked for strong dramatic effects with a good ensemble. Mesdames Amalia Materna, Marianne Brandt, Auguste Kraus (wife of Anton Seidl), and Anton Schott were the principal singers in the company. The German opera season began on November 17 1884 with T a n n h ä u s e r. The following February Dr. Damrosch died. His son Walter accompanied Mr. Edmund C. Stanton, secretary of the Metropolitan, to Europe to organize a company for the next season. One of their most felicitous achievements was the engagement of young Anton Seidl as conductor. Seidl had been secretary to Richard Wagner and had been a member of his household for six years. Of him Wagner had said: "Ich kann ruhig sterben wenn Seidl lebt." ("I can die peacefully, as long as Seidl is alive.")

Alvary, Lilli Lehmann and Emil Fischer were among the artists engaged for the season of 1885-86. A year later Patti too was singing at the Metropolitan, in a "little Italian season." Colonel Mapleson had quietly given up his operatic endeavors at the Academy of Music. In the two or three preceding years, various other Italian companies had essayed a New York season, and there had also been an American Opera Company which endured one season and was then, because of the hopeless condition of its finances, reorganized as the National Opera Company, with Theodore Thomas as musical director.

German opera flourished for seven years in spite of Mapleson's conviction that "sauerkraut opera" could not last, but toward the end of that period some members of the fashionable faction had been getting restive. The art offered to them was too serious. Still, their objections availed them little; the season of 1888-89 saw only one presentation of Italian opera in all New York—a benefit performance of L u c i a   d i L a m m e r m o o r. Immediately after the close of the season, however, an Italian company, under the management of Henry E. Abbey and Maurice Grau, took possession of the new opera house, and about the middle of January 1891 the directors of the Metropolitan announced that they had leased the house to these men, who would give opera in French and Italian the next season. Patrons were amazed. It seemed that instead of going forward Grand Opera was to remain at a standstill or even to retrogress. The public was not slow to show disapproval. Thenceforth, every time Mr. Seidl conducted he was called upon the stage to receive tributes of confidence and admiration. The directors were compelled by popular demand to desert the announced list for the rest of the season, and of the thirty-five performances given after January 20, twenty-five were operas of Richard Wagner.

The season's final performance was D i e   M e i s t e r- s i n g e r. The packed house recalled Mr. Seidl and his singers again and again, and instead of leaving after the last act, summoned one after another of the persons who stood for the system that was being abandoned. This demonstration, according to report, was not participated in by the occupants of the boxes, who preferred Italian opera. They were blithely indifferent to artistic proprieties, being chiefly concerned with the display of gowns and jewels, which were duly admired by the cavaliers who fluttered from box to box during the intermissions. It was said that the management had even been requested to have the last act of D i e   M e i s t e r s i n g e r sung first, as it was "the only act of the opera that had music in it," and the fashionable patrons did not care to listen to the rest. The conduct of the box-holders was anything but compatible with common ideas of good behavior in public places, and on January 21 1891 a notice was hung against the wall in each of the boxes as follows:

January 15 1891

Many complaints having been made to the directors of the Opera House of the annoyance produced by the talking in the boxes during the performances, the board requests that it be discontinued.

BY ORDER OF THE BOARD OF DIRECTORS [46]

Considering all the circumstances, the directors could not be too severely criticized for their readiness to lease the opera house to Abbey and Grau. The German period had not paid very large dividends to the stockholders. Prices of admission had been reduced, whereas the demands of artists had increased. It was only natural that the management should listen to Mr. Abbey when he suggested that a revival of Italian and French operas would swell the coffers of the Metropolitan. Little did they realize that they had appointed Beelzebub—in fact two Beelzebubs—to cast out Satan.

THIS, THEN, was the troubled operatic sea upon which Jean and Edouard de Reszke embarked in the autumn of 1891; for Mr. Abbey had engaged them both for the Metropolitan. The Atlantic Ocean was likewise troubled during the greater part of their crossing on the SS. *Touraine*. Edouard complained bitterly that not all the power of his stentorian voice, issuing from his tremendous body, could still the waves, and it irritated him even more to be ill. Sadly he went to his cabin, there to tend his malady and his mortification, and wait patiently for the rude sea to grow civil. Upon arrival in New York the company did not prepare at once for the Metropolitan season. They were scheduled to go first to Louisville, Kentucky, and then to Chicago for five weeks. On November 9 1891 they inaugurated in Chicago what was later so aptly called "The Golden Age of Music."

The de Reszke brothers, heralded as "the most striking figures on the European stage in the past ten years," had been awaited with much curiosity. The first performance was L o h e n g r i n, of course in Italian. It was the first appearance in America of all the principals. The house was packed. The double tier of boxes, gayly decked with all that wealth and fashion could command, formed a live frieze stretching across both sides of the Chicago Auditorium. And even these decorative listeners had arrived punctually; almost the entire house was seated before the overture began. This audience was familiar with L o h e n g r i n, and consequently was extremely critical. Not a sound issued from them when the curtain went up, but when Edouard began to pour out his Niagara-like voice they became alert. He sprang into immediate favor, and during the intermission his name was on every tongue. The impression deepened as the opera proceeded; Edouard's first American appearance was a triumph. Emma Eames received a welcome enhanced by the fact that she was an American who had achieved decided success abroad. Other members of the cast were likewise well received, but when Jean de Reszke swept into view in his swan-drawn boat, tall, fair as a Viking, the light playing on his shining armor, he was hailed king of the night by only a small part of this strange audience in a strange land.

Curiosity and interest in him had certainly been great and were in a measure satisfied, but complete approbation

was withheld. Oddly enough, the *Daily News* critic, whose
comment follows, voiced the opinion of a minority.

> Jean de Reszke ... is an ideal of the hero. He dressed
> the rôle lavishly and strikingly, though in good taste. His
> voice—which he seemed to economize last night—is rich,
> penetrating, and quite free from the nasal quality which
> afflicts so many tenors. From the opening solo, "Cigno
> gentil," in which he made an admirable impression, to
> the final farewell, it was absolutely true in intonation.
> M. de Reszke is, however, less a singer than a dramatic
> artist who sings. The perfection of his work lies in its
> happy development in the union of both faculties. Re-
> fined, appreciative intelligence governs this art, in which
> the vocalist is forgotten in the interpreter. For the rest,
> he is handsome in appearance, wears glittering accouter-
> ments with easy dignity, and rarely or never goes false in
> gesture or by-play.[47]

In general it was agreed that from the standpoint of both
individual artists and brilliant ensemble such a performance
of L o h e n g r i n had never been given in Chicago, and
probably never in America. It was Edouard, however, who
was most warmly applauded. A few nights later he sang Il
Conte Rudolfo in S o n n a m b u l a, and scored another triumph. Again when R o m e o was first given, it was Edouard
who was applauded at his every appearance, though on that
occasion Emma Eames also "scored a hit," and to her singing
critical observers attributed the awakening, at last, of the
Chicago opera audience, which had been niggardly in bestow-
ing applause. The attendance of the first night was not
equaled again until F a u s t was given. The general attitude
had remained rather lukewarm. Towards Jean de Reszke especially, opera-goers persisted in being hypercritical; and yet,
though he seemed overshadowed from the start by the sheer
force of his big brother (and perhaps by Edouard's genial
personality as well), he rose steadily if not rapidly in the
public favor. Critics became more generous. His Romeo was
warmly praised and his Raoul was considered the best ever
presented in Chicago. His greatest triumph, however, was as
Otello.

By the time F a u s t was produced on November 27, there
was a little grumbling about the idolized Edouard. Even

though he was genial, even if he could give out thunderous volumes of sound "with no more effort than a street car conductor asking for fares," why, asked some people, should he be wildly applauded no matter what he did, to the neglect of the other artists? Not that his Mephisto was underrated by those who voiced this objection. They agreed that his conception of the rôle was "undeniably grand," that he looked as if he had been cast in the very mold of Mephisto, the incarnation of all that was infernal, yet withal a dandy from the lower regions; void of all that could offend, and still offensive—"the Mephistopheles that Gounod gave to the world." They felt that he had the right to claim the rôle as his to hold and use in fee simple; that there had never been a more prepossessing agent of evil; that in making Mephisto jocose and worldly instead of fiendish, he was right. Their affection for him was not lessened by one tittle, but they began to object, or at least the critics did, to having him applauded to the skies, while the "Salve Dimora" of his brother, which was "almost the acme of excellence," was greeted with applause that was barely audible. Volume seemed more highly valued than finished artistry. Still, notwithstanding the excellence recognized by the few, Jean's Faust was described in one place as merely "a fitting third in this trio of artists" (Emma Eames was the Marguerite), though he had used his voice with the taste and artistic perception which characterized all his work, and there was little lacking either histrionically or vocally.

This apathy was, however, transformed into excitement when Aïda was performed on December 11. It was Jean's last appearance in Chicago that year, and his Radames was voted the best performance given by any artist during the entire season. "He cannot be inartistic, either as a singer or as an actor," was the conclusion. "Each succeeding rôle he assumes only seems to prove his genius anew." At last the audience was roused to an appreciation of his greatness, and when the season was over it was generally acknowledged that while Jean had a smaller voice than his brother, he had more intelligence.

There were then, as now, many Poles in Chicago, and they were ecstatic over the success of their countrymen. They gloried in the critiques which lauded their superiorities, they praised the de Reszkes for their qualities as men, they were proud of the fact that they were "artists for art's sake and not simply for pay." "Besides, they are such good Poles," said the

Dziennik Chicagoski, "such loving brothers, so amiable to all
with whom they come in contact, that they compel not only
admiration, but love. It is impossible to speak to them several
times and not be attracted to them with the heart, and only
one conversation is needed to appraise them as real men."
They felt flattered that the brothers regretted their lack of
time to get acquainted with their fellow Poles in Chicago, but
they understood the demands of frequent rehearsals. They
hoped the fame of the de Reszkes would help to glorify their
beloved Poland. But they were not to see their idols again for
nearly two and a half years, because Chicago was getting ready
for its Columbian Exposition in 1892, gave it in 1893, and
suffered with the rest of the country in the financial panic
which reigned the same year. Under these conditions Chicago
could afford neither time nor money for Grand Opera.

The de Reszkes, of course, went through the usual ordeal
of interviewing in America. Their factotum, Willie Schütz,
encountered the first reporter.

"Italians, aren't they?" asked the latter, addressing Willie
as though he were their trainer.

"No," from Willie.

"Well, they sing, don't they? So they're Italians!"

Then the reporter cornered the singers themselves. What
did they think of America? What did they think of the American cuisine? "The meats are better than in Paris, and served
in a more liberal manner" (which sounds enough like a de
Reszke to be an accurate report). What did they think of the
streets and the people? Jean had never before seen such
straight streets, such wide streets, or such dirty streets. And
then, never-failing question asked of visitors to America:
What, please, did he think of the American girl? Of course
Jean hadn't met very many, but he'd noticed their ability to
dispense with the chaperon.

One bright youth, writing in the *American Art Journal,*[48]
admitted that Jean spoke very little English and no American,
and then proceeded to give what he generously termed a "free
translation" of the tenor's chief impressions:

> America is a great country, and one of its greatest
> institutions is ice-water. I never drank water until I came
> here. We use water on the other side to wash, but not
> to drink. When I reached New York I stopped at the
> Hoffman. I wanted some writing materials and rang my

bell. When the boy came I explained as best I could what I wanted. He nodded his head, ran off and returned with a pitcher of ice-water. I rang again. Another boy appeared with ice-water. At breakfast the first thing was a vast pitcher of ice-water to be consumed before I could reach soup. I have been hounded almost to distraction by ice-water. I never saw ice-water until I came here, and it has become a nightmare....

I never saw people rushing along the streets with such speed and energy. When I arrived here I saw thousands of people running down a great wide street, and I said to my brother, "Let us prepare to save ourselves; some great calamity has occurred." We seized our small bag and told the carriage driver to take us to a place of safety. He didn't understand us, but kept on driving in the direction from which the multitude was flying. I stopped him and we both jumped out and tried to learn what terrible evil had overtaken the city. Nobody would listen to us. They hustled and jostled us about and when we attempted to speak they shook their heads. The driver motioned us to reënter the carriage and in a rather nervous condition we obeyed and were driven to the hotel. There I learned that the Chicago Board of Trade had just adjourned and that the sprinting on the streets was the everyday Chicago gait....

The baggage checking system is incomparable. I have two valets lying in premature graves on the Continent from trying to keep track of my baggage, but my present one is growing fat from inaction. What I have seen of Chicago is like a chapter from the *Arabian Nights*. The bar-rooms and barber shops surpass the grandest dreams of Oriental luxury.

All of which was probably largely apocryphal and the contribution of somebody who felt it his duty to help advertise Chicago and its Great Exposition. However, America did make a deep and lasting impression on both the de Reszkes. Their affection for the American people endured, and though they thought the stage of the Paris Grand Opera the best in the world, the people they most enjoyed singing for were the Americans. Edouard wrote glowing accounts to his family in Poland, praising this new country and adjuring his children to love it. "It was as though another commandment had been promulgated," his daughter Minia told me. "We used to repeat to ourselves, my sisters and I, 'You must not lie. You must not steal. You must love America and the Americans.'"

In 1885 Edouard had married Hélène Schütz, sister of the Willie Schütz who for years acted as secretary to both Jean and Edouard, and of Felia Litvinne, who sang with them. Minia (Emilie) was one of four daughters. She it was who had the deepest understanding of both her father's and her uncle's natures and art. On days when her beloved father was to arrive home from his journeys, it was Minia who got up by candle-light and stood shivering on the porch with Edouard's favorite dog, both straining their ears for the first sound of approaching carriage wheels; Minia who in later years was the confidante of both her father and her uncle, and whom Jean wanted with him after his dearly beloved brother had died; Minia who was with Jean when he himself died. Her father seemed to her the "most good" man the world had ever known. And as to that quality great numbers of other people agreed. "He was so *good*," is almost the first comment they make when Edouard de Reszke is mentioned. "He was like a great big St. Bernard. You always wanted to pat him," said Madame Emma Eames. As father he was sometimes stern, but never cruel. However, on those rare occasions when he was really angry about something, the great voice boomed through the house, making the windows rattle. The de Reszke children could never try to excuse a non-appearance with an "I didn't hear," for they knew, and they knew that their father knew they knew, that the torrential voice could be heard almost in the next village if Edouard felt like exerting himself, which was very seldom.

But dearly as Minia loved her father, much as she admired his voice, it was her uncle Jean who filled her with the greatest wonder. "It was glorious to listen to my father sing," she told me. "It was a wonderful voice. But the other man—he did something to the inside of one that my father couldn't do. I can remember when we were all small—I was only about ten years old—what a thrill it was to go to see Uncle Jean when he was living with my Aunt Michalska. He would sing and I would sit and stare, I don't know at what. And then all the way home in the carriage, while the rest would be laughing and joking, I would have to take hold of something and cling to it hard, I would try to think of rags or something else ugly, so that I wouldn't cry. I didn't know what it was, but I thought something inside me would burst whenever I heard my dear uncle sing."

Thousands and thousands of other people, grown men and women, echoed that thought through the years. They knew not what it was that moved them so profoundly when Jean sang, but they felt that their hearts would break. They heard sounds such as must have reached Caliban; such as Caliban could only describe by saying he had heard voices,

> That, if I then had wak'd after long sleep,
> Will make me sleep again; and then, in dreaming,
> The clouds methought would open and show riches
> Ready to drop upon me; that when I wak'd
> I cried to dream again.

Though not all the critics had written in superlatives, though audiences had for the most part been only moderately enthusiastic, Jean himself, it seems, felt well satisfied by the reception accorded him in Chicago, if one may judge from the following letter: [49]

Auditorium Hotel, Chicago
December 9 1891

MY DEAR FRIEND:

I beg to inclose some press cuttings from this place in order that you may learn of the success of your friends in America. I have sung twice in Lohengrin, twice in Faust, twice in the Huguenots, once in Romeo, twice in Otello, and once in Lohengrin at Louisville. That makes ten representations in a month. The public is very warm, very enthusiastic towards us. Edouard, for his part, besides the operas with me, has sung Leporello and in Sonnambula. You would confer on us a great pleasure by showing the cuttings to Harris, to Higgins, and to your colleagues, in order that London may know how the artists of its choice have been winning honors here. Tomorrow I sing Aïda, with Lilli Lehmann, for my farewell in this city; then on Thursday I leave for New York, where I am to make my début on Monday in Romeo. Trusting you are in good health, with a hearty handshake, believe me,

Your devoted and ever grateful,
JEAN DE RESZKE

It may be that this eagerness to let his London friends read favorable criticisms was due to an uneasiness akin to that which prompted the letter Jean wrote to a critic the day before his London début as a tenor. As he had been uncertain of his reception in England though he was then the idol of operatic Paris, so he had been uncertain of his success in America though he had become the favorite tenor at Covent Garden. He expressed his doubts quite frankly during the negotiations with Mr. Grau, saying that he thought it wiser to make a flexible arrangement instead of stipulating a fixed salary; so that if he proved unpopular Mr. Grau would not suffer too great a loss, and, on the other hand, if America liked Jean de Reszke, the singer himself might derive some benefit therefrom. It was finally agreed that Jean was to receive $10,000 a month for eight appearances (two a week), plus 25% of the gross proceeds of a performance in excess of $5,000. Edouard's salary was considerably smaller, but he also shared in the surplus receipts, of which he received 10%. These were verbal agreements. The de Reszkes never had a written contract either with Mr. Harris or Mr. Grau. The impresarios had complete faith in the brothers, they in the impresarios. But although Grau was very fond of them and accepted their recommendations and advice, a contract, written or spoken, was a contract. He observed its every detail, but was not inclined to allow any extras. Jean used to say that Grau would be glad to give a man a cigar but would refuse to give him a match to light it with.

On December 14, the opening night of the 1891 season in New York, the Metropolitan was filled. New York had no scions of royalty to lend radiance to first nights, but it had its Diamond Horseshoe, it had its first families, who saw to it that no undesirables elbowed their way into a box at the Metropolitan; for ownership of a box signified that one had been "accepted," a distinction not lightly bestowed. It was of course a Monday night, and on Monday nights resplendent dowagers and their expensive jewelry were then, as now, on display in the grand tier boxes, against the somber background of their cavaliers.

New York, which remembered Mario, was very curious about the much heralded Jean de Reszke, though that faction which wanted German opera rather resented his coming. For was he not to restore Italian opera? Comparisons with German singers and singing were therefore inevitable, though the

JEAN DE RESZKE AS LOHENGRIN

opera—R o m e o—was French. But as in Chicago, Edouard made the greater impression in this first New York appearance. Said the critic of the *New York Evening Post:*

> In voice and method both of them are more closely related to the French and German schools than to the Italian. Jean lacks that *Schmelz,* or sensuous beauty of tone, which is characteristic of the best Italian and German singers. Edouard has more of this quality, although his voice is less warm and sympathetic than Fischer's or Reichmann's. Both the de Reszkes, furthermore, proved somewhat uneven in their work.... Edouard... sang superbly in the marriage scene, with a magnificent, resonant voice, while in the following act his voice sounded forced, constrained, and puckered up, as if he had eaten alum. So, too, Jean, some of whose tones were most agreeable to the ear, while others were harsh and overloud. Both the tenor and the bass, however, phrase like genuine artists.

The *New York Times* reported as follows:

> His [Jean's] voice has something of the baritone quality in the middle and lower registers, but the upper notes are true tenor tones. His voice has none of the radiant mellowness of the Italian tenors. It resembles the German voices somewhat, but comes nearer to the French voice. It is an agreeable, though not a surprising, organ. The tenor is, however, a man of genuine artistic feeling and of high vocal accomplishments. His phrasing is good and his taste is charming. He showed genuine dramatic feeling in his work last night, and will undoubtedly become a favorite with this public.
>
> The hit of the evening, however, was made by the basso, Edouard de Reszke. This singer demonstrated in a single scene that he is a really great artist. His voice is magnificent in power and range, and is of double quality. His phrasing is superb, and his delivery of Friar Laurence's music last night was imposing in its breadth and dignity. The audience was quick to recognize his superlative merit and applauded him with enthusiasm.[50]

A few days after this performance John C. Freund wrote in his *Music and Drama:* [51]

Jean de Reszke, the tenor, who has a full, almost massive voice, sang with masterly skill.... He sends out his high, robust notes with splendid power. He always sings with taste and judgment, and his personal bearing, if not answering to the ideal of the youthful and impetuous Romeo, is always graceful and spirited. His greatest triumph will come in other operas; but as Romeo the critics as well as the audience welcome him as a great tenor, such men as Campanini and Errani joining in the chorus of unstinted praise. The new tenor triumphed gloriously.

But more instantaneous was the triumph of his brother, the basso, Edouard. His opportunity was but slight, for as Frère Laurent...he has but little to do. Yet in the short scene in the friar's cell, where he blesses the union of the two lovers, his magnificent voice startled the audience into wild applause and three recalls at the close of the act were evidently intended chiefly for him. His voice is of amazing power. It is metallic rather than rich. It is best in the middle register, but even in the lower notes is pure and melodious.

Still another critic appraised Jean as the greater of the brothers. He held that although the new tenor's voice did not have the great volume and force of some of the German singers who had been heard at the Metropolitan for several seasons, it had what those singers lacked—sympathy and sweetness, and it could be heard from every point of the auditorium.[51a]

The third experiment that season was L e s H u g u e-n o t s, and then New York learned that Jean was also equal to the sterner and more arduous work required in a part like Raoul. He scored his greatest triumph in the love scenes and more particularly in the wonderful duo with which the opera closes. Once more his tasteful phrasing, his charm and tact, were impressive. The Marcel of Edouard confirmed and deepened the impression made by his Frère Laurent. His rich, round, resonant voice never failed him for a moment. From beginning to end it conveyed a sense of strength and beauty.

New York had to wait to hear the Mephistopheles it afterwards loved, because Edouard fell a victim to influenza. F a u s t became an immensely popular opera in New York. It was given eight times during that short season, and so frequently during the next few years that a certain New Yorker, parodying the name of the Bayreuth institution, facetiously dubbed the Metropolitan "Das Faustspielhaus."

On January 2 Edouard sang Plunket in M a r t a; on the 4th both he and Jean appeared in L o h e n g r i n, and on the 11th in O t e l l o; on the 13th Edouard sang—and success- fully—Rocco in Beethoven's F i d e l i o, an opera in which he had never sung and which he had never even seen. On the 18th he showed the New York audience what he could do as Leporello, and was voted by one critic not so very funny. An- other found him somewhat ponderous in action, but thought that the music had never been better sung. On January 20 Jean sang Don Jose for the only time that season, with Calvé as Carmen.

A ï d a was given on January 30 and L' A f r i c a i n e on February 3, when it was reported that Jean fully sustained his reputation as Vasco di Gama and that the Don Pedro of Edouard gave a new idea of a part too often slighted. That occasion marked Lassalle's first American appearance with the de Reszkes. On January 2 L e P r o p h è t e was produced, and was pronounced the most brilliant performance of the season. Writing years later, W. J. Henderson, the learned New York critic, said that on this occasion Jean achieved one of the most imposing pieces of dramatic singing ever heard in America.[52]

The list of the operas Edouard sang in that first season is enough to make a less robust singer gasp. He appeared in fourteen rôles: Frère Laurent, Marcel, Count Rodolfo (La S o n n a m b u l a), Zacharie (L e P r o p h è t e), Plunket (M a r t a), König Heinrich, Rocco (F i d e l i o), Don Pedro, Leporello, Ramfis, Mephistopheles, King Claudius (H a m- l e t), Nilakantha (L a k m é), and Daland in an Italian ver- sion of D e r F l i e g e n d e H o l l ä n d e r. But although, as in Chicago, Edouard made the greater impression at first, Jean's place in the affections of New York music lovers be- came more secure with each appearance. If New York had doubted whether the newcomer would displace the memory of Mario, such doubts were gradually dismissed; for Jean proved that he had all the best qualities of Mario and in addition sang heroic rôles such as Radames and Jean de Leyde, which that singer would probably not have attempted at all. Financially, however, the season was far from successful. Those who heard the new company were high in praise, but there were not enough of them to gladden the hearts of the officials in the box office. Messrs. Abbey and Grau had spared no expense in assembling artists, but sometimes operas were hurriedly put on, without regard to the minor details essential to a perfect whole. The stage management was anything but adequate. The German *régisseur* was acquainted only with the works of Wagner. Of his two assistants one spoke only French, the other only English. "When the three come together," remarked Edouard, "it is as good as a farce. When O t e l l o was announced for production none of our three stage managers had seen the opera, so my brother Jean, Madame Albani and myself had to rehearse the people."

The fortunes of the impresarios mended during the last few weeks of the season, which closed without actual loss, but there were rumors that Abbey and Grau might not lease the Metropolitan for the following season. Then statements attributed to Willie Schütz appeared, to the effect that he, or Jean de Reszke, or he and Jean together, would turn producers; in which case operas like Reyer's S i g u r d and Massenet's L e C i d would be performed, and all French operas would be given in that language, not in Italian. In the end, however, contracts were renewed all round, and by Mr. Grau. There was general satisfaction in the certainty that the de Reszkes and Lassalle would return. Those three, a triple-leaved musical clover that had proved a genuine talisman for the management, had endeared themselves to the New York public.

They were not very often seen in the popular gathering places. Their calling did not permit late hours or any other dissipation, but occasionally Broadway had a chance to see the trio of giants strolling after a late breakfast, and then eyes would gaze in ecstasy and many a heart would flutter. "That's Edward, the big one. And the one in the middle, that's *Jeen*," came in awe-struck whispers. They were in truth a trio to dispel any notion one might have about the puniness of male opera singers. Lassalle, swarthy of complexion, large-gestured, had a chest which measured fifty and a half inches. Edouard de Reszke, the "Singing Cannon," was six feet two inches tall. (One account credited him with six feet four, but there really was no need to fib about Edouard's size.) Jean was about six feet tall, and just as the robust ring in his voice put his hearers out of humor with the pretty warbling of the usual *tenore di grazia*, so his manly figure gave the lie to Hans von Bülow's slightly blasphemous gibe that God had spoiled a man when he made a tenor, and to that other caustic but too much quoted observation that a tenor was not a man but a disease. A baritone once repeated the latter to Jean, who promptly retorted, "I wish you could catch it." Here was the sweetest-toned, the most fervid Romeo the world of the theater had ever known. Here was a Vasco di Gama who could make love to two out of a possible three ladies so convincingly that the audience—and perhaps the three ladies too—were quite sure he was in real earnest. Here was a Lohengrin, the very embodi-ment of gentleness. And yet, here was one, "the glass of fash-ion, and the mold of form," of whom all had to say: "There goes a man."

These three were singers, but they were athletes too. They played tennis and swam and fenced, and they were fre-quently seen at prize fights and at the six-day bicycle races at Madison Square Garden. They were excellent huntsmen, and they were all superb horsemen. The de Reszkes not only rode, but they had large and valuable stud-farms in the homeland, and their horses won many prizes. One year Jean's horses Pickwick and Le Sorcier won the Russian Derby and the International Stakes on the same day in Moscow. On another occasion the Tsar of Russia gave him a prize of ten thousand roubles for having the best stud-farm in Poland. To have one of Jean's horses named after her was considered a real honor by more than one New York and London lady.

Edouard was a man of enormous personal strength. He would let Lassalle clasp his hands round his neck, and, by merely inclining his head, could lift the two-hundred-and-fifty-pound baritone off the floor. Once Edouard was in St. Louis when a famous "strong man" happened to be there. When somebody produced a horseshoe the latter tried with both hands to bend it, but had to give it up. Edouard took it in his powerful right hand and with one twist bent the points together. When he slapped a man on the back, the recipient of the friendly greeting thought his bones were crashing together. And though James Huneker described Willie Schütz as being "not very strong above the eyes," physically he too was a large, strong man, and when the quartet of giants foregathered and laughed at the same time, the volume of sound was prodigious. And they laughed a good deal.

On those rare occasions when Jean could be lured to private homes he and his brother kept every one in gales of laughter with their imitations of other singers, of musical instruments and of animals. When they felt at home they acted like boys out of school. They would sing some popular song at the top of their lungs, winding up, perhaps, with the finale of F a u s t. Then Edouard would give a selection from a piano-organ, runs, trills and all, using his huge voice as lightly as a Patti. Next he would imitate a negro spiritual on the phonograph, the two vocal qualities comically mixed, with Jean assisting in the chorus. Then perhaps Edouard would sit down at the piano and sing "Hello, Mah Baby!" or "All Coons Look Alike to Me."

Jean's forte in such "goings-on" lay in mimicking members of the opera company. One of the minor conductors was a source of constant amusement to him. Jean would pucker his nose, squint as if looking through ill-fitting glasses set down too far, bend his knees, turn in his toes, and walk as if he had the "blind staggers," looking for all the world like the poor conductor, to the delight of his informal audience. Next he would imitate Anton Seidl, a cigar in the corner of his mouth, muttering unintelligible directions, so that that beloved conductor seemed to stand before them; or Castelmary, rejoicing over his rôle as the Dragon and the beautiful emptiness of the stage, with no chorus, no ballet; or David Bispham, with his wonderful vitality and the ready, cheerful smile curling up the corners of his mouth. He could imitate Plançon's splendid bass to the life, and just as Plançon was ready to go on the stage in M a n o n, Jean used to call him into his dressing-room and roll out "Elle est vraiment fort belle" exactly as Plançon did. It made Plançon laugh so that he could hardly get through his lines, and he begged Jean not to call him. But he always went at the call!

They were all fine artists and they were social assets as well; so New York was relieved to learn that their contracts had been renewed. Gradually even the German faction became mollified, for it learned that almost immediately upon his arrival Jean had begun to agitate for the presentation of all operas in their original languages. But New York knew not where this was to lead, though already Jean himself had vague yearnings toward singing Wagner in German. From the very beginning of his work on D i e M e i s t e r s i n g e r, following his first visit to Bayreuth, he had been impatient because he had to sing Walther in Italian. All this was to bear rich fruit, but not for a few years.

After the close of the New York season the new company

gave a few performances in Boston, where Jean was liked best
as Raoul and Romeo. The reaction to Edouard was the same
as in Chicago and New York. As his cape swept behind him
the first time he sang Mephistopheles, one young woman,
forgetting that she was surrounded by other people, exclaimed
aloud in delighted amazement, "Well, will you *look* at those
legs!" And, like George Meredith's Sir Willoughby, Edouard
did have a leg. So did his fellow artist Plançon. Once when
they were all at the home of a society hostess in London, the
discussion turned upon the gorgeous picture of Plançon in
a new costume. "Yes, and have you noticed his legs?" asked
Jean. "No," came the properly Victorian assurance. "Oh but
you must see them!" insisted Edouard. Whereupon he and
Jean forced Plançon to roll up the bottom of his trousers and
display his calves, to the confusion of the dignified hostess and
the huge delight of the company. How the ordeal affected the
victim can be appreciated only by those who remember Plançon's meticulous elegance in both dress and manners.

The first de Reszke season in America proclaimed the
dawn of a new operatic day not only in that country but in
the entire musical world. And yet the powers of the two Polish
artists were only partially developed. At that period, when
some one murmured, "Inspiring, isn't it?" to Lilli Lehmann
during a de Reszke performance, she could still reply, "Yes,
and they might be as fine artists as they are men if they would
but study." The time was not far off when she too would speak
nothing but praise, when even she was to do better work
because her singing partner was Jean de Reszke. Concerning
the brothers and Lassalle Mr. Krehbiel wrote in the *New
York Tribune*: "A marvelous artist indeed is this Frenchman,
and if he and the brothers de Reszke are in next year's
company, the lovers of the lyric drama as distinguished from
the old sing-song opera will look into the future without
trepidation." That sentiment must have surprised the carping
English critic who had informed his readers: "I am not very
sanguine as to the result of Messrs. Abbey and Grau's experiment, for I fancy that M. Jean de Reszke will not prove the
revelation to the Yankees that is expected. . . . It is quite on the
cards that when the time comes comparisons will be made,
and that many of these will not be favorable to the Polish
warblers." [53]

The strain of the New York season and of much traveling
took its toll, however, and throughout the following term at

Covent Garden Jean was far from well. The season was not considered really started until his and Edouard's first appearance, which was in R o m e o; but as a result of Jean's illness, there were only four performances of L o h e n g r i n during the season, and he sang but once in C a r m e n. M e i s t e r- s i n g e r and H u g u e n o t s were not given at all. Le Pro- p h è t e was performed, but again Jean's singing was marked by fatigue, and he did not win quite his customary success in the solo "Pour Bertha mon cœur soupire." He sang only ten times during the season, probably saving himself for the per- formance of E l a i n e, written by his friend Bemberg. This was given on July 5, with Melba, Plançon, and Edouard also in the cast, but the opera won only passing interest, securing its chief value from the impersonations of Jean and Melba as Lancelot and Elaine. The composer, more than pleased, wrote the following letter to Jean:

> My dear Jean:
> I am writing you from my bed, where I am obliged to stay, to take care of a bad cold which has suddenly seized me. That is why I do not come down to embrace you and tell you of all the gratitude that is in my heart! You have done more for me than my best friend could have done, and I shall remember "to my last day" that I have had this immense joy of having my opera sung by you, the greatest and most admirable of all the artists I have known in my lifetime. I am not making polite phrases, my dear Jean, in writing this, but I consider it such a piece of good *luck* as to be almost unfair for a talent so small as mine, and I know I do not merit such a great favor from Providence.
> I shall work hard when I return to Paris. I shall try to write a rôle more worthy of you, if I can; with what Elaine has taught me, to put into it more understanding and perhaps more charm.
> Thank you again with all my heart.
> Tell Edouard too how touched I am by his kindness to your
>
> H. Bemberg

Lancelot was Jean's last performance that season. His sudden departure from London caused many rumors: that he was going to retire; that he was going to be married; that

LA TOURAINE

PROGRAMME DU CONCERT

---

1   OUVERTURE POUR PIANO   X

Consuelo Domenech

2   GRAND AIR DE L' AFRICAINE   MEYERBEER

3 A.   CHANSON DE PRINTEMPS   GOUNOD
   B.   LES DEUX GRENADIERS   SCHUMANN

Pol Plançon

4   SICILIENNE DE CAVELLERIA RUSTICANA   MASCAGNI

Fernando De Lucia

5   CHANSONS ESPAGNOLES   X

Emma Calvé

6 A.   EXTASE   VICTOR HUGO & SALOMON
   B.   CHANT PROVENCAL   MASSENET

7   AIR DE RIGOLETTO   VERDI

Nellie Melba

8   A UNE FEMME   UGO ERRERA

Edouard de Reszke

9   CHANSONS   X

10   AIR DE LA JUIVE   HALEVY

Jean de Reszke

11   LA ROBE   EUGENE MANUEL

C. Coquelin

12   DUO DE LA TRAVIATA   VERDI

Nellie Melba   *Jean de Reszke*

13   MONOLOGUES A DISCRETION

C. Coquelin

LE PIANO SERA TENU PAR MLLE C. DOMENECH & M. JEAN DE RESZKE

---

4 MAI 1894

he did not care to sing Otello, because he and Maurel were not on the best of terms and Maurel's Iago was too good. It was also said that the proprietors of the copyright would not allow a performance of O t e l l o unless de Reszke sang the Moor's music. But Jean's refusal to sing the exacting rôle was quite in keeping with his artistic standards, which forbade his singing when the condition of his health prevented good work.

Edouard fared better that summer. "Sing on Garcia's method when you are dead by all means," wrote Bernard Shaw, "but whilst you are alive you will find Edouard de Reszke's more useful: only don't abuse your power when you have gained it by willful bawling for the mere fun of making a thundering noise, as he sometimes does." [54]

Though the season as a whole had not been satisfactory either to Jean or to the London opera public, the presence in the city of a very successful German opera company lent it indirect importance; for the German singers spurred Jean's slowly formulating decision to sing Wagner in his own language. That decision might have shown its first results in New York the following winter, but a scene painter's carelessness changed all plans. In August there was a fire in the Metropolitan Opera House, so destructive that it was necessary to forego opera during the winter of 1892-93. This caused some elation in Paris, which thought the circumstances might bring their beloved Jean back to them for at least one season. Parisian dilettanti could not reconcile themselves to this annual exodus of the greatest operatic artists to the United States. The New World had taken away some of their best paintings—wasn't that enough? Was Paris to become nothing more than second fiddle to New York from the point of view of all the arts? Unfortunately, Jean's health continued indifferent, and although he was anxious to comply with Gounod's request that he should sing in the five-hundredth performance of R o m e o, in Paris, that event had to be postponed several times. With what effect he sang when he did feel ready for it may be guessed from the letter which the composer sent him the day after the performance: [55]

MY DEAR JEAN:
        You literally surpassed yourself last night. Perhaps that surprises you? It does me, too. Nevertheless, it is true. Never have you carried to such a height that beauty

of diction and gesture, that correctness and expressiveness of accent, that control of voice production—in a word, that perfectly balanced proportion which alone makes the artist great by placing him beyond the danger of extremes, the perpetual temptation of the incompetent. Thanks and bravo, again and always! May heaven preserve you and leave us your beautiful art as long as possible! Of such as you we have great need. Remember me to dear Edouard, who, like yourself, has the air of having been born in his rôle, and believe me, both of you,

                                   Cordially yours
                                   CH. GOUNOD

THE FOLLOWING SEASON (1893) at Covent Garden was un-
eventful except for the special performance of R o m e o given
in honor of the marriage of the present King and Queen of
England, when the brothers sang. Alvarez took the leading
tenor rôle in that opera for the rest of the season, but it was
said that although Parisian audiences might accept this embodiment as worthy of succeeding the ideal impersonation of
Jean de Reszke, London amateurs, "certainly more critical in
these matters," were not likely to endorse such a favorable
verdict.

Jean was again in poor health during most of the season,
but when F a u s t was given on the last night he was in excellent voice and carried off first honors as of old. The prolonged
applause finally brought out Sir Augustus Harris, accompanied by Nordica and the de Reszkes, and the impresario
announced: "I have much pleasure in informing you that my
good friends Jean and Edouard de Reszke have just told me
they intend to return to London and sing for me next year,"
a statement which was greeted with deafening cheers. The
experience of that year dictated the precaution of guarantee-
ing, in the brothers' contracts, a month's rest between the
New York and London seasons.

If one only knew which newspapers the de Reszkes read
while in London, or which critics' comments they took most
seriously, it would be easy to decide how much of the credit
which Mr. Shaw claims for their finally singing the mature
Wagner should actually be assigned to him; for he continued
to complain about their failure to do so, and he refused to
subscribe to a testimonial to Sir Augustus Harris because
Covent Garden, with all its boasted resources, could not produce the N i b e l u n g e n l i e d without sending for German
artists. He did not blame Sir Augustus for this. The real difficulty was "the incorrigible *fainéantise* of the de Reszkes, with
their perpetual schoolboy Faust and Mephistopheles, Romeo
and Frère Laurent, and their determination to make Covent
Garden a mere special edition of the Paris Grand Opera." [56]
He berated Jean for allowing Alvary to take Siegfried from
him, and Edouard for leaving Wotan to another singer.

In the meantime the two brothers had been preparing
for their second season in America. When the Metropolitan
opened on November 27 1893 it was with F a u s t. It was a

great night for Society, which found the refurbished house even better suited than the old one for the display of persons and adornments. That part of the audience which was in a critical mood found the performance exquisite, but, as before, it was the genial Mephistopheles of Edouard which won the greatest applause. "M. Edouard de Reszke's glorious voice is as full and round, as majestic in quality and as big in volume as it was when he was last here," said the *New York Times*. "He is a superb Mephistopheles, and throughout the evening his work was that of a great artist rejoicing in the plenitude of his powers."

"Edouard de Reszke is the ideal Mephistopheles unquestionably," declared the *Evening Post*. "Whether in the demoniac or the ironic moments, he always suits his mien to the situation, his word to his actions, and his tones to his words. Singing is no impediment to his speech; he repeatedly moved the audience to laughter. Jean de Reszke is less interesting as Faust, and he does not always use his voice properly, yet, take it all in all, it would not be easy to replace him or M. Lassalle as Valentine."

Rather mild praise that, for Jean, and not too heavily supported by Mr. Henderson's criticism: "He was in good voice, though it must be admitted that one has to become used to hearing him again before being quite sure of this. His 'Salve Dimora' was charmingly sung, but it was not till the duet, 'Dammi ancor,' that he rose to the full measure of his powers. In the closing measures of that he sang with all the reserve power of his voice, with eloquent style, and with a genuine warmth that was inspiriting."

Even the L o h e n g r i n which followed did not call out superlatives from the critics, one of whom said that though Jean sang the music beautifully, though his acting was "graceful and interesting," he was "somewhat deficient in weight and repose." Edouard's Henry the Fowler was "superb," and his singing of the music "somewhat better, if anything, than usual." Jean fared better when L e s H u g u e- n o t s was given a little later. His singing with Nordica in the grand duet of the fourth act brought a storm of applause, and it was predicted that if the opera were repeated even the immense Metropolitan would not be large enough to hold the public. Jean was a romantic and graceful Raoul. He sang the music with taste and sentiment, and when the climax came he rose to its demands with vigor. The simple words of love in the immortal duet vibrated with new power when a Valentine sang them with such a Raoul as Jean, who charged both words and music with blended fear and delight, lending to the urgency of peril and the approach of death both fascination and yearning tenderness. As the lover he was always supreme, and no condition of voice or health ever prevented him from giving exquisitely lovely performances, even when every tone might not be perfect in itself, or when, as with Nellie Melba, his partner gave to a duet her voice but little warmth of acting.

That was the most successful season, artistically and financially, that had ever been given in New York. In all there were ninety-one performances, and the total receipts amounted to something over $500,000. Nineteen works were given, in which Jean sang twenty-six times and Edouard thirty times.

Early in March the company went to Boston. The Damrosch opera company was there at the same time, with Mr. Amherst Webber as *solo répétiteur*. He had worked with Lillian Nordica at Bayreuth, and when she found that he was in Boston the work was resumed. Madame Nordica's hotel rooms adjoined those of the de Reszkes. Jean, who had already made up his mind that to his Lohengrin and Walther, Tristan would have to be added, was impressed by the playing he heard in the next room. He asked Nordica for an introduction, and immediately upon meeting Mr. Webber invited him to go to Poland that summer.

But there were other engagements to be fulfilled before this one could be kept. The Abbey and Grau artists proceeded to Chicago: Nordica, Eames, Melba, Calvé, Plançon, de Lucia, Lassalle and the de Reszkes, all in the same company—no wonder the advance sale of seats exceeded all hopes of the management! On the first night every seat was filled and about five hundred eager listeners lounged in the foyer. Speculators on the streets were demanding—and receiving—double prices. Before the first carriage had driven up to the main entrance the clerk at the window was wearily repeating "standing room only" to an endless line of would-be ticket buyers.

The opera was F a u s t. There was a dead silence while the audience caught their breath after the orchestral prelude, and then the storm of applause broke and kept pattering steadily until the bell tinkled for the curtain to rise. Jean de Reszke sitting at his table in the old alchemist's shop was greeted by excited hand-clapping and murmurs of delight.

Then Mephistopheles shot upon the half-darkened stage in a blaze of red light, and received a wild welcome in turn. Jean's Faust was perfectly sung, his "Salve Dimora" was exquisitely given, and the music of the garden scene was sung with fine expression and fervor; but as before, Chicago preferred the performance of Edouard, being pleased that a virile part should be played by so virile a personage. "A finer example of declamatory singing has never been heard in this country than this artist's work in the cathedral scene," concluded a critic, "while the Calf of Gold, the Serenade, the first act duo and the fourth act trio were never given more impressively. He develops the sardonic humor of the rôle in capital style. In short, M. Edouard de Reszke's Mephistopheles is a master-piece akin to Goethe's, equally great in its way." [57]

He was also declared the best Marcel ever seen on the Chicago stage, and in some quarters he was likewise considered the best impersonator of Assur (S e m i r a m i d e) who had appeared in that city. His facility in managing such a large voice in the elaborate roulades of Rossini was thought most remarkable.

But while Edouard roused the greater fervor, the audi-ence was now by no means indifferent to the more quiet art of Jean. In the spirited duo in the third act of L'A f r i c a i n e he and Edouard achieved a volume of tone and such a vitality of acting that one listener insisted "it was worth going to the Auditorium to hear just this one *tour de force.*" Jean's Lohen-grin, his Romeo, his Raoul, his Radames, all were enthusiasti-cally received and praised, and he rose higher and higher in the appreciation of Chicago audiences. His greatest triumph, however, and the event which gave him the season's deepest satisfaction, was the first American production of Massenet's W e r t h e r, on March 29 1894. W e r t h e r is, of course, all Werther (except for a bit of Charlotte), and unless it is sung by a tenor of most unusual caliber the opera can easily be a failure. But for Jean the rôle was a very great personal tri-umph. Massenet sent a cablegram saying: "I owe you my greatest pleasure since C i d. I embrace you with emotion. Vive Amérique." And Jean wrote a revealing letter about this per-formance to a friend in England. [58]

CHICAGO, March 31 1894

MY DEAR FRIEND:

In an artist's life every new rôle is a stage in that long journey towards the summits of art, towards the beautiful, the infinite. Werther, the other night, was for me one of those unanimous successes wherein the heart —the science of causing it to beat in one's audience and before one's audience—stood in true proportion to every artifice. The true path—that of emotion—that goal for which I am striving all my life—was reached in the presence of a public which did not understand the words, but which divined by instinct that my conception of the character arose from that simplicity, that pure, unexaggerated truthfulness which age and maturity alone can confer upon the thinking artist.... I am sending you the cuttings from the newspapers here; show them to Harris, who, I hope, will stage the opera for me. Mancinelli conducted the orchestra admirably. Eames and Arnoldson are two adorable little sisters. In a word, I believe that to the cultivated London public, accustomed as it is to novelties, it will come as a delightful surprise. I sing regularly three times every week, and my voice is excellent. At this present moment I am reaching my forty-first performance. Accept, my dear friend, from Edouard and myself, a thousand affectionate remembrances, together with a hearty shake of the hand.

Your devoted,

JEAN DE RESZKE

When Werther was given in New York upon the company's return for a supplementary season, this triumph was repeated. The large audience fairly went wild over Jean. His voice was rich with emotion as he sang "C'est moi qu'elle pouvait aimer," but in the love scene of the third act his art rose to sublimity. His first appearance in the following London season was in the same opera. He realized that its success depended upon him, and he discharged his responsibility magnificently. "His beautiful tones fairly compassed the entire gamut of passionate longing and despair." But the opera itself found little favor with the London public, and was removed from the company's repertoire. There is a story according to which Augustus Harris had not been over-anxious to produce this work in the first place, feeling that the English would not care for it; but he yielded to Jean's wishes. At the end of the performance he said to Jean: "Well, you have had your way. Werther has been played, and for the present season, this one representation will be enough." Nevertheless, to oblige

SHOOTING PARTY AT BOROWNO

Baron de Kronenberg

Viktor de Reszke   Edouard de Reszke   Jean de Reszke

Adam Michalski   Jeanne and Hélène de Reszke

Minia de Reszke   W. Johnstone-Douglas

his star tenor, he consented to give it a second time. On the afternoon before the performance he was grieved to find that the seats were not selling. Suddenly a letter arrived from de Reszke containing a request for a couple of stalls "if there were any left."

"Come in here," said Sir Augustus to the messenger, and he took him to the box office. Then he addressed the official in charge. "Give me eighty stalls, twenty boxes, and a hundred amphitheater stalls. Make them up in a parcel, please." He handed the bundle to the messenger and instructed him to say that if M. de Reszke wanted twice as many tickets he could have them. Half an hour later he received a telegram informing him that the tenor was ill and would be unable to sing that night.[59] This is only one of several similar stories circulated about the withdrawal of this opera. The real explanation, according to Mr. Klein, "was not the menace of an empty house, but an intimation from an exalted quarter that the *grandes dames* of the grand and pit tier boxes had no wish to see their beloved Jean de Reszke in costumes so drab and uninteresting as that [sic] of the Goethe period. Accustomed as they were to feasting their eyes upon his superb, manly figure in the picturesque attire of one of his dazzling heroes of romance, they simply refused to put up with a repetition of the saddening display. And in his heart Sir Augustus quite agreed with them."[60]

To Bernard Shaw Jean's Werther seemed masterly, and he wrote of it in glowing terms. In Werther there are several formidable declamatory passages, accompanied by the full power of the orchestra. "He attacks these," said Shaw, "with triumphant force, and the next moment is sing ɡg quietly with his voice as unrestrained, as responsive, as rich in quality as if it had been wrapped in cotton wool for a week, instead of clashing against Massenet's most strenuous orchestration with a vehemence that would put most tenors practically *hors de combat* for several minutes."[61] Jean seemed to Shaw both to be at the height of his physical powers and to have perfected his artistry. His grip of Werther and Romeo was "extraordinarily firm and intimate; he is in the heart of them from the first note to the last. Not a tone or gesture has a touch of anything common or cheap in it: the parts are elaborately studied and the execution sensitively beautiful throughout, the result, aided by his natural grace and distinction, being in both operas an impersonation not only unflaggingly interesting, but exquisitely attractive." Still, though on de Reszke nights, when Covent Garden was at its best, there were moments when Bayreuth was left "positively nowhere in point of vocal beauty and dramatic grace," it irked Shaw that the chief Wagner rôles were being sung not by Jean but by Alvary. He felt that the latter had to summon Wagner to his aid because he was a much less attractive singer than the Pole, and Shaw's formal criticisms of Jean de Reszke in *The World* ended with the sentence: "I have appealed so often and so utterly in vain to de Reszke in these columns to do for the sake of art what Alvary does because he must, that I do not propose to waste any more ink on the matter." [62]

He should have been comforted somewhat by the announcement which Sir Augustus made in the middle of the season, namely, that Jean intended to sing in Massenet's M a n o n, and would play T r i s t a n in German. Wagner did receive cosmopolitan interpretation on the closing night of the Royal Italian Opera that season. M e i s t e r s i n g e r was sung in Italian: by a Polish Walther, M. Jean de Reszke; an Italian, Signor Mario Ancona, who took the part of Hans Sachs; an American, Mr. David Bispham, who represented Beckmesser; a Frenchman, M. Plançon, who appeared as Pogner; an American woman, Emma Eames, who took the part of Eva. A German woman, Fräulein Bauermeister, did what little could be done with a secondary female part. It was high time for de Reszke to make his contribution to the proper representation of Wagner. Perhaps that M e i s t e r s i n g e r cast gave a special impetus to his work on T r i s t a n at Borowno that summer.

JEAN DID NOT HAVE a home of his own in Poland at this time. Borowno, which lies between Warsaw and Cracow, was the home of his sister, Emilja Michalska. There have been so many varied—and some ridiculous—stories about the properties and "castles" of the de Reszkes in Poland that it seems proper to give a matter-of-fact account of them, based on what Édouard's daughter Minia told me and on my own observations. In the first place, there is no truth in the story that Jean's father had been deprived of vast estates because of his part in the uprising of 1863 and that his sons bought them back years later with the proceeds of their singing. The father had no properties outside of Warsaw. Jean acquired four estates in his own name; Skrzydlow,* purchased first, and three others—Chorzemice, Witkowice, Zdrowa—on which there has never been a dwelling, much less even a modest castle. Skrzydlow, which lies near the village of Klomnice, a five hours' ride from Warsaw, was bought, about 1890, from the man who owned and lived on it; so that there were already a house, a guest-house, a servants' house, and, of course, equipment for conducting the activities of a large country estate. The Skrzydlow château is built in typical Polish style, which means that it is one story high, with large, high-ceilinged rooms and many large windows. Here are the old family portraits and many of the souvenirs of Jean's triumphs, including the huge silver tankard presented to him by Queen Victoria, said to be the handsomest individual gift she ever bestowed upon a guest. It was here that he lived and studied during the summertime, and his wife sometimes joined him. The fantastic stories about his having engaged a Chicago architect to build a wonderful palace in Poland became current at the time of his marriage. He was said to be preparing this home for his bride, who was the Comtesse de Mailly-Nesle (she had been born Comtesse Marie de Goulaine) and whose own station in life, whose great beauty and accomplishments, required a regal setting. "The plans contemplate the erection of one of the grandest structures on the Continent. . . . The palace, with all its magnificence, however, is to have a modest name, for, in compliment to his admirers in this country, M. de Reszke will call it the 'Cottage Américain.'" So ran the story in the conservative *New York Times*. De Reszke had, in truth, begun negotiations

* Pronounced Skshidloof.

with an architect, only he was French. He did intend to prepare a suitable home for his bride, only it was to be the one
already standing there, remodeled. As for the "Cottage Américain," that came into existence when Jean so christened the
old guest house. It had been reported that every part of this
cottage was to be completed in Chicago and sent to Poland
in sections. Now, some of the de Reszkes' ideas were on as vast
a scale as their really immense estates and their vast incomes,
but the absurdity of this story, which was well circulated, is
obvious.

Together Jean and Edouard owned "Klobukowice,"
where there was a simple dwelling. About 1895 Edouard built
the home at Garnek in which he always lived when in Poland
and which his daughter Hélène now occupies. Jean's name
is most frequently associated with Borowno, where both he
and Edouard spent their summers before either of them was
married. And the Borowno château was really an ancient
castle.* It was rebuilt about 1791, and from that time on has
remained unchanged. The architecture is a mixture of French
and Russian. The walls are of stone and very thick. One enters
through a semicircular façade supported by massive pillars.
Beyond this is a square entrance-hall of ample size, and from
that one reaches the banquet hall, which was probably used
as a feast chamber by court nobles in olden days. From each
side of the large hall a double stairway leads to a gallery where
musicians played during feasts and for dancing. In front of
the château is an oval track for exercising horses; for it was
at Borowno that the de Reszkes had their first stud-farm. Behind it are several acres of "kitchen garden," and a huge brick
wall surrounds the house and garden. Beyond this there are
thousands of acres of forest.

All these estates are near each other and the river Warta
winds its leisurely way through them, forming little lakes here
and there. Like most Poles, the de Reszkes were ardent
patriots and quite apart from a natural wish to comply with
the accepted standard whereby a Pole's importance was judged
by the amount of landed property he owned, there was also
the desire to utilize their earnings in contributing to the improvement of the homeland. Jean employed hundreds of

---

* At the time of my visit the house was for sale and all its furnishings were
being sold at auction. There was a rumor that a rising young Polish tenor had
made overtures for its purchase, hoping, perhaps, that some of the tones which had
been heard there in other days might descend on him.

peasants. A small army of his less fortunate countrymen enjoyed his generosity, and they adored him.

Edouard also felt a deep sympathy with the Polish peasants. When some one asked him whether he was conscious of the audience while he was singing, he replied that it was his habit, while in America, to raise his heart and his eyes to the topmost gallery, where he knew so many of the music-loving people of his own country were gathered. "I do not see them," he said, "but I know they are there. I rejoice to know that they are in this great free country, where they learn to carry their heads like aristocrats and look every man straight in the eye. I see them sometimes waiting for the side doors to open. I am proud of their fine black clothes, their gold watches, their air of prosperity and sturdy independence. I compare them to the poor peasants in my own country, and I thrill with gratitude toward this new country, that has transformed, in a few years, the servile peasant into the thinking man."

Their love of Poland was a sentiment the de Reszkes shared deeply with Paderewski. At a luncheon given in New York in honor of Paderewski, the pianist suddenly got up from the table, went over to the piano, and began to play the Polish national anthem. Jean and Edouard promptly sang the words. Never was love of country more thrillingly expressed. The late William Steinway, who was present, exclaimed in his emphatic manner: "I thought I knew all the worlds of music, but this is a new world to me." Another guest, deeply moved, declared dramatically: "Poland is not yet lost!"

Jean spent vast sums in building roads and otherwise improving his estates, but except for his great love of horses he was less interested in the details of this phase of his life than Edouard. When Jean returned after a season abroad, his agent informed him about what had been done, what needed to be done. He listened half interestedly, but "C'est bien" was usually his only comment. Edouard, on the other hand, missed nothing. He remembered every little ailment any horse might have had the previous summer; he noticed every change. And when he was engrossed in the subject of horses the angels singing in heaven could not have distracted his attention. With Jean it was different. If a group were standing around after a hunting party, no matter what the topic of conversation or how lively the discussion, let a sound of singing come from the house and his interest was immediately transferred. Without any thought of intruding, he would interrupt a conversation with, "Mais, non, c'est impossible! She mustn't do it that way." And then he would either go into a long explanation of what was being done wrong or right, or go to give counsel direct.

It was to Borowno, then, that Amherst Webber went in the summer of 1894, to work with Jean on T r i s t a n. And it was anything but a holiday. At seven Jean would be up, watching his horses exercise. Work began immediately after breakfast and continued intermittently until lunch; not merely *répétition,* but a thorough study of technical difficulties. He would sing each passage in many different ways, until he was satisfied with it. That went on throughout the morning. Most of the afternoon he worked spasmodically, stopping only for a vigorous game of tennis. After dinner he sat in a chair half asleep until about eleven o'clock, and just when his companions were hoping to get to bed, up he would jump. "Essayons la voix!" Then all the phrases were tried over that had ever worried him in any of the operas in his entire repertoire. He might even wind up by singing most of a rôle. But whether he got to bed at two o'clock in the morning or later, he was up at seven just the same. This capacity for doing a great deal of steady and concentrated work without much sleep endured throughout his lifetime. To the last he complained bitterly about any scoundrel who might want to retire before midnight.

Jean worked hard on T r i s t a n that summer, but it was not yet to be included in the repertoire. The 1894-95 New York season opened with the ever popular R o m e o. The perfection of Jean's every enactment of the rôle was by this time confidently expected. Not only was his Romeo ideal, but now his Faust too was so characterized. In the first scene he managed to make Faust an old man, despairing but yearning, surfeited but eager. And then when the miracle had been worked, grace, manliness, ardor, passion, personal magnetism, combined to make the rejuvenated Faust a glorious, winning human being. The public responded with wholehearted approbation. When L o h e n g r i n was the opera of the evening, the same gratified audience echoed the same kind of praise. Somehow his portrayal seemed more finished, although it had always seemed beyond improvement. "His Lohengrin is every inch a knight, his action aristocratic, stern, affectionate, pathetic, as the occasion requires, and his song is incomparable. After his great narrative in the third act the audience could not help interrupting the music to show its enthusiasm, and if anything could have been finer than this it was his farewell, which made every sympathetic spectator feel his departure as keenly as Elsa."

The audience had more facilities than the critics for expressing wonder and delight at the new beauty unfolded at each successive performance. They could send their verses, their wreaths and roses and violets, they could clap their hands until they tingled, and recall the artists again and again. They could show where their preferences lay by packing the Metropolitan. They could crowd to hear even the feeble E l a i n e, given once that season; not because they wanted to hear the opera, but because they wanted to sink down in luscious enjoyment of the voice of their favorite. The poor critics despaired of making mere language express the moving power of Jean's art. Of what avail are words in trying to express the tenderness of

> Music that gentlier on the spirit lies
> Than tired eyelids on tired eyes.

When Romeo, Lohengrin, Raoul, Walther, were to be described, critics had to admit that they had "lived long in the alms-basket of words," and resort to a prosaic: "There is no more to be said about Jean de Reszke's performance in this part. Enough to say that it was up to standard." They could tell their readers that it was worth the price of admission just to hear him sing the "Preislied," or his farewell to Elsa; but what words could serve to express the countless nameless graces which enhanced his every attitude; as when, in the vault of the Capulets, his cloak dropped from his shoulders, not by any perceptible motion, but as it were borne down by the very weight of Romeo's grief? What language could describe the stream of silvery tones which flowed from the lips of the singer and entered into the souls of his listeners like some enchanted wine, quickening their senses, clarifying and glorifying emotions which they had experienced but had not quite understood?

It was a little easier to describe Edouard's good humor, which was as never-failing as his torrential voice. That year he sang Hans Sachs for the first time. With kindly mischief and a substratum of sentimentality, he made Hans a big, burly, unpolished, tender-hearted fellow, a poet by nature, a man of the people by birth, and a shoemaker by trade. Always friendly, always generous and lovable, Edouard's place in the hearts of his public was incontestably secure. People felt slightly less awed by him than by his brother, perhaps because of Edouard's spontaneity. The difference between them is delightfully illustrated by what happened one night when they had returned to the Gilsey House after a performance. They were met in the lobby by a group of people who seemed to know them. Jean was just as ignorant of their names as Edouard, but he talked away with his customary tact. Edouard stood there in a puzzled silence. After some moments, his face suddenly lighted up. He had remembered their names. "How do you do!" he bellowed. "How do you do!" and he shook hands all around as though he had just at that moment met them.

This most gratifying season in New York was followed by one in Chicago that was equally brilliant and successful. One evening the receipts exceeded $13,000. Huge audiences were the rule rather than the exception, and they roared their appreciation of the great artists who graced the stage of the Auditorium. Chicago felt that it was really getting the cream of the opera in the spring of 1895, the New York performances having been in the nature of mere rehearsals. They acted like a crowd of maniacs in their enthusiasm for Melba, Nordica, Plançon, and the de Reszkes. They stood up and applauded, sat down and applauded, unfolded their programs and folded them up again, glared at one another in ecstasy, and declared that such opera had never before been heard anywhere. But in the middle of the season Jean became ill with influenza. The Poles, who had been ecstatic over the triumphs of their countrymen, begged them to attend a charity concert, but Jean was compelled to decline.

Auditorium Hotel, Chicago
March 23 1895

DEAR SIR:
    With real regret I must let you know that it will be impossible for me to attend your concert, owing to severe influenza, which has attacked me for the second time, and which does not allow me to sing today in Les Huguenots.
    I am afraid that this illness will be prolonged and I doubt whether I shall be able to sing even once more in Chicago. The whole repertoire had to be changed and Die Meistersinger, which was announced for Monday, is to be replaced by Le Nozze di Figaro.

At this very moment my brother received a rehearsal bulletin for tomorrow evening; so he also will not be able to attend the concert. In such a way an illness shatters all the plans of a singer.

We ask you, dear sir, to make our apologies to our countrymen, and accept from me a sum of $200 and from my brother $100 as a small donation to be distributed among our poor.

Respectfully yours,
JEAN DE RESZKE

That change in repertoire caused at least one minor disaster. A young woman, hysterical because her adored Jean was not in the cast, was carried out of the Auditorium shrieking: "I want Jeen! I want Jeen!"

The demonstrations in Chicago and New York, especially the hysterical outpouring of applause and gifts at the season's closing performance, were alarming to the more serious-minded people who were as much concerned about the opera itself as about the artists who performed therein; for the demonstrations were for individual singers. Jean had sung Des Grieux for the first time on January 16 and the performance won little comment; yet on that closing night, when he sang selections from M a n o n again, it would have made little difference had he sung from that or from a child's song book. As in the case of the other singers, his farewell ovation was for himself, and not for Wagner or Massenet or Gounod. The "star system" was in full sway. The public had discouraged the introduction of novelties. Old favorites had to be repeated again and again. Those concerned for opera as such worried about what might happen should disaster befall the stars, more particularly the de Reszkes, whose dominance caused a London newspaper to call the Abbey and Grau artists the "Jean de Reszke troupe."

Covent Garden did not, however, hear Jean that summer, although enterprising journalists blithely referred to him as being in the company. It was his first absence in eight years. When it finally became definitely understood that he was not to appear at all, many reasons were assigned for his absence: that he refused to appear because Tamagno had sung early in the season, and successfully; that he was going to sing Siegmund at Bayreuth; that he was going to retire; and, as usual, that he was going to be married. Jean himself was rather worn out with the winter's operatic work, and the frequent changes of climate experienced in traveling from New York to Washington, to Boston, to Chicago, had brought on colds and influenza. Besides, he had special need of the summer's rest that year, for the autumn was to see his most ambitious work. For that reason he declined the Covent Garden engagement. It is significant that the principal tenor work was divided, in his absence, between Tamagno, de Lucia, and Alvarez.

EVEN IN THE spring of 1895 Jean de Reszke had striven to bring about a performance of Tristan und Isolde in German. It was due to his efforts that Die Meistersinger —in Italian, to be sure—had been incorporated in the repertoire, and for several years he had advocated that all the Wagner operas should be given in German. He himself was especially eager to sing Tristan, having caught a glimpse of what it could be during that first visit to Bayreuth in 1888. Nevertheless, he had his moments of misgiving; as once, when he heard Tristan, and in answer to his question, "Why does the orchestra play so loudly that the voices can't be heard?" was told that for Wagner the orchestra was of paramount importance. To this Jean sadly replied that then he would never sing the opera, because his voice was not big enough to be heard above such an orchestra. Soon thereafter, however, he heard Anton Seidl conduct Tristan, and was beside himself with delight. He fidgeted about, folded and unfolded his hands, muttered to himself, and after the first act rushed behind the scenes to congratulate the performers and Seidl. He told the conductor he hadn't dreamed Wagner could be so beautifully sung in German. Seidl responded: "You ought to be singing Tristan yourself," and Jean replied, "If you will promise to conduct, I shall learn it." Not a new thought, but it had added zest to the preparation of the rôle.

Jean's contribution toward the resumption of German opera in New York was an important one, but the people themselves had clearly indicated their desires by their unexpectedly liberal support of two performances of Die Walküre, which Walter Damrosch had produced in the spring of 1894. These had been followed by representations of Götterdämmerung and Tannhäuser, the latter produced by the German Press Club. Things were astir in the German camp, but rivalry between Mr. Damrosch and Anton Seidl prevented concerted action toward a general program. On April 27 the supplementary season at the Metropolitan ended, and under date of April 28 a circular letter appeared, signed individually by friends of Mr. Seidl, soliciting subscriptions for a season of German opera in 1894-95. The plan called for forty performances between November and May, on dates which were not to conflict with the regular performances of Italian and French opera.[63] A Wagner Society was organized, designed to support a four weeks' season of Wagnerian operas at the Metropolitan, beginning November 19 1894. An attempt to reconcile the differences between Seidl and Damrosch was unsuccessful, and as a result Mr. Damrosch organized a company of his own. The following spring he launched a season of German opera which exceeded all hopes from a financial point of view, even though it left something to be desired artistically. Writing to H. E. Krehbiel at this time, the impresario commented on the fact that people came to hear the dramas instead of the singers. Nordica and the de Reszkes had given as exquisite performances of L o h e n-g r i n as any one could wish to hear, and yet, he said, "the public crowded into the German representation as if expecting a special revelation from Fräulein Gadski, a novice, and Herr Rothmühl, a second-rate tenor." [64]

Walter Damrosch had thus saved the day for Messrs. Abbey and Grau, who now realized that the public wanted not only Italian and French opera, but German as well. But that German opera could be imbued with the tenderness, the clarity, the charm with which Jean de Reszke (and Edouard de Reszke too) enhanced it, neither directors nor public, nor even critics, could guess; though some of the last named had been urging Jean for years to sing more of Wagner and to sing it in German.

The 1895-96 season opened, however, with the perennial R o m e o, which, with Jean in the cast, always meant a special Society night, particularly on the first night of the season. That Monday of November 18 Society was on dress parade. Duchesse lace and diamond crescents, black velvet and ai-grettes, bright red tulle "with corsage fastened with diamond stars," purple velvet with point-lace and diamond-and-opal crescent, vied for admiration; the boxes were effulgent with the best-gowned women in New York. On that opening evening the representation was also such as had never been equaled. It was difficult to think that the audience would ever accept any future Romeo, so completely was Jean de Reszke identified with the rôle. The critic of the *New York Times* wrote:

We have frequently said in these columns that the popular tenor never had one of the great voices in the world, but he has incomparable art. He is past master of the art of singing, and behind that art there is the soul of a true artist. Last night he sang and acted with all his old-time grace, passion, and intelligence, and the result was a beautiful musical and dramatic embodiment of the ardent lover. His work called forth, as usual, long and loud applause.

M. Edouard de Reszke was the Frère Laurent. This grand basso is now in the plenitude of his powers, and the sonorous tones of his noble voice delivered with matchless art, not only filled the auditorium last night, but satisfied the ear and fired the imagination.

As it was difficult to find new words with which to express the beauty and artistic perfection of Jean's Romeo, so too with his Faust and his Walther; so too with Edouard's genial Mephisto and his Frère Laurent. And when, in January, Massenet's M a n o n was performed, Jean's Des Grieux was likewise entirely adequate and satisfactory. "The tenor and the prima donna seemed in the critical scenes to stimulate each other," reported an observer. "Nothing could be prettier than their delivery of the pretty music of the second act, while the climax of the opera was really thrilling in its dramatic intensity. With Melba and Jean de Reszke M a n o n ought to be brought out of the comparative neglect of an occasional production to become one of the mainstays of an opera season. The applause at the end of the third act was not limited to hand-clapping, but from all parts of the house came the cries of admiration that denote real enthusiasm." [65]

But that 1895-96 season included an event which made Walther, Des Grieux, Faust, Raoul, Jean de Leyde, even Lohengrin and Romeo, seem less important. Not that they diminished in splendor, or that affection for them languished; but "there is one glory of the sun, and another glory of the moon; and another glory of the stars, for one star differeth from another star in glory," and as all other operatic stars, though brilliant, seemed lesser orbs in the presence of Jean de Reszke, so the glory of his own earlier rôles paled to that of the moon before the grandeur and intensity radiated by the sun of his Tristan.

The prospectus for that season read in part: "The management has also decided to add a number of celebrated German artists and to present Wagner operas in the German language, all of which operas will be given with superior singers, equal to any who have ever been heard in the language." [66] Just how "superior" some of those singers were, was demonstrated, and unforgettably, by those who that season essayed opera in German for the first time in their careers.

There is no need to repeat all that had been said about the unsingableness of Wagnerian opera. The chief arguments were that there was insufficient melody (or none, according to some); singers could not learn the notes, could not manage the intervals; the instrumentation was such that any singer would be overwhelmed by the orchestra. Those who tried to contend with the din soon shouted even a powerful voice away, and in the few cases where that had not happened it was simply due to the good luck which attended the singers. As for Jean de Reszke's undertaking heavy Wagnerian rôles, it would be his ruination. He had been trained in the Italian school and in the traditions of the Grand Opera of Paris. No one who had acquired his chief fame in parts like Romeo and Faust could hope even to approach the austerity and power of Tristan. Faust had suffered greatly when portrayed by German Wagner singers. Romeo they had not even tried, and, as W. J. Henderson pointed out, "the fact that they had never really sung Tristan had not dawned on them." That they had never read Wagner's own ideas on the subject was also clear. Concerning a certain performance he once wrote: "If at the performance it was always only the music, nay, commonly only the orchestra, that attracted attention, rest assured that the vocalists fell far below the level of their task."

Jean had worked on Tristan even before that summer of 1894 when Amherst Webber went with him to Poland. He had, in fact, studied it intermittently for three years before the 1895-96 season in New York. He was ready to sing it at the beginning of the 1894-95 season, but he got no support from his associates, who clung to French and Italian operas. Lillian Nordica had, however, sung Elsa at Bayreuth, and her success made her eager to study Isolde.

At last Tristan was scheduled for production in New York in the autumn of 1895. Then, though Jean knew his part letter-perfect, before the opera was finally produced he attended every orchestra rehearsal, so that he might know every shade of the instrumental music as well as the vocal parts. In this willingness to study every detail that could contribute to a perfect whole both he and Edouard were almost unique among their fellows. Many a time they could be seen sitting in the auditorium during rehearsals, content to munch an apple for luncheon, so that they might learn from other artists. They were always ready to listen to a conductor's suggestions too. Theodore Thomas, for instance, would never have had to declare his position to them as he did one day to Patti. She felt outraged at his refusal to let her have her way; after all, she was the prima donna. "Excuse me, Madame," said Thomas, "here *I* am prima donna."

The evening of November 27 finally arrived, and Jean, always nervous before a performance, was even more agitated than usual. Edouard was to sing King Mark, and for him too it was a first appearance in German, but he could not stop to think very much about his own new part. It required all his and Webber's efforts and all those of Seidl and Jean's factotum Louis to calm and reassure him.

In the great auditorium there were many admirers and friends, and some of them too wondered what the outcome of the new undertaking would be. Could Jean rise above the gentleness of his Romeo and Lohengrin and yet not lose the old tenderness? For T r i s t a n   u n d   I s o l d e was as much a love poem as R o m e o   e t   J u l i e t t e; like L o h e n g r i n it called for renunciation. Would he be able to convey, in a new language—one which had been called unpronounceable —through music in an unfamiliar style, the strength and the scope of the character Wagner had created out of the old Celtic legends? Could this singer, imbued with the traditions of an alien stage, command not only the German declamatory passages, but stamp with his artistry and personality a character that had hitherto been portrayed only according to the German school of singing and acting, and yet not lose the power of what was best in that style?

The first scene, with its quaint, peaceful song of the sailor, could not, of course, answer these questions. The audience awaited its close.

Then the curtain was drawn aside. Tristan stood at the helm, quietly, silently, the embodiment of self-restraint. His serenity was not disturbed when Kurwenal brought the warning that Brangaene was coming with a message from Isolde, but a scarcely perceptible start betrayed the subject of his thought as he gazed out upon the sea. Isolde could disturb his peace if he let her. Tristan held his repose throughout the passage with Brangaene; nor could Isolde's chiding ruffle it. Even when she asked him to tell her how to achieve the revenge she had sworn for Morold's death, he still re-

mained calm. Wan and mournful, he handed her his sword.
And when, not yet knowing that Isolde loved him too, he
sang "War Morold dir so werth?" the quiet but deeply sorrowful majesty of his utterance and action gave his listeners
a new concept of nobility. Only when he had quaffed the cup
which held, not the death-dealing draught both he and Isolde
thought it contained, but the fatal love potion, did he stand
there as the lover; perplexed—but urgent, yearning, passionate. Even yet he waited until Isolde sighed "Tristan." Then,
as though of Lethe he had drunk, a veil of oblivion shrouded
"Tristan's Ehre." Then, as the light of the new happiness
dawned in his heart, "Tristan's Elend" became a joy; not less
a joy because fraught with uncertainty and pain. Then, all
self-control abandoned, the lover in him roused to distracted
eloquence, came the dramatic answering cry, *"Isolde!"*—complete, shot through with the glory and the longing and the
wonder of love. Naked soul faced naked soul, defenseless
before what was now the only reality—the elemental desire of
the man for the woman, of the woman for the man. Tenderly
he took her in his arms, and in their love duo these two rose
fully to the majestic heights of the tumultuous music through
which the composer portrayed the driving, irresistible force
of the passion which engulfed them.

If there had been some vague uncertainty about Jean de
Reszke's capacity to portray this first act, there could have
been little in the minds of those who knew the opera and
knew him too, about the second. They already knew him as
the very embodiment of romance, and they expected him to
bring the love element in this great love drama into higher
prominence than any other interpreter; but that any singer
could invest the part with such intense tenderness, with so
much of grandeur and noble strength, so much of overwhelming ecstasy and sadness and sweet anguish, they had never
even imagined.

Here in this second act, in ever shifting tone-colors, like
the shadows of clouds passing over downs, the singer de-
picted with astonishing poignancy every shade of love, from
tender, sweet affection to flaming, consuming passion. Here
he made all listeners feel that for such a lover any Isolde
would willingly forsake all else, repeating with Ruth,
"Whither thou goest will I go, and where thou diest will I
die." Every word could be understood. Every word was
clothed with deepest tenderness. Every word went winging

Photo Dupont, N. Y.

JEAN DE RESZKE AS TRISTAN

on tones so beautiful that the entire audience, and Isolde herself, must have felt:

> Now more than ever seems it rich to die,
> To cease upon the midnight with no pain,
> While thou art pouring forth thy soul abroad
> In such an ecstasy.

The "Sink hernieder, Nacht der Liebe" passage was ineffably beautiful, sung there in the garden, the brooding trees on one side, the ancient castle on the other; sung there in the stillness of the late spring night. Every woman must have yearned to be an Isolde to such a Tristan, every man longed for the power so to convey passionate love to an Isolde.

But when, just as cool morning dawned, Marke returned and confronted Tristan, "den treu'sten aller Treuen," the "truest of the faithful" became once more immovable. At first bewildered by the gradually dawning horror of his treachery toward his king, then stern with remorse, he admitted sorrowfully, in the accents of one not yet awakened from a dream: "Das kann ich dir nicht sagen; und was du fragst, das kannst du nie erfahren." And now, after the rich beauty of the duet, he sang, with a world of love and despair concentrated into a single phrase: "Wohin nun Tristan scheidet!" In asking Isolde whether she would follow him into that dreary land which Tristan once had known, he kept the lovely tones, but clothed his voice with darkness and sorrow, losing nothing of his dignity. This was less delirious singing than the love duet; it was more human, and poignant with human tenderness. Absolutely convincing was this singing which revealed the very deeps of emotion. One could believe that Isolde might gladly welcome exile with this man in whom were met such human tenderness and such surpassing human nobility; that she would have no regrets if

> They, hand in hand, with wandering steps and slow
> Through Eden took their solitary way.

In his singing of Italian Jean de Reszke had worked this magic, transmitting by means of his bearing, his tone-coloring, the meaning of the poetry. When, later, he sang in French, it was more clearly, more beautifully articulated than by the French themselves. Camille Bellaigue, long music critic of the *Revue des Deux Mondes,* once wrote that the French language had never been pronounced and accented with such accuracy and force, or if need be with such charm and tenderness, as on the lips of this foreigner. And now, in hearing his Tristan, the Germans themselves were amazed at the tenderness with which this language that had been called unsingable could be charged by one who had the soul of a true man and a true artist. Until Jean de Reszke taught them that they had been too indulgent, they had been content to

> Let the singing singers
> With vocal voices, most vociferous,
> In sweet vociferation out-vociferize
> Even sound itself.

The day after the performance a German wrote to a friend in Munich: [67]

> Man erwartete zwar viel von Jean de Reszke's Tris-
> tan, aber er hat alle Erwartungen weit übertroffen....
> So schön gesungen wie gestern kann das Duett im zweiten
> Akte noch nicht dagewesen sein; es war eine Wonne,
> diesen Klangwundern zu lauschen.... Aber was mich
> am tiefsten gerührt hat, war im dritten Akt Jean de
> Reszke: Alle, selbst die Unempfindlichsten, waren hier
> vollständig überwältigt.*

The third act did indeed embody all that human contemplation could bear of beauty, of ecstasy, of anguish. Here
also Jean satisfied in full measure the exacting demands of
this trying rôle. From the lyrical beauty of the second act he
rose to tragic heights almost intolerable in their intensity,
and yet he never once passed a hair's-breadth beyond the
limits of artistic restraint. Lying there in the garden, mor-
tally wounded by his betrayer, unconscious alike of the sultri-
ness of the atmosphere, the pounding of the sea, and the
desolate melody of the shepherd, he sang, in his delirium, of
the one emotion which was still supreme. He began with a
cold, empty tone that sent a shudder through his listeners.
Then gradually, as he fancied he saw Isolde coming to him
in a ship, the tones became warmer and richer, till they

---

* "Of course one expected a great deal of Jean de Reszke's Tristan, but he
exceeded all expectations by far.... Surely the duet in the second act can never
before have been sung so beautifully as last night; it was blissful to listen to the
wonderful sounds.... But what stirred me most deeply was the third act of Jean
de Reszke: here every one, even the least impressionable, was completely overwhelmed."

vibrated with the fullness of passion; and as despair once more overcame him, the timbre was again marked by the chill of the beginning, and it seemed as though a sudden gust of rainy wind had blown through the theater. Hopelessly he dropped his arms as the shepherd's pipe conveyed to his fevered mind the emptiness of the sea. One thought of Tennyson's *Princess:*

> Ah, sad and strange as in dark summer dawns
> The earliest pipe of half-awakened birds
> To dying ears, when unto dying eyes
> The casement slowly grows a glimmering square;
> So sad, so strange, the days that are no more.

Then once more came the delirious strain, with its eager repetition of "Siehst du Isolde?" its unspeakable yearning, and, at last, again that most wonderful cry, *"Isolde!"* full of infinite love and longing and worship, stark with the despair of coming darkness, yet melodious with the deep joy of seeing once more, though for the last time, the woman he loved above all else.

In singing the declamatory speeches Jean gave every word its full force, every tone its full musical value; the boundary line between speech and song was almost obliterated. Wagner had said that if Tristan were equal to his task in this act the complicated orchestral score would sound subordinate to the vocal part, as though it were a guitar accompaniment to a simple tune. So it proved, owing to the marvelous artistry of the singer. Jean could achieve this magnificent effect because, in the first place, his natural sympathies made the rôle of Tristan an appealing one. He was a good musician, and he had studied the music patiently and lovingly. Deeply he understood the poetry of the opera. He had a profound sense of the artistic and dramatic value of a word; knew when it should sound blush-crimson, when cool blue; sensed the fragrance and the whispering and rustling of some, the fury and recklessness of others. He could achieve this great creation because he was a great artist—intellectually, musically, dramatically.

It was such a performance of Tristan as had never been witnessed, uniting as it did, so beautifully, all the essential elements of this tragedy of love. Sharing in the glory of it were Lillian Nordica and Edouard de Reszke. Like that of Tristan, the part of Isolde requires that the artist who would give an adequate representation shall have a magnificent equipment. Tremendous vocal resources she must have, deep insight and the power to transmit the emotional content of the work, limitless physical strength and endurance, and intellectual discernment of shades of meaning and emotion. In her portrayal of Isolde, Madame Nordica showed that she possessed this equipment in a degree which, if not completely satisfying to the most critical, was yet agreeably surprising even to her enthusiasts. She did not quite overwhelm her audience, but that was due less to a lack of finished artistry than to something which art can neither create nor transcend. There was lacking in her voice a certain necessary sensuous quality, and she simply did not have the temperament which could portray the impetuous, volcanic passion of the first act, the blissful, mad rapture of the second, or the overwhelming grief of the last.

Edouard gave a new quality to the character of Marke. Audiences had been used to hearing the part droned or shouted. Edouard gave the monarch his proper measure of nobility. The German words rolled out on the stupendous tones with the same admirable enunciation that characterized his brother's singing, and his speech at the end of the second act, weighted with a grandeur of sorrow and reproach, was delivered with magnificent certitude. He sang away the boredom with which portrayers of Marke usually fill the atmosphere, and because of his own profound feeling, invited sympathy. When, in bewildered grief at seeing Tristan and the faithful Kurwenal dead before him, Isolde dying too, he sang

> Todt denn Alles!
> Alles todt?

one thought again of the sorrow of that other who asked:

> All my pretty ones?
> Did you say all?

But even these singers could perhaps not have shown their talents in such superb degree had the man who wielded the baton been any other but Anton Seidl, who knew every nuance of Wagner's music and poetry, knew the great composer's great intention, and knew and loved the artists; Anton Seidl, who could make the orchestra sigh and sob and thunder. Seidl knew that Jean de Reszke would realize the dream of the composer, who had loosed the torrent of his tremendous talents in this opera. "Here," wrote Wagner, "in perfect trustfulness, I plunged into the inner depths of the soul, and from out this inmost center of the world I fearlessly built up its outer form.•A glance at the *volumen* of this poem will show you at once that the exhaustive detail work, which a historical poet is obliged to devote to clearing up the outward bearings of his plot, to the detriment of a lucid exposition of its inner motives, I now trusted myself to apply to these latter alone. Life and death, the whole import and existence of the outer world, here hang on nothing but the inner movements of the soul. The whole affecting action comes about only because the inmost soul demands it and steps to light with the very shape foretokened in the inner shrine." [68]

Seidl remembered, too, "how impressively and with what a variety of voice he [Wagner] was able to sing the different rôles for those who had been chosen to interpret them, and how marvelously he phrased them all." [69]

Some said that Seidl had, in this production of T r i s t a n, supplied the work with more delicate tints than usual, for the sake of Jean de Reszke and Nordica. But he himself says: "In rehearsing T r i s t a n I did not change a single note or expression mark, but only carried out what the composer had written down, and gave effect to the vocal and orchestral parts in their true complementary values. I am flattered to know that I achieved the desired and prescribed success, for it was the general verdict that every word was understood from beginning to end; that was my wish, and that should be the wish and the accomplishment of every conductor." [70] Seidl knew that the orchestral coloring had to be adjusted to the acoustical properties of the auditorium, and he knew how to do it without violating the composer's thought. He knew that there was an instrumental *forte* which could be governed and a vocal *forte* which remained very nearly if not absolutely a fixed quantity. Wagner, he remembered, had been most anxious, even when conducting mere fragments from his operas, that the singer's every syllable should be heard. At the close of a vocal phrase he would frequently arrest the sound of the orchestra so that the last syllable might be heard. "How often did he call out angrily: 'Kinder, you are killing my poetry!' "

Wagner had despaired of hearing his T r i s t a n sung as he felt it should be. In a letter he wrote:

Was ever work like mine created for no purpose? Is it miserable egoism, the stupidest vanity? It matters not

what it is, but of this I feel positive; yes, as positive as
that I live, and that is, my Tristan und Isolde, with
which I am now consumed, does not find its equal in the
world's library of music. Oh, how I yearn to hear it; I
am feverish; I feel worn; perhaps that causes me to be
agitated and anxious, but my Tristan has been finished
now these three years and has not been heard."[71]

If, as Liszt said, this work marked "a new epoch in the
evolution and creation of music," certainly Jean de Reszke's
singing of it marked a new epoch in interpretation, and that
performance of T r i s t a n   u n d   I s o l d e on November 27
1895 represented, above and beyond the success of the de
Reszkes and Lillian Nordica, a new triumph for Richard
Wagner. Jean stilled once and for all the objection that Wagner could not be sung musically, tenderly. Indeed, there were
a few who said that this music was never intended to be sung
so beautifully. Other singers, they said, who had shown
more rude strength, more barbarism, more feverish abandonment, had come closer to the composer's intention. And yet,
there was the whole tradition of courtly love, all the historical
records of chivalric bearing, the very legends from which
Wagner had taken his story, to support Jean in emphasizing
the fact that love was Tristan's most powerful emotion.
    Nor could the charge that the human voice would
crumble under the strain stand before Jean's achievement in
the third act; for though he did not tear passion to tatters, he
did not spare himself either, and his voice held out gloriously
throughout all the trying demands made on it. His listeners,
far from feeling that it might break, never gave the matter
a thought. The artistry was so superb that they thought not
of voice or song or singer, but only of the wounded and
yearning Tristan, whose heart,

> 'Twixt two extremes of passion, joy and grief,
> Burst smilingly.

They knew it had "burst smilingly," because Isolde asked
them to see, "Mild und leise, wie er lächelt."
    There was no mistaking how the audience felt about
these singers in their new opera. Breathless they sat during
the performance, but when the curtain dropped after each
act the dead silence was broken by tornadoes of bravoes, in
which Mr. Seidl richly shared. At his first appearance he was

welcomed by three volleys of applause, and after each act he was forced to join the singers before the curtain. Once he escaped through a side door, but Jean de Reszke marched out after him with great strides and determined air, and brought him back in his iron grip. When, after another act, Seidl again refused to respond to the calls, Jean and Edouard brought him back once more, a very meek little man between two giants.

But from the standpoint of both operatic and personal history the largest single achievement of the evening was Jean de Reszke's. The critic of the *New York Times* wrote: [72]

It was Philip Gilbert Hamerton who wisely said, "You cannot put an artist's day into the life of any one but an artist." Yesterday was an artist's day for Jean de Reszke.... He has achieved the grandest triumph of his career. He stands today with the proud record of being the first lyric and the first heroic tenor of his day. He sings Faust and Tristan with equal beauty. But Tristan is a tremendous tragic hero, and the music in which his utterances are embodied is utterly different in style from that in which M. de Reszke has gained his world-wide fame. Today the tenor has to his credit an impersonation which, in vocal beauty, excels every Tristan ever known, and in dramatic power is a broad and commanding creation. Even to say that he sang every note in tune is to credit him with a new record, for, so far as New York is concerned, it is a refreshing experience to hear this music correctly intoned.

Not only did he sing it in tune, but he sang it with declamatory power that was simply magnificent where power was necessary, and with such a wealth of yearning tenderness in the love passages that he almost eclipsed all memories of his own former fervor. He enunciated the German text perfectly, and with such care that not a word was lost. What is to be said of it all? What words can be used that will not seem extravagant? It was a great performance of Tristan, and it revealed for the first time the complete musical beauty of Wagner's declamation. More must be said about this creation at another time, when the emotions are not under the immediate influence of the work. The Germans must admit that it was "ganz wunderbar schön."

The Germans did admit that. One of them wrote:

> Jean de Reszke stand in jeder Scene vollständig
> auf der Höhe seiner aufgabe.... Seine Aussprache des
> deutschen Textes war durchaus eine vortrefflich reine
> und klare. Sein Spiel war in jeder Scene—und ganz beson-
> ders in der letzten und schwersten, der Sterbescene—von
> überwältigender Schönheit und Wahrheit.*

Jean was deeply moved by the reception accorded this
new undertaking. Generously he gave to Anton Seidl a large
share of the credit for its success. The conductor's wife went
to congratulate him after it was over, and found him standing
in the center of the stage with his arms around Mr. Seidl, saying: "How you help us! You always make it easy for us. Ah,
surely the spirit of Wagner hovers over you tonight."

There had been no need for de Reszke to study this new
rôle for the sake of adding to his glory. He was admired and
loved. He was the idol of two continents. Honors had been
heaped upon him. In most respects he stood higher than any
other in the art of the lyric drama. And yet—it was at the
beginning of Jean's career as a tenor that the Bayreuth master
had begun to exercise his posthumous fascination on lovers
of the musical drama. A man with the soul and the artistic
ideals of a Jean de Reszke could not remain indifferent to that
influence. Did he sense, when he first heard the Wagnerian
operas in German, that in interpreting Wagner in his own
language he might triumph as greatly as he had in Italian and
French operatic art? No matter. At middle age he entered a
new operatic realm, driven by the "insatiable hunger of the
genuine artist to achieve the one grand and noble thing that
was left for him to achieve in the whole realm of lyric art, to
enter a new domain of vocal and dramatic beauty, to be the
central figure in the inspiration of a new world." [73] And this
though it meant learning a new language and absorbing a
quarter of a century of traditions in which he was unschooled.
It is as though the great soul of the man itself became articu-
late within him and said: Here is an opportunity to communicate in mellow music, for your own deep satisfaction and that
of thousands of others, the beauty and strength of a passion

"In every scene Jean de Reszke completely met the demands of his task....
His pronunciation of the German text was throughout splendidly pure and clear.
His performance was in every scene—and most especially in the last and most diffi-
cult, the death scene—of overwhelming beauty and truth."

that is great and universal; here you can show what a great-souled man can be and do for honor and for love.

In range and sincere endeavor, if perhaps not quite in intellectual discernment, Edouard kept pace with his beloved brother. After a later performance of T r i s t a n, W. J. Henderson answered an inquirer:

> If "Old Stager" desires to hear how a passage can be declaimed in the most satisfactory Wagnerian style, and at the same time in a manner that will not offend, but will rather deeply move any lover of pure singing, let him go and hear Edouard de Reszke as King Mark in Tristan und Isolde.

One had thought the first performance could not be improved so far as the de Reszkes were concerned, but the next time the opera was given this actually seemed to have happened. "In two places," wrote the critic of the *Evening Post*, "the first meeting of the lovers in Act II, and in the climax of his [Jean's] last scene, he was even more thrillingly dramatic than before." The *Times* critic thought, however, that he had shown a tendency to lose some of his dignified repose in the places where that was most necessary.

Nordica's Isolde showed great improvement. (There was a story that she had had a thousand rehearsals before the first performance, a circumstance George Moore is said to have used in drawing his Evelyn Innes.) Some people think that Lillian Nordica was always in love with Jean. That circumstance, added to the strain of a rôle like Isolde, might easily explain why she was sometimes so carried away with emotion as to impair the artistry of her performance. In the great duo on the first night, Edouard de Reszke stood in the wings and when she neared his side of the stage he would call out, "Non si allegro!" and Jean would whisper, when she went over to him, "Pas si vite!" thus keeping her in check and preventing her from marring the effect of the whole. It brings to mind a story about the tragedian Young, who, when playing with Mrs. Siddons was so violently moved that not even the prompter could make him proceed with his part. Finally Mrs. Siddons herself had to touch him on the shoulder and say: "Mr. Young, recollect yourself!"

Jean loved Isolde's glorious music in the last act, and when he was properly protected against draughts, enjoyed listening to it as he lay on his couch; but during one of these early performances he took cold, just as Schnorr, the first Tristan, had done thirty years before in Munich. Schnorr died from the effects of that exposure, but Jean wisely made changes in his dress and in the position of the couch.

As a matter of artistic exactitude he always went to the theater several hours before the rise of the curtain, to see personally that every bit of stage property with which he was concerned was just right. For Tristan he took special pains. He had the couch arranged and then stretched himself out upon it, adjusting the furs and pillows so as to get the most effective position and also to protect himself against any draught. The couch was then moved to the back of the stage and practically sealed up until the last act of the opera. Nevertheless, as a result of that one evening's lapse, he was prevented from singing for a time, and the disappointed public was probably not quite fair in judging the tenor who tried to fill the rôle of Tristan in his absence. As for Jean's own impersonation, it seemed that in every performance he towered above the splendor of the last, and the customary comment became: "Upon the whole, the latest presentation of T r i s- t a n was the most brilliant and successful of all." The verdict of German critics may be judged from the following critique in *Daheim*.* The writer had heard three performances of the opera in America, the first with Rosa Sucher and Max Alvary, the second with Katharina Klafsky and Wilhelm Grüning. Then came the third, with Lillian Nordica and Jean de Reszke, which he described thus:

We expected both the de Reszkes to give distinguished performances, and probably had the right to do so; but for such overwhelming grandeur we were not prepared. Only yesterday did we hear and see, for the first time, such a Tristan and such a Marke as Richard Wagner created. And with that realization a wistful thought stole upon us. Isn't it a thousand pities that two such men, through the accident of birth and the consequent musical education, were trained in the Italian- French instead of along the neo-German channels! For surely the Bayreuth master himself could not have dreamed of two heroic figures more completely Wagnerian! Jean de Reszke, for example, what a Siegmund,

* The original German will be found in the Appendix.

what a Siegfried, what a Walther! Edouard de Reszke—
what a Wotan, Hagen, Hans Sachs!

A more ideal Tristan than Jean de Reszke we cannot
imagine. He surpasses that miserable singer and de-
claimer Alvary, as well as Grüning, who recites like a parrot, as the Eiffel Tower in Paris looms above the local
water-tower. In Jean de Reszke everything combines to
form a perfect Tristan: fervor, refined and dramatic acting, and glorious vocal interpretation. This Tristan
doesn't wail and bellow; he sings the glorious Wagnerian
tones ever nobly and in highest fulfilment. Yes, such a
Tristan makes Isolde's self-sacrifice understandable.

On artistic heights just as eminent stands the König
Marke of Edouard de Reszke. Only the day before yesterday did we really comprehend this creation of Wagner.
This Marke was no dish-rag, but remained, though with
a deeply injured pride, the proud King! And how he
sang! Every tone shook our inmost being.

The enthusiasm during that third performance had been
extraordinary, indeed unprecedented. Six frantic recalls after
the first act and seven after the second, and at the close of the
opera the audience lingered long, hoping for "just one more
look" at the artists who had moved them so profoundly. They
went home emotionally exhausted; worn out from suffering
with Tristan, but with expanded souls. It was Sidney Lanier
who said: "Music is love in search of a word." That word had
been found in "Tristan."

So moving an effect did Jean's acting and singing have
that once, during an impassioned scene, a young woman in
one of the dark upper boxes leaned over and kissed her husband convulsively, exclaiming in rapture: "Oh, Jean!" But
for the most part the audience sat motionless, in utter silence.
During the first matinée performance a very famous singer
was among them. At the fall of the curtain after the second
act she turned to her companion and said: "Did you notice
how absorbed the people were? Not even a cough was heard!
Wonderful!" [74]

But it was not only T r i s t a n that was glorified through
Jean's assumption of its leading rôle. His work on that opera
lent new understanding and color to his other rôles as well.
Though his Lohengrin had been thought perfection itself, it
now became still more effective, both vocally and dramatically.

Some of the languorous grace of the traditional chevalier, some of the sentimental elegance of the Italian knight, now gave way to the imposing stature of the genuine German Lohengrin, large-gestured and more profoundly emotional. One example will illustrate why it seemed that Jean actually surpassed himself in this part, after all superlatives had already been exhausted in the attempt to convey the effect of the consummate art with which he united beauty of voice, perfect intonation, artistic phrasing, distinct enunciation, and swiftly changing facial expression. Lohengrin's declaration of love consists of the four words: "Elsa, ich liebe dich!" The music to which they are set places the accent on "liebe," and the effect of the whole phrase is almost destroyed when through translation the accent is placed on another word. When Jean now sang the words in German he could give a richer tone to their emotional content. This one phrase alone enraptured his hearers and made them impatient with every other Lohengrin.

AFTER ONE of Jean's especially beautiful performances that season a critic wrote: "Jean de Reszke is the greatest tenor of the nineteenth century; his retirement from the stage would practically mean the collapse of opera as at present given in New York." [75] Chicago, on the other hand, might have felt that opera as given at the Auditorium would collapse should his brother Edouard retire from the stage. For in Chicago Edouard still reigned supreme. His Mephisto continued the most popular characterization offered by the brilliant company visiting the city in these years, though Jean's Faust was considered "an accepted standard" because its nobility and genuine virility made Faust seem not a mere poltroon, but deserving of the sympathies of men and women. And even Chicago grudgingly admitted that the new T r i s t a n discovered to them the grandeur and the subtle beauty of the formidable Wagner score. What an answer these performances were to the skeptic who had, a few years before, ventured the following prophecy: [76]

> And what is Jean de Reszke, after all? Good looking and shapely fellow, with a colorless voice of little resonance and small range, and an impassive countenance. De Reszke phrases well and acts well; but I lay any reasonable wager that the gifts and talents he possesses will not produce the slightest impression upon American audiences that have had the good fortune, in years bygone, to listen to the finest voices in the world. I predicted over my signature, ten months ago, that Signor Tamagno would fail to please in the United States and events fulfilled my prophecy. I venture to give the same assurance in respect of Jean de Reszke, whose artistic feeling and refinement of style, however, will win critical regard where Signor Tamagno's leather-lunged vociferation never once commanded it.

If Jean's was a "colorless" voice, then Americans thought colorless voices well worth listening to. And Londoners confirmed that judgment. They envied America its opportunity of hearing the new Tristan first. As early as 1889 English musical commentators had promised both S i e g f r i e d and T r i s t a n, as well as W a l k ü r e with Jean playing Siegmund,

for the "next season." Now at last Covent Garden was to hear
at least one of those rôles, but not before it heard Jean and
Edouard again in more familiar parts.

The de Reszkes were joyously welcomed back in May
1896, after their year's absence. Jean's German Lohengrin was
admired, though it was admitted that "so long as M. Jean de
Reszke warbles the farewell to the swan as mellifluously as on
Friday, he can sing it, if he pleases, in German, Italian, or,
for the matter of that, in Choctaw." Edouard sang Hans Sachs
for the first time in London that season. His humorous impersonation, his full and rich tones, his dramatic accent, made
Londoners forget all previous impersonations of the famous
old cobbler.

One there was, especially, who would have greeted the
new Tristan joyously—Sir Augustus Harris. But, he, alas, was
denied the joy of witnessing the crowning achievement of his
career as an operatic manager—the production of Wagner's
tragic masterpiece sung in its original language by some of the
world's greatest artists. He died suddenly in the middle of
June, about ten days before the first London performance of
Jean de Reszke's Tristan. The success of the occasion would
have made Sir Augustus ecstatic. Despite increased prices, the
house was crammed. Londoners were quick to acknowledge
their joy that no longer would it be necessary for them to
choose one of two imperfect things in opera—singers of slight
vocal attainment using the original language, or a foreign
version sung by great artists. The de Reszkes and their fellow
artists proved to England as to America that Wagner could be
beautifully sung. The performance was thus described in *The
Times*:

> At last we have seen and heard Jean de Reszke's
> Tristan, and it must at once be pronounced a perform-
> ance of unsurpassed nobility, strength, passion, and ten-
> derness—the highest example of superb histrionic and
> interpretative musical art offered to this generation. Not
> until some hours after the event is it possible to realize
> its completeness, its entire magnificence; for the last act
> of T r i s t a n u n d I s o l d e is so piercing in its pathos,
> the merely human appeal stirs the spectator to such acute
> anguish, that the artistic effect of all that has gone before
> is obliterated, and at first the artistic effect of the act
> itself is to a degree overshadowed. But . . . thinking only

of the artistic effect of Jean de Reszke's singing and acting, of his interpretation of Wagner's thought and emotion, the recollections of the exceeding splendor of the
conception and of the superb art with which the conception was put objectively before us, rush in, as it
were, upon the mind and drive one on to superlatives.
And in the first fervor it seems that Jean de Reszke is
surely the greatest operatic tenor who has yet lived; for
none of the celebrated tenors of the older time was ever
set such a task as the impersonation of Tristan, and not
the best of them could have done it more finely.

...He has never acted—in London at least—as he
acted on Friday; his dignity in the first act, his fervor in
the second, and his most touchingly expressive singing
and gesture in the last, showed the artist who is absolute
master of his art.

Tosti, who was a warm admirer of the brothers, sent Jean
the following letter after this performance: *

12 Mandeville Place
15 juillet 96

Mon cher Jean,
Votre Tristan m'a donné la *plus grande* jouissance
artistique dont je me souvienne! Permettez-moi de vous
le dire et de vous en remercier. Vous vous êtes surpassé
hier au soir; c'est tout dire! C'est une soirée que je
n'oublierai jamais! Adieu; je voudrais aller vous serrer
la main ainsi qu'au cher Edouard; malheureusement je
ne le puis! Je le fais donc ici de tout cœur, en souhaitant
vous revoir l'année prochaine.

Votre tout devoué
Paolo Tosti

But not only critics and composers were moved to put
their feelings down in writing. London audiences, though
traditionally less demonstrative than those in New York, were
just as devoted to the de Reszkes. There was always a curious

* My dear Jean,
Your Tristan has given me the greatest artistic satisfaction that I can
remember. Permit me to tell you so, and to thank you. You surpassed yourself last
night; to say that is to say everything! It is an evening that I shall never forget!
Adieu; I should like to clasp you by the hand, and dear Edouard too; unfortunately
I cannot. So I do it this way, with all my heart, hoping to see you again during
the coming year.

Your devoted
Paolo Tosti

sort of effervescence in the theater on a de Reszke night, an excited feeling that something special might happen. A genuine affection existed between the brothers and their audiences. After the performance one heard, on all sides, eager, delighted discussions, warm with friendliness. Thousands of men and women, if dowered with the gift of adequate expression, would perhaps have written a tribute such as the one following, sent to Jean anonymously. Nowadays its tone may seem fulsome, yet I feel it is worthy to be preserved:

To
　MONSIEUR JEAN DE RESZKE
　　　The Opera Season is nearly over, and I, who with a little band of enthusiasts, have spent many a wonderful night in listening to you, feel now so burdened with our debt to you that I am going to try to put into words something of the gratitude of which our hearts are full.

　　　We are not in the *beau monde* of London; we have not got it in our power to express our admiration by such means as they have who live therein. We are just unfashionable musical students and enthusiasts who have long enjoyed your superb art from the gallery in Covent Garden and who now for the first time are venturing to draw a little nearer to you, to rid our hearts in words of a little of their load of thanks and praise before we go back again and become mere items of enthusiasm in that huge sum of noisy applause that greets you from the inexpensive places in the Opera House.

　　　In speaking for myself throughout this letter, I know I speak for many, for thousands; if I did not know that I should not dare to take this liberty, for the praise and worship of one unknown individual can have little value for you who have won the heart of the "great world," and the admiration of artists, wherever you have been; but I hope, when you realize that the "I" of this letter represents a great number, you will not condemn me as impertinent, but will look at least with charity on this our little tribute.

　　　How may I put it into words?

　　　You have been a revelation to me; the *greatness* of feeling in all that you do is an inspiration to me; you create an atmosphere in which nought that is mean and unworthy can live. In the presence of your genius and

A toi mon cher Jean en
souvenir de la grande et
inoubliable émotion artistique que tu m'as fait
éprouver hier

CHARTRAN

N.Y. 31 Xbre 1896

A mon cher ami et collaborateur
Amherst Webber, en souvenir de nos
études et de la 1re de Siegfried
à N. York, le 30 Dre. 1896.
Son dévoué

JEAN DE RESZKE AS SIEGFRIED

your supreme art, I feel my heart on fire with high as-
pirations; a priceless boon to me, for I too am an artist
after my fashion. All my life I have hungered and thirsted
for great art, and in you I have found it as I think I can
never find it again. For God has given you a nature made
on such grand lines that nothing poor, petty and mediocre
has a part in you. It would seem to us who watch you and
listen to you with such joy, that your blood has never
moved in the tame ebb and flow of everyday life, but only
at the impulse of the splendid passsions, of splendid love,
splendid hate, splendid despair; and hence your power
of great impersonation—a power so lamentably lacking on
the operatic stage as a rule, where a singer's poor and
undignified acting so often spoils the pleasure we take
in his voice.

I have heard many singers, in Germany and Italy as
well as in England, but I have never heard, and I fear I
shall never hear again, any other man who so *absolutely*
becomes the character he personates; no, nor who will
always give the highest and noblest interpretation of that
character too. Surely, for the time you are *wholly* Romeo,
with his exquisite love and pathos. (Ah! how you wring
our hearts with *O ma femme! O ma bien aimée!* ending
with *mes lèvres, donnez-lui votre dernier baiser!* You seem
to gather all the love and heartbreak of the rich Italian
love-story into your voice, in that part.) And just as surely
you are wholly Tristan, at first holding his passion at
arm's length, and then, under bewitchment, losing himself in it, a creature blinded, bewildered, possessed by
passion. You take our breath away over that! We who
heard you on your first night in London as Tristan, will
never forget the quiet tragedy in your voice when the
disloyal friend, the dishonored knight, answers his
beloved King's reproaches, *O König, das kann ich dir
nicht sagen*—nor the poignant despair of your conclud-
ing cry, *Aus Eifer verrieth mich der Freund, dem König,
den ich verrieth!*

You are just as wholly Faust; and especially in the
first act do you seem to me great. Never have I seen any
other who could so wonderfully personate that restless,
miserable, splendid old man, weary of all his load of
learning, and craving for his lost youth and its forfeited
power of passion, at any price, at any price!

You are wholly Lohengrin, the radiant and pure-hearted lover, *chevalier sans peur et sans reproche,* the stainless knight, with the faint, fine halo of mystery and holiness, around his whole bearing and voice. When you sing your great declaration beginning *Da voi lontan, in sconosciuta terra, a voi un castel,* etc., I think you have all Heaven in your voice; and when you speak your last to Elsa, it seems to me that every note falls from you like a drop of your heart's blood.

Not the whole world of Society with all its wealth and its honors, nor we enthusiasts with all our worship, can ever repay you for what you are to us; the worth of the highest art can never be gauged. We can only applaud you and thank you and bless you, and tell you that you have made our lives richer and happier, and that whether you go away, dear and great Master, to return again next year, or whether, as rumor sometimes says, you go away and will never come back and gladden us any more, the memory of you will be a splendid inspiration, a joy, a glory for ever in our lives.

July 1896

That same season a unique acknowledgment of their talents and services was sent to the beloved brothers. The majority of London musical critics affixed their signatures to the following testimonial, which was inscribed in two albums, each containing all the signatures.

To the Brothers Jean and Edouard de Reszke:
To the great artists, who have ever upheld the Dignity of their profession, and enjoyed the Confidence and Respect of the Public. To the Men whom Success has failed to enervate, and abounding Honors to deprive of manly Modesty. To the Vocalists in whom survive the Traditions of a glorious Past, and through whom the Succession of all that is illustrious in their Art has continued to the present hour. To the lyric Actors who have given Substance and Vitality to Creatures of Imagination, and made them live in sight and memory. We, whose names are hereto appended, being musical journalists in London, desire to offer the homage of our admiration and gratitude—admiration of brilliant talents, gratitude for high example and the rare delight of perfected art.

Thus had Jean and Edouard added to their glory and fame on two continents. But they were not yet satisfied. "Enthusiasm makes everything possible," Wagner once wrote; and enthusiasm for Wagner's work was the force that urged Jean de Reszke to new achievements at a time of life when most singers, especially if they have amassed a fortune, are willing, if not to retire, at least to rest on the laurels of ancient accomplishments. Not so with the de Reszkes. They had both begun to study Siegfried as soon as Tristan was well under way.

As it had expected to hear the new Tristan first, so London also thought to have the first experience of Siegfried, and there was some grumbling that the two beloved Poles were spending so much time in America. But there was no particular decision on the part of the de Reszkes, or on that of any manager, to favor America instead of England with these important first performances. Events simply so shaped themselves that Siegfried was not ready for performance anywhere until well on in the 1896-97 season at the Metropolitan. While the endless rehearsals were in progress the brothers continued their triumphs in other impersonations. Edouard's Leporello was especially popular. He himself was very fond of it. The actual enjoyment of a rôle seemed to him the first condition of successful operatic work. "I never tire," he declared. "I think I could sing through three operas, one after another, with just as much freshness and buoyancy at the finish as in the first act. I have often been compelled to repress the mood of gayety, so carried away have I allowed myself to be in some of the finer flights and the jollier passages. This jubilation, too, I know to be infectious; but it is honest and legitimate, putting my audience *en rapport* with the artist as nothing else can." That jubilation he never felt more heartily than when he sang the air about Don Juan's "mille e tre" conquests in Spain alone, and waved aloft the huge list of the victims' names. Edouard's portrayal of this rôle has been variously criticized, some feeling that his tremendous size and his naturally dignified gait were a handicap, and that he could not fool without becoming a grotesque buffoon. But the discriminating critic of the *New York Times* felt thus about it:

It is a good thing once in a while for the big basso to
· make his appearance among the lesser lights of the com-

pany, so that people may discern just how big he is artistically. His Leporello is simply superb. It is a joy without alloy to hear him read the recitative with all the skill of a perfect actor and vocalist, and with such brimming and unctuous humor that every line is funny. As for his "madamina," it is one of the most admirable of all achievements in the art of buffo singing.

And in spite of some objections, the fact remains that Edouard's great size was very much in his favor in making humorous contrasts. Then too, he was unusually nimble. As Don Basilio his efforts to hide behind the diminutive Fräulein Bauermeister were side-splitting. But he did not often abuse these opportunities. He was a true artist who could modulate his tremendous voice, which had a working range of about two octaves (from E below to E above the bass clef), so that he could out-coo the dove as well as outroar the lion. Soft or loud, high or low, it always sounded easy and spontaneous. But the sheer volume of the voice was so amazing that that quality was most spoken of; and, naturally, was humorously exaggerated too. It did reverberate through a large auditorium like thunder echoes rolling among the Alps, but some wag said that people living near the opera house, upon first hearing his voice but not knowing whence it issued, ran out into the streets, fearing that the city had been visited by an earthquake, and could not be convinced of the exact truth until the big basso had personally appeared before them and sounded his fundamental note. Certainly Edouard would never have experienced the difficulty which distressed a certain trumpeter who was accompanying a vigorous-voiced soprano. The conductor felt that the trumpeter was not using sufficient force and called to him in a subdued tone, "Louder, louder!" This was repeated so often that finally the poor man—a German— threw down his instrument and, turning to the audience, exclaimed in passionate indignation: "It iss easy to cry louder! louder! but—by gar—vare iss de vind?" De Reszke, under such provocation, would probably have sent singer, conductor, and orchestra scurrying to shelter.

It was during this 1896-97 season that Emma Calvé first sang Marguerite in F a u s t. Calvé was a favorite with American audiences, and though her singing of the part was somewhat faulty, nobody but the critics minded that. At times she was a little trying to Jean. She loved to improvise new "business," and she did so almost every time she appeared. As Carmen she once stuffed a rose into Jean's mouth just as he was ready to begin a tender melody. In another scene she decided to run to the other side of the stage so that he would have to run after her. Since that would have meant getting out of breath just before a long and difficult bit of singing, Jean refused to pursue, thus leaving no need for Calvé to run away, and that piece of business was not repeated. In F a u s t she dropped her prayer-book as she was coming from church, expecting him to pick it up before he began his tuneful appeal. This he likewise refused to do, preferring to let one of the village maidens assume this duty. He said afterwards, when some one joked about the incident: "Well, if she thought I was going to bend down and split my elegant brand-new tights she had better think again!" But the famous Carmen must have liked to sing with Jean in spite of his refusal to indulge her whims, for she sent him the following letter: *

MY DEAR FRIEND:

I feel like throwing my arms around you, to embrace you and thank you for being willing to sing Don Jose.

Without you, I should feel myself lost, and my Italian Carmen would seem to me to be a dismal failure. You come to save me, and I shall never forget it.

Believe in the gratitude of your little Carmenita, who sends you a very affectionate "shake-hand."

EMMA CALVÉ

M e i s t e r s i n g e r, L o h e n g r i n, and R o m e o were repeatedly given, with the perfection that was now always expected and nearly always realized; although one critic was irritated by the constant praise of Jean's interpretation of young Montague, which he found unsatisfactory. He objected: [77]

Italian love as Shakespeare has pictured it—that quivering, ungovernable and semi-tropical amorousness that breaks through all restraints and expends itself in defiant hyperbole or rapturous exaltation—is not de Reszke's gait at all. No one denies him the possession of matchless staying power, or of prodigious lung energy, but no one can detect in him those Paduan nuances that

* Translated from the French.

creep sweetly to the ear from between the lines of that immortal love story. It is a startling heresy to say that there are several singers in the Metropolitan company who would make a better Romeo than de Reszke, but it is a heresy that somebody ought to temper the monotonous praise of this season with. There is no one admires de Reszke more than I do, but I do not admire him with the same degree of enthusiasm in everything he does. I think he often falls off in quality while he is being praised for quantity.

An occasional dissenting voice did no harm; but "quantity" is exactly what Jean de Reszke did not specialize in. He had no desire to "split the ears of the groundlings." Indeed, he was sometimes criticized for not observing the boundary between music and the unmusical in the Wagnerian recitative. Even so ardent a champion of his as the critic of the *New York Times* felt that because he sacrificed the ruggedness of the true Wagnerian recitative to pure beauty of tone Jean's "Tristan in one or two places, and his Siegfried in more than one or two, fell below the possible measure of eloquence. But it is far better to sing than to shout Wagner." [78]

L E C I D was also produced that season, probably because the New York company included three of the artists who appeared in the opera when it was first produced in Paris on December 1 1885. Jean was again Rodrigue, his brother was again Don Diègue, and, as on that occasion, Pol Plançon was Le Comte de Gormas. But in New York L e C i d met with small success, perhaps because the people preferred sentiment, such as they were accustomed to having ladled out in generous portions, to the heroics of an opera by the composer whom a French wit dubbed "Mademoiselle Wagner." Though opera-goers adored Jean no matter what he played, it was considered a mistake, not to say actual retrogression, for him to sing Rodrigue. As with some other operas, this one was enhanced through his portrayal, but the rôle held no opportunities for the subtleties he was master of. One complaint ran: [79]

> The famous tenor had little to do, save stand in picturesque attitudes and declaim music upon which his voice bestowed unmerited favor. . . . Not all his art could save Rodrigue from being a mere operatic figurehead. His brother was more fortunate, for in Don Diègue he found a rôle which afforded him some opportunities for the display of his noble voice and his finished style. The audience, in the early part of the evening at any rate, preferred M. Edouard de Reszke to M. Jean, and with reason.

Not every one concurred in this judgment. "From first to last it is Jean de Reszke's opera," we read elsewhere. "He appeared in eight out of the ten tableaux, and was sung about in the other two. He made love; he fought a duel; he sang farewell; he led in battle; he conquered all foes; he was hailed as the hero of the world. His acting and his singing fully justified these honors. Never was he in better voice than on last Friday night; never did he more charm the audience by his sweetness, and thrill them with his vigor, and rouse them by his enthusiasm. It was a gala night for him and for Director Grau, and he seemed to be doubly inspired. L e C i d will never become a popular opera . . . but it will rank as the best opera in which to hear and see Jean de Reszke in all the phases of his excellence." [80]

In Chicago, oddly enough, this opera caused a furor in

a season which only de Reszke performances kept from being consistently dull. In the duo between Rodrigue and Chimène at the close of the first scene in the third act, enthusiasm which had been accumulating all the evening burst forth tempestuously, and there followed the most memorable ovation ever accorded artists appearing on the Auditorium stage. "The magnificent dignity of the thrice repeated 'Je le jure' was the keynote of Jean's whole impersonation and from that it sounded every depth of passion, martial ardor, pathos and despair."

But just as all the triumphs of the previous season had paled before the magnificence of Jean de Reszke's Tristan, so everything that happened at the Metropolitan during the 1896-97 season took second place to his Siegfried. And just as there had been misgivings as to whether he would be equal to the elemental Germanic forcefulness of Tristan and still not lose the delicate shadings which his artistry lent other rôles, so some wondered whether Jean, now forty-six years old and by no means slender, could make one feel the boyishness of the younger Siegfried. Could he portray the freshness of life's springtime? Would he seem convincing talking to birds and darting among trees? For Wagner's woodland hero was both legendary and human, a more complex nature than those which Jean had excelled in portraying. He was playful and grave, youthfully innocent and manfully passionate; a combination of frisky colt, adventurous young giant, and thoughtful, mature man. Could Jean seem heroic, grandly remote, and yet the kind of youngster one would enjoy picnicking with in the forest? All doubts were definitely silenced long before the end of the first performance, which finally took place on December 30 in the presence of one of the largest audiences in the history of the Metropolitan Opera House. Let those speak whose eyes were trained to impartial observation, and had looked on other Siegfrieds, some among them notable. The critic of the *New York Times* said: [81]

His physical proportions are indeed admirably suited to the rôle, and in vigor and power of action he left nothing to be desired. There were grace and strength in his every movement, and he acted with a freedom which was made possible only by an absolutely perfect acquaintance with the entire score of the music drama. Those who wish to understand how completely he has mastered the

score should note at the next performance the unerring
accuracy of his hammer beats in the forge scene. He never
misses a single stroke of the troublesome rhythms which
Wagner has given him.

So careful was Jean to make sure that no detail would be
overlooked that he asked Amherst Webber to sit *in* the forge
with the score to prompt him; not as to the music, but as to
what piece of action came next. But it was never necessary
for Mr. Webber to make a move or say a word.[82]

To continue with the *Times* comment:

> To rise from the mere physical aspects of his Sieg-
> fried to its intellectual and emotional qualities, let us say
> briefly that his conception of the part is complete, just,
> and masterful. As it was in T r i s t a n, so it is in S i e g -
> f r i e d; there is not a single word of the text or phrase
> of the music whose meaning he does not understand and
> reveal. Furthermore, he sets the character of the young
> Siegfried before us. He gives us the impetuous energy,
> the fiery will, the fearless courage, the pathetic yearning,
> the overmastering love, and the youthful ingenuousness
> with the unfailing skill of a commanding artist who has
> at his call all the resources of lyric art and knows how to
> employ them with the most delicate discrimination. In
> the sum and in the details his Siegfried is a complete and
> satisfying embodiment of Wagner's ideas. And it is
> always entrancing to both eye and ear. Jean de Reszke
> charms the senses, fascinates the fancy, and fires the
> imagination. He is Baldur the beautiful, prototype of
> Siegfried. He is Sigurd, the son of Volsung. He is Sieg-
> fried, lover and warrior.
>   It is like uttering a truism to say that he sang the
> music beautifully. It would be perhaps nearer the truth
> to say that it never was sung before. Jean de Reszke has
> not now to prove his ability to voice the declamation of
> Wagner's later style, but it came upon us like a new
> revelation last night. Nothing more touching could be
> conceived than his reading of the lines in the forest:
>
>> Doch, ich bin so allein,
>> Hab' nicht Bruder noch Schwester;
>> Meine Mutter schwand,
>> Mein Vater fiel;
>> Nie sah sie der Sohn.

The purely lyric parts of the rôle he sang as no one has ever sung them before. The "wander song" was glorious in its verve and rhythmic richness, and the celebration of Nothung at the forge and the anvil was a superb example of all that is noblest in lyric art. The whole of the scene of the forest was sung in a manner altogether lovely, and in the final duo, warmed to the highest glow of emotional force, the great singer soared into regions of eloquence in song where the hearer could follow him only in that triumphant exaltation of spirit which it is the dearest privilege of music to establish in common between performer and auditor. M. Jean de Reszke's Siegfried must go into the annals of opera as one of the master creations of the century.

Alvary too had made his Siegfried début in New York, but he, German, and long trained in the rôle, had not kept an audience spellbound every single moment by song and action and mimic expression. He had not, in the forest scene, after trying in vain to learn the language of the bird, sung with such delightfully naïve drollery and disappointment: "Vöglein, mich dünkt ich bleibe dumm." (Birdie, methinks I'll stay a fool.) Jean both looked and sounded half vexed, half amused, as a real boy would in such a circumstance. To be sure, his youthful appearance was not achieved without cost. To shave or not to shave his mustache had been an important question, the subject of long meditation and discussion, even the musical writers arguing for and against. De Reszke himself was very uncertain what to do. Siegfried was no doubt intended to be clean shaven, but Jean had a large, sensuous mouth, no more in keeping with the character than a mustache. No decision on this very grave matter was reached until one hour before Jean left his hotel on the night of the performance. Then he summoned his valet and instructed him to proceed, but very slowly. Jean sat, mirror in hand, and around him stood his secretary, Edouard, and several friends, anxiously judging the effect as snip by snip came off. Then when that stage was reached when to part with another sixteenth of an inch meant either disfigurement or complete removal of the mustache, a halt was called in the operations. After a few moments of further pondering Jean laid down the mirror, and with a wave of the hand decreed that the de Reszke Siegfried was to be smooth-faced.

And if the result was not too pleasing to Jean when he visualized himself mustacheless in mufti, as it were, the audience was enchanted with the youthful Siegfried. In the first act, Jean seemed a very schoolboy in taunting Mime with his inability to forge the sword and with a fine offhand superiority finally forging it himself. The audience demonstrated its delight, and Jean's superb climax brought cheers and six calls. At the close of the next act the enthusiasm was not so great, but that was not surprising; the spectators were too profoundly moved by the tenderness and poetry of the scene to rouse themselves to hand-clapping. They were storing it away in their memories as one of the exquisite experiences life had brought. Before their very eyes an amazing metamorphosis was taking place. The gay, enthusiastic urchin, who had led a kind of Alice-in-Wonderland existence, was swiftly striding into manhood. When he came on the stage in the third act and gazed at the sleeping Valkyrie, his face was transfigured with an ecstasy of beauty which seemed born not of histrionic art but of real love. (Jean did love his Siegfried, as a man loves his bride.) Majestically he sang "Erwache, heiliges Weib!" And now, big with this new strength, he became the heroic Siegfried apostrophized by Brünnhilde:

> O Siegfried! Herrlicher!
> Hort der Welt!
> Leben der Erde!
> Lachender Held!

In the final duo Jean allowed himself the high C which his artistic principles forbade using when it could not take its place simply as one part of an artistic whole. The compass of his voice was two octaves from C to C. Had he wanted to, he could have sung half a dozen high C's in quick succession, and he used to amuse his friends by lying on the floor in his room and roaring out a few; but he refused to do that in public, saying: "If I begin that sort of thing I shall always be expected to indulge in it. I prefer to make my successes in more artistic ways." There is a story that once at a H u g u e - n o t s performance he threw an unwritten high C into the chorus. In the wings he was congratulated; but, contrite, he exclaimed: "For shame! That was not art." He felt that at the close of S i e g f r i e d a high C served a dramatic purpose, and he therefore sang it, though it came at the end of a long and exhausting part, where the "high note stunters" would have left it discreetly alone. The composer indicated in the score that the singer might choose whether to use that note or not. Most Wagner singers of an earlier day could not sing it, and therefore it was not heard. But, as one of the New York commentators observed, de Reszke's high C rang like a triumphant "shriek of joy" as he clasped Brünnhilde to his heart in the rapture of love.

There may well have been something of pain, too, in that "shriek of joy." So thoroughly had Jean become Siegfried, he forgot that in life he had had no experience in a smithy. He worked away like a real blacksmith, but once his right arm came down with too much vigor and speed, and he chopped off the tip of his left forefinger. No one detected the accident, and Jean finished the opera as though nothing had happened.

For Edouard too, Siegfried represented another triumph. With his huge hat and his thunder-compelling spear, his massive figure and the dignity of his bearing, he seemed in very truth the father of all the gods, and when he thundered out the sonorous music, enunciating every word clearly, one said, "Here is the ideal Wotan." Wagner wrote some of his loveliest orchestral and vocal music for the Wanderer, and Edouard made Wotan a figure instinct with majesty and sympathy; yet he lost none of the sense of mysteriousness. Like his Marke, his Wotan brought a realization that if the character had previously seemed a bore, that was because the singer had made no effort to portray a personality, perhaps because he himself could boast none.

Once more these two Poles demonstrated that Wagner could be beautifully sung. "For the first time we have heard all the music of the rôle of Siegfried sung," wrote Mr. Henderson, "and now let any person capable of rising above 'Annie Rooney' come forward and say it is not beautiful!" Some one asked Mrs. Anton Seidl: "You have heard George Unger, the originator of the rôle, have you not? Tell me frankly, what is the difference?" She hesitated a fraction of a second, and replied: "Unger was a very tall man!"

But this first and astonishingly lovely performance of Siegfried could hardly be called a complete success. Not the supreme artistry of Jean de Reszke, not the inspired conducting of Anton Seidl or the rich outpouring of song from the throat of Edouard de Reszke, could make Madame Nellie Melba even approach the possibilities of the rôle of Brünnhilde. Suffice to say that she sang it once and once only, and then even Melba admitted that she had made a grave mistake. Why she was not persuaded by some one that it was, to put it kindly, a ridiculous attempt, is one of those things one must simply accept when dealing with the vagaries of a prima donna's inclinations. There were those who said Jean de Reszke had urged her to study the rôle. One journal placed the entire blame for the lamentable fiasco squarely on de Reszke's shoulders. A writer in another said that he had it "according to Stage Manager Parry" that "Melba was scared to death at rehearsal until encouraged by Jean de Reszke, who told her [in his presence] that Wagner had evidently in mind just such a voice as hers when he wrote the music of Brünnhilde in S i e g f r i e d, and that he (Jean de Reszke) had every confidence in her success, inasmuch as she possessed the proper training, one essential portion of which is breathing power." When some one asked Jean afterwards whether he had urged Melba to study the rôle he smiled and said: "I suggested that she sing in S i e g f r i e d, yes, but I told her to be the Stimme des Waldvogels." Had the silver-toned Nellie, endowed, as some one observed, not only with the voice but also the soul of a lark, been willing to assume a minor rôle for the sake of contributing to a beautiful whole, she might, by singing the part of the bird in S i e g f r i e d, have achieved one genuine triumph in a Wagner opera. But this of course was too much to expect. She who had soared into the operatic empyrean could no longer be content to move in a more restricted orbit. Melba herself removes all blame for the disaster from Jean de Reszke. "I had long wanted to sing the rôle of Brünnhilde in S i e g f r i e d, in German," she writes. "In Paris I had mentioned to Madame Marchesi this desire, always to be met with a horrified expression and great fluttering of the hands.... I was well aware that Brünnhilde was not by any means an ideal rôle for me, but I thought that Madame Marchesi's horror was exaggerated, and much against her wish, I had asked Herr Kniese over to Paris to coach me in the part.

"But as the day approached for the first performance... I began to grow more and more nervous. And from the moment when the curtain went up and I began to sing, I knew that Madame Marchesi had been right and I had been wrong. The music was too much for me.... How I got through the performance I do not know, but when it was all over I threw a dressing-gown round my shoulders and sent for my manager...and said: 'Tell the critics that I am never

going to do that again. It is beyond me. I have been a fool.' " [83]
It may have been her panic not less than her unfamiliarity
with Wagnerian traditions which caused Melba to be guilty
of the conduct David Bispham describes in his own reminiscences of this event. Apparently Melba forgot the Wagnerian
tradition to remain well within the scene, and Jean, in the
heavy fur coat of Siegfried, "was kept busy patrolling the forward part of the stage to keep the white-clad Melba from
rushing into the footlights." [84]

After this Melba mishap, Felia Litvinne, sister-in-law of
Edouard de Reszke, and sister of Willie Schütz, assumed the
rôle, and though she was not overwhelmed with praise by the
New York critics, that deficiency was remedied in Chicago.
There the S i e g f r i e d representation was thought "a lifetime's memory," and Jean's performance the greatest of that
season or any other in the history of opera in Chicago. The
eulogy which follows expresses the universal opinion: [85]

> It is an effort of heroic proportions, rich in long-sus-
> tained flights of inspiration as to both acting and singing,
> and marked by unfaltering and unwearied certainty. In
> the earlier passages he frankly conserves his resources,
> but we are more than compensated by the later and un-
> reserved outbursts of passion which mark Act III.
>
> Boyishness, the exultation of a warrior who knows
> no fear, the flaming passion of youthful love and the most
> delicate note of mysticism, are all voiced in the de Reszke
> Siegfried. It is a conception that must inspire something
> more than admiration for this divinely gifted man. Only
> reverence can measure the extent of our regard for him.
> He seems capable of the most widely divergent mani-
> festations of emotion—from almost boyish pettishness in
> the bird-note scene to that final transport of passion with
> which the opera closes.

Edouard, Chicago's favorite, also took new honors; was
voted as having every quality for Wotan; was counted pic-
torially the greatest Wotan ever seen there. But the de Reszkes
could not make a whole season. It was a financially unhappy
year, but, as a local commentator remarked, it was significant
that Jean de Reszke was "concerned in every important success, both artistic and financial, of the season." The truth of
that statement seemed to others to have given Jean a swelled
head. There were objections to the increased prices for admis-

sion on de Reszke nights, but it seems to have been Society
that was deficient in respect of attendance. There may have
been a little exaggeration in the suggestion that many of those
worth over a million dollars had clubbed together for seats
that year, and less in the statement that "Grand Opera is a
Society fad when Society is feeling flush; when Society is
pressed, Grand Opera is the first of the fads to go by the
board, because it is a fad that makes some demands on the
intellect, and Society is careful of its intellect." One performance of Aïda was attended by only eight hundred people,
though it was perfect in every detail and caused one critic to
write enthusiastically: "There may be moments in life when
one is more thrilled by the human voice than when Edouard
de Reszke thunders:

> Radames, Radames: tu es disertasi
> Dal campo il di che precedea la pugna.

But if there are, they come like angels' visits, and the angels
make few calls."

Prices were reduced, but still the attendance did not in-
crease. Whether the reduction of prices and Jean's simul-
taneous withdrawal had any linked significance one cannot
say, but he did not participate in the lower-priced performances, and the less expensive seats were not bought in larger
numbers. Even on a night when Jean appeared in a great
rôle, the total receipts were only $1,600. Certainly, if he
received his customary fee, it would require few such evenings
to deplete the managerial coffers. Mr. Grau raised a fund of
$30,000 to finish the season, and to this fund the artists con-
tributed, Jean $4,000, Edouard $2,000. Sadly Grau brought
his company back East, and as he noted them admiring the
beauties of the Catskill Mountains he admonished them in
mournful tones: "Gaze on, my children, and gaze long at this
wondrous spectacle, for it is the last time that any of you
will ever view it at my expense." The four weeks in Chicago
had eaten away the profits of the New York season, where,
despite the absence of Melba and Emma Eames, and the death
of Mr. Abbey and two artists, the company had earned a profit
of about $30,000.

In Boston things were no better. Of course there was a
panic abroad in the land that year (the condition was not yet
graced with the euphemism "depression"), which may have
had something to do with this situation; but Mr. Apthorp,

the Boston critic, did not take that into consideration in his
forcible comment on the sparse attendance when S i e g f r i e d
was performed. "The artistic reserve of the de Reszkes' singing and acting seems tame," he lamented, "to a generation
used to having its hair raised by the mere mass of din accomplished by conducting as frantic as the whipping-up of an
army mule-train, and its ears split by very Titans of tenors
and Brobdignagians throughout the cast. *Tout Boston* found
Wagner could be delivered with as decent an observance of
the ordinary proprieties of life as the libretto of prehistoric
passion permits, and hardly concealed its disappointment at
being balked of its barbaric orgies of the past with the cave
dwellers." [86]

However, on their return to New York the artists once
more received ovations of numerical as well as appreciative
strength. On April 14 Jean again sang Siegfried, and Wagnerian etiquette was violated when he came on the scene.
After the third act the curtain-calls were innumerable. Hundreds crowded near the stage doors to get a closer view of the
greatest tenor of the century. Three days later F a u s t was
given with Calvé and the de Reszkes. Lest I seem inclined
towards exaggeration in mourning "the tender grace of a day
that is dead," here is a description by the distinguished critic
of the *New York Times,* written immediately after the
event:[87]

> The house was packed to suffocation and the en-
> thusiasm was of a somewhat wild sort. The calls at the
> close of each act were numerous, and the artists became
> tired of tramping across the stage. But at the close of
> the performance the audience could not be denied. The
> curtain rose six times upon the prima donna, the tenor
> and the basso. By that time the audience had itself going.
> People crowded down to the rail, surrounding the
> orchestra pit in a dense mass, while those in the rear
> stood on their seats. Upstairs men and women leaned
> over the rails, waved handkerchiefs, and cheered. Back
> and forth across the stage went the three singers, amid
> screaming, whistling, and cries of "Speech! Speech!"
> Finally Mme. Calvé waved both hands to the audience,
> and said in French, "Thank you, and good-by." That
> was on the eighteenth recall.
> Then the audience made more noise than ever, and,

Leporello (Don Giovanni)   EDOUARD DE RESZKE   Mephistopheles (Faust)

on the twenty-first recall, M. Jean de Reszke said: "I will say au revoir, and not good-by." He spoke in English. Three times more the audience called out the singers, accompanied the third time by Mr. Grau, who said: "The Messrs. de Reszke and Mme. Calvé wish me to say to you that they are so fatigued that they cannot express to you their gratitude for the magnificent reception you have given them today. And they also wish me to say to you that they hope to be with you soon."

Such scenes were frequent during the heyday of the de Reszkes, and especially during the season that had just closed, for Jean sang in every single performance for which he had been scheduled. The standing space at the rear of the orchestra circle was sometimes so crowded that a dozen or more women fainted during the performance. It was well that attendants kept a generous supply of ammonia handy, for at one matinée as many as fifteen overwrought ladies were under treatment at once, and the corridors resembled a hospital. An amused observer said of the crowds: "I doubt if they would take as much trouble to get into Paradise." And listening to Jean was indeed a celestial experience for the ladies. He himself agreed with the journalist who complained: "This craze at the Metropolitan cannot be duplicated outside of a lunatic asylum," and he tried his best to escape the attention of his adorers. Sometimes he had to persuade Willie Schütz, whose physique resembled his, to pull his hat down rather far, turn up the collar of his overcoat and bury his face in it, and hurriedly make his way through the mob waiting at the stage door, bowing to the worshipers, who, happy in thinking they had been bowed to by Jean, then dispersed, whereupon that gentleman could go home in peace.

This adulation and the steady outpouring of letters and flowers and laurel wreaths and gifts was a source of constant amazement to Jean. Sometimes he felt almost disgusted with the demonstrations, and yet he required them too. During an opera season, he said, the tenor was king, and it seemed only natural that he, who had kingly attributes, should also receive the homage paid to other monarchs. He was very conscientious about acknowledging "fan letters" and usually sent the requested photograph, but he drew the line at doing all the autographing himself, and many a treasured signature was the handiwork of Willie Schütz. Among the thousands of

letters there were, however, an unusually large number of
thoughtful ones, written out of a deep sense of appreciation.
People who obviously were not sentimentalists told him how
they prayed for him nightly, that it "did them so much good"
to listen to him, that in the midst of his singing they thanked
the Almighty for having created such a voice in such a man.
Jean destroyed the great majority of these letters, including
most of those sent to him by people of social and artistic importance. A few he saved, some because they amused him,
some, like that which follows, because he cherished their
sincerity:

Murray Hill
19 East 37th Street
February 6 1896

My dear Mr. Jean de Reszke:

As the opera season is drawing to a close, and as
at my advanced age one can hardly be expected to live
to enjoy many more, permit me now to express to you
and to your accomplished brother, Edouard, my gratitude for the infinite satisfaction you have given me by
your art. It is an art that has no defects,—only perfections;
and may you both live long to delight the world by its
exercise.

Yours very truly
Parke Godwin

And here is one which, though in quite another tone, is
just as sincere and generous:

Dear Mr. de Reszke:

I have the mania. I am simply Jean de Reszke mad!
You are undoubtedly the greatest *actor* I ever saw, and
I have seen them all. One could almost be wicked enough
to hope you would lose your voice, and take to the drama.

This is not a "mash" note (excuse the phrase) but a
tribute to art from a poor sinner who has been trying to
act for six years. My experience has only taught me how
great others can be.

With much regard
Incognito

There were plenty of other letters, however, which *were*
"mash notes," of which the following (one of the very few
preserved) is a sample:

Mon Dieu! cher Monsieur! je suis enchanté! tout mon cœur est plein d'enthousiasme pour vous, oh! quel délicieux Vasco vous avez joué ce soir, j'ai entendu pauvre Gayarre dans cet même opéra. Oh! la douce et divine voix de ce pauvre homme qui *devrait* être de ce monde! mais hélas! il n'est plus. Mais vous, oh! vous êtes beau, divin dans ce rôle. J'étais heureuse en vous entendant, je vous ai applaudi beaucoup! J'adore la musique, j'ai chanté en duo avec un de ma famille, ce duo que vous avez enlevé avec un si grand brio avec Nordica, oh! comme vous savez aimer en scène, et je suis sûr que quand vous aimez, c'est de vrai, ne riez pas, Monsieur! Je sais que vous devez recevoir beaucoup de lettres, peut-être pas autant qu'à Paris, moi, je vous écris parceque je vous connais de Paris. Je vous ai entendu mille fois dans le Cid où vous êtes superbe, enfin, quoi de plus puis-je vous dire? que je voudrais vous voir, que je serai heureuse, mille fois heureuse de vous recevoir dans cet hôtel où je suis. Puis-je avoir cet espoir? Vous seriez gentil, bon, de venir ici. Je serai toujours de 4 à 5 heures, à vous attendre, cela ne vous engage à rien, mon cher ami, ne me croyez pas une femme intéressée. C'est vous que je veux connaître, pas votre argent, du reste! Grand Dieu! Je n'ai besoin de *rien, rien!* répondez-moi quand j'aurais la joie, le plaisir de vous voir, deux minutes tout au plus, je me conforme, mais venez, je vous en prie. Je vous en supplie! mais écrivez-moi, dites, franchement, si je puis compter sur vous, si je puis attendre votre visite, il me semble qu'il ne manque qu'une choise à faire et c'est, que je me mets à genoux devant vous et croyez-moi, j'ai tant au cœur de vous parler que je n'aurais aucun inconvénient à le faire.

Donc—adieu ou à bientôt, mon cher ténor—j'attends avec impatience, votre résponse, je me fie à votre délicatesse de gentleman.

Tout à vous et du cœur
C. DE S.*

* Good heavens! dear Sir! I am enchanted! all my heart is filled with ecstasy for you. Oh! what a delicious Vasco you played this evening. I heard poor Gayarre in this same opera. Oh! the sweet, divine voice of this poor man who *ought* to be of this world! but alas, he is no longer. But you! Oh, you are beautiful, divine in this rôle. I was happy in listening to you, I applauded you so much! I adore the music;

C. de S. was one of those who did manage to have a meeting with Jean, but apparently, judging from the letter a part of which follows, she was, like so many other woman, rather more ardent than the idol she begged to see her once more:

MY MOST DEAR LOVE,

... But enough of me—it is of you that I wish to speak, to tell you that I have read your last letter over and over again—and I believe—no, I am sure—that I love you, if that is possible, more than ever! Apropos the subject you mention, you are wrong. I have such confidence in you that I should find myself in no matter what place, no matter what situation, without any fear! Dear soul, you would not wish to do me wrong, not even in thought.

You say, however, that you have not wanted to see me again because you were afraid of losing your head. But you did not lose your head the other day, and I have not changed since then; grown a little uglier, it is true, but that would only have made you more strong, wouldn't it? And even *if* you lost your head a little because of me, that would be charming! Then what is there to be afraid of? You are always impeccable, and as for me, I have enough ... for two! But seriously, you have hurt me by not seeing me again—*nothing* could happen—I have *absolute* confidence in you! In any case, I should have such happiness in seeing you a second time. There is much that is lovable in your consideration on my behalf, but I should have preferred a thou-

I sang the duet with a member of my family, this duet which you sang with such great vivacity with Nordica. Oh! how you can make love on the stage, and I am sure that when you love, it is real. Do not laugh, Sir! I know that you must receive many letters, perhaps not so many as in Paris. As for me, I write to you because I know you from Paris days. I heard you a thousand times in Le Cid, where you were superb. Finally, what more can I say? That I should like to see you, that I shall be happy, a thousand times happy, to receive you in this hotel, where I am. May I have this hope? You would be kind, good, to come here. I shall always be here between four and five o'clock, to wait for you. This will not involve you in anything, my dear friend; do not think I am a woman with ulterior purposes. It is you that I want to know, not your money, however! Great God! I have need of *nothing, nothing!* Answer me, when I shall have the joy, the pleasure of seeing you, two minutes at the most; I shall comply with that, but come, I beg of you. I implore you! Write me, tell me frankly, if I may depend on you, if I may expect your visit. It seems to me there is only one thing to do, and that is to go on my knees before you; and, believe me, I have so much in my heart to tell you that I shall have no objection to doing so.

Then—adieu, or good-by for the present, my dear tenor—I await your response with impatience, I rely upon your delicacy as a gentleman.

Sincerely yours and with all my heart

C. DE S.

sand times to see you; I have seen you so little, I have talked with you so little! Truly, dear, you fear things that could *never* happen—I shall answer for you, and for myself—for, at bottom, I am not frivolous at all! Then lose your charming head a little because of me; you owe me that, at least, since I lost mine the very first time I saw you, and when I heard you, I was finished. Most dear one, you are so very wrong! You see only the idle fancies and the nightmares. There is no place in our friendship for these somber ideas. Dismiss them, and tell me that you will see me again as quickly as possible, and that all these ideas have disappeared forever! ...

Even if some day we should no longer be friends, I must always bow down before you because of this celestial voice! But, most dear, if I should be in New York, are you going to see me again? I shall never embarrass you, for you would scold me afterwards and make me feel that I should not have done it. Ah! Chéri, you don't understand me at all, not the least little bit! I am not a child, and if you have no confidence in yourself, it is not flattering to me for you to believe me a thing without will-power—and without principles; for I have enough, I must confess. Shocking, isn't it? "A woman with principles!"

You do not wish that I should love you; very well, I no longer love you! And now are you content? Then you will see me again, won't you, Chéri?

CECILÉ

It is significant that the women who might be expected to express injured feelings toward Jean, explain that they were the ardent ones; that he never encouraged them to hope that the adoration was mutual; that he advised them to find some good man and marry him. Here and there among Jean's effects one finds some slight evidence that once in a while they were rewarded for their steadfast devotion, as, for example, a note which accompanied a gift sent to him at the close of a season and which ends: "Last year I sent my thanks anonymously, but I think now it is due to both you and myself not to be ashamed to do so openly." And if some of them feel that they might have become the bride of the most popular tenor in the world, had he not felt more or less compelled to marry the woman who did become his wife, that is

perhaps only natural, and can hardly be attributed to phi-
landering on his part. Jean was unusually modest about this
worshiping.

Long years after his retirement his favorite niece asked
him: "Which prima donna did you like to sing with best
of all?"

"That," replied Jean, "is difficult to answer. Lilli Lehmann and Ternina were superb Isoldes. Nordica and Eames
were fine artists too. I always liked to sing with Emma Eames;
there was always an odor of violets about her."

"Then tell me, Uncle dear, which of the women who
loved you did you really love?" After a moment's hesitation
came the answer: "My art."

"But wasn't it Lady ——?" And the reply to that was a
gentle smile.

"My art" was, in the opinion of those closest to Jean de
Reszke, an honest answer and not a subterfuge. His art was
everything to him. On the stage he was the great lover; off
the stage he was kindly, friendly, but, to quote one who knew
him well, "as void of passion as an oyster." Even the memory
of the Natalie he had loved in his youth can probably not be
said to have represented a passion as great as that he felt for
the art of singing; which does not mean that the feeling for
her was not deep. Late in life one of his pupils who was on
intimate terms with Jean said to him: "Master, you have told
me so many things, tell me just one more. Of all the women
you have known, whom did you really love?" Jean played
softly on the piano keys and began: "There was a Polish
girl——" and then went on with the lesson.

And just as he tried to avoid the mobs who stormed the
stage entrance after a performance, he refused to become a
social lion. Jean was seldom seen at the opera house on nights
when he did not sing, but he was just as seldom persuaded to
accept social engagements on his free evenings. There were a
few places where he and Edouard liked to go, and there they
went freely; here where they could be sure of good roast
beef, there where the baked potatoes were just right, still
another place where perfect green apple pie was to be had.
Not that they accepted invitations from only those hostesses
who were considerate of their preferences at table; but they
happened to feel sufficiently at home to make those preferences known and to express their pleasure in specific terms.
They were simple-hearted men, and their pleasures were

simple too. When they were not working or singing at the opera they wanted to relax utterly. (It was amusing to hear Baron de Kronenberg explain that one of the few faults his illustrious brothers-in-law could be taxed with was a tendency to go rather far at times in telling risqué stories; but this, he insisted, was due to their rigid mode of life.) There was many a proud mansion in New York whose mistress would have parted with a good deal of money to bring Jean under her roof, had money been a bait. One wealthy husband of such an ambitious wife once offered him ten thousand dollars if he would come and "sing just one simple little song." Baron Rothschild made him a similar offer in London. This Jean absolutely refused to do, although his brother sometimes consented to sing in private. There were only two conditions under which the great tenor sang: at the opera, and when he was simply a guest and happened to feel like singing for his friends. When he was singing at the opera he was not Jean de Reszke; he was Romeo, Lohengrin, Tristan, Siegfried. When he left the theater he became Jean de Reszke. He would sing for hours just to give his friends pleasure, and he enjoyed that; but to agree to be at a certain place at, say ten o'clock in the evening, to be exhibited as a part of the evening's entertainment, that was an idea so distasteful that no amount of money could have induced him to accept such an invitation. Thus, if he could not avoid causing ladies to faint at the opera, he at least was spared the embarrassment of drawing-room gushing, and, for instance, such an experience as befell his famous predecessor Mario. Mario was also a magnificent stage lover, and many women fell under his spell. Once he was singing in a salon in Paris. As he sang the last line—"Come, love, with me into the woods," a young woman who had been listening in a semi-hypnotic state rose to her feet and tottered towards him, murmuring: "I am coming." [88]

Even if Jean had been willing to help adorn the parties of Society matrons, there was one who kept a sharp eye on his master's activities. This was Louis Vachet, who served him, first as valet, then as secretary, from 1887 until Jean's death.

"Louis," Jean would say to him, "next Tuesday evening I'm going to dine at Mrs. Smith's."

"Non, non, monsieur. Ca ne va pas."

"Oh, come now."

"Non, monsieur. There's a Huguenots rehearsal at ten o'clock Wednesday morning and you must be in shape for that. Besides, you're singing Thursday evening. Tell Mrs. Smith you'll be able to come on Friday."

Occasionally, if Jean's heart was particularly set on doing something, he would quietly get Edouard to intercede for him. Louis also made it his business to see that Edouard studied, and followed him around with the score, telling him it was time to work. Edouard obeyed. Louis himself came to know every phrase of the Wagner operas. In the midst of blacking Jean's boots he would sing out at the top of his voice: "Nothung, Nothung, neidliches schwert." When other singers were cast for his master's rôles he resented it, and exclaimed indignantly: "Here's a fine state of things. Mr. —— is to sing Lohengrin! A fine mess he'll make of it!" When he heard any one sneeze he rushed into the room, asking anxiously: "Monsieur, did you sneeze?" To which Jean would respond: "May not a man sneeze in his own house?"

Louis was always glad when the season ended and he could be sure his master would rest in Poland, far away from the multitudes against whom he had to be protected. He took his duties so seriously, watched over Jean so carefully, suffered so with Jean on account of the singer's nervousness, that shortly after de Reszke retired his secretary had a nervous breakdown and became very ill. Not until then did Jean realize what a strain Louis had been under, and he did everything possible to aid his recovery. It is said that no man is a hero to his valet, but Jean de Reszke is still worshiped by Louis Vachet. With bated breath he says: "Il était une âme élevée," and then, proudly: "Il était mon ami." So absorbed was he in the master's work that from the very beginning of his service, which lasted almost forty years, he sent his mother a full account, once a month, of everything that had happened. These invaluable letters, which had been given back into his possession, the faithful Louis was going to turn over to me, but alas, while I was on my way from Poland to France, fire broke out in the little villa which Jean bequeathed to Louis and his wife, and completely destroyed the room in which the letters were stored.

"Au revoir" and "À bientôt," Jean and Edouard had said to the crowds who had come to see them off on the SS. *St. Paul*, but the beautiful women whose delight at the good news had been so great that they never noticed how awry their beribboned and be-blossomed hats had become in the crush, were not to see their beloved singers "soon." After several half-hearted statements that he would produce Grand Opera during the next season as in the past, if he could secure the artists, Mr. Grau formally declined to renew his lease on the Metropolitan. Calvé and Melba were unavailable, Emma Eames and Nordica were uncertain, the de Reszkes had announced their intention of remaining in Europe the following season. Mr. Grau knew that the public could not easily be induced to try out newcomers, at least not in paying numbers. There was a good deal of grumbling among patrons who, though disappointed at not having their favorites, would have been content with inferior casts. They insisted that if the de Reszkes could not be secured, other singers were available; no one was indispensable. Finally one of the directors issued a statement to the effect that it was all very well to utter the ancient platitude about the dispensability of individuals, but that certain circumstances did prove it unsound. If a singer became ill, he contended, due allowance was made, the illness being considered just an unfortunate occurrence; if he died, then surely that provided an excuse for not securing him; but if he was alive the public seemed to think the managers were in duty bound to secure him, the inclination of the singer notwithstanding, and if he was not produced large audiences might be expected to be extremely rare.

The public had missed one of its favorites during the season just ended. Lillian Nordica had not sung her accustomed rôles. In preceding years, she had won high praise as Isolde, and it had been announced that she would sing Brünnhilde in D i e W a l k ü r e and S i e g f r i e d, in both of which Jean was to appear. Then came an announcement that Madame Nordica had refused to renew her contract, and there was much speculation as to the reason. She had demanded $1,500 a performance, it was said, and had been denied, but she herself insisted that financial matters had been easily settled. Her own story was that she had been told D i e W a l k ü r e would be abandoned because Edouard de

Reszke was unwilling to learn the part of Wotan in both that opera and S i e g f r i e d. Next she learned that Madame Melba was to have the rôle of Brünnhilde in S i e g f r i e d, leaving Nordica the only member of the company who would not have an opportunity in a new rôle that year. She was quoted as saying that she understood Jean's influence had secured the rôle for Melba, and that she felt, when she heard this, as though she had been struck in the face. Those two singers and Mr. Grau replied, of course, that Madame Nordica had been misled, but the misunderstanding persisted. At Christmas time, so the story goes, Mr. Grau called upon her and said that Jean desired her to sign the following letter for general publication:

> I am happy to be able to state publicly that I was misinformed when I accused my fellow artist, M. Jean de Reszke, of having used his influence against me. Now that I have conclusive proofs to the contrary, I feel it is my duty to retract my former assertion, and I am happy, I repeat, to do justice to an artist who has always been friendly toward me.

She did not feel that she had had "conclusive proofs," and so asked to talk the matter over with de Reszke at Grau's office. This, she said, Jean refused to do. Several months later, according to reports, Grau asked her to help him on his Chicago tour, as Mesdames Eames and Calvé were both ill, and Melba had been incapacitated by her Brünnhilde experience. She sent de Reszke a note asking for "a quiet talk," and he returned the note unopened.

By this time gossip had it that the two famous singers had decided never to meet again. De Reszke denied the charge that he had tried to manipulate the operatic strings so that Felia Litvinne might be engaged, and was said to have counseled the latter to refuse an offer from Covent Garden because he wished to avoid giving any semblance of truth to Nordica's charge that he was using his influence for the benefit of his relatives. A cable came, saying that Nordica, as evidence of her desire to end the quarrel, had taken a box for the first London performance of T r i s t a n (in 1897), "for the purpose of applauding the great tenor." [89] A few weeks later, another cable, this time to the *New York Herald*:

Having had an interview with M. Jean de Reszke, it proved I had been misinformed and misled when I believed him the cause of my absence from Opera last season. Now I wish to state that I am thoroughly convinced, and happy to say that it was not M. Jean de Reszke. My impulse in declaring this publicly is my sense of right and justice to my fellow artist.

LILLIAN NORDICA

Then when Mr. Seidl returned to New York an interview yielded an account of the reconciliation.[90] Seidl had met Nordica during the intermission, and she could not conceal from him how deeply affected she was by Jean's impersonation, which recalled memories of nights at the Metropolitan when she had sung with the great tenor. Seidl had always regretted the breach between the singers. "Come, now," said he, "why be childish any longer about this affair? Why not write a frank, womanly letter to Jean and ask him to meet you like a brother artist, talk over your differences and settle them once for all?" Madame Nordica was, it seems, in a melting mood, and took his advice.

Small wonder if that performance of Tristan filled Jean's erstwhile companion with longing to resume her place beside him. Jean had been ill for a fortnight, but when he felt well enough to appear he sang magnificently. He had attained a degree of perfection in the part that must seem nearly incredible to those who never saw and heard him. Again the performance was hailed as a stupendous achievement. Later in the season he gave one equally impressive, and Bernard Shaw wrote to Ellen Terry: "O Ellen, Ellen, Ellen, think of it! De Reszke, at 48, playing his *second* season of Tristan, to a perfectly crazy house, and cursing himself in his old age for not doing what I told him years ago when I cannonaded the Opera and himself just as I now cannonade the Lyceum and Henry." [91] Jean de Reszke probably did not curse himself very much or very often, and if one may say so without offending Mr. Shaw's estimate of his own influence, his growth toward Tristan had been natural and steady. Mr. Shaw should have remembered his Epictetus: "No great thing is created suddenly, any more than a bunch of grapes or a fig. If you tell me that you desire a fig, I answer you that there must be time. Let it first blossom, then bear fruit, then ripen."

Siegfried, which London heard for the first time that

season, was variously received, being considered by some the
finest impersonation ever witnessed there, by others not much
like Siegfried at all. "Of the real Siegfried's exuberant vitality, and eternal youthfulness, there is nothing," objected one
critic. "For the most part it has scarcely even energy enough;
and when there is energy it is of the wrong sort—the adult's
cool, determined energy, not the fresh, spontaneous, bubbling
vigor of youth." [92] But even this writer admitted that "as a
mere piece of vocalism it would be impossible to beat, or indeed to match." In other quarters it was felt that Jean's Siegfried eclipsed his own Tristan and Lohengrin; that in addition
to the juvenile appearance of Max Alvary in this part he
brought a voice which in charm and nuances could not even
be approached by that of any German vocalist. In *The Lute*
we read: "His Siegfried was a delightful revelation, and mere
words cannot do justice either to his robust singing in the
forge scene, or his delicate and exquisite treatment of the
music during his progress through the forest in the second
act." [93]

And in *The Times:* [94] "Nor is it only the buoyant side of
Siegfried's nature that finds expression, though the Schniede-
lieder were sung and acted with superb brilliance and vigor;
the meditations of the Waldwehen scene were given with exquisite poetry, and the first dawning sense of the tragedy of
life in the question 'So starb meine mutter an mich?' was
beautifully shown." Still another critic thought that although
Jean was splendid until the last act, he fell short of the powerful climax expected in the closing scene.

The *Musical Courier* of New York seized on these by no
means entirely adverse criticisms, it seized on the Nordica
misunderstanding and on the Melba fiasco, and used them to
bolster up its anti-de-Reszke campaign. Ostensibly a campaign
against "the high salary crime," and designed to combat the
undue influence of foreign singers who were keeping American talent from coming to the fore, it was in reality, according
to those who were then closely associated with Jean, a campaign launched in retaliation for his refusal to pay for having
his photograph reproduced in the magazine. There is not an
iota of evidence that Jean de Reszke ever paid for a sixteenth
of an inch of advertising or publicity throughout a singing
career of more than a quarter of a century and almost a quarter century of teaching after that! Whatever the motive, the
points of attack were, so far as they concerned an individual

singer, absurd, and as they concerned Jean, malicious and vulgar.

Modestly this magazine announced that it considered as the most marked feature of New York musical life in 1896, "the amiable crusade against operatic high salaries and 'bossism.'" If "amiable" means to say that a man has lied, schemed, conspired, ridden roughshod over others' sensibilities, all dictionaries had better be revised. The *Courier* prided itself on being "the first, the only newspaper that dared to unveil his [de Reszke's] scheme to monopolize the Metropolitan Opera House." Later it held that his machinations included Covent Garden as well. He had "used Melba as a cat's-paw." Nordica had been "literally railroaded out of the opera house because she got too much applause . . . as Isolde"; "Maurel was forced out"; and as for Calvé, "her stand against his extravagant participation in the C a r m e n receipts which, she claimed, were due to her, ended in her banishment for one season." [95]

Emma Eames was warned that she was next. All this scheming was designed to provide places for ever more members of the de Reszke family. Jean was plotting against American singers. He could not brook Nordica, because she had been very successful, "and in order to provide for the emergency, which must have been foreseen by Reszke, his relative, Madame Litvinne, was prepared to fill the rôle in which Melba was to fail." (As a matter of fact, the reason Melba happened to sing Brünnhilde was that Katharina Klafsky, who had been engaged to sing Wagnerian rôles with Jean, died just before the opera season began.) Reszke was condescending "to make women the main victims of his tremendous egotism and his monumental vanity"; he was "engaged in the chivalrous task of intriguing between women"; and he was doing it all without regard for art, his artistic instincts being "mere pretensions and sham." He had tried to get Nordica to sign a "lie." Why, was the virtuously indignant question, should Nordica apologize to a man who had been charged with "deliberately issuing a falsehood over his own signature?" ("With a perfectly well balanced mind he never would have written or signed such a lie—for that is what it amounts to.") [96]

Even Melba's poor health in the early part of 1897 could be traced entirely to de Reszke's operations, the magazine had maintained. The truth seems to be, however, that Nellie

Melba owed a great deal to Jean de Reszke. Herman Klein puts it thus: [97]

> But more valuable by far, in an artistic sense, to one who was still comparatively a stage novice, was the practical advice that she received from the famous Polish tenor who was her constant associate during her second season at Covent Garden. Then it was that she really began to master certain fundamental principles of her art of which she had previously commanded little more than a smattering. From him she acquired the old Italian system of breathing, which Mme. Marchesi too frequently allowed her pupils to pick up as best they could. Until that time Melba had been a vocalist *et præterea nihil.* Jean de Reszke practically taught her how to act, how to impart ease and significance to her gestures, how to move about the stage with grace and dignity.
>
> ... Because he inspired her, Melba always appeared to greater advantage with Jean de Reszke than with any other tenor. When he was the Faust her acting in the Garden and Prison scenes would wax warmer and even a trace of passion might glow in her silvery tones.

Melba herself writes of Jean: [98]

> So utterly wonderful was he that when some time later I found myself singing in Lohengrin with him without a rehearsal, I burst into tears in the last Act, and thanked my stars that my singing rôle for the evening was practically finished. Jean de Reszke—so perfect, so gallant! Never has there been an artist like him.

When the *Courier* assumed a protective attitude towards Melba, she declared that she was on the best of terms with her colleagues, and added: "The de Reszkes have hearts of gold and are sincere friends." Her statement was promptly admitted to be true in so far as hearts of gold were quite natural in gold-bugs, of which those two were "the most perfect specimens ever made in Europe and shipped over here to devastate the green American dollar." To be sure, Jean and Edouard de Reszke, Felia Litvinne and Willie Schütz did, between them, carry off a good many American dollars in an operatic season. But America had no titles to confer, no decorations to offer its favorites. It was glad to give its love and its gold. Besides, Jean was not the only high-salaried singer at the Metropolitan. Melba, Calvé, Eames, Lilli Lehmann, Pol Plancon, and Lassalle could hardly be called penny-a-nighters. The question of whether the star system is created by the stars or by the public is analogous to that ancient one concerning the precedence of chicken or egg. The public, more especially the American public, would be satisfied with nothing but the best, particularly if the best was also costly; and when that best was not forthcoming at the Metropolitan Opera House the public simply stayed away.

New York had decided that Jean de Reszke was the greatest tenor in the world; it would be satisfied with no other. Tamagno, Van Dyck, Alvary, all took second place, not entirely because of secondary qualities, certainly not because of maneuvering on the part of Jean de Reszke, but simply because that singer had endeared himself by his personality not less than he had established himself as a supreme artist. A famous Kurwenal once complained that Bispham always sang the part at the Metropolitan. Mr. Grau's answer was: "Do you think it makes a dollar's worth of difference which of you sings Kurwenal so long as Jean sings Tristan?" The tenor Salignac, for long years one of Jean's good friends, who suffered comparison between his own and Jean's singing, protested: "If I were as great a singer as he, I would not be receiving the salary I do, and I can't understand why I should necessarily have been compared with the greatest tenor of his time and a giant among singers. What will happen after he stops singing here? Will there never be toleration for another tenor? Will they all be compared unfavorably with him?"

Early in the campaign the *Courier* (in fairness let it be recorded that the magazine is now under different management) had resurrected the controversy about Jean's age, and various other writers also attributed more years to Jean than he could claim. Finally he sent the following letter to the *New York Herald*:

> I read in one of this evening's papers: "Like Alvary, Jean de Reszke has honored New York with his début in Siegfried, and, like Alvary, it is to be hoped that he will live to delight us with his hundredth Siegfried."
>
> This graceful wish must have called forth a smile on the face of many readers of the New York papers,

which seem to delight in ascribing to me a number of
years which I have not yet attained. It is, therefore, not
from any feeling of coquetry or vanity, or from any desire
to pose as a young man, but merely from a love of truth,
that I am writing to ask you to rectify, once and for all,
an error which seems to be gaining ground in this
country.

My real age is forty-six years. I was born on January
14 1850. I have not with me my certificate of birth, as it
is not an article with which one usually travels, but in
order to remove all doubt on the subject I have written
to Warsaw for it, and shall forward it to you as soon as
I receive it.

This fact being established, even if I do not arrive at
my hundredth performance of Siegfried, I can reasonably
trust I may not be too decrepit to reach at least my
fiftieth. In this hope I remain, dear sir,

Yours truly,
JEAN DE RESZKE

NEW YORK
December 31 1896

Had he been engaged in any other profession, Jean would
probably not have cared how old he was thought to be; but
the public prefers its tenors young, especially as lovers, and
therefore it did make some difference whether the public
thought Jean was closer to sixty than to forty-five, particularly
since he was growing rather stout. The salaries of noted opera
singers have always been a subject of gossip, but rarely has
discussion been so continuous or so "interested" as in the case
of de Reszke. This may have been owing to the fact that in
England, France, and America he was paid higher fees than
any other singer before him had received. To be sure, he was
not the first member of his family to earn large sums of money
for singing. Many years before, when his sister Josephine was
at the height of her career, she had received $65,000 a season.
And, of course, Mr. Grau did not invent the all-star cast system. When Tristan was first performed in America, on
December 1 1887, Lilli Lehmann was the Isolde, Niemann the
Tristan, Marianne Brandt played Brangaene, Emil Fischer
Mark, Alvary the Seaman, and Anton Seidl conducted—surely
not a cast of second-rate artists.

Jean himself was not much disturbed by the quarreling

ANTONIO COTOGNI

ANTON SEIDL

about his remuneration. An impudent American reporter
once asked him: "Don't you think you are very much over-
paid for what you do, Mr. de Reszke?" To this Jean replied
imperturbably: "On nights when I am in good health, voice,
and spirits, it does seem that I am highly paid for doing what
I love best to do; but when I am out of health, voice, and
spirits, and yet have to make a superhuman effort not to disappoint my manager and the public, no sum in the world is too
great to compensate me for what I have to go through." The
New York Herald finally secured an interview [99] which may
be presumed to state Jean's attitude toward the whole question of singers' salaries. Since it was an authentic interview
and marks one of the very few times when Jean was induced
to speak of his own position in the musical world, it is here
reproduced in full.

I am aware of the opinion entertained in some
quarters that the principal operatic artists are paid excessive salaries, which they are supposed to wring heart-
lessly from a reluctant public. While I have my own very
positive conviction on the subject, I feel a hesitancy about
committing my views to writing for publication, lest my
intentions be misconstrued. The *Herald,* however, has
been at all times so fair and impartial in its treatment of
matters relating to the lyric and dramatic stage that I
cannot with good grace refuse an answer to the question.

Of course you must understand, to begin with, that I
am simply speaking for myself, although I think it is safe
to presume that my opinion on the matter is quite generally shared by my brother and sister artists. I say, therefore, that it is my belief, based upon a long experience,
that the singer is a laborer who is "worthy of his hire,"
and I am sure that there is no artist who is a member of
the Metropolitan company—and I include Madame
Melba, who, I feel, is still one of us—who does not earn
every dollar he or she receives.

With regard to myself—and here I will again ask
your indulgence for my personal references, inasmuch
as the question you put to me is so directly personal—I
must say that I do not think I have ever made any exorbi-
tant demands upon the management of the Metropolitan
Opera Company.

I receive a guarantee for the same amount a night

in this country as I do in the principal cities in Europe, plus twenty-five per cent on the gross receipts over $5,500.

It may surprise some to know that this is less than I have received in former seasons, when the percentage allowed me was upon the excess of $5,000. Messrs. Abbey, Schoeffel and Grau have been my friends, however, and I cheerfully assented to the modification of our terms in view of their difficulties. Furthermore, notwithstanding the fact that neither M. Alvary nor M. Van Dyck will be available next season, I have consented to return to America next autumn on the same terms, although if I were a man who sought to make a purely selfish application of the law of supply and demand, I might have used this fact as a justification for demanding increased terms. But since I first came to America I have never asked an increase of salary, have never said the more the public favors me the more I must be paid. In fact, I formerly got a larger percentage, though I draw larger audiences now.

I am very grateful for the kindness shown me by the public, but since we are talking plainly on this delicate and personal question of operatic engagements, let me say that if I consulted nothing but my own inclination and personal comfort, coupled with my best business interests, I would not come back to America next season. Aside from purely domestic reasons there is much to induce me to spend the season in Europe. Delightful to me as my New York engagements have been, I have my home, my people, my closest associations abroad, and for several years most of my life has been spent here.

I have warm personal friends of influence in Vienna, Berlin and St. Petersburg, who have been urging me most earnestly to return to those cities and appear in opera, especially as Siegfried and Tristan, and I assure you it has been very difficult for me to resist their kindly pressing invitations. In any one of those cities I am not far from my own home in Poland, and would have frequent opportunities between engagements for rest and recreation and social enjoyment there, all of which are entirely denied me while here.

The profit to me and my brother, financially, would be quite as great should we remain in Europe instead of coming here. Special engagements in London, Paris,

Vienna, Berlin, St. Petersburg and elsewhere would give us almost as much as we earn here. For you must consider that we lose a whole month on the journey coming and going, with a rest of a week each time, and that our expenses for five or six months here are double what they would be on the other side. Our personal enjoyment, if our engagements were abroad, would be incalculably greater.

In the five months we spend here each season we have few leisure hours. It is a period of incessant rehearsal, for I never sing the same part two nights in succession. While in Europe I could sing the same opera over and over again, in America the bill is constantly changed, and I am continually trying over the scores to keep them well memorized or to have rehearsals with other singers. Between work at the opera house or in my own apartments and being house-bound during climatic changes or bad weather, I am fairly a prisoner.

I am always in dread of catching a cold and being unable to sing, which might mean a disarrangement of the repertoire and my non-appearance when announced. I am so careful to avoid possible colds that I abandon almost all social enjoyments during the long operatic season. I have not once failed to appear this season when announced, but I have only succeeded by giving myself up entirely to my duties at the opera house.

The sole reason, indeed, for my promise to return next autumn is the assurance by Mr. Grau and by the gentlemen who are the stockholders of the opera house that my coming back will materially aid their plans for the next season of opera. I beg you will not think me egotistical, vain, or as over-estimating my worth in saying all this, but when I am discussing such purely personal questions I must be pardoned for speaking freely about myself. The directors have told me again and again that I am needed next season, and I feel that under these circumstances it would be ungenerous on my part to say "No" to those who have been such good friends to me. To abandon the company now would make me feel like a soldier deserting his post before the losses recently sustained by those in command have been fully retrieved.

To return to the original questions of artists' salaries, and speaking only for myself, as I am not presuming to speak for others, I will repeat that I really do not regard my terms with the Metropolitan management as excessive. When a singer has devoted twenty-five years to the earnest, serious, thoughtful, expensive and trying study of vocal art and his efforts have been crowned with what the public have been pleased to call success, don't you think that the singers' services are worth whatever they will bring in the open market?

Should he not ask as much as managers are willing to pay, just as he should be content to receive as little as his place can be filled for? Are the artists of the Metropolitan receiving too much in salary if they can draw an audience that pays for their salaries and a profit besides?

The group of singers whose art was crowned by that of the de Reszkes did earn large profits for the manager. That is a matter not of conjecture, but of fact. Mr. Grau made enough money during the last few years of his administration, the years when Jean was paid the largest salary he ever received, to enable him to retire with a fortune.

THE SEASON of 1897-98 found the de Reszkes in Europe, singing chiefly in Paris and St. Petersburg. There had been a repetition of the periodic rumors that they were to sing in Germany; this time it was to be at the Imperial Opera of Berlin, but, as usual, these reports were unfounded. There has been much speculation as to why Jean and Edouard never did sing at Bayreuth, or, indeed, anywhere in Germany. The question was frequently put to them, but they preferred not to give the real reason. It was easier to say, what was true enough, that they could not spare the six weeks for rehearsal which Madame Cosima Wagner demanded of all Bayreuth singers, though she would probably have been willing enough to waive this stipulation in order to secure the illustrious brothers. It is also true that Madame Cosima said that Jean sang certain phrases in H u g u e n o t s incorrectly, and that he, not considering the widow of Wagner an authority on interpreting Meyerbeer, chose to ignore her suggestions; but Jean was hardly the man to let such a slight incident control a decision. Moreover, while he was preparing Siegfried he did go to Bayreuth, to find out exactly how Wagner wanted the rôle interpreted. "Madame Wagner," Baron de Kronenberg, who went with him, told me, "knowing what sort of student Jean was, did not wait for him to ask questions, but had thought out carefully everything that she might tell him. We spent hours going over details, and she would sing certain parts, saying: 'This is the way he wanted it done.'"

Richard Strauss, a young man then, was there too, and he sat staring at Jean and Cosima with his big eyes, like one transfixed. Julius Kniese was also present. He was preparing singers for Bayreuth, and wanted to convey to them as much as possible of Jean's interpretation. How earnestly Madame Wagner wanted Jean himself to sing there may be gathered from the following letter, written to him by Mr. Kniese: *

ESTEEMED MR. DE RESZKE:

I thank you heartily for your dear letter from Borowno. As you suggested that we should get into touch with Mr. Harris from here, we did so, but I regret to say that up to today there has been no result: Harris has not answered.

* Translated from the German. The letter is reproduced in facsimile on pages 200-202, and a transcription of the German text appears in the Appendix.

Verehrter Herr de Reszke!

Herzlich danke ich Ihnen für Ihren lieben Brief aus Sorrento. Wie Sie es rieten, daß man sich von hier aus mit Herrn Harris in Verbindung setzen möge, ist es geschehen, leider bis heut ohne Erfolg; Harris hat nicht geantwortet.

Nun komme ich noch einmal zu Ihnen, um Ihnen wieder unsre herzlichste und dringendste Bitte um Übernahme des Siegfried vorzulegen. Sie können nachfühlen, daß wir hier nicht loslassen dürfen, sondern Alles versuchen müssen, um den

Siegfried von Ihnen zu = erwägen; um des herrlichen Kunstwerkes und um der vom Meister hinterlassenen Institution der Bayreuther Festspiele willen, die es gebieterisch fordern, daß man den vorhandenen besten Vertreter einer Rolle gewinnt. Mit Ihnen die Parthie zu studiren, soll mir eine innige Freude sein, und ich erwarte nur Ihren Brief, um mich Ihnen zur Verfügung zu stellen, sodaß wir für Ende September unsre Bitten und Hoffnungen auf Ihr = Ja = erfüllt sehen dürften?

Was das Arrangement mit Harris betrifft: darf ich Sie um die Ermächtigung bitten, sagen zu können, daß es in Ihrem Auftrage geschieht?

Dann wird ja wohl die Antwort an unsere Verwaltung nicht ausbleiben.

Mit sehr ergebenen Empfehlungen Frau Wagner's und herzlichsten Grüßen an Sie und Ihre verehrte Frau Gemahlin, sowie mit schönstem Danke für Ihre freundliche Antwort bin ich Ihr

verehrungsvollst ergebener

Bayreuth, Juli 1895.
31.

Julius Kniese.

Now I come to you once more, to lay before you our most hearty and urgent request that you take charge of Siegfried. You can understand that we cannot give up, but must try everything to get you to represent Siegfried, for the sake of the glorious masterpiece and to maintain the institution of the Bayreuth Festival bequeathed by the master, which insistently demands that the best living impersonator of a rôle be secured. To study the rôle with you would give me deep pleasure, and I am but awaiting your letter to place myself at your service, so that we may see our prayers and hopes about your "Yes" realized before the end of September.

Regarding the arrangement with Harris: may I ask you for the authorization to tell him that it is done at your request? Then the answer concerning our control would probably not be delayed.

With most humble compliments from Madame Wagner and hearty greetings to you and your honored wife, as well as with best thanks for your friendly answer, I am

Respectfully and obediently yours

JULIUS KNIESE

BAYREUTH
31 July 1895

Jean's "Yes" was not given, and about a year later Madame Cosima wrote in a letter to Anton Seidl: "I am dreadfully sorry not to be able to have these two great artists, Jean and Edouard, with me. I have done all I could to secure them." The reason she could not secure them lay in their friendship with the Princess of Wales, later Queen Alexandra of England. Every now and again the Princess would say to them, half jokingly, half seriously: "Now you're not going to Germany, are you, to sing for that horrid old man?" meaning the Kaiser, whom she personally detested. At first they made non-committal replies, but finally she extracted a definite promise, and they, being very good friends of Her Royal Highness, gave their word of honor not to sing in Germany.

In a letter dated October 25 1898 Jean wrote to Mrs. Henry T. Finck:

This year I have again refused to sing at Bayreuth for Madame Wagner, the Princess of Wales having insistently begged me not to leave Covent Garden. I regret this much, for I have a great desire to sing Parsifal.

Whether this state of affairs was responsible for what happened on the occasion of the Kaiser's state visit to the Opera in 1891, it is impossible to say. Jean was to appear in scenes from Lohengrin, Huguenots, and Romeo, and when, towards noon, he sent word to Harris that he would be unable to sing because he was suffering from a bronchial attack, the impresario was, quite naturally, greatly perturbed. Herman Klein happened to be at Covent Garden when the news arrived, and undertook to go round to the Continental to see what could be done. He found Jean slightly indisposed, but by no means voiceless, and begged him not to disappoint entirely "so mighty and puissant a personage as the Emperor William II," suggesting that he might sing in at least one of the scenes scheduled. Finally Jean sent the following note to Sir Augustus: [100]

> MY DEAR FRIEND:
>   Klein has just asked me to sing at least one act of the three that I had promised you. Consequently I chose that of Romeo as the least fatiguing. Look upon this, my dear friend, as an evidence of my desire to spare you a portion of the trouble occasioned by my indisposition. And in doing so I risk hurting my voice! Make an announcement. A thousand greetings!
>
> JEAN

Well might Madame Cosima lament her failure to secure Jean. She admitted that if Wagner had heard him sing Tristan, his highest dreams would have been realized. In other rôles too she thought Jean unsurpassed. Amherst Webber once sat near her during a M e i s t e r s i n g e r performance at Covent Garden. "She was in ecstasies," he told me. "She kept exclaiming that she caught new beauties of melody that no German singer had ever suggested."

For Jean it would probably have been a deep satisfaction to sing in Wagner's own theater. He revered and loved the art of the great composer in whose operas he had reached his own highest artistic stature. Then too, he could have returned to Bayreuth a part of the great master's legacy, for Jean worked closely with Anton Seidl, Wagner's intimate associate. He considered Seidl the greatest of Wagner interpreters, and insisted on his conducting certain operas, among them T r i s - t a n, if he was to sing in them. On one occasion he made Mr. Grau and the conductor sign a contract in his own room, so that he might be sure his wishes would not be frustrated. And, of course, his wish was law. When some one voiced misgivings as to whether a certain plan involving Seidl would be carried out, he drew himself up and, eyes flashing, announced: "Si je le veux, je le veux!" Later, when a friend of the conductor's thanked him for what he had done, he said, simply: "You must not thank me. It is for myself also."

And now, during this 1897-98 season, while the de

Reszkes were singing in Europe, Anton Seidl died. As friends and as artists they mourned his loss. When, some time later, a memorial volume for Seidl was prepared, Jean and Edouard welcomed the opportunity to attest his greatness. They sent this appreciation of his talents:[101]

The death of Anton Seidl was felt very deeply not only by those who, like ourselves, were privileged to call themselves his friends, but by the whole musical world at large. It would indeed be difficult to overestimate what his loss means to all lovers of opera.

Nowadays so much is expected of a first-rate conductor that it is no marvel if he be a *rara avis*. The purely technical knowledge which is required for a leader to master the intricacies of a modern orchestral score well enough to secure merely a correct and smooth performance of it is in itself considerable, and yet this is but the A B C of the conductor's art. At the performance of any orchestral work, whether ancient or modern, the conductor alone represents the composer, and it is he who must put into the interpretation not only the spirit and atmosphere of the work as a whole, but all those thousand and one subtle nuances which it would be well-nigh impossible for the composer to indicate in black and white in his score, and which nevertheless contribute so greatly to the life of the performance. And in the case of an operatic work even this is not all that is required of the ideal conductor. Here he must be in sympathy with the singers, he must understand their individual interpretation of their respective parts and help to give it its full expression, without, however, detracting in any way from the unity of the whole performance. And it was just in this that Seidl was so wonderful. He was thoroughly imbued, from his boyhood, with the spirit of the works he was destined to interpret, and he added to this an instinct which is indeed rare among orchestral conductors of the modern school; he understood singing, seemed to know by intuition exactly what the singer would do in every case, and always helped him to do it well. But he did not accomplish this by following the singer slavishly. There are many conductors who can follow a singer in a *ritardando* such as singers love to make at the close of a musical phrase, but there are few

who know exactly how to catch up the rhythm again
and restore the equilibrium, as Seidl did, without apparently affecting the shape of the musical period in the
least.

   And how dear Seidl's heart was in his work! What
trouble he took over every detail! At rehearsals he was
conductor, stage-manager, mechanician, electrician—all
in one; and when it came to the performance the artists
had only to look at his authoritative glance and inspiring
beat to gain absolute confidence, and feel that they would
be ably steered through any difficulty that might arise.
In the course of our work with Seidl our admiration for
him soon grew to warm affection, and we lose in him
not only an incomparable artist, who always gave us
invaluable assistance and support in all our work, but
also a very dear friend, who enlivened many an otherwise dreary hour for us with his genial companionship.
We shall never forget him.

JEAN DE RESZKE
EDOUARD DE RESZKE

Soon after Seidl's death a benefit performance was planned
for his wife, and again Jean proved himself a friend in deed
as well as in word. He had such a winning personality, and
his position in the company was so exceptional, that he could
give both advice and orders, not only to his fellow artists, but
to Grau, without giving offense. He pacified prima donnas,
he telegraphed artists here and there, he put pressure on Grau
when that gentleman was inclined to play the manager game.
"Webber will see Grau" meant business. When the benefit
plan was abandoned and it was decided to ask all the singers
for monetary contributions, it seemed to some of those in
charge of the project that this was a polite form of blackmail,
but when Jean heard of it he promptly wrote that he would
be glad to contribute a thousand dollars. He felt that he was
indebted to Anton Seidl for much of the success of his Wagnerian portrayals, and was happy to repay him in the only
way now possible.

   During the Covent Garden season of 1898 Jean devoted
himself almost entirely to Wagner. T r i s t a n, with Lillian
Nordica back in her old rôle, won ever greater favor. Always
it seemed as though Jean had reached the very pinnacle of
artistic achievement, and always he towered above himself,

especially as Tristan. In S i e g f r i e d he was less fortunate. He was ill rather frequently on dates when he was scheduled to appear in it, and there was grumbling when he disappointed the public by not appearing, but a more serious cause of complaint were the cuts made in the opera. There were probably no more than during the previous season, but this year the entire R i n g was given, and the Wagner Society regularly attended *en masse*. They sent a letter to the management demanding that if Jean and Edouard de Reszke could not sing the operas without cuts, other singers should be substituted. The blame for the situation was shifted alternately from singers to management, the burden of it falling upon Jean. But Jean made no retort. He maintained his customary dignified attitude towards all cavilling and simply learned the sections that had been omitted, although it seemed to him that their inclusion impaired the artistry of the performance. The most rabid Wagnerites could protest no further.

London had been somewhat annoyed that New York was first to hear both Jean's Tristan and his Siegfried. Now London had the opportunity of hearing his first representation of the elder Siegfried. Singing Brünnhilde with him in G ö t t e r d ä m m e r u n g was Madame Milka Ternina, fit companion for the world's leading tenor. She enjoyed singing with Jean, saying that "as Tristan the lover he had never had his equal, while as Siegfried the singer he would never be surpassed."

Universal praise for the new Siegfried could hardly be expected, but to the critic of *The Times* and to the London correspondent of the *Revue Internationale de Musique,* two responsible writers, his conception of the rôle seemed dazzling, and his performance on the same high level of excellence as his best work in other operas. *The Times* commented as follows:[102]

> As is his wont, the great artist gave a real interpretation of the part, setting thereby the crown on his achievement up to the present time. His rendering of the part is on the same level of excellence as his Siegfried of last year in the drama of that name, and it would be impossible to give it higher praise. At every point some new beauty was revealed which all, or almost all, the former Siegfrieds had missed. None of these, for instance, have assumed the baritone voice of Gunther, in the scene

where Siegfried sees Brünnhilde in his friend's shop, with such complete success. The final narration, with its imitations of the woodbird song, was exquisite; and the death scene is one of the very few things that deserve the epithet memorable. Here, as elsewhere, he eclipsed all former representations of the part in the heart-rending poignancy of vocal expression. That the part was interpreted mainly from the vocal point of view seems to have displeased some of those who have lost sight of the fact that Wagner meant his works to be interpreted by singers, and in whose eyes a Siegfried who omits to carry the "*tarnhelm*" ... in the first act commits a fault that the most perfect singing cannot atone. It is quite true that M. Jean de Reszke's principal medium of interpretation is his voice rather than his gestures, but when a singer can convey all that he conveys by the perfect art of his vocalization, all intelligent hearers must feel that a more restrained style of acting contents them than would be required of a performer whose singing was the least of his merits.

New York did not hear the new Siegfried until January 1899, for Jean did not arrive until late in the old year. Indeed, there had been rumors that he would not return to America at all. Why, after all, should he go back season after season? He was a very rich man. He had achieved all that an operatic artist could possibly hope to achieve, and more than any other had achieved. All that the social world could offer was his for the accepting. Kings and Queens were his devoted friends. He enjoyed his Paris home and his vast estates in Poland. His wife did not like his journeying to America. He had not escaped harsh treatment by some newspapers and magazines, and the last time he had sung in Chicago the people had seemed not to appreciate his art. The joys of travel had long since ceased to hold any charm for him, and the rigors of the New York climate regularly took their toll in the form of colds and influenza. Moreover, his own respect for the art of Grand Opera would not allow him to rest on laurels already won, and since he could not be satisfied merely to sing old rôles, each new season meant new work. And, added to everything else, he had been far from well.

Why, then, did Jean de Reszke return to New York after this absence of more than a year? For one thing, Maurice

Grau needed him. Jean was very fond of Grau. When, a few years previously, the impresario's receipts were dwindling, Jean volunteered to reduce his own salary, offering to sing for $1,250 a performance, without anything additional. And when, in the summer of 1896, it seemed that Sir Augustus Harris would not recover from the illness which had suddenly overtaken him, Jean at once thought of Maurice Grau as his successor. He wrote Grau a letter, to which the latter replied:*

Friday, 19 June 1896
9 rue Auber

My dear Jean:

Your letter flatters me enormously and overwhelms me with joy! What a crowning of all that you have done for me! For if such a thing should happen for me, it would be to you and you only that I should owe it, and my only aim would be to prove myself worthy of the confidence in me and of the friendship which you have proved you feel for me. I hope that the condition of Sir Augustus is not so grave as one fears, but if unfortunately a catastrophe should occur, I shall do everything that you want me to do, and without empty talk and big words. I shall say only that I shall be proud and happy to do whatever I can at Covent Garden, above all for you and Edouard. It is needless to tell you that you can count absolutely on my discretion, as I count on yours.

I embrace you both, and with all my heart.

Your very sincerely grateful
MAURICE GRAU

After the death of Sir Augustus, Maurice Grau was appointed managing director of Covent Garden, an opportunity he appreciated deeply. It is no wonder that Jean inspired devotion and affection even in his impresario. Some time after Grau's own death, his wife found, upon opening the case of a watch she had not seen for a long time, an early portrait of Jean, in the first rôle he had sung under her husband's management.

Mr. Grau needed Jean in New York, and partly because of that the great tenor decided to go back; partly, too, because he loved an American audience; but most of all, because to sing was life for Jean; because, in spite of all the nervousness and apprehension which never left him, he was completely

* Translated from the French.

happy only when he was singing, and not merely that, but singing his way into the furthest depths of the character he was portraying, and into the hearts of his listeners. So he came back to New York, and New York wondered. Would he seem older? Had he grown too fat? Would he have all the old-time grace and sweetness? Would he seem less poetic, and had the velvet of his voice worn thin? Would he still transcend all other singers, still be the incomparable Romeo? For there was a new Romeo that year, Alvarez, an excellent artist. Naturally he had had to face, in addition to the strain of a New York début, the certainty that every note he sang, every gesture he made, would be compared with that of the one artist who had set so high and so beautiful a standard that the public would accept no other interpretation as "just as good"; so completely had Jean become identified with the rôle.

Jean had wanted to make his *rentrée* in L o h e n g r i n, but Van Dyck had been announced in that opera for the same week and Jean acceded to the wish of Mr. Grau that he should sing Romeo. Well did Grau know that meant a crowded house; one can almost see him rubbing his hands in glee. Then there was the question of who would be the Juliette. There were five Juliettes in the company, some of whom had established enviable records in the part. Suzanne Adams had been announced, but she became ill. Then Melba wanted to sing with Jean on the first night. Marie Engle and Emma Eames and Madame Saville all would have loved it. Finally Mr. Grau asked Marcella Sembrich to sing the part, and the evening of December 26 1898 saw as Shakespeare's most beloved lovers two who were facetiously called "the Poles of Art."

Every seat in the Metropolitan Opera House had been sold out. Row on row of "standees" pressed toward the brass rail behind the orchestra circle. The house had not been so packed since the opening night. The atmosphere was tense with the cumulative tenseness of several thousand men and women who were waiting to see and hear what they longed once more to experience but did not quite dare to expect. Juliette appeared, and was applauded, but mildly; the thousands were waiting. The beloved Romeo walked upon the scene. And then the vast audience burst into applause; not the hysterical cheers which greet a man who has done something spectacular in the eyes of the world, but the kindly sincere roar that is the only expression available to a crowd

To my dear Tolmanina
Edouard
1903.

1581

By Courtesy of Colonel Creighton Webb   Photos Dupont, N. Y.

JEAN DE RESZKE   EDOUARD DE RESZKE

of men and women who want to show their love and admiration both as individuals and as a group. Jean stood with head
bent low, waiting for the tumult and the shouting to die. He
was visibly affected by the ovation. He tried to go on with
his part, but the clapping and the cheers continued in full
strength. He came forward and bowed again and again, hands
clasped as though to greet each one of those thousands personally. After each scene the uproar broke out anew, and at
the close of the balcony scene the young lovers were called
out eight times. That the ovation was intended chiefly for
Romeo was certain. Modestly he insisted on having Juliette
and Capulet share it, but the house would not be satisfied
until he came out alone. At times it seemed the performance
could never proceed, and much as Jean appreciated this ovation, which he knew was heartfelt, he was a very weary man
when he was finally allowed to go home at midnight. A reporter described the scene thus:[103]

> Well, well, we had a great time at the opera last
> night. It was the return of M. Jean, and a lyric love-feast.
> Nobody cared for Gounod or the sorrows of Romeo and
> his Juliette. The tenor was our chief concern. Had he
> grown older, or less poetic, or diminished in good looks,
> or become lethargic in acting or lost the quality of his
> famous voice? These were problems of perturbation.
> The anxiety of them filled the Metropolitan from doors
> to dome.
>
> It was the occasion which the opera-goers long had
> sought, and mourned because they found it not. It was
> the reappearance of M. Jean after his long absence. It
> was the first night of the season *par excellence*. It was
> the return to town of the most popular singer that Grand
> Opera has known since the days of Mario. Soft eyes
> melted in the boxes and snowy bosoms heaved tumultu-
> ously, and Saleza, Salignac, Dippel and Van Dyck, tenors,
> too, but lesser ones, suddenly fell from the eminence into
> which they lately climbed in the absence of their rival—
> and M. Jean was crowned anew in the Metropolitan.
>
> A roar of applause greeted him as he strode into the
> palace of the Capulets. Yes, he had grown stouter. What
> of that? He wears his weight well. His cheeks, hollow
> during the quarrel with Mme. Nordica, are now filled
> out. Handsomer than ever. Even M. Pol, the professional

beauty of the company, must now be secondary. The basso, who sang Capulet, seemed almost insignificant beside M. Jean. The tenor, arrayed in a new and extremely becoming costume, eclipsed even his own record of good looks. M. Jean, as a spectacle, was the finest picture the opera-goers have looked on this season.

Dramatically and morally admirable, as well as visually. No nasal tenor this; no singer with a single high C and nothing else; no fiery Frenchman burning himself up with a fever of fervor; no thin Italian running through the score like scarlatina; no solid German with housemaid's knee before the tomb of Wagner.

Romeo—the very Montague—enraptured with his lovely lady, and so far from being selfish over the matter, taking all the audience into his passion. The lover of all lovers! Full of sentiment—embracing the spectators as well as Juliette, and spreading his tenderness over the footlights into the boxes. What wonder that the ladies wished with Desdemona that Heaven had made them such a man!

Now let Saleza, Van Dyck and Dippel, who have lately been putting on airs as well as singing them, make way for M. Jean. The Polish tenor has come into his own again, and all the singers who hoped to supersede him are bowled over.

M. Jean returns to us in fine shape. His voice never sounded better, richer, fuller, sweeter, more eloquent or more sympathetic than it did last night. His acting has rounded now into completeness of dramatic art. His performance of Romeo, animated as it was by the quick and cordial spirit of the audience, was replete with all the charms of romance, dignity, power, and song.

M. Jean once more lifts opera from effort into grace, from talent into intelligence, from labor into art. The Metropolitan season, already brilliant in incidents, has attained its climax of achievement in the Romeo of Jean de Reszke.

The auditorium was as tumultuous as the stage was melodious. Every man and woman in the house suddenly found a singing voice, and all sorts and conditions of cries issued from the audience. The fall of the curtain raised Cain, Babel, Bedlam. People embraced each other hysterically and fell to shouting vehemently.

Such an inarticulate and appalling clamor was never heard in a public building, for everybody wanted to shake hands vocally, so to speak, with the tenor.

But all that was sensational at the Metropolitan that night was in the auditorium. On the stage there was perfect restraint, perfect suiting of action to singing, singing to action, not once an effect for the sake of effect. Jean always obeyed all the instructions Hamlet gave to the players, especially that one: "For in the very torrent, tempest, and, as I may say, whirlwind of your passion, you must acquire and beget a temperance that may give it smoothness."

His Romeo, always lovely, had grown in depth and pathos since his study of Wagner. He knew this. To a young woman friend he gave a photograph inscribed "Souvenir of Romeo become Tristan." "The refinement he has reached in phrasing," wrote a critic, "the variety of nuance in light and shade he is capable of, the perfect balance of the registers of his vocal organ, all this is hard to describe, and even the most eloquent description could not give a remote idea of the effect it has upon the audience. Such a perfect art of singing is hypnotizing." [104]

That the demonstrations just described had not been merely a welcome after a long absence, but bore witness to a genuine love of the great singer and his art, seemed clear when, at the season's seventh R o m e o, there were some four thousand people in attendance.

In his Tristan Jean out-Reszke'd de Reszke that year. A part of the reason for the special beauty of the performances was the superb art of Lilli Lehmann, who sang with him rather frequently during the season. She liked the rugged quality of Niemann's Tristan, but thought de Reszke the greater singer. He also considered her a supreme artist. She wrote Jean a letter after one of their Tristan performances, to which he replied:

GILSEY HOUSE
NEW YORK, 19 January 1899

DEAR MADAME:

You cannot believe what pleasure and joy your charming letter gave us. My brother and I cannot find enough words to thank you for it; as for me, since I consider you the greatest artist of the century, your flattering words are the greatest recompense for my artistic

efforts. As for the reciprocal sympathy, that can be explained only by the great admiration which I have always
had for you and which increases upon experiencing your
kindness and your frank friendship.

Believe, dear madame, that I shall always keep the
memory of our beautiful evenings, when, inspired by
you, I believe I have given the best that is in me.

Count always on my unchanging friendship.

Your devoted

JEAN DE RESZKE

Jean's modesty about his own achievements was touching. When Mrs. Finck, wife of the critic, told him that she
had wanted to meet Tristan, to thank him for all the happiness he had given her, he replied simply: "It pleased you,
Madame?" And now that Lilli Lehmann expressed her joy
over his interpretation, he (whose photograph was begged for
by thousands) wrote her a note, saying that "if she would permit it" he would like to send her a portrait of himself as
Tristan. When Mr. W. J. Henderson visited her in Germany
many years later he saw on the wall a large photograph of
herself as the Irish princess and near it this large photograph
of Jean, which she treasured. He asked her whether she remembered a certain performance of Tristan with Jean on
a Saturday afternoon when everything was perfection, when
the audience seemed breathless and the representation one
long thrill. "I remember it well," replied this great Isolde. "It
was the ideal Tristan performance of my life."

In both London and New York opinions about the
amazing beauty and depth of Jean's Tristan were never
divided. Not so with his elder Siegfried. His portrayal of
that rôle had been variously criticized in London, and when,
on January 24 1899 New York first heard it, the result was
the same. Henry Finck gave unqualified praise, saying:

The second Siegfried made as deep an impression as
the first. Wagner's hero was presented to the eye as a
living being who had the immense advantage over ordinary mortals of being able to express his feelings in song,
and though backed up by an immense orchestra, he
dominated it every moment. No detail escapes his attention; did he not enunciate so distinctly, one could read
in his face what he is saying—and what the others are

saying too. . . . He is called upon to recall to the audience practically the whole substance of the Siegfried drama, poetically and musically—a feat which M. Jean de Reszke performed last evening with a beauty of voice, art of phrasing, and variety of emotional expression never before witnessed here in that part.[105]

The *Times* critic did not discuss the new creation in full immediately after the performance. He felt that he would have to hear it again, but it seemed to him to fall short of the proper weight in the early scenes, although it improved immensely in the second act. Another hearing did not, however, change Mr. Henderson's impression of the "apparent lack of spontaneity" which characterized Jean's singing of the first act. "At the first performance and again last night," he complained, "he sang the music without breadth or power, and was weak even in the brotherhood oath, which ought to suit his voice." But the second and third acts, particularly the third, were closer to what was expected of the singer. "Not one of the women has equaled the airy lightness of his delivery of the bird music, and his entire work in this scene is that of a master of vocal art. But Siegfried in G ö t t e r- d ä m m e r u n g, it must be admitted, is the least convincing of all M. de Reszke's Wagnerian impersonations." [106]

Jean, with his equipment and standards, might of course have been expected to remedy such a situation. The next time he appeared in the rôle, we find Mr. Henderson saying that he sang with fine abandon throughout, and gave a much more convincing impersonation. "The increased plasticity of his action was in a considerable measure the cause of this."

Jean had very definite ideas about the elder Siegfried. He believed that Wagner intended him to be entirely secondary to the heroine; in fact, he felt that the composer should have called the opera "Brünnhilde." G ö t t e r d ä m m e r u n g, he said, represents the degeneracy of Siegfried, who is, in that drama, a much less manly and sympathetic character than in S i e g f r i e d. It is only through Brünnhilde that he accomplishes anything. She gives him his horse, his arms, everything; it is she who wishes him to leave her to become a real hero. And after he drinks the potion Siegfried loses his individuality entirely; he becomes a mere tool in the hands of Hagen and Gunther, lending himself to every suggestion. It is for this reason that after the opening duo, in which he allowed his emotional voice to glow, Jean kept himself in the background, so that Brünnhilde might come into stronger relief. As a reward for this artistic unselfishness, some people accused him of saving his voice! Jean did not take the public into his confidence and ask them to watch him efface himself in order to make a graceful background for Brünnhilde. Nor did he insist that every one ought to consider his interpretation as the one and only correct one, but he resented the suggestion that he economized his resources. "To say that I deliberately spare myself during a performance," he protested, "and save my voice for this reason or that, is to charge me with bad faith towards the public and my manager. I have never been guilty of that." No one could doubt his complete absorption, who saw the groping expression in his eyes as he struggled to remember Brünnhilde after he had drunk the potion brewed by Hagen, or the sudden change in his mien and action when, after taking the second potion, his memory returned, and he once more became a man capable of thinking and acting for himself. Certainly no Brünnhilde could harbor doubts as to this Siegfried's intensity. Some one said to Lillian Nordica: "I have never seen the struggle for the ring enacted as you and Jean did it," and she answered: "That was a real fight. I was struggling for my very life, and still carry the marks of the struggle. My arms and hands were scratched and bleeding."

By the time the last performance was given, even Mr. Henderson recorded that it "had the full freedom of declamatory vigor needed to give the utterances of Siegfried the heroic authority demanded by the character. As heard yesterday this rôle won its proper place in the gallery of Wagnerian portraits given us by this great master of operatic impersonation."

Edouard's Hagen sprang into immediate favor, being judged perfect in conception, make-up, action, and declamation. In looks he was the very incarnation of the word sinister, and he suited song and action to the gloomy text. His portrayal would have represented a signal achievement for an artist who made a specialty of cheerless, tragic rôles; it was even more so for one who, like Edouard, had made immortal his conception of such comic characters as Leporello and Don Basilio. When Edouard stood on the rock, and, with his powerful, sonorous voice, called together his men, the effect was tremendous.

DURING THE FOLLOWING London season Jean was ill very frequently, and his enforced retirement was freely predicted. Sensible people, however, realized that the strain of a long New York season was bound to have some effect on the voice. Obviously, not even the greatest artist can sing with the same freshness after several months of steady hard work as after the same period of absolute rest. Jean avoided, that season, the more melodious rôles which demand a truly fresh voice, and confined himself almost entirely to declamatory music. But even if his voice seemed less electrifying than formerly, he was never anything but artistic. His worst would have been considered a notable achievement for any lesser artist; he suffered only through comparisons with his own record. The more he felt out of voice the more he revealed the resources of his astounding technical skill. Naturally, when he undertook to sing before he had fully recovered from an attack of influenza, his resonance chambers were not entirely clear and there was not so much volume or brilliancy, but there was never any diminution in his art. Indeed, to some it seemed that he had done the impossible—that he had actually improved his Tristan, as witness the review in the *Musical Standard* of May 20 1899:

> On Thursday, and again on Tuesday, he sang with a force and meaning which I have never before heard from him. It takes a good deal to move a critic who during the last week or so has been hearing more music than is good for him; but Jean de Reszke succeeded in moving me as I have never been moved before. And a strange thing in his singing is that though he conveys every bit of pathos, he never overacts or oversings . . . and the whole effect is at once beautiful as music as well as touching as drama. But the thing which has particularly struck me this season is that de Reszke's voice in such music as the third act of T r i s t a n is at its best. . . . My theory with regard to the new de Reszke is that he feels the dramatic moments in Wagner's music-dramas more than he used to feel them some three years ago, and proportionately he is less interested in the lyrical beauties of the set order— the subtle lyrical beauties still appeal to him, as in Lohengrin's Farewell to the Swan—and that when he

feels strongly, as when Tristan in his delirium pictures Isolde sailing to him in her ship, "full of grace and loving mildness,"' his voice rings out with a tone of which no mere operatic climax can be the cause any longer. I do not know if this be the real reason of de Reszke's present greatness as a dramatic singer, but I should like to find out how we can train singers to get such intelligence in their voices, such pathos as he realizes in this third act of T r i s t a n. Would it be possible, for instance, to get a lyrical tenor to sing those two wonderful cries of "Isolde" which are heard in this drama and haunt one for hours afterwards; the first when Tristan sees the barriers which separated him from Isolde thrown down; the second when he recognizes, as he turns his dying eyes on Isolde, that the last and eternal barrier is being set up by death? I think the lyrical tenor could not touch us at all, however beautifully he might sing; if he learned to feel and then brought his lyrical art to the expression of that feeling, he might come within measurable distance of Jean de Reszke. But how long is art! For certain it is that if Jean de Reszke had not studied in the *bel canto* school he would not now be able to portray all the poetic and emotional beauties of Wagner's music.

But Jean was really in no condition for a heavy season. From the very beginning of his career he had suffered from a susceptibility to colds which easily developed into bronchitis. A less zealous person would soon have abandoned a career so dependent on the condition of his respiratory apparatus, but to Jean that circumstance simply meant a challenge to overcome the difficulty. With him it had never been a question of whether it was possible to sing with such a handicap, but merely of how best to cope with it. The perfection of his technique was not confined to one method of singing. He could sing—and sing well—even when his bronchial tubes were so congested that most other singers would not have dreamed of attempting a performance. He was sometimes in real distress, but such mastery was his that his audiences never suspected it. Such mastery was his that when one method of voice production was not proving satisfactory, he could change to another with perfect ease and without a shadow of uncertainty.

Of course a physical condition such as his was aggravated

by frequent and pronounced changes in climate. The rigor
of New York winters demanded the greatest caution. Jean
seldom left his hotel except to go to the opera house to sing.
The very severity of the climate in New York probably in-
sured fewer cancellations than were necessary in London, for
in America the necessity of guarding his condition was always
before the singer, whereas in London, the opera season being
in the summer, a little carelessness was natural. Jean frequently went to the country for week-ends, as he liked to
indulge his fondness for bicycling, but both he and the public
suffered on account of his relaxation, because he caught cold
so easily.

Newspapers and musical magazines had always paid much
attention to Jean's physical condition, particularly in London.
From the very beginning of his career there (as a tenor, of
course), paragraphers seized upon every instance of a cold or
attack of the *grippe,* to predict the ruination of his voice
and the abandonment of his career. In Paris and New York
also there was great disappointment when, because of some
indisposition, the beloved singer could not appear; but it
seemed to be recognized that he was a human being and not
a machine, and that by reason of such a self-evident fact he
was susceptible to the same conditions and influences as other
people; his devotees were happy to hear him when that was
possible. But in London, where, for the reasons indicated,
Jean was compelled to disappoint his public more frequently
than elsewhere, each non-appearance gave rise to dire pre-
dictions. Some, remembering that he had not always been a
tenor, nodded wise heads and said that no "pushed-up baritone" could expect to force his voice as de Reszke had and not
pay the penalty. Those who had been sure that Jean's voice
could not withstand the strain of the heavy Wagnerian parts
were certain that his ambition had o'er-vaulted itself. Others,
who had insisted on his great age, seemed almost to delight in
pointing out that he was "no spring chicken," and would have
to make way for younger men. The actual illness was grossly
exaggerated; lung trouble, burst blood vessels, tumor, cancer,
all were assigned as the ailment. It became necessary for Jean's
physician to issue an official denial of the report that a serious
operation had been performed on the eminent tenor's throat.

For years such rumors had persisted. Many of the an-
nouncements that Jean was to sing on some special occasion in
London or on the Continent were erroneous, but that did not

prevent statements that his failure to appear was due to the "precarious" state of his health. Even the extremely intelligent and kind critic of the *New York Times,* a de Reszke enthusiast, said, as early as 1894: "It is possible that the best years of his voice have passed." He suggested, however, that what were called signs of wear should more properly have been characterized as signs of weariness, and added: "But it would be hasty to say that signs of decay are now visible. On the other hand, it is quite certain that the singer is at the maturity of his splendid growth as an artist.[107] This before Tristan! before Siegfried!

However, in spite of his frequent inability to sing because of bronchial trouble, Jean never earned the sobriquet "The Great Indisposed," which was applied to one of his famous Juliettes. His sincerity was recognized; his audiences knew that when it was announced that he could not sing because he had a cold, he really had a cold. Once when he was unable to appear at Covent Garden a London journal published a story to the effect that he had been singing in private houses on the dates of his scheduled appearances. Jean was furious and threatened to leave London for good if he did not receive better treatment at the hands of the press. The story was retracted and an apology published. But the state of his health in the summer of 1899 made it necessary for Jean to ask release from his contract.

Before this happened, however, he sang, with Edouard, Nordica, Schumann-Heink and Bispham in a L o h e n g r i n performance before Queen Victoria on her eightieth birthday, May 24 1899. Her Majesty had never heard the opera before, and found it "the most glorious composition, so poetic, so dramatic and, one might almost say, religious in feeling and full of sadness, pathos, and tenderness." The singing of the two brothers she thought "beyond praise. Jean looked so handsome in his white attire, armor, and helmet, and the electric light was turned strong upon him, so that he seemed surrounded by a halo." After the performance the Queen requested that the principal artists should be presented to her. Jean and Edouard, not knowing that it was customary to wear evening dress for the presentation ceremony, had decided to save time and avoid the inconvenience of dressing at Windsor Castle by donning the costumes of Lohengrin and Henry the Fowler in their hotel rooms. Thus they rode out to Windsor in comfort, but consternation reigned among the Court officials when they learned how tradition was threatened, for they knew of the Queen's fondness for these singers. They were quite right in supposing that Her Majesty had no objection to the slight irregularity. The brothers were summoned, and a very picturesque addition they were to the formal gathering. Jean received the cross of the Royal Victorian Order (fourth class) on this occasion. Edouard was similarly decorated fourteen months later, after a representation of F a u s t, which was the last time Queen Victoria listened to an opera.

Jean sang at Covent Garden only a few times after the royal birthday celebration. His last appearance was as Tristan. Even the inhumanly superior Wagnerites, whom any demonstration during a performance exasperated, would perhaps have have been mollified had they known that the wreath which was presented to Jean at the end of the first act was no mere costly bouquet sent by a rich admirer, but a token of appreciation from the chorus. It bore the inscription: "To the superb artist, Jean de Reszke, the honor and glory of the *bel canto*, the Italian Chorus offers these humble flowers with best wishes for a prosperous journey."

The following winter Jean did not sing in America. His absence was responsible for one of those fantastic episodes that can occur only in an opera company. Among his and Edouard's acquaintances was a Pole who went by the name of Maurice de Nevers and who occasionally wrote articles on musical matters. He came to New York with Edouard in the autumn of 1899, and it seems that other members of the company thought he had been commissioned "to scatter flowers on the tomb of Jean de Reszke, and keep his memory green" until he returned. While the company was in Boston, a reporter called to interview Edouard and was referred to de Nevers. That gentleman delivered himself of the opinion that the troupe was a good one, barring the fact that it contained no tenors. Now as the names of Van Dyck, Saleza, Alvarez, Dippel, and Salignac, who were members of the company, comprised a list of all the famous contemporary tenors, this was regarded as a somewhat surprising statement from Jean's "representative," and there was great excitement among the singers. Ordinarily Mr. Grau paid no attention to disputes of a purely personal character, but this one involved the reputation of the entire company, and he therefore summoned his artists to his office, and asked de Nevers, who had denied the truth of the interview, to meet them and the reporter there.

The reporter arrived, and embellished his published story with some pungent comments on the tenors made privately by de Nevers, which the reporter had, as a matter of delicacy, refrained from publishing. The tenors writhed anew under the stinging remarks. De Nevers declined Grau's invitation, but sent letters of apology to the men he had offended, one of whom replied, forbidding him ever again to notice his existence in any way. De Nevers's answer was that his seconds would call on the singer in Paris. The duel never took place, however, and the only injury was to the feelings of the group of tenors.

In the meantime the cause of all the trouble had been ill. He tried to fulfill his contract at Covent Garden, but during the entire 1900 Covent Garden season Jean sang only five times. His first appearance was as Romeo on June 12, and although he was not in good voice, his impersonation had distinction, charm, and beauty of vocalization. But in America headlines were displayed, blaring: *"Famous Tenor's Voice Lost."* After saying "Jean de Reszke, the world-famous tenor, has lost his voice and it is feared that his career on the operatic stage is ended," the account quoted an impresario as reporting that Jean's "breakdown was pitiable. His voice diminished and faded away, astonishing his audience and frightening him. Melba was so affected by the scene that she cried like a child. Some one had to go before the curtain and ask the indulgence of the audience. De Reszke is very courageous, insisting that his failure was only temporary and the result of long vocal illness. He believes he will get back all his old powers, but his friends say to one another that they fear he will not have that happiness."

Jean had indeed been ill, and there was a bad congestion of the bronchial tubes. He did, in fact, break down, but when Jean de Reszke was not at his best nobody knew it better than he himself. He did not attempt to sing again until July 4, when M e i s t e r s i n g e r was given. The public did not know whether they would ever hear him again. As one commentator put it: "Lively speculations as to the day on which Mr. Jean de Reszke would next appear in any public place other than the advertisement columns of the newspapers have kept opera-goers' wits in a healthy circulation." However, when he did reappear, any lingering grudge against the management, or against the great tenor for his frequent disappointments, was quickly dissipated. Even yet the singer did not seem to be in very good condition, but again his performance could suffer only in comparison with his own previous work. For Jean the evening's portrayal was not perfection; for any other singer it would have been a truly great success. A critic observed: "It would be absurd to say that he sang well; it would be equally absurd not to say that, under obvious circumstances of great difficulty, he accomplished really an extraordinary feat."

In some quarters, nevertheless, commentators found the performance entirely unsatisfactory. According to one of them, he was "entirely out of voice, and, except in the Prize Song in the last act...he sang almost throughout *sotto voce*." [108] Another reported: [109]

It was clear before the curtain had been up many minutes, that the beautiful voice is by no means what it was, and that the ringing quality of his tones has apparently disappeared; it may be hoped, only for a time. The impersonation is as beautiful and sympathetic as ever, and this would have won him success even had his vocal condition been so satisfactory as to do away with the necessity of saving himself for the Prize Song at the close. When it came, it was of course artistically phrased, but in power and effect it was a sadly faint reflection of what it used to be. The wreck is beautiful, but a wreck it is, and the performance could not but excite painful memories.

This criticism was refuted by an indignant listener, who wrote:

As I was present at the performance, I may be entitled to protest against such a violent conclusion as Mr. Fuller-Maitland, of *The Times*, reaches. M. Jean de Reszke has been ill, and did not intend to sing. The clamor of the papers was such, however, that the many disappointments could not be indefinitely continued, and the tenor, contrary to his best judgment, agreed to sing. His voice was not so vibrant as it is when he is in health, but, as to its being a wreck, I can only say that such an expression is too radical to deserve the consideration due to a usual *Times* criticism. M. Jean de Reszke will prove the justice of this next season in America. [110]

In the *Saturday Review*, J. F. Runciman wrote:

He did not sing well; neither did he act well; he, the
pet of stalls and gallery alike, seemed to suffer from extreme nervousness. None the less, from the moment the
curtain rose one saw the folly of talking about "tenors of
the future." It may or may not be true that he thinks of
retiring; but if he does retire, no tenor who has yet sung
at Covent Garden can be reckoned on to fill his place. In
acting and in singing he is first and the rest out of sight.
None match him in appearance and address; there is
none whose gestures compare with his in gracefulness and
expressiveness; there is none whose tones have the expressiveness and beauty of his; certainly there is none who
can manage the voice, coloring it from moment to moment as the moment's emotion requires, as he manages
his. For Jean, Wednesday evening was not a huge success; for any other than Jean, it would count as a stupendous hit. He had undoubtedly been ill, and will not,
I trust, retire disgusted with his own shortcomings. He
is our only Tristan, our best Siegfried, our only Walther,
and nearly our only Lohengrin.

That "nearly" had to be gently recalled when, three
nights later, Jean repeated the part. Mr. Fuller-Maitland rejoiced with every one else that "even as the first notes of the
'Farewell to the Swan' were given out at the back of the stage,
it was clear to every one in the house that M. de Reszke's voice
had come back, and from this point to the final 'Erzählung'
all was perfect in phrasing, conception, and interpretation." [111]
    Two nights after this he sang Walther again, and then, on
July 13, concluded his appearances with Romeo, for which he
was in fine voice and in which he again showed all the old
magic. But he had been singing under distressing handicaps,
and went away to rest.
    Edouard, fortunately, did not share the ill health of his
brother, and sang better than ever all through the season. His
great voice always rolled out over the orchestra without the
slightest suggestion of strain. His Leporello, "free from ex-
travagance," was, as usual, immensely popular. His Marcel
was "an inspiration." His make-up as the sturdy, loyal fol-
lower of Calvin was perfect, and he sang the famous "Piff-
Paff" air with such martial fervor, and intoned "Ein Feste
Burg" with such rugged vigor that no other star, however
radiant, could dim the luster of his performance. His Ramfis

continued to show many noteworthy points both in acting and singing, and his Friar Laurence had lost nothing of its imposing quality. Always amiable, always ready to sing, Edouard's place in the affections of his public never once, throughout his career or afterwards, lost its secure hold. Not that those who heard Jean lost their regard for him, but there had been a good deal of complaining during this last London season because prices were raised when he was to appear in the cast and no refund was made when he was unable to sing. Few stopped to think that any manager would have had a pretty kettle of fish on his hands if he so much as hinted at making a refund because Jean de Reszke could not sing in a certain opera when, say, Nellie Melba or Emma Calvé was also scheduled to appear! Of course most people would have been satisfied to hear Jean no matter how he felt, preferring him out of voice to any other tenor in voice, but his own artistic standards forbade yielding to this preference. When he decided to leave London after his second appearance as Romeo, which, be it remembered, was an excellent performance, he said to a critic-friend: "I cannot tell you how profoundly I deplore having had to disappoint the public in this way, but I have hoped against hope and now I must really give up the struggle. There is nothing the matter with my voice; you could hear that when I sang Romeo on Friday week. The trouble is in my chest, and in a general sensation of lassitude and prostration which the doctors tell me can only be cured by complete change of air. . . . As to the future, I can say nothing definite at this moment. I fully expect to go to America with Mr. Grau in the winter, and in any case I shall hope to return to London next year. But if I do it will be at the beginning of the season, when I shall not run the risk of such a heat visitation as you now seem to get here every July. . . . I have sung five times under the most adverse conditions, and I dare not run any further risks." [112]

In AMERICA the story of Jean's "breakdown" had spread like a prairie fire. It was not entirely reassuring to learn that Mr. Grau had urged him to sign a contract for the following season, because one also learned that de Reszke had replied: "No. Wait a little. If my voice is impaired you will not want me, and I am sure I shall not wish to sing in America." The *New York Times* requested a definite statement for the benefit of the many anxious people who had nothing to rely upon but opinions of London critics. To this Jean replied, under date of July 30 1900:

> I have been very much touched by your solicitude in regard to me. I hasten to tell you that I am very well indeed. The influenza which I contracted on the way to London has not left me because of the terrible heat which has prevailed during the whole month of July. Nothing but a change of air could set me on my feet again. But be assured as regards my voice, which has never been better. Moreover, if I go to New York, you can convince yourself of it by hearing me. As for certain papers which have loudly announced the loss of my voice, they belong to that category which will not admit that Jean de Reszke can be ill like other people. They insist that he has lost something. Happily my "business" is beyond the reach of these insinuations.

This letter was published [113] with the following comment: "M. de Reszke is the most consummate vocal artist now before the public and his own opinion of the state of his voice should be authoritative. He knows when he can sing and when he cannot." In October it was announced that Jean had assured Mr. Grau by letter that his voice was never in better condition and that he would positively leave for America on December 15. His reappearance was scheduled for December 31 in L o h e n g r i n. There had been anxiety as to how the great tenor would sing on that other occasion after he had been absent from the Metropolitan for a year, but that uneasiness was now greatly intensified by the alarming reports, followed by news (albeit false) of an operation, which emanated from London. When it became certain that Jean was really to appear, the house was at once sold out. On the long-

Edouard de Reszke as Hagen

GÖTTERDÄMMERUNG

Jean de Reszke as Siegfried

awaited night there were more than a thousand persons standing. The very atmosphere seemed nervous. How every one wanted to believe that the old-time sweetness would be there! that the old-time charm would be found not only in graciousness of personality, not only in every gesture, but in the voice too. One wanted to believe; and yet, the story of the "ruined voice" had been spread far and wide—one couldn't be sure. The great tenor was now in his fifty-first year. It might be that he would make "a swan-like end, fading in music."

The Herald sang his few lines bravely. The men of Brabant welcomed their King heartily. But König Heinrich was not himself. His tones faltered unmistakably. He sang the prayer out of tune. And Elsa's nervousness showed plainly that this time she awaited the arrival of her knight in truly great perturbation. The immense audience was tense with the same anxiety. "You might have taken a sword and run it across the backs of a whole row of people," said one man afterwards, "and nobody would have felt it." Lesser artists wandered through the house uneasily, wondering whether the prince of tenors would break down and leave the field clear for them.

On the aisle seat of the fifth row sat one man who alone seemed strangely calm. Maurice Grau knew that there was no need for all this uneasiness. When, a few months earlier, he had heard the rumor of Jean's announcement that he would never again sing in public, Mr. Grau had cabled for the facts and received Jean's prompt answer: "I shall never sing again until I am sure that my voice and my health are in perfect condition." That summer Grau went to Poland to visit de Reszke. Another season without Jean would, he felt, mean disaster to his operatic endeavors. He found that all was well. Not a question was asked. Grau knew his man. He knew that he could depend on the artistic perfection implied in Jean's promise to come to America. And so he sat in calm expectation of beautiful sounds, though all the rest of the packed house might pray as Elsa did, "Oh, as I saw him once, let me see him once more."

"Der Schwan! Der Schwan!" cried the men of Brabant. And then, floating down the lazy Scheldt, came

> The swan, with arched neck
> Between her white wings mantling proudly,

bringing her dear burden—the Lohengrin of Lohengrins, robed in shimmering armor; the Knight of the Grail best beloved of the musical world. His eyes, had one looked closely, showed the faintest trace of fear that the brightness of the glory which had always come trailing in the wake of his shallop might seem slightly tarnished.

Edouard was trembling so that he could hardly hold his kingly sword. Lillian Nordica strained every nerve to meet, this time, the need of the savior who had so often met her own.

The vast audience had been leaning forward in breathless stillness. That quiet tenseness could not be endured. The pent-up excitement now burst its bonds, and Jean de Reszke's thousands of admirers abandoned every impulse toward restraint. The protesting hisses of the ultra-Wagnerians, who were indignant at this vulgar affront to the music of the master, went unnoticed. Both chorus and orchestra were drowned in hand-clapping and cheers which grew more tempestuous every moment.

It was the duty of old Tom Bull, now dead, to time every performance. He timed the curtain when it went up and when it came down, he timed the intervals between its going up and its going down. He timed the beginning, middle, and end of every opera. He timed the crotchets and the quavers and the semi-demi-semiquavers. And he entered these timings in little books which he preserved for reference. There is a man in New York who says that old Tom Bull swore that the welcome to Jean de Reszke on the night of this performance delayed the first act for half an hour! Walter Damrosch, who conducted on this occasion, writes that the return of Jean "was like the triumphant entry of a victorious monarch."

That jubilation was at once balm to Jean's spirit and agony too; for while he rejoiced in the kindliness of the greeting, it made it difficult for him to begin his song. But as Lohengrin stepped from his bark a hush fell upon the audience. Out into the silence floated

Nun sei bedankt, mein lieber Schwan!

tender, beautiful, sweet as of old. The multiple sigh of relief was almost audible. That voice, then, even though it trembled slightly, was still "propertied as all the tunéd spheres." Strangers smiled at each other. One enthusiast nudged another and whispered: "Good as ever, old man! Good as ever!"

Jean's voice was nearly always a trifle veiled when he began to sing, and some thought this condition gave the tones an appealing, haunting quality. But as the mists of early morning are put to rout by the oncoming sun, laying bare a fairer view than the watcher thought to behold, so this film disappeared from the voice as the artist sang his way into his rôle, revealing clearer, sweeter tones than any listener had ever thought to hear. That night Jean seemed to require less "warming up" than usual, and when he uttered his soul's desire in the words, "Elsa, Ich liebe Dich!" his voice rang with such splendid power that the impression he had made on his entrance was intensified tenfold. "Good as ever?" retorted the second enthusiast to the first. *"Better* than ever!"

Throughout the first act his voice sounded clear and fresh, and the most anxious could detect no trace of weakness. He attacked difficult notes carefully, of course, but he had never been a reckless singer. At the end of the act there was a delirium of applause. Again and again the curtain had to be raised. After the first time the other artists, knowing full well for whom the uproar was meant, insisted on Jean's appearing alone. Then the tumult broke out anew. Ecstatic "Hurrahs!" and "Bravo, Jean!" rent the atmosphere of the dignified Metropolitan Opera House, in such a scene as New York had perhaps never known before. When Jean finally reached his dressing room, which had been hung with garlands of evergreen, he was almost exhausted with emotion. "What can I say? What can I say for all this kindness?" he repeated. "My heart is too full to speak."

A young tenor rushed up to say: "You never sang so well!" Nordica expressed her delight, knowing full well that because of nervousness on behalf of her Lohengrin she had not sung her best throughout the whole first act. Madame Schumann-Heink shed a motherly tear, put her hand on Jean's shoulder, and said, "Mein Kamerad!" Brother Edouard, anxiety now dismissed, announced with a wink, "I knew it would be all right, and it was." That night there was no jealousy behind the scenes. Every artist, every stage hand, every member of the orchestra, thought of only one person's success, and that person was Jean de Reszke.

The general excellence of the performance steadily increased as the other artists regained their old security. It was an evening to linger long in the memory. Every one present not only thrilled to a deeply moving operatic. performance, but shared in the joyous certitude that the greatest operatic artist in the world had lost neither voice nor charm, nor yet

his power to act. The most adored tenor had not yet to
say "a long farewell to all his greatness." The audience was
hysterical. Men shouted themselves hoarse and mopped their
brows, and women wept. More than thirty years later a rather
stolid business man said to me: "I remember every detail of
that performance as though it had been last night. I don't
know how I ever lived through it. I remember being afraid
that I should take cold on the way home, because I was so excited; I perspired so that at the end of the opera my shirt, and
even my collar and tie, were wringing wet."

The quality of subsequent performances proved that it
was not only the hysteria of this event which was responsible
for the judgment that Jean's voice and art had not deterio-
rated. All the old nobility of utterance and deportment was
there when F a u s t was given a few nights later, to a crowded
house. Then it was obvious that the public had decided for
itself when the Grand Opera season was to begin. Jean de
Reszke was back, and everything was in full swing.

> So doth the greater glory dim the less:
> A substitute shines brightly as a king,
> Until a king be by.

On this second appearance Jean was in even better voice
than in that historical performance of L o h e n g r i n. "His
lovely tones came out with a comforting plenitude," wrote
Mr. Henderson, "and with that old, winning quality which
has always reached our hearts.... No prodigal of tone, he
made his effects by the most delicate touches, but was ready
to peal a trumpet note to delight the gods when that was
needed." [114]

Two nights later the "broken-down tenor" sang in A ï d a.
Jean had not sung the opera in New York for several years,
and in those earlier years, he had sometimes omitted the
"Celeste Aïda" aria in the first scene. But that night he sang
it with such splendor of voice that "celestial!" was the only
word which could describe it. This scene is rarely applauded,
but at its close there were excited expressions of delight. The
high level set at the beginning Jean maintained triumphantly
to the end. In the third act he poured out his magnificent
tones generously, "and he sang through the long passages of
high-pitched music to the 'Io resto a te,' with its three successive A's, with energy unflagging and voice to spare." [115]

The friendly folk who had joyfully been spreading the

stories of the great tenor's "decay" must have been filled with
consternation to hear the vigorous tones of the energetic
young warrior. For of such a "broken voice" the public could
not get too much. It flocked to hear the second L o h e n g r i n;
when F a u s t was given again, it thrilled with Marguerite to
the beauties of her lover's wooing; and if it lamented the
fact that L e C i d offered little scope for the refinements of
Jean's art, it could yet feast eyes on a champion of the Moors
who looked like a youth of twenty, and it rejoiced that this
operatic wreck could still fling out robust B flats, B's and high
C's. It was as though de Reszke had deliberately chosen to re-
vive this barn-storming part, which had not been performed
in New York since 1897, not only to set at rest tales of a de-
teriorated voice, but to convince the world that he was in
better physical and vocal condition than he had ever been
before. Needless to say, his Romeo was the same piercingly
tender portrayal as of yore.

Jean was deeply gratified with the season's work and regretted that he could not also sing in London. He sent Herman Klein the following letter (hitherto unpublished):

Gilsey House
New York, January 26 1901

My dear Friend:

I received your charming little note enclosing the
article from the *Sunday Times*. With your kind heart,
you could not do better. During this month I shall
have sung ten times: 2 Lohengrin, 2 Faust, 1 Aïda, 3
Cid, 1 Tristan, 1 Romeo. As you see, it is the entire
gamut of tenor rôles—I have not felt the least exhaustion,
finishing my operas as fresh as I began them.

The coming month I shall sing Les Huguenots, Siegfried, Götterdämmerung, Prophète, etc. What wouldn't
I give if you might hear me in London under similar
conditions! Yesterday Tristan put the audience in a
frenzy—they were weeping; I sang like one inspired. For
the rest, I send you the critiques. What a pity that a
large paper like the *Herald* should be deprived of a
musical critic; since the retirement of S—— they are all
simple reporters.

The death of your dear Queen [Victoria] grieved us
very much. She showed me such touching kindness, and

I shall never forget her. What will Covent Garden be during this period of mourning? Will there be music just the same? It is true that "The King is dead, long live the King," and we have our new sovereigns to entertain. For my part, I wish to refrain from going to London this season; at least, only the desire of the new Queen, which, for me, would constitute an order, would make me change my plans.

   With a thousand tendernesses for your family and a good and cordial shake of the hand for you, my dear friend, believe me always

Your devoted
JEAN DE RESZKE

Jean's Tristan, which had given audiences of two continents an entirely new and a deeper understanding of Wagner's masterpiece, had only to be announced during this season to ensure crowds that overflowed into all available standing room in the Metropolitan and strained the very walls of the sturdy building. The first performance of that work came on January 25. This is the evening Jean refers to in the letter just quoted. "The greatest presentation ever known of T r i s-t a n u n d I s o l d e," it was called by one who admitted that the statement was perhaps "too dogmatically assertive," and then declared: "It was a night to fill the critic with despair. Any attempt to do justice to it must read like ill-judged sentimentalism to those who were not there; and those who were there need no reminder of the beauties of this great work as they were so eloquently set forth." [116]

   That was it. It was impossible to describe Jean's Tristan adequately, and when it was matched by such an Isolde as Madame Milka Ternina the whole thing became so strangely, awfully mystic, and yet its ineffable beauty was so directly and completely communicated to every listener, that the audience hung upon the tones as though here, at last, they themselves were sharing such a love as they had longed to experience; for that of Tristan and Isolde was perhaps more wonderfully rich, more glorious, more poignantly sorrowful than anything they themselves had known. The release came when they could applaud, and then it was as though each one strove to realize the wish,

> I would applaud thee to the very echo,
> That should applaud again.

Thus the "broken down" tenor held his own. Not that there was no vestige of carping criticisms. These persisted. In fact they reached such a point during this season that W. J. Henderson published the following signed statement: [117]

...Some foolish attempts have been made to discredit the statements of the newspapers of this city as to the condition of Mr. Jean de Reszke's voice. Now, there is no ring or cabal among the critics of this town. None of them write in accordance with policy, other than that of faithfully discharging their duties as reporters. They frequently agree because of that. Sometimes in matters of opinion they disagree. Whether Mr. Jean de Reszke is still in possession of all the notes he used to sing and is able to give them forth with sufficient power and good quality, to sustain his phrases, and to command the dynamics of his voice, are not matters of opinion, but plain facts, which a man must either recognize with his ears or prove himself unfit for the business of chronicling the doings of musicians.

Every reporter of musical matters in this town has recorded that Mr. de Reszke's voice is equal to all the demands of such parts as Lohengrin, Radames, Faust, and Rodrigue in Le Cid. A man who can sing these parts can sing anything. There are no holes in Mr. de Reszke's voice yet, praise heaven. He can and does still sing from C below the clef up to C sharp above it with free and abundant tone. As for his art, that is another matter. It is not just what it used to be; it is better. Mr. Jean de Reszke is still a student of his profession, and will continue to be till he dies. If Mr. Jean de Reszke had come to America this season a broken down tenor, that fact would have been recorded in these columns, in great grief, but in perfectly plain type. The contrary being the case, that is printed with delight and the printer's best ink in the market.

At the third performance of Tristan Jean suffered from the draughts that played across him as he lay on the death couch in the final scene. Bronchitis resulted, and kept him from singing for three weeks. He reappeared as Lohengrin, in full power and beauty of voice. Then he went to Philadelphia, and on his return to New York there was a re-

vival of L'Africaine. He used his *mezza voce* a great deal,
but when it was necessary, he took the high tones with full
voice. When Huguenots was performed some time later,
Jean still showed signs of his illness, but his superb art conquered the handicap. Again he saved himself a little, until
the duet of the last act, and then he was the great master of
old. He sang the high C in the sextet and also in the last
scene. When he chose to use this note, it rang out pure and
without any sign of effort. "Admiral of the High C" a punster
called him.

It was a season of revivals for Jean. He had always felt
that each season would be his last, but this year, he said, he
had a deeper premonition, which his admirers shared. The
public realized that a man who had passed the half-century
mark, and who had been singing during fully half that period
(even if not every year), would not return many more times,
especially since he had ties across the seas. They wanted to
hear their best-beloved as often as possible, and although it
is true that in earlier years the Metropolitan was not crowded
every time he sang, during this particular season the announcement of Jean's appearance in the cast meant difficulty
in securing even standing-room, and for every appearance.

He had not sung the younger Siegfried in New York
since 1897, but when that event took place on March 19 1901
any doubts as to his capacity for resuming so youthful a rôle
were dispelled simultaneously with his entrance upon the
scene. Not that he had become a stripling, or that Siegfried
himself would have worn the mustache his interpreter could
hardly have been expected to part with for a single performance, but there was an incontestable air of youth about him.
He really seemed a stalwart boy. His movements were free.
He had something of a gay blacksmith's air while forging his
sword, and then went off adventuring with a high heart, bantering with a dragon and killing it for fun, and listening to
the birds like a big bird's-nesting urchin. Not the slightest
detail was overlooked in making the scene realistic. In cutting
notches in the reed, he did not even forget to blow away the
chips he cut out. He danced off the stage in the most natural,
spontaneous way. Here as the young Siegfried he showed that
even if he had devoted the greater part of his career to tragic
rôles, he could also be a superb comedian, almost rivaling
his brother. And in the finale of the first act, where the
melody suddenly makes that thrilling change to major, just

before the anvil is split asunder, it seemed as if Jean had reached the climax of his career. Then, in the second act, when he learned that a beautiful lady lay slumbering on a flame-encircled mountain, waiting for him to claim her as his bride, this carefree boy throbbed into passionate manhood. By every gesture, every tone, every facial expression, he showed the development of character, singing the music at first with poetry, caprice, humor, then more thoughtfully and with increasing intensity, until in the last act, his companion (Ternina) taking her part gloriously, the love duo was sung with overwhelming passion. To Jean, S i e g f r i e d seemed one ceaseless flow of beautiful melody, without a single un-vocal phrase, and as such he sang it.

But while Jean's work that entire season was on a magnificently high level of artistry and beauty, Edouard had been ill a large part of the time and his work had suffered accordingly. He had not sung for some weeks before this performance of S i e g f r i e d, and for a few moments even his mighty voice seemed somewhat weakened and uncertain, but that soon passed away, and he sang the music of the Wanderer with the vocal opulence, the sonority and dignity and power, which he alone could command in the rôle. His Hagen seemed even more subtle in its grimness, more significant than it had been.

Soon after this Edouard sang Hans Sachs in German for the first time, and he showed plainly that his study of the rôle in its original language had deepened his understanding of it. He seemed more poetic in the monologue "Wie duftet doch der Flieder," and the scene where Hans notes down Walther's prize song was more delightfully realistic. David Bispham, with whom the de Reszkes greatly enjoyed singing, says of Edouard's Hans Sachs: "But of all the Sachses with whom I ever did sing, Edouard de Reszke was the best, more completely in nobility of voice and of personal appearance realizing the part, to which he brought a greater degree of bonhomie than any other of the numerous artists, even Van Rooy, with whom I have sung in T h e M a s t e r s i n g e r s."

Both the de Reszkes realized how much their study of German had improved their work. Their decision to sing Wagner's operas in his own language was not lightly made. They were men of intellect, who looked beyond the surface of things. They knew that as artists they must either deteriorate or advance, and they realized that the Wagnerian dramas offered opportunities for growth. They had long "travel'd in the realms of gold" represented by Italian and French opera, and had exhausted their last possibility. It may well be that when they discovered the wide expanse which Wagner "ruled as his demesne" it was with a feeling such as Keats experienced upon first reading Chapman's Homer—

> Then felt I like some watcher of the skies
>   When a new planet swims into his ken;
> Or like stout Cortez when with eagle eyes
>   He stared at the Pacific, and all his men
> Look'd at each other with a wild surmise,
>   Silent, upon a peak in Darien.

Having discovered the greatness of Wagner, they were quite ready to pay him homage by studying his works with the most minute care, undaunted by the prophecies that they could not sing the music without danger to their voices. They were sufficiently familiar with the methods of German singers to understand their love of declamation, and knew when to sing and when to declaim. That is why one heard heart-rending melodies where none had been heard before, and why intervals which had appeared extremely difficult seemed transformed into the most natural, melodious mode of expression. "Of course it is no holiday pastime to interpret Wagner," said Edouard. "But the strain on the voice and the physique which it involves has been absurdly exaggerated. No great artistic achievement is possible without fatigue, but with the training and experience that are necessary to make a man or woman an artist, such fatigue is reduced to a minimum and will produce no ill effects." 117 [a]

Concerning the much discussed injurious effects of singing Wagner, Jean expressed himself thus:

> In all the range of operatic music there is nothing which compares in greatness of effect with the works of Wagner. He stands alone—the master whom many have striven to imitate, but who never once permitted himself to borrow an idea from another. Wagner's music stands above considerations of country and period. It is the music not alone of the future, but of the present, and not alone of the present, but of all time. It is universal and all-embracing. It interprets all human emotion, all passion.
>
> It is true that the singing of some Wagner parts involves a physical tax on the singer, but it is true only in

a measure. All depends on the artist. To interpret the
master's music demands the most perfect and severe
training. It demands that the singer shall be as perfect
in his or her art as the limitations imposed by nature will
admit of. That means the artist must have absolute command of his or her voice. Given such conditions, there
need be no fear of injuring the voice or of suffering more
fatigue than should be expected after hours of hard physical and intellectual work, to say nothing of the emotional strain incidental to any artistic effort. At this
moment, for example, I have just returned from singing
the most trying part I know—that of Siegfried. And I
certainly do not feel sufficient fatigue to interfere with
my enjoyment of affairs outside the Metropolitan Opera
House.

But this is a proposition which hardly needs demonstration. If the singing of Wagner produced injurious
physical effects, artists would not rush to their doom
quite so eagerly. And what operatic artist is there who
is not anxious to sing in Wagner opera? [117 a]

Having sung their way into the deeps of Wagner, it was
inevitable that Jean and Edouard should have broadened
their other rôles, and each season showed, instead of sameness
or deterioration, a growth in understanding and artistry which
communicated itself to the audience. What consternation
would have reigned had it been known that the last performance of L o h e n g r i n in the spring season of 1901, given on
March 29, was also to mark Jean de Reszke's last New York
appearance in a complete opera! It was as beautiful a portrayal as ever. After every act the applause rang out vibrant
in spontaneity and in volume, reaching its climax at the end
of the opera. The audience refused to leave, keeping calmly
to their seats, the while the singers were forced to come forward again and again. Finally the curtain went up and the
tenor appeared alone. Then the storm broke in all its fury.
Fourteen times did the devoted ones insist that Jean de
Reszke come forward to receive the expression of their love
and thanks, in the only way possible to a vast audience. He
made a short speech in English and said that he hoped to sing
for them again.

After a few performances in Boston, Pittsburgh, and Chicago, with a final appearance as Lohengrin in Chicago on

April 7, the company returned to New York for a farewell appearance in scenes from various operas. The program included not only all the leading operatic stars of the season, but also an act by Sarah Bernhardt and M. Coquelin. The audience was as brilliant a gathering as had ever assembled at the Metropolitan even in the height of the subscription season, and it was a larger one than had ever been packed into the immense auditorium. At two dollars a head at least two thousand people squeezed into the standing space between the orchestra seats and the wall, and the majority of them were women. Soon they began to faint; they stood in the heated atmosphere until they fell and had to be carried out by the attendants. The management, familiar with the excitement and crush of a season's final appearance, had supplied each attendant with ammonia; before the evening was over nearly six bottles had been used. The second act of T r i s t a n proved the most trying time of all. The doors had to be closed during that number, and by the time it was over sixteen women had fainted, and one of them was completely prostrated and had to be taken home. An officer of the company said that it was a record-breaking night for "faints." (The ladies caused the management a good deal of trouble during the heyday of Jean's career. On the last night of another season a number of them crept under the orchestra rails at the close of the opera, leaned against the stage, and when their idol came near the footlights they touched his knees and his feet in mute adoration, as devotees in the Middle Ages worshiped the sanctified leaders of the Church. The officials of the Opera House were compelled to order the lights to be turned out, to stop this astounding demonstration.)

This second act of T r i s t a n was sung by the de Reszkes, Nordica, and Schumann-Heink. At its close the de Reszkes received a frantic ovation, and after the singers had bowed their last good-bys, many women, and a large number of men too, secured permission to go behind the scenes to bid Jean adieu. The excitement of the crowd continued for some time after the house had been darkened, for people had difficulty in finding their carriages, which stretched in a double line up Broadway from Thirty-seventh Street to Forty-second and one block each way along every intervening cross street from Broadway. It may be remarked in passing that that evening closed an operatic year in which the Metropolitan paid a dividend of 150 per cent.[118]

DURING THE LATE spring and summer of 1901 there was much conjecture as to whether there would be any opera at all in New York the following season, and the prospect seemed to depend on the Polish tenor. In London there was no uncertainty, for Jean's decision not to sing there had been definitely announced. But London journalists were now annoyed by stories published in America as to the cause of that decision. Respect for the dead Queen Victoria, dissatisfaction with his salary, bitterness towards a public that had declared him finished when he happened to have a cold, were among the reasons assigned, to which was added the solemn opinion that the strenuous Wagner work had finally taken its toll.

In the meantime Jean was quietly resting, preparatory to his coming season at the Paris Opera. His health and his voice were in such good condition that he was able to appear even earlier than had been expected. Paris had not forgotten that evening when Jean de Reszke had eclipsed the great Patti in the *reprise* of R o m e o. It remembered his first appearance in H é r o d i a d e and L e C i d. It remembered how he had given significance to even an inferior opera like L a D a m e d e M o n t s o r e a u, and how he had restored L e P r o p h è t e to the place of honor from which it had fallen because of poor interpreters. Paris had watched with jealous interest Jean's progress through the startling variety of his rôles, reading in amazement that he sang in one week in T r i s t a n, M a n o n, and A ï d a, and in another S i e g f r i e d, L'A f r i c a i n e, and W e r t h e r, each in its original language. The French had envied English and American audiences their privilege of hearing him every year, of experiencing the wonder of his Wagner impersonations. But France had been proud, too, of how much Jean had done, in those years before he became a Wagner enthusiast, to popularize the use of the French language in French operas given abroad, and for that service it made him, in 1901, Chevalier of the Légion d'Honneur.

Paris had no fears that the great tenor would come back to it with voice or dramatic power diminished. It was confident, and it was satisfied. Jean created Siegfried in French; the first artist, it is said, to sing any Wagner rôle in that language. He had also been requested to sing Tristan in French in Paris, and agreed to do so, but on condition that he might use a new text made under his own supervision. When he was asked whether the translation made by Catulle Mendes, who knew both French and German thoroughly, was not a very good one, he said: "Listen to this," and then sang "Tristan's Ehre, höchste Treu" in German, followed by "La gloire de Tristan," showing how the notes that properly belong to "Ehre" fell on the last syllable of "Tristan." "What do you think of that?" he asked. "No, I'll not sing such stuff. I must make a literal translation note for note, and then a poet may put it into lines."

But Paris never heard Jean's Tristan, and this French opera lovers regretted keenly, for they had heard so much of the wonders of his portrayal. They were consoled, however, by his Siegfried. They noticed no signs of deterioration in this strong, exuberant young Siegfried. They felt, on the contrary, that he sang with even more energy and freedom than formerly. They realized, too, that to carry the double weight—pictorial and vocal—of this exacting rôle, a singer had to be in full possession of all the resources of his art. Before the end of the season Jean had appeared in most of the rôles in his repertoire. He sang Siegfried some fifteen or sixteen times, and after the Paris season sang in Monte Carlo for a month. All who heard him must have wondered whence came the stories of de Reszke's decline.

That spring there were rumors that he was to return to Covent Garden. Queen Alexandra, it was said, had requested him to come, and since there was to be a real "gala," in connection with the coronation ceremonies, it was hoped that he would participate. He decided against the Covent Garden appearances, and of course he could not appear at a State representation without taking part in the regular season. It is not likely, however, after all the mingling with royalty which had fallen to Jean's lot, that this represented a very poignant deprivation, just as it had never caused him any pangs to decline to sing at a Command performance, although, for the sake of appearing before a Queen and getting a souvenir, most other singers would have sung had they been as hoarse as ravens. In the same way, Jean had never taken notice, while singing, of the fashionable occupants of certain boxes. Lesser singers might try to get a nod of recognition from some exalted person, but Jean was always, in the first place, too much engrossed in his part, and in the second place, too much the *grand seigneur,* to condescend to such maneuvering. A protégée of his, who made her début as Juliette at the Paris

Opera with Jean as Romeo, delighted in defying his counsel in this respect. Observing that she played directly to a be-whiskered gentleman in a stage box, he chided: "My dear child, you must observe no one; you must be impersonal. Ig-nore that stout person who seems so much interested in you." "Yes," came the reply, "but one does not always make one's début before a King. That is King Oscar of Sweden, and I wish very much to please him."

In the autumn of 1902 the Paris Opera announced a *reprise* of Gluck's O r p h e u s for Jean, but this was never given. He did, however, sing one entirely new part. It was said that he had signed a contract for that season on the con-dition that he was to appear as Canio in Leoncavallo's P a-g l i a c c i, and that the management had objected to the work as not quite worthy of the Paris Opera, but had finally agreed to take Jean on his own terms. Whatever lay behind that de-cision, the opera was given, but although the pain, humilia-tion, and rage of Canio were portrayed with intensity and truth, and though the impersonation was called a triumph by some, the general feeling was that the rôle was unworthy of the great de Reszke, and he did not sing it again. His own instincts had been against it from the start, but he yielded to the pleas of his wife, who was always ambitious for him and urged him to ever new conquests.

Some months later distressing messages came. Even Mr. Henderson reported: "Jean de Reszke is failing rapidly. His voice, as a voice, is quite as good as it ever was, but his breathing is so poor that he can no longer phrase anything as he used to." Reyer's S i g u r d was in rehearsal, with Jean in the title rôle. He fell ill with the ever-recurring bronchitis. He went to Poland for a rest but returned too soon, and after several re-hearsals became ill once more. There was grave anxiety on all sides. A certain prominent tenor had made it a part of his terms that he would not sing if Jean were in the company, and if Jean could not appear the directors had to close a contract with the other singer. Jean learned of this predicament, and the decision to retire quickly followed. During his entire career he had never been guilty of jealousy and intrigue, and he would not now be party to any situation which could pos-sibly implicate him in anything smacking of that atmosphere. He had never stooped to conquer. He had always taken his profession *en grand seigneur,* and he would leave it in the same manner. He therefore simply announced that he would

sing no more. He did not, as most other singers do, return
again and again in "farewell" performances, until it becomes
necessary for their friends to apologize for their persistence.
There is nobody who heard Jean de Reszke after his voice was
"gone," for he never "lost" it.

He was now prevailed upon to become "Artistic Director"
of the Paris Opera, but it was impossible for him to accomplish anything, because, he said, "il y avait toujours la mait-
resse de quelqu'un à se faire entendre," and he soon resigned.

Edouard had, in the meantime, gone back to New York.
Whether it was solely owing to the fact that he relaxed his
efforts somewhat in the absence of his more studious brother,
it is difficult to say, but his work was plainly not of its former
quality. The big voice was still there, the style was good, but
the breathing was labored. At the opening performance of
T r i s t a n he delivered himself of Marke's reproaches in a
rasping voice and with uncomfortable phrasing. His Marcel
was, happily, as good as ever, and the famous Piff-paff song
brought him the wonted applause. His Hans Sachs was even
better than it had been; more significant in detail, more consistent and effective in general characterization. But the following season unfortunately showed growing weakness. In
appearance and action there was little to criticize, but the voice
was not the voice of old, and the style showed many evidences
of carelessness. The Chicago season of 1903 yielded comments
that made strange reading for those accustomed to enjoy
Edouard's singing a second time as they read the criticism of
an opera they had heard the night before. Of T r i s t a n it
was lamented: "The second act would have surpassed the first
but for the very bad singing of Edouard de Reszke as König
Marke. All that can be said for Mr. de Reszke is that he looked
the part. His phrasing was fragmentary, his intonation uncertain, his German often not to be understood." His Mephistopheles was full of the same old good-natured devilry,
although in that too the breathing was faulty when he combined singing with action. But while there was general dissatisfaction with his falling-off in artistry, his Leporello was
still a delight, even if, like his Mephisto, it may have been lacking in craftiness and malice.

The next season a concert tour of the Metropolitan Orchestra, with Edouard and Madame Nordica as soloists, was
undertaken by one John S. Duss, but it was far from success-

ful. Edouard enjoyed concert singing, but it allowed him a dangerous laxity. There were late dinners and late parties, and his indulgence of course showed in his performance. He seemed less concerned about his work, however, than about enjoying life. One day he called on an old friend in a Detroit conservatoire of music. He told his friend the director that he would like to hear some of the pupils play and sing. His sincerity and easy manner banished the nervousness of the youngsters, who forthwith gave an informal *musicale*. The big basso shook each one by the hand and spoke a few words of appreciation in his broken English, then announced that he would like to take his turn, and the little group had the thrill of hearing some of Edouard de Reszke's greatest arias. Having finished them, he swept his accompanist off the piano stool, sat down himself and began to play "Hello, Mah Baby," singing a bar of the ragtime song here and there, then getting up and demonstrating his agility in cake-walking. If any of the frequently announced plans for Edouard's appearance in vaudeville had materialized he would probably have had a thoroughly good time, but happily some restraining influence prevented this. He himself had a predilection for the English music hall. While Jean was in town he could instill into Edouard a proper fear of the real or imaginary dangers of rheumatism and lumbago lurking in the Variety Halls of London, but when he had left the city things were different. As Jean's train slowly pulled out of Charing Cross station one day Edouard, solemnly removing his hat, remarked that now he proposed to go to the Alhambra, and while his brother laughingly shook his fist at him, he hailed a cab and drove straight off to secure a box. What he saw pleased him so much that on the following evening he went to the Empire. The result of these excursions was seen when he sang Basilio the next night. With another huge member of the company as partner he attempted to imitate the gyrations of the *corps de ballet* he had seen, and to dance a two-step. The house roared and so did all the artists on the stage, as these two performed their elephantine dance.

A second concert tour was arranged for Edouard, but it was broken off, resulting in what was probably the only lawsuit involving either of the de Reszkes. Edouard sued Duss, successfully, to recover $20,000 for alleged breach of contract. Thus his last appearance in a complete opera in New York was as Mephistopheles on March 31 1903 and he sang in

America for the last time in a "mixed bill" at the Metropolitan on April 28 following, again in F a u s t.

When he returned to Europe he joined Jean in Paris. The brothers were never completely happy when apart from each other. For years they had been constant companions both in work and in such recreation as their arduous duties permitted. At the beginning of Jean's career as a tenor, Edouard, who had been singing with much success for some years, received a most attractive offer of a season in South America, but the younger brother did not hesitate to decline it when he found that Jean needed him. Throughout their careers they had helped each other, going over all the details of a rôle together. They were not deeply religious men, but all their lives they wore medals of religious significance, and whenever one of them went on to the stage, the other made the sign of the cross for him. Whenever Jean came back into the wings, there stood Edouard with a cloak to put over his shoulders so that the beloved brother might not take cold. Edouard had no need to take such precautions. "Il est fort, ce grand petit garçon," said Jean. But when, as Hagen, Edouard was supposed to use some of his strength to harm his brother, he seemed indeed "the least o' the cut-throats." He could never make his eyes look fierce, although otherwise he presented a sinister figure; neither could he bear to strike sufficiently hard to hurt Jean, let alone kill him. A friend suggested that it would be better if Jean turned more towards the audience, so that they might not see this mild stroke which would hardly have pierced his tunic. "That is just it," he replied. "I say, 'Strike, Edouard, strike hard,' but he doesn't want to, and he barely touches me."

In New York the brothers used to experiment in the Metropolitan with different kinds of voice production, one listening from the gallery to the other on the stage, and each note would be separately criticized until the ideal was attained. Sometimes Jean would sing a whole part through, or a whole act, with various methods of production, until he was satisfied that he had found the best. After each performance they criticized each other honestly, painstakingly. Jean would say (or Edouard, perhaps, but very infrequently): "You sang like a pig tonight." Or, after a performance of L e C i d, Jean might ask: "Well, how was it?" and Edouard would reply: "You sang very well, but you can't go calling a man a goose," and then Jean would try to make his "O roi, O roi, O roi" sound less like "O oie, O oie, O oie." Sometimes they went over words, action, tone, make-up, until three or four o'clock in the morning. Edouard did not always stay up quite so long as his brother, being contented with the reflection that the next day would do just as well. Not so with Jean: he *could* not leave off until he had mastered whatever was troubling him. One morning at three o'clock, Edouard woke their secretary. "Listen," he said. From the living-room came the sound of Jean's voice, singing. They stole to the door, and Edouard called out, half jokingly: "Bravo, Jean!" "Oh, Edouard," cried Jean, "listen to this phrase now. It goes perfectly well this way and it gave me a lot of trouble last night. It wouldn't let me sleep." He had sung in H u g u e n o t s the previous evening, and had been warmly applauded, but everything had not gone to his satisfaction, and he could not rest until he had corrected what had not pleased his own sense of the truly artistic. There was nothing to do but get out of bed and work on the troublesome phrase. He had infinite patience in studying and working out details. One afternoon a friend was sitting in the room while Jean was going over a certain phrase in O t e l l o again and again, the phrase "E stanca, e muta, e bella," in the last scene. Curious as to why this great artist spent half an hour repeating nine syllables, he asked Jean what he was working for. "Well," came the answer, "I am standing here, gazing at the strangled Desdemona. She is very near me; that is, her body. But the soul of her is already far away. When I sing, 'So pale, so still, so beautiful,' I want to convey not only the sense of paleness and stillness and beauty, but the feeling that soon all that will be far away too. I am trying to convey the sense of distance, through my tone."

A little girl once had an exciting afternoon watching Jean practice. A guest in the same Long Island home, she stole behind him as he boarded a yacht for some quiet practice, imploring him to let her read in a corner of the yacht, as it was very hot on the porch. He helped the child up, but paid no attention to her, sitting with his back towards her, while he ate his lunch. In a little while he held his hand over his shoulder, extending a chicken wing, which she ran over to get. Soon came a piece of huckleberry pie, handed over as though he were feeding scraps to a pup, all in dead silence. Poor Dorothy's eyes almost popped out as she saw his diaphragm swell until it looked like a huge watermelon, for she thought he must surely explode. He began to sing Romeo, addressing his songs to the thirteen-year-old girl, any audience being better than none. Dorothy became almost hysterical at having the famous man on his knees before her, gesticulating and imploring. He saw her blushing and trembling and, perhaps deciding that this was too much for a sentimental youngster, suddenly switched to a tragic rôle calling for rather fierce gestures and facial expressions. The child was thoroughly frightened. Her lips puckered up and she began to sob. Immediately Jean stepped back, all penitence. "Ah, child," he said, "if I could only find a heroine with such facial expression! And I suppose you will never sing a note."

Sometimes Victorian inhibitions interfered with artistic expressiveness. The first time Emma Albani was to sing Isolde with Jean, he asked Amherst Webber to work out some of the details with her. "After drinking the love potion," Mr. Webber reminded her, "it is Isolde who speaks first, and as you say 'Tristan' you take a step forward, towards Tristan."

"Oh, but I couldn't!" exclaimed Madame Albani in dismay. "I *couldn't* take the first step. Why, that would be contrary to all my principles and training."

Jean worked out practically every detail of his rôles in private, leaving as little as possible to regular stage rehearsals, because after the season had opened and he was singing two or three times a week, he could not, since he tried to avoid rehearsals on the day of a performance, have as many of them as he would have liked. The first time he was to sing Tristan to Lilli Lehmann's Isolde, he had been suffering from a bad cold, and the doctor said that he would be unable to sing unless he kept to his room until the night of the performance. On the day before the performance, Madame Lehmann called on him at his hotel, bent on having a rehearsal. Refusing all assistance, she pushed sofas and chairs about until she had made the room look as much as possible like her state-room in König Marke's yacht. While this was going on, Marie Brema, who was to sing Brangaene, appeared. She had just arrived from London, and when she heard at the pier that there was to be a *Verständigungsprobe* in Jean's room, she deserted her luggage rather than miss anything in the nature of a rehearsal. Soon the Kurwenal of the evening arrived, and as König Marke was already present in the person of Edouard, there was an impromptu rehearsal lacking only orchestra and scenery. The rest sang out in full voice and went through the complete stage action, but Jean merely indicated his part, using his voice very sparingly.

Whether at rehearsals or actual performances, Jean never seemed to be making heroic efforts. It was always plain that he sang with much emotion, but the gestures were perfectly natural and the voice was produced as freely and easily as ordinary speech. Indeed, close at hand the singing voice sounded almost smaller than his speaking voice, which was very deep and hardly seemed to belong to a tenor. But as with other arts, this appearance of creating something beautiful and profound without effort was very deceiving. They did not know, those men and women who swallowed hard or quietly wept whilst they listened to the flood of silvery music which this man poured into the auditorium where they sat, they did not know at what cost not only of labor but of suffering he was able to reveal to them the innermost meaning of the poetry and the music he sang. They did not realize how much more than mere technique was required to recreate in their hearts what the singer felt had been in the heart of the poet and composer who made the opera. Jean de Reszke knew that if a new rôle did not move him to tears upon reading it he could never succeed with it. He knew that unless his own heart had been torn by it he could not carry his listeners out of themselves. When he was learning Tristan he felt the music so deeply at times that he could scarcely proceed with the singing. But the pain had to be absorbed, the very beauty had to be analyzed; just as a poet does not write while the fullness of powerful emotion is still upon him, but waits until it has penetrated heart and brain, until, in Wordsworth's sense, he can recollect it in tranquillity, and then, free from its hampering excitement, he can create with greater truth a poem which conveys the force of the experience which impinged on his sensibilities.

By the time Jean sang a rôle on the stage he had so completely mastered its emotional effect on himself and he had so thoroughly and skillfully worked out the outward signs by which he could produce in the audience the emotions he himself had felt—having, as it were, learned the emotion by heart —that he could go through it *à froid,* devoting his entire attention to his singing. When a man told him that he had been moved to tears by Caruso's singing, and explained that he believed the reason lay in the fact that Caruso himself had been moved to tears, Jean replied: "How can you say that! A singer must play on his audience as though it were a violin, but he must keep himself calm." Again he expressed his views on this matter as follows: [119]

> It is true that in order to do my rôle justice I must live it, I must get into the skin of it. But if, when I am playing before an audience, I were actually to experience every emotion that I express and to undergo every sensation that I portray, how do you suppose I should be in a fit condition to sing? It would simply be impossible. The physical and the psychological would so clash as to injure if not destroy each other. My remedy is a preventive one. I mold my action, I study and prepare my movements and gestures, I let myself go without reserve; in a word, I expend my real energy—all at rehearsal! When the performance takes place I have merely to simulate as an actor the delineation that I have accustomed myself to shape in detail. I devote my thoughts exclusively to my singing, which, I need not assure you, demands my entire attention.

Even in a rôle as absorbing as Tristan, Jean was usually so at ease that he could, while singing and listening to impassioned music, observe another singer's method. He said he learned a great deal about taking high notes from watching the operations of Lilli Lehmann's uvula while they were singing duets. He remembered only one occasion when he was not consciously directing himself, and that was while he was singing Tristan to Ternina's magnificent Isolde. He was completely carried away, when suddenly he saw the conductor watching him, trying to find out what the singer wanted him to do.

Whether or not Jean de Reszke was conscious of being an exponent of the Aristotelian theory of tragedy, he certainly did body forth its principles: although Aristotle did not acknowledge such a thing as a creative imagination and held that music was the most "imitative" of the arts, and de Reszke's supremacy derived from creating, by means of music and through his vivid sympathy and his extraordinary mental and physical plasticity, an illusion of not merely representing but *being* the character he was personating. Mounet-Sully, the great French tragedian, said, even long before Jean assumed Wagnerian rôles, that if he lost his voice he could still become one of the greatest actors in the world.

Most of the characters he portrayed had been cast in the heroic mold. They were not perfect, but their slight imperfections only enhanced their natural grandeur, and de Reszke, who had "that within which passeth show," got, as he said he tried to, into their very skin, and gave utterance, through them, to his and their most inward feelings. He had no need to assume conventional attitudes to express feeling, or to exaggerate the spectacle of which he was a part; he employed none of those artificial arts which make the actor and not the character seem most important. His own inherent dignity, the nobility and large humanity of his own character, gave the stamp of reality to the fiction of the opera, and created that impression of rich harmony, of wholeness, which enabled his listeners to identify themselves with the experiences they witnessed, and purge themselves of the feelings of pity and fear aroused through the contemplation of those emotions in another. Thus he produced that certain kind of *katharsis* which Aristotle held to be the function of tragedy.

Another element which tended to lift the spectator out of himself was the fact that Jean sang most poignantly of human love. The men and women who heard him could feel themselves at one with him in that, and through him with all humanity. Not that love in itself is a fit subject for tragedy, but when it constitutes a tragic *motif*, it is properly combined with other conditions which heighten its dramatic interest and give it universality. When Jean de Reszke sang, this emotion seemed an exhalation of his very soul, for he himself was

> Dowered with the hate of hate, the scorn of scorn,
> The love of love.

He was himself a being who called forth the exclamation: "What a piece of work is a man!" and it was a part of his greatness to lend his own personal grandeur, along with the amplitude and generosity of his style, to fictional situations and characters; and to sustain the illusion in beauty and depth and truth, not only throughout an evening's performance, but throughout a career. Nor did he ever grow careless. He never reached the point where he seemed in a hurry to get through his part, could never have been content with merely an occasional flash of tremendous power, as some actors seem to be when they have reached the pinnacle of success. He was born to the graces of life, and he observed them in great things and in small. Violence, which is easy to portray, was always absent. There was always an ease about Jean, none of that restlessness which is conveyed through hasty, jerky bodily motions. His performance always conveyed to the audience the unaffected nobility of his character. How many a Faust has begun to talk of love to Marguerite with his hat on: Jean removed his as though the gesture itself were a part of his devotion. Every move he made had its significance, and every detail of his make-up and costumes was planned to enhance the effect of the whole portrayal. Again, of course, he had some natural aids. He had beautiful hands, and by having his sleeves fitted very tight, with lace coming over the hands, he made them look even more slender and graceful. He had shapely legs and small feet, and he made sure that they would show to the best advantage. The skin of his face was rather porous, and this enabled him to work out an infinite variety of effects. The assortment of lotions and other make-up materials which he kept on hand made his dressing-room look more like a prima donna's than a man's.

Sometimes Jean's make-up was criticized. For instance, his Lohengrin beard was objected to, because it made his face seem less strong. His answer was that Lohengrin was not a lover like Tristan, a man with a man's passion. He was a half-divine being whose love was celestial. Elsa was not the first maiden in peril whom he had rescued, that being his mission in the world. He felt that his large mouth, with the deep lines on each side of it, would destroy any illusion of a supernatural being; therefore he not only wore a beard to cover it, but he laid the beard over gold-leaf, in order to give a luminous radiance to his face, letting his expressive eyes picture his emotions. (Similarly, in the banishment scene in Romeo he did not gesticulate, but stood motionless, and let his face tell the story of his despair.) He was perhaps the only Lohengrin who did really create an atmosphere of other-worldliness.

He enjoyed talking about these things to people who listened sympathetically and understood. When he found such a listener he willingly showed his own thoughts about his work. At a jolly dinner table, while other guests were busy with small talk, he discussed his art with his companion. He would explain, in answer to the latter's suggestion that Calvé's terrified little cries as he towered over her sounded very real: "I do not want to kill her, but I lose my head. I think I feel the opera more than an Italian tenor I once saw, who whetted his knife in preparation for the murder. You see, Don Jose *loves* Carmen." Or if one mentioned that the saddest moment in Götterdämmerung was that when Jean shook his head with a tragic, lost expression in his eyes, struggling hopelessly to remember Brünnhilde, he would remark philosophically: "That is the real death of Siegfried. After that, the death of his body means nothing. But one must be very sensitive and sympathetic to see those touches. The general public understands nothing of them. For instance, most people seem to think that Siegfried is nothing but a happy, boisterous youth, bubbling over with life. My reading of Wagner tells me that he is sad. He has his prankish impulses, but they don't last. He has moments of the exuberant joy perfectly natural to a healthy youngster, but after these outbursts he relapses into pondering about his father, and especially about his mother, and then he becomes wistful."

"What joy it must be to receive such ovations," some one said to him one day, and he replied: "After a great triumph one does not feel happy. One is sad. It is past, finished. The moment may never return. One may never sing that part again." When Jean was absorbed in a discussion of this kind he was entirely oblivious of the rest of the gathering. If his neighbor at dinner happened to look away momentarily he would recall her by gently laying his hand on her arm and saying "Ecoutez, Madame," and would continue with details about his work. But, the spell broken, he suddenly became the wit and star entertainer. Once some one broke in upon such a serious conversation with the question: "Who do you think is the most popular artist in New York, M. de Reszke?" and like a flash came the answer: "Pas de Reszke"; for Paderewski was present. Another time he was showing how the fashionable Englishwoman applauded, and he pretended to be holding in his hands opera-glasses, lorgnette, bouquet, handkerchief and other sundries, the lady's applause becoming a noiseless tapping together of the backs of her hands.

Or he might imitate his fellow artists coming into his dressing-room to offer congratulations. First came the French tenor, polite, reserved, saying in a slightly patronizing way: "Vraiment, mon cher, vous avez chanté très bien ce soir, très bien, je vous assure!"

The German baritone, in a double-breasted frockcoat and a most polite attitude, came next: "Erlauben Sie mir, Herr de Reszke, Ihnen meine grosse Hochachtung auszu-

drücken für den wirklich ausgezeichneten Genuss den Sie uns
heute Abend bereitet haben."

The Italian baritone followed, rushing in impulsively,
kissing Jean on both cheeks, and exclaiming, as the prelude
to a flood of Italian: "Caro mio, carissimo!"

"Then came the real climax of the scene. Enter the electrician who, thrusting a 'horny hand of toil' into that of de
Reszke, would exclaim in real 'Yankee' accents: 'Jean, you
done fine!' " [120]

Once a fellow guest protested that it was hardly fair for
Jean to make fun of these sincere expressions of appreciation,
adding that she herself could not sleep after hearing him.
"Webber can't sleep either," replied Jean with a wink. "My
valet goes to call him and he says: 'Let me sleep. I am broken
with emotion.' That touches my valet, and he lets him sleep."

But on the day of a performance there was none of this
fooling. There were, on the contrary, long hours of agony.
For notwithstanding Jean's own certainty that his interpretation of a rôle was correct and the assurance that the public
and the critics agreed, and in spite of the fact that he worked
out every detail of his part so carefully, he was a very miserable man the day he sang. He never allowed any one to see
him, and he preferred to be left to his thoughts even the day
before, so that he might shake off entirely the nature of the
last character he had portrayed. As soon as he had laid aside
the armor of Lohengrin he became preoccupied with the
doublet of Romeo. The ways and manners of the one had to
be exchanged completely for those of the other, from a gesture
to the slightest inflection of the voice. So absolutely did Jean
strive to become the character he was representing that he had
special underwear made for each costume, in the style of
undergarment the prototype of that character would have
worn.

During this process of "getting into the skin," as he put
it, of a different rôle, Jean paced the floor, his hands clenched,
his face drawn, exclaiming from time to time that the evening
would be a fiasco. His secretary, Edouard, Webber, all would
suffer with him, but were powerless to help him. Then at five-
thirty, all nervousness gone, he went to breathe the atmosphere of the theater, but, almost without exception, while he
was dressing the panicky state would return for about ten
minutes, and again he walked restlessly up and down, trying
his voice in every possible way.

Usually, however, he was quite calm from the moment he stepped on the stage. Then it made no difference if Lohengrin's swan suddenly lost its long white feathery neck and a long black pole came into view instead; or if, as once in Chicago, a madman jumped on the stage and the progress of a Montague's wooing of a Capulet was impeded by more than parental objections. On this occasion, as Romeo stood under Juliette's window and began to sing "Oh Night, spread thy pinions about me, and hide me now," the conductor stopped the orchestra almost in the middle of a note. Jean turned, to see, standing at the left of the prompter's hood, a slender, pale-faced young man, garbed not at all like a Veronese of centuries ago. He had clambered upon the stage, tossed his overcoat and hat before him, strode across the footlights and addressed the audience. "People say I'm crazy," he shouted. "Well, why don't they do something about it?" Romeo, who might well have usurped part of Juliette's lines and asked,

What man art thou that thus bescreen'd in night
So stumblest on my counsel?

chose instead to anticipate the duel scene. His right hand grasped his sword and the bright blade gleamed. He did not know just what the trouble was, but he felt that a bomb explosion or a shot from a lunatic were possibilities. He had a sword at his side, and was prepared to use it. The maniac insisted on delivering his speech to the audience. The curtain was dropped, and stage hands removed him. The curtain rose again, and there stood Jean de Reszke as though nothing had happened. A round of applause rewarded his cool-headedness and nerve, and the scion of the house of Montague again began to serenade the daughter of Capulet, as though no interruption had occurred.

When Jean actually was nervous during a performance, his fears were not about forgetting music or words or points of action. A sudden dread sometimes struck him that he might be troubled with phlegm, which would interfere with perfect singing, and this was an agonizing thought. One evening when his Tristan seemed even more wonderful than usual, Amherst Webber, who was of course accustomed to the dazzling effect of Jean's every performance, hurried behind the scenes after the second act to congratulate him. The audience was applauding tumultuously, but there stood the singer with a half terrified look on his face. Before Webber could utter a word Jean said, holding out his handkerchief: "Voilà ce que je crache" (See what I coughed up).

Concerning this anxiety of Jean's, Emma Eames writes in her memoirs: "Jean de Reszke was one of the most apprehensive singers imaginable, and wore an expression of terror in his eyes during the whole performance. He always had with him a laryngoscope and frequently examined his throat and larynx." Then she goes on to say that Jean made it the fashion for singers to be treated by a certain throat specialist even if there was nothing the matter with them, and adds that he went to this doctor before every performance and that he always smelled of iodoform and ether throughout the evening. Occasionally Jean's nervousness on the day of the performance did result in actual illness, and then some other tenor would in turn become half ill with apprehension about filling his place. Sometimes the substitute received the call so late that he had to get into his costume in a cab going from his hotel to the opera house. It was Edouard, however, who suffered most because of Jean's great nervousness. But if Edouard had to make sacrifices occasionally because of Jean's dependence on him, if he sometimes had to neglect the preparation of his own rôle in order to calm Jean on the day of a performance, surely the example of his brother's industry and the inspiration of his artistry more than repaid him for "sacrifices" that Edouard himself did not consider such at all. His nature made the preparation of a rôle a less exhausting labor. Not that Edouard was always entirely at ease about his work. He was frequently extremely nervous, but a smoke always calmed him. He was a great smoker, and he preferred cigarettes to cigars, whereas Jean preferred cigars.

The story of how the "De Reszke" cigarette originated illustrates at once the devotion of Jean's admirers and the devotion of Jean to Edouard. One fine day Jean found that smoking, one of his few pleasures, was interfering with his singing. He decided to give up cigars, and experimented with every kind of cigarette available, but they all produced the same effect. Word of this situation reached Mr. Jacob Millhoff, a Russian, who had settled in London as a cigarette manufacturer, and had long admired the art of his fellow Slav. He now set about blending a tobacco which the great tenor might smoke without danger to his voice. He finally succeeded, and out of gratitude Jean allowed Mr. Millhoff to call the new cigarette by his name—out of gratitude, and also, according to his secretary, because his beloved brother was so very fond of cigarettes.

But the stories of Jean's generosity must not be allowed to overshadow those of his brother's. Although Edouard sometimes complained a little wistfully that composers and the public were inclined to neglect bassos, and lamented that "all the big fees go to the prima donnas and tenors, while a basso has to worry along on the pay of a chorus girl," and though he had a larger family to support, he also was extremely liberal. Once Jean broke his rule not to sing anywhere but in opera, and gave a concert on behalf of a charitable institution in Paris. The president handed him an ivory egg filled with gold coins. Jean handed the money back with the remark: "I eat only the white of an egg. Please give the yolk to the poor." Edouard could make just as pretty a gesture. One day when he was singing at a private house in London he noticed how eagerly, almost hungrily, a careworn, shabbily dressed clergyman was taking in every note. Inquiry revealed that he was a very poorly paid, overworked vicar in a town about forty miles from London, and was such a passionate lover of music that he had walked the whole distance in order to hear the famous singer. Some time later a concert arranged by sympathetic parishioners was to be given for the benefit of the vicar. A few hours before it began the latter received a letter from Edouard, saying: "I had intended running down to your little concert tonight. I intended singing a few notes. However, as I cannot sing you these notes, may I send them instead?" One hundred pounds in banknotes fell from the letter.

The affection between the two brothers was never tinged with the slightest jealousy or unpleasantness throughout the long years of their close association. Their love for each other was so well known that a legend grew up to the effect that Jean had changed his voice from baritone to tenor because he loved his brother too well to compete with him. When, at the close of his career, Jean's decision to retire became known, some said it was owing to his desire to give his brother a better chance. Jean refused to sing in certain operas unless Edouard also appeared in them, and when Jean was in the company his brother had the first chance at all the bass rôles in his repertoire. One of the other bassos objected to being "sent around the country like a trunk" because Edouard de Reszke was singing all his rôles in New York.

Edouard, of course, thought Jean the greatest artist in

the world, and it made him furious when anybody criticized Jean adversely. "How dare they write anything bad about an artist like my brother!" he would exclaim in indignation. And if he himself had not sung as well as usual and the morning newspaper reported that fact, he worried whether Jean would read it. "I do hope Jean won't know about it," he said. Still, this respect for Jean's opinion, this pride in Jean's art, did not blind Edouard to the qualities of others. One night he went to hear Caruso in London, in the early days of the Italian tenor's fame. Edouard's companion, anxious for an opinion but mindful of the fact that he was with the brother of the world's most famous tenor, asked timidly: "Well, what do you think of it?" Edouard responded without hesitation: "It's the greatest voice that God ever gave to man!" He called on Caruso in his dressing-room to tell him of his delight. Not content with that, he sent him the following letter as soon as he reached his hotel:[121]

> DEAR CARUSO:
>
> I am so sorry I could not manage to come and bid you good-by before leaving London, and tell you again *viva voce* all the pleasure I had from hearing you sing. I never heard a more beautiful voice.... You sang like a god. You are an actor and a sincere artist, and above all, you are modest and without exaggerations. You were able to draw from my eyes many tears. I was very much touched, and this happens to me very very seldom. You have heart, feeling, poetry and truth, and with these qualities you will be the master of the world.
>
> Please do accept these few words from an old artist who admires you not only as an artist but as a very dear man. May God keep you in good health for many years!
>
> Au revoir, until next year.
>
> Your friend and colleague
>
> EDOUARD DE RESZKE

Caruso, according to his wife, had this letter framed, and counted it his most precious possession. He had been deeply impressed when, on a previous occasion, both Jean and Edouard had visited him in his dressing-room at Covent Garden, and Jean had said to Edouard: "This boy will one day be my successor." Caruso shook his head and replied: "If I can only do half as well!"

Edouard's generous attitude was not confined to tenors. The same man who had half feared to ask his opinion of Caruso went with him one night to hear Chaliapin. Here was a still more delicate situation. Obviously one wanted to discuss the performance, but could one suggest the greatness of the artist to another bass? He waited carefully for what he thought the opportune moment, and then asked in a non-committal tone: "Well, what do you think of it?" "Ha!" said Edouard enthusiastically, throwing back his head, "he's the greatest actor the stage can boast!"

The jealousies that are usually rife in an opera company could hardly have touched the de Reszkes in the ordinary way. Jealousy, after all, assumes a certain parity, which, strictly speaking, cannot be said to have existed between them and their fellow artists, great as some of them were. Contemporary artists speak of them in the most generous way, both as to their art and their attitude toward other singers. In the book *Lillian Nordica's Hints to Singers* that artist mentions the petulant response of another singer to the suggestion that some of her notes could be improved, and comments: "But if I should happen to ask of Mr. Jean de Reszke, 'Why do you take a certain note in this way?' he would at once talk the matter over and enlighten me."

Lilli Lehmann wrote of Jean and Edouard: [122] "One can be proud and glad at the same time to work with such artists. It gives me especial pleasure to indicate to the world, in this place, all the good and beautiful which they give us." Of Jean she also wrote:

> He takes account of every word, every trait of the character which he presents; he is always careful to step into the background as soon as another becomes more important. Hence the lack of great, overflowing passion. The effects of his noble singing consequently remain unbroken, effects which can be attained solely, and alone, of perfect beauty. Every artist ought to reflect on this, for what is offered to the public and to art ought to be perfectly beautiful, perfectly satisfying. Thus I understand art, thus I love it.

After a certain performance Nellie Melba sent Jean a letter the full effect of which cannot be conveyed here because it contains so many words underlined so many times that mere type could not do her emphasis justice. In subdued form it reads:

MY DEAR JEAN—
Excuse my poor French—all that I write comes from the heart.
Is it possible for you to know how *great* you are? You gave me an emotion last night such as I have never experienced in all my life. What art, what *perfection,* in short, what everything! *Mon Dieu,* how can I tell you? I am *moved,* MOVED. There never was an artist like you and there never will be—*never*—you can be *sure.* I should like to tell you in person all the emotions that I had. And Edouard, bravo, both of you, from all my heart. God bless you both and give you the happiness you deserve.

NELLIE

Adolf Mühlmann, another contemporary, says in his published reminiscences [123] that he owes his international career to Jean de Reszke. His story attests Jean's influence with impresarios. Mühlmann's contract with the Breslauer Stadttheater still had three years to run when Jean suggested that Maurice Grau should secure him for the Metropolitan. Grau had never seen or heard Mühlmann, but on Jean's recommendation he paid the Breslau management ten thousand marks to secure his release from the contract. Mühlmann also tells an amusing story about a Command performance at Windsor Castle. Jean was scheduled to sing Lohengrin, but, feeling unwell, was uncertain whether he could appear. Singers are not, of course, paid for such engagements. Andreas Dippel was asked to accompany the other artists to Windsor and step into Jean's place if necessary. He consented, but only for a consideration of five hundred dollars. Jean sang, and his potential substitute received the five hundred dollars —an unusual instance of hush-money.

And if some of the other singers felt a little envious of Jean's art, if they wished they too might achieve the beauty which Jean communicated to his audiences, the feeling was only natural. They could not, however, help admiring him and loving him. Well did these other stars know that he never aspired to be the entire operatic constellation, and they appreciated his greatness the more. In appraising his unique

BOROWNO

THE BROTHERS AND COQUELIN AINÉ
IN MID-ATLANTIC

qualities, David Bispham says that the other members of the company could not, "alone or together, fill the vacancy Jean de Reszke left. Dippel was not heroic enough in figure to fill the eye, Van Dyck's mode of singing left too much to be desired by the ear, Burgstaller had too small a repertory, Kraus was so vast that his Siegfried in armor looked like a huge armadillo, even Tamagno the Italian and Alvarez the Spaniard, admirable artists both, could by no means vie with de Reszke in the extent of their own repertories. Taking him for all in all he was the finest artist of his generation, a tower of strength to our company, and a vocal and physical adornment to the stage he elevated by his presence." [124]

THIRD ACT
THE TEACHER
1902-1925

AFTER Jean's announcement that he would not sing in public again, a great variety of offers were made to him, invitations for concert tours and to make phonograph records among them. Henry Mapleson organized a syndicate to induce him to come to America. He was to be supported by a small company and appear in scenes from opera, visiting forty American cities. This was to be in the nature of a farewell tour. The terms were $5,500 a performance, plus traveling expenses. To this proposal Jean replied: [125]

> My dear Friend:
> The brilliant proposition you have made to me is exceedingly tempting, and I am sure that, under your able direction, all would work well for my interests and my peace of mind—a matter of the last importance to a lyric artist. But I am so happy in Paris, and my strong desire to create Siegfried [in French] being satisfied, I have for the moment no other ambition.

The idea of singing in concert was never entertained by Jean. In the first place, it gave him no scope for half of his art—his acting. In the second place, he realized that his voice itself was not of the greatest, though there can be no doubt that if he had sung some of his arias in concert they would have made as deep an impression as they had on the operatic stage. But he required the show of pageantry. He needed freedom to use the gestures he had learned to make so eloquently, and although supreme in himself, he required the support of other artists to transmit the best of his own art. It was as the great lover that he had been most successful, and even if his imagination could body forth the forms of things only dreamed of by his listeners, and could give to their vague longings "a local habitation and a name," he still needed a partner in all this. It was all very well to suit facial expression to the meaning of songs, but Jean sang best to his audiences through singing to and with his fellow artists. To be sure, he

may not have been conscious of these reasons when he refused
to consider concert singing.

He felt somewhat the same about recording his voice for
the phonograph. Various companies offered him enormous
sums of money to do so, and one of them left its apparatus
in his Paris home for months, so that he might make the
records when he felt like singing. The mood did sometimes
come upon him, but he was never satisfied with the result.
Others did not share this opinion, but he said: "No: Jean
de Reszke cannot put his soul into that wax," and ordered
the records to be broken to bits before his eyes. Every now
and again there has been an excited report that some one
was on the trail of records made by Jean, but the only one
in existence is in the possession of the British Royal Family.
Once when Jean was a guest at Windsor Castle, Queen
Alexandra asked him to sing into one of the old-fashioned
cylinders, and he complied with her request, although it was,
of course, far from a work of art.*

Just as there were periodic reports that phonograph
records by Jean were about to make their appearance, so the
opening of each musical season brought the promise of his
return to America. It is true that Heinrich Conried, Grau's
successor, negotiated with de Reszke for a return to the
Metropolitan. Various reasons were assigned for the failure
of this plan: that Jean had demanded twice as large a fee as
formerly, that he would not return without Edouard, and
that he had sent his refusal when he heard that Conried had
sought to reduce Edouard's fee. Mr. Conried was criticized
by many people for not persuading these favorites to revisit
the scene of their great triumphs. He had, however, made
the effort, as indicated in the following telegram which he
sent to his agent in Paris: [126]

> My offer for Jean was ten performances in six weeks,
> three thousand dollars each performance, with right to
> renew for ten more performances at the same terms.
> This is absolutely the highest salary possible. Would
> have to know at once. If I had known before, would not
> have engaged * * * *

* Edouard did make three records for the Columbia Phonograph Company,
Inc. of New York the last time he was in America: "Infelice" from E r n a n i,
"Serenade de Don Juan" (Tchaikowsky), and the "Porter Song" from M a r t a. Two of
these, the "Infelice" and the "Porter Song," were recently re-recorded and are now
available through the International Research Collectors' Club of Bridgeport, Conn.

To say that there was any actual enmity between Conried and the de Reszkes because of these negotiations or their failure to bear fruit, is nonsense. Mr. Conried, as his biographer points out, frequently visited de Reszke's singing class, and suggested to various artists that they should go to Jean for coaching.

Naturally Jean would have liked to return to America. He had enjoyed his greatest success there, he had many friends in New York, and he liked the American people. "But," he said, "with me it would not be so much a question of selling my art, as of selling my leisure, which, all things considered, I prize as highly as anything else in this world." Herman Klein's way of commenting on Jean's refusal to return to the United States would seem, however, to bolster up the case of those who insisted that there was a "difference" between the tenor and the manager. According to Mr. Klein, Conried had entrusted the negotiations to him, and, says the London critic: "I went to see M. de Reszke in June 1903, but he positively refused to go back to New York, or, indeed, to sing for Mr. Conried at any price." [127]

Plans for a conservatoire and theater for Jean in the Champs Elysées had been discussed, in the papers if not in fact, ever since 1898. Now they were revived. Jean was to choose his colleagues, and supervise pupils from the beginning through every stage of training, until he could produce complete operas with them. This project was also abandoned. Then there was talk of his securing Sarah Bernhardt's theater —she was a good friend of his—for a season of Wagnerian operas. Later cables arrived from Paris saying that M. Gailhard and Jean were to take over the management of the Paris Grand Opera. In the end Jean decided to teach at home in his house in the Rue de la Faisanderie. At once applications for lessons began to pour in. Beginners with no money but some talent, the very rich who thought a voice and a career could be bought, artists already famous, all went flocking to Jean de Reszke, hoping that by some miracle he could mold them in his image. Of course he could not accommodate them all. At first he taught only four hours a day, in the afternoon, and by classes, four pupils in a class. The lessons were given in a little theater he had built in the rear of his residence. The auditorium seated a hundred people. A movable bridge led across the orchestra pit, which accommodated thirty musicians, to the stage, and on either side above the orchestra was a box. The stage, conventionally but picturesquely set, was of ample proportions for a theater of this size.

Jean employed an assistant to play the accompaniments and a secretary to make arrangements for lesson hours and fees, thus allowing him to devote all his own time to teaching voice production and dramatic interpretation, which he loved. It was, of course, not a new occupation for him. In his student days he had insisted on giving lessons to the servants in his parents' home; later, most of his prominent fellow artists profited by his instruction and advice, and, as related elsewhere, many a beginner received help from him. His new duty to the music-loving world lay, he felt, in preparing other artists, and he threw himself into this phase of his art with the same zeal that had characterized the preparation of his own rôles. He wasted no time, he put up with no nonsense, but this does not mean that he terrified applicants or pupils. On the contrary, although they might tremble at the thought of an audition with the world-famous tenor, his friendliness and cheerfulness and his winning smile soon put the most nervous aspirant at ease. It was natural enough that even a girl with a big voice should give out thin little notes because she was frightened. "You sing like a child," Jean might say, and when she explained that she had been afraid, he would add, "You need not tell me that," and, taking her hand, lead her to the piano. "Now I want you to take this note for me. There. That's very pretty, but nobody would hear it. Try it once more." Soon all fear would vanish, and then he said delightedly: "Voilà! Mademoiselle, that is your voice. Now come and sing again this song that I could hardly hear when you first tried it."

Or perhaps some one came for an audition half doubting that a man who had sung only in opera would also know oratorios and simple songs. One day a young baritone appeared, and when Jean asked "What will you sing?" he replied loftily: "The aria from Mendelssohn's *Elijah*." Immediately Jean began to play and sing "It is enough" and then inquired, "Is that the aria?" It was. Again, a young woman endowed with a good voice, dramatic talent, and ambition, but not with money, might take courage and write for an audition, telling de Reszke about her situation and explaining that his judgment alone would help her to decide whether to continue to make sacrifices for the sake of an operatic career. Perhaps a friend had warned her that she could not dare to hope for an audition without a letter of introduction from some influential person, and that she would probably have to pay several hundred francs for his opinion. Imagine her surprise when, after the ordeal, she wanted to know the price and he took her hand in his and said: "My dear young lady, it was a great pleasure to hear you. I will cost nothing at all." And what joy of joys if he could crowd her into his own time-table!

The actual teaching process is difficult to describe. Jean himself objected to calling it a "method," for he knew only too well that no single method could possibly be effective for all pupils, and he was suspicious of teachers who claimed to have one. He preferred to speak of his "ideas about the voice," and his ideas constantly increased in number, as did the analogies and metaphors by which he illustrated them. He refused to write a book on voice production or to issue any detailed explanations of his science, saying: "How can I write a book on my method when I don't use the same method with any two pupils?" He took account not only of differences in voice, but of differences in physique and intelligence. A suggestion which might, for instance, help one person to bring forth a full tone, might yield a flat, unpleasant sound when followed by some one else. A metaphor understood by one might bring utter confusion to another.

Broadly, he outlined his working plan in three parts: breath control, secured from the diaphragm; resonance; and head sonority and overtones. Then came the focusing and coloring of tone and the countless details which make up the æsthetics of singing. He had a genius for vocal diagnosis, and seldom erred in analyzing needs and applying remedies. Naturally, he tried to get pupils to imitate him, since he himself had begun that way. Naturally, also, he was primarily interested in training pupils for the operatic stage. Although he did not confine his efforts to that, opera was the ultimate goal.*

* In preparing these notes on Jean de Reszke's way of teaching I have consulted many of Jean's pupils, and here present the substance of their observations. Many of them wrote me exceedingly interesting and helpful letters, and some of them took the trouble to write rather full articles. I regret that it is impossible to list all their names; nor can I use the complete articles or quote them extensively. For the sake of a unified work, it has seemed best to fuse all these generous contributions, with the exception of one, which seems to me to present with such clarity and truth the endearing humanity of the great master and so largely to embody the attitude of most of his pupils, as well as his to them, that I feel it ought to be reproduced as written. It therefore appears in the Appendix, together with the valuable article by Mr. Walter Johnstone-Douglas which appeared in the July 1925

It was to be expected that what the greatest operatic tenor of his time—perhaps of all time—had acquired through a lifetime of painstaking and devoted study, could be absorbed only in part and only by a few of the most intelligent pupils. He did not take them into his confidence about all the whys and wherefores of each suggestion or exercise. Although he was modest, he was aware of his unique position in the musical world, and simply took it for granted that any one who came to him for lessons knew that he understood what he was about. But it was not surprising that some of his pupils were bewildered and thought he contradicted himself. When he found that one means was not achieving the end he sought, he tried another. He treated each phase of development as though it were the most important—as it was, for the moment —and sometimes, according to the pupil's needs, dwelt on it longer than seemed necessary. Then when that stage was mastered he might suddenly switch to something which seemed to be directly opposed to it. A German pupil who had been working for mask resonance for some time was suddenly given exercises which seemed to set at nought all that Jean had told him about the importance of the mask. In amazement he exclaimed: "Na also! nun soll's *ohne* Nase sein!" ("So! now I should do it without the nose!") But he had sense enough to realize that his teacher probably had a good reason for what he told him, and that he himself might soon see daylight.

Nor could a pupil suspect, when he arrived for a lesson, what the order of the day would be, "Bon jour, mon grand ténor," might be the greeting, or, "How are you, Romeo?" Then, turning to the accompanist: "Let me have E flat," and a familiar phrase like this would be practiced:

If the exercises were satisfactory the request to sing something followed. Perhaps it was an aria from W e r t h e r, and

number of *Music and Letters,* and is here, by permission, reprinted in full. Mr. Johnstone-Douglas knew both Jean and Edouard intimately from 1907 on, acted as secretary to Edouard, was a pupil of both brothers as well as accompanist, and for some years assisted Jean in teaching. In introducing this article, Mr. Amherst Webber, Jean's associate and friend for more than thirty years, said: "If any one has to write about his teaching, Jean himself would have preferred nobody to Mr. Johnstone-Douglas."

then a look of•sadness came over Jean's face as he said: "Well, my dear, you do that well, but I doubt if the London public will like this opera. I sang it there many years ago and it was a fiasco. It is too morbid and sad for the public." Or perhaps Lohengrin's Narration was being studied. The pupil might have thought it dull whilst he worked over it by himself, but as soon as Jean began to sing *In fernem Land, unnahbar euren Schritten,* what had seemed prosaic became poetic, what had seemed dull became luminous. But if the young tenor expected to perfect the entire Narration in one lesson he was doomed to disappointment, for the first phrase required most of the time. "Draw back the uvula," Jean would say, "pinch the tonsils, push from the diaphragm and use no nose or head resonance; it is the uvula that controls and directs the quality of tone." But the *r* in *fernem* had to be remembered, also the fact that there were two *t's* in *Schritten.* In his momentary confusion the student might bellow out something far from musical, and then the master would rebuke him: "You, who are an intelligent musician, I'm astonished that you can begin this phrase as though you were calling a waiter in a café!" But as the line improved a pleased smile passed over Jean's face and he would say: "*Now* is right." Then he himself might sing the phrase, *Liegt eine Burg, die Monsalvat genannt.* "How hopeless to get the sort of passionate reverence he got into the word Monsalvat!" writes one of his pupils, "a sort of *ripæ ulterioris amor,* very simple, very personal, but all accomplished by a definite technique; a tiny upward portamento, a half-smothered *M,* a sudden piano, his marvelous *voix étouffée;* it was like a recipe, Shake the bottle and apply the Elixir of Life. *Ein lichter Tempel stehet dort inmitten.* 'Throw light into the voice, strike right above the uvula.' So over it again. 'But why in such a hurry? Take your time; don't say it as though you were a schoolboy saying a piece as quick as you can; sing as though you were improvising it; it gives you authority over the stage, over the orchestra, over the audience; you compel them to wait for you, to pay attention to you.'"

Take the phrase:

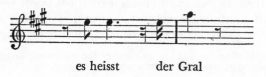

es heisst   der Gral

Here he would say: "Get your support on the note preceding
the high note, and just carry the resonance of the high note
further up by drawing back the uvula as far as possible, and
when on the note itself, expand the ribs to support it 'like the
pinions of a bird.' " *

It was a great strain, trying to store away all that the
master had given, and sometimes a pupil seemed to be suffering from a kind of vocal indigestion, but Jean would shake
him by the hand and say: "It was a good lesson, we didn't let
anything pass that was wrong."

He had infinite patience, but it did irritate him when
pupils failed to do their part. He felt that they might at least
learn their music by heart. He felt, too, that they ought to
realize that the little tricks by which he secured a certain
result were not intended to embellish an aria. If, however, a
pupil was going through a particular trying stage, he gladly
gave extra time to help him to overcome the difficulty. Occasionally Jean's secretary interrupted: "Maestro, do you know
that you have been working with Mr. —— for one hour and
fifteen minutes?" and the master replied: "That doesn't
matter. I'm interested. I will work longer." At times the years
seemed to roll away and Jean lived again in one of his own
performances. His voice rang out like that of a young man,
and the listening pupil said in despair: "Ah, Maestro, if I
could sing just one note like that!" Modestly Jean replied:
"Thank you. If I had known as much about singing some
years ago as I do now, I wouldn't have suffered so much and
I would have sung much better."

That rare combination of modesty and dignity, gentleness and severity and kindness—all genuine—linked with the
natural authority of his presence, filled his pupils with respect
and admiration for the teacher and love for the man. They
were overwhelmed by his grandeur, but they were not made
to feel self-conscious or afraid to try. Lesser artists might
paralyze a sensitive student by their affectations and egotism;
not so Jean de Reszke. On some dripping grey morning a
pupil might go to her lesson rather half-heartedly, feeling
that the gloominess must surely show in her voice. She entered
the studio timidly, not even amused by the servant who flitted
around with an atomizer, showering the spray which answered
for a change of air between lessons. Then came the master,

* For some of these details I am indebted to the anonymous article in *Music
and Letters,* July 1925, entitled "A Lesson with the Master."

and the whole room, the morning itself, seemed brightened by his smile as he greeted his pupil with a delighted "Ah!" as though she were the one person in the world he really wanted to see. And if the earlier mood returned for a moment during the lesson and the lips trembled, he would say: "But you must never let me see you cry real tears when you are singing. Crying is crying and destroys the voice. Any one can cry, but to simulate weeping so well that you make others cry, is art."

Let a pupil be in real distress and the master was quick to show his sympathy. Not infrequently the need was for practical aid. It was generously given. It is an amazing—and moving—experience to go from pupil to pupil and hear the stories of Jean de Reszke's kindness. From the beginning he had adopted the practice of accepting large fees from the wealthy in order that those without money might also develop their talents. So entirely without ostentation was his help given that one hears over and over again: "You know he didn't charge me a penny for my lessons. I think I was perhaps the only one." And again: "Then one day he said to me, 'You aren't eating enough. Here, take this and buy yourself a good steak. Then come back and we'll try again. Forget about paying for awhile. You can't sing when you are not eating properly. Use the money for food.'"

But as great virtues often carry inherent defects, so Jean's very kindness concealed a weakness. He was always helpful, always generous and kind, and a marvel of patience, but at times he seemed unable to face realities. (He had spent many years in the unreal world of opera; that helps to account for it.) Whenever anything unpleasant had to be said or done, it was delegated to his secretary, or to one of his assistants or friends. Was a servant to be dismissed, he received word of it from some one other than his master. Did Jean find that the personality or manners of a pupil irritated him, some one else had to explain, so that the student might mend his ways. It was the same when a pupil had to be told that de Reszke could not continue to teach him. Not that Jean especially wanted to be thought kind, but that he could not bear to be, or to be thought, *un*kind. He was accustomed to receiving homage, and although his humility with respect to his art and his achievements was genuine, he enjoyed his own artistic and social standing; he was an aristocrat among men and among artists, and seemed to take a quiet pleasure in the consciousness of that fact. Figuratively speaking, he moved naturally towards the head of any table, and no one disputed his right to sit there. That tacit acceptance of his rank he would not have cared to disturb by any conscious or unconscious act of his own.

During his singing years Jean had mingled in the affairs of the world only so far as his art would allow. Now that he was free from the restrictions imposed by his profession, he and his wife entertained lavishly. Perhaps he found the distinguished guests at his dinner table an agreeable substitute for the audiences of the theater which he had voluntarily renounced. If some one happened to ask who would be present at dinner on a certain evening, Jean replied nonchalantly: "Oh, the King of Portugal, the Duke of Connaught, the Grand Duke Vladimir of Russia, le Duc de Morny, et ainsi de suite," quite unaffectedly, but a little pleased all the same. Usually artists, actors, musicians and litterateurs were also included among the guests. Now that he was no longer delighting audiences on the stage, Jean regaled these informal gatherings with his reminiscences. The talk seldom strayed from the subject of singing and opera for very long. Now and again some one launched into another topic, but although Jean seemed attentive, frequently he was only half listening. To quote one of his devoted friends, "In some ways he was a most selfish man, but he was so charmingly polite about it that one was hardly aware of it." Yet, in spite of his seeming inattention, he seldom failed to notice the person who seemed shy or uncomfortable, or excluded from the general conversation. He had the knack of putting such people at their ease. Generously he invited his pupils to attend receptions and dinners, and the most timid was made to feel at home among the socially exalted. Occasionally a pupil was requested to sing, and afterwards a wealthy guest might proffer financial assistance, thinking his impulse quite spontaneous—blissfully unaware of his host's intentions. Sometimes, also, an American pupil was asked to play jazz music, then something of a novelty in Paris. Jean and his wife were both fond of it and liked to engage negro jazz orchestras. "Niggers!" Jean would announce with delight. "Niggers. Real ones!"

Madame Adelina Patti was frequently a guest in the de Reszke home. One evening after dinner, the guests implored their host and Patti to sing together. Jean did not wish to, but his wife said, "Sing even if you die after it," and he

obeyed. It was deeply moving to hear the two artists sing a
duet from R o m e o e t J u l i e t t e, for it seemed doubtful
that they would ever again hear Adelina Patti and Jean de
Reszke sing together. Afterwards, Patti, the top of whose head
did not quite reach Jean's shoulder, stretched up and threw
her arms around his neck. They were both in tears and said
sorrowfully that they had probably sung that duet for the
last time. So it proved. But in May 1907, when she was in
her sixty-fifth year, Patti did sing in Jean's theater again—her
favorite rôle of Rosina, in a private performance of I l B a r-
b i e r e, with Edouard as Don Basiiio. That was her last appearance on any stage in a complete representation of an
opera.

Madame Patti had watched the progress of Jean's pupils
with much interest, often listening in the next room, sometimes asking questions and making suggestions. In the summer of 1905 she and the de Reszkes were, as usual, at Mont
Dore, where many singers went for an annual cure. Patti was
planning a charity concert tour, and was having a little difficulty with her upper notes. She consulted Jean, and he
observed that if she knew his way of singing she would have
less trouble. "But," she replied, "I can't stay in Paris to study
with you. What shall I do?" Jean responded, "I can send
some one to you." Among his pupils was Miss Florence
Stevens, an American who understood his teaching so well
that when other pupils failed to grasp his suggestions, or
when his time was too crowded to accept new applicants, he
sent them to her. It was, however, an astonished young woman
who received this letter from Madame Jean de Reszke:

PARIS, Aug. 4 1905
53 Rue de la Faisanderie

DEAR MISS STEVENS:

I have just a few lines to write to you which I believe
will be agreeable to you. Madame Patti has heard some
of my husband's pupils sing, and she became most enthusiastic over his method. She immediately begged of
him to show her the ways and expressed a desire to take
lessons in November, but as she cannot come to Paris
before, my husband proposed that you, if you wish, go
to her home in England the first days of September and
prepare her for her lessons, as he says you are capable of
doing so, having well prepared a number of pupils. I am

sure it will be very pleasant for you, as Madame Patti is a most charming person. She will send you your ticket and you shall stay at her home in Wales for about two weeks.

Will you let me know at once if you accept, as my husband hopes you will? And believe me, my dear Miss Stevens, yours very sincerely,

MARIE DE RESZKE

Miss Stevens found it hard to believe that it was the great Patti who was referred to, and wanted to be certain. Madame de Reszke reassured her in a second letter.*

PARIS, Aug. 8 1905

DEAREST MISS STEVENS:

I have just received your reply, which gives me great pleasure, and I hasten to tell you that it is really the famous singer, Madame Adelina Patti, who wishes to work with the Master. She has always sung like a marvelous bird but she is greatly surprised and very enthusiastic over the wonderful methods of the Master, and wishes to see what his skill could do for her voice, which is always divine as to quality. You see that Madame Patti, Baroness Cederström, gives a beautiful example that one can always learn even after the most extraordinary career such as hers has been. It is a very flattering homage to my husband....

Write me as soon as you have received an answer from Madame Patti and I shall hope to see you as soon as you have returned from her. Many thanks for your affectionate words, my dear little Stevens. We are relying on you to do honor to the school and I am certain that you will have a brilliant career.

Au revoir, with my best love,

Yours ever sincerely,

MARIE DE RESZKE

To Craig-y-nos Castle, in Wales, Florence Stevens went, to give instructions in Jean de Reszke's way of singing to a woman who had achieved international renown as a very great artist and who was then past sixty. The letters sent home by the young teacher so signally honored throw interesting

* Translated from the French.

AT WORK
Jean de Reszke, Amherst Webber, and
Madame de Reszke

sidelights on the famous singer. She wrote that Patti did really open her mouth like a bird and did really sing like a bird, that she had been astonished to find that Patti had two sets of eyeteeth. She described her manner of living, and related how the diva constantly admonished her tutor to keep within her income and put aside something for a rainy day. Extracts from letters sent by Miss Stevens to her mother follow:

> Patti is a darling. She looks and acts like a girl and seems to adore me. Her voice, of course, is wonderful, but some of the muscles are weak and it is for that, I suppose, that de Reszke sent me here. He is sure his method will help her and I think it will....
>
> Patti and I are better friends than ever. She is very enthusiastic over my work and says she is coming to Paris for my début and talks about it all the time. She tells me more stories about herself, and she really thinks there is no one like Patti; but she is about right, for she is a most wonderful woman.
>
> We are doing the scores now. The weather is horrid, it rains every day and we can't go out at all.
>
> She is so impatient about her work. It is so funny, yet she does try so hard. She doesn't believe in getting up in the morning and says I should stay in bed until 9 and then dress very quietly. She doesn't approve of any violent exercise like tennis, riding, etc.—nothing but walking, but a good walk every day which lasts an hour. Then to bed at 10, eat lots of oysters, but don't let anything ruffle or disturb you. Keep everything unpleasant far from you.

That Patti found the lessons valuable is plain from the letters she sent to Miss Stevens. "I know you will be glad to hear that my tour was an immense success," she wrote. "I had great ovations and enthusiastic receptions everywhere. I certainly *do* open my mouth now, and those exercises are positively excellent for avoiding the fatigue of too many scales." A few months later: "I sing my scales every day and of course think of you all the time. *Open your mouth.* My mouth has become so large that I can hardly shut it up properly after I have done singing."

Jean de Reszke's teaching has been criticized by some of those who studied with him, as well as by others who did not and do not know what or how he taught. He has also been criticized for not producing great singers from among his pupils. Mr. Douglas answers such critics in this way: "That is not the standard by which he must be judged. His triumphs were rather the improvement out of all recognition of voices which were neither magnificent nor generous by nature. His absorption in teaching was such that he preferred a voice which he had to "make," rather than a voice to which he had only to add qualities not already there. But cultivated voices, like cultivated flowers, tend to revert to their wild state unless they are carefully tended. His pupils were also expected by their friends to be able to reproduce at once the characteristics of the great de Reszke, their friends forgetting that great singers are the combination of great voices and great brains and great instincts."

Certain it is that most of his famous contemporaries in opera went to Jean for instruction at some time. They did not always want that fact known. Madame Patti, for instance, was greatly annoyed when she discovered that newspapers had published the story of her taking lessons from one of de Reszke's pupils. Madame Nellie Melba went to him frequently for counsel. She was another who did not care to have the world know about it. When she was singing in Australia with John McCormack, she constantly insisted: "No, Jean did that *this* way," and: "But de Reszke sang that *so*," until Mr. McCormack, himself a warm admirer of Jean's, could endure it no longer and protested: "I don't care *how* Jean de Reszke did it. I'm John McCormack!"

On days set aside for auditions a strange company of people might be found in the waiting-room outside the studio. Once, after all the others had been heard, a tired-looking, rather shabbily dressed man was ushered into Jean's presence. The master listened in amazement while this person, who had the appearance of a commercial traveler, sang difficult operatic music with beauty and artistry. When he had finished, Jean said excitedly: "Mon Dieu, mon ami! with a voice like that you can sing anywhere!" but the queer-looking stranger refused all offers of introductions to impresarios. This attitude puzzled Jean until, a few weeks later, a letter of thanks arrived from Munich, revealing that the stranger was Heinrich Knote, the well-known tenor, who had disguised himself in order to insure an unbiased opinion.

As for Jean's regular pupils, where else but in his studio

could they find an artist with such equipment and experience? Where was there another teacher with such eclectic taste, one who had himself sung Italian opera better than the Italians, French opera better than the French, and German opera better than the Germans! And quite apart from his specialized knowledge of the operas themselves, de Reszke's pupils, who came from all parts of the world, enjoyed the unusual advantage of having the lessons explained in their own language. Jean seemed to have a special gift for imparting pronunciation and accent. Whenever possible he spoke French in teaching, as that was the language he habitually used in conversation, but to German pupils he spoke in German, to Russians in Russian, and he was a master of Italian. He spoke English fairly well, but seldom used it. However, he gave invaluable lessons in English diction to his pupils, including those to whom English was native. Incidentally, he was rather proud of his repertoire of American slang and some carefully memorized "cuss words."

His pupils received, also, the full benefit of his thorough musicianship. He read easily at sight, and he could play the piano well enough to accompany himself in his rôles. If need arose he could play when giving a lesson, but piano music he played only by ear, although he could perform the works he knew in any key.

He was as conscientious about the work of his pupils as he had been about his own, and the more a pupil mastered, the more Jean expected of him. He has been condemned for giving praise where others thought no praise was due, but he based his demands upon the possibilities of the pupil and he praised accordingly. One day his niece objected: "But, Uncle, how can you tell that girl that she sang well?" His reply was: "For her it was good. She has not much to work with, but she is sincere. She does the best she is capable of; I can ask no more." Let some one reach unexpected heights some day, and Jean would be satisfied with nothing less thereafter.

When the time came for a début, the teacher was almost as nervous as the pupil. Jean did not attend the first recital by de Reszke pupils, but he walked the floor at home until it was over. When Florence Stevens, she who had given lessons to Patti, made her début (at Nice) he sat at the telephone in his Paris home and listened to the entire performance.

Sometimes he did attend débuts, and occasionally he was pleasantly surprised. One of his earliest pupils was a young

woman with a fine voice and sufficient artistic temperament,
but rather awkward in her movements and without taste in
the matter of personal appearance. She made her début as
Elsa at Covent Garden, and Jean went to London for it,
not without misgivings. The girl's success was sensational.
Friends rushed to Jean's box after the first act to congratulate
him. He was bewildered. "Oh, yes," he said, "Yes. What?
Excuse me, but I'm—excuse me, I am a little confused." So
had the singing and acting of his pupil astounded him. He
was much amused, later, at the interviews the young lady
granted to reporters who inquired where she had learned to
sing. Feeling that she must relate something strange to match
her unexpected success, she solemnly explained that she had
spent hours in a certain Paris garden, communing with the
birds and the rocks, getting knowledge and inspiration. When
Jean heard of this he said: "What's this nonsense you've been
giving out! There isn't a rock in the world that taught you
a single note. Whatever you know about singing and acting,
you have learned from me!" In later years this woman said,
as did many another: "All that I know about singing I learned
from Jean de Reszke."

But he was not always so fortunate in the performances
of his pupils. Another young woman also sang in London,
and in her eagerness to do things right, carried over into her
songs some of the sounds Jean required in exercises, with the
result that critics raised their eyebrows and asked: "What is
our dear Jean teaching in Paris—Chinese?" One of the other
students rushed into the studio, clutching the offending
newspapers, and begged him to allow her to reply to the
insulting remarks. "Thank you, my child," he said, "but don't
bother. I am Jean de Reszke."

Also among the first pupils was the German tenor Sembach, who wanted especially to study Lohengrin with Jean.
They worked at it for several months, but when, a year or
so thereafter, a friend asked him how he was getting on,
Sembach complained: "They wouldn't let me do half the
things de Reszke taught me." Jean could hardly expect that
all of his pupils would be accorded such deference as he
himself had received during his career, for his position had
been unique. No conductor ever questioned his style, because
whatever he did seemed perfect and it would therefore have
been folly to tamper with it. This does not mean that he
resented honest criticism. He was amused at those who did.

He delighted in describing the vehement reaction of Signor Ancona when a fellow artist showed him an adverse critique. Ancona could not read English, so he asked: "What does it say?"

"It says that you have no voice and that you can't act," was the humiliating information, somewhat exaggerated by the translator.

"That's not so!" declared Ancona, pounding his fist on the table. "If God Almighty Himself were sitting there and saying that, I'd tell Him the same thing."

During the first few years of Jean's teaching, Edouard also lived in Paris and assisted him. It was a real privilege for an aspiring young singer to receive lessons from both of them, and a novel experience it was to sit down on the floor with the two giants, while they drew diagrams to explain stage action. Edouard's plans for his own future were still uncertain. For a time it seemed that he might return to the United States, as had often been promised. He did want to; again and again he said so in letters. He had good friends in America whom he wished to see once more. Dearest among them was Laura Tolman, a 'cellist. Their friendship had begun in the early nineties and continued until Edouard's death. On many an evening when some socially prominent lady lamented his absence from her dinner table, Edouard was enjoying the informality of his "Tolmanina's" home, sitting around the fireside, happy in listening to the music which the diminutive dark-haired beauty drew from the 'cello they both loved. To her, when he retired, he gave the little heart encasing a red figure of Mephisto which he had worn whenever he sang the rôle. There are various heart-shaped pieces of jewelry, many photographs, and other mementoes of this friendship in the little house in Maine where "Tolmanina" now lives. There you will find a decanter and six dainty glasses which Edouard brought before he left American shores for the last time. Still in the decanter is a little of the liqueur from which they drank a toast to that next meeting in America which never occurred. They made a game of it, each sipping a few drops from each glass in turn, except one, from which Edouard alone drank. Then Tolmanina put decanter and glasses away. Nobody ever touched them, or sipped of that liqueur again, until years later, when Tolmanina and one other drank a toast to the book in which Edouard's memory was to be enshrined.

A Great St. Bernard dog Edouard also gave to Tolmanina, to guard her, now that he was going away. He named him "Leporello" and Leporello seemed to understand that his charge was precious.

Edouard de Reszke wrote few letters, and those rather laboriously, but he wrote to Tolmanina to the end, and from these letters one can tell how restless he was away from the theater, far from his brother and his friends. Always he hoped to return to America. In November, 1904, he wrote to Tolmanina from his home in Poland:

GARNEK, 28 November 1904

MY DEAR AND GOOD TOLMANINA,

You are always charming to think of me. I thank you for your excellent photograph, which has given me great pleasure. I know that in you I have a true and devoted friend. It is a long time now since we have seen each other, but that does not prevent my thinking often of you and your dear parents! Where did you spend the summer? I am sure that you have made great progress with your inseparable 'cello. What has become of your little friend, Red Head? Give her greetings from me.

As for me, at the moment I have bronchitis, which confines me to the house. The rest of my family are well. My brother Jean is in Paris, where he teaches singing. My three daughters are working hard; one of them will finish her studies in the coming year. I have spent two months away from home. In July Jean and I went to London, at the invitation of their Majesties, the King and Queen of England. We spent two weeks there, and we sang. Their Majesties were most amiable and decorated us with the Order of Arts, Sciences and Music. From there we went to Mont Dore to take the cure, then to Deauville, and then we came home to the country. I do not know yet whether I shall sing this winter; it is more than likely that I shall stay in the country with my family. I have been offered a concert tour in America, but did not accept because of the absence of guarantees.

In short, God alone knows whether I shall see you again. I hope that your health is good, also that of your family. My best wishes to your dear parents!

You, my dear and good Tolmanina, I embrace you very affectionately and send you my best greetings.

Your very devoted friend,

EDOUARD DE RESZKE

Merry Christmas!   MEPHISTO

When, in 1906, Oscar Hammerstein opened his new Manhattan Opera House in New York, he announced that after much difficulty he had secured Edouard de Reszke, and that he expected to secure Jean as artistic director. Hammerstein made a contract with Edouard and paid him a generous sum as advance salary and guarantee. Some months later it was rumored that Edouard had sent a cable saying that he would come to America and sing in concert but would have nothing to do with Mr. Hammerstein. The latter countered with a statement that he had been shocked when, the previous spring, he had heard Edouard sing in concert. He had told him that he would have to get his voice into better shape before appearing as a member of the Hammerstein company. "Mr. de Reszke promised to do this," said Hammerstein, "but instead of practicing with his brother Jean, he spent the summer idling in Poland. After a few weeks I wrote him a long letter telling him he must not forget his promise, but I received no answer. A few weeks afterward I learned that he had returned to Paris, and I immediately cabled him asking the condition of his voice. No answer to my cable. I sent another one; no reply, nor have my letters been answered. Now I learn that he refuses to keep his contract."

What Edouard was really doing in Poland and how he felt about the Hammerstein affair is revealed in a letter he wrote to Mrs. Henry Finck under date of January 3, 1907, a part of which follows:

If I have been unable to reply to your letter immediately it is because of the revolution and the events which have taken place in Poland during the last two years. It has been going on for three years now. I have not been able to leave my family, for fear that evil might befall them, what with the agrarian movement and the menacing bands of robbers, bandits, and men on strike, or that they might any day be burned or assassinated. I have spent whole nights, with my guards, armed to the teeth, protecting the repose of my wife and children. I assure you that it has not been very cheerful, and that we have suffered a great deal. The country is disorganized, everything is at a standstill, and we don't know what the end will be.

I should have rejoiced to go to America, and should have been so happy to see you again! Mr. Hammerstein has violated the conditions of the contract, and has, moreover, slandered me in saying that I have lost my voice. There is certainly some one who has intrigued and has biased Hammerstein against me, out of professional jealousy. Unfortunately I cannot name the person. Bad luck pursues me. I have taken advantage of a calm interlude and am spending the Christmas holidays with my brother Jean, to rest my poor nerves.

Edouard's disappointment at not going to America was keen, for that country was as dear to him as his own. Shortly before the Hammerstein affair he wrote a letter to Max Hirsch, treasurer of the Metropolitan, again expressing his longing. It represents one of his rare excursions into English, which he wrote, as he played the piano, "by ear." He was very self-conscious about his use of English, and it may not be entirely fair to publish a letter showing his spelling and construction, but in a peculiar way these letters written in English convey the man's lovable personality. One of them follows:

GARNEK, 20 January 1906

DEAR MAX

I heartily thank you that you kindly remember me, and also many thanks! for all you good wisches of New Year! Please accept also my best wishes of health, and filicity for you and your dear family!——

I am very anxious to know, if I will have still the pleasure to see you again??? 3 years passed over my *tournée* with Duss, and also over the nice days of our friend's Maurice Grau direction! You can't imagine how musch America misses me! We left there, so many sincere friends and so many good remembrances! It seams me so queer not to be among you!

I suppose that all our friends are in good health? Please be so kind to transmit them my best wishes of happy New-Year! My family and I we are quite well. This war during two years was a real disaster for Russia, and the last revolutionary movement is ruining the country! Since a year the workmeans impulse made a great deale of harm. With all these disorders I couldn't leave the country and my family, but now I am quite decided to retake the theater. In two weeks I am going to Paris and there surely I will find to sing somewhere. I feel my self quite well and my voice is in perfect condition.——

John is always in Paris with his wife and boy.

Dont forgett me my dear friend!

With my best affection and friendly remembrance I remain

Yours truly

EDOUARD DE RESZKE

In discussing the projected return to the United States, Edouard told a friend that "that jealous Nellie," whom he himself had urged Hammerstein to engage, had maneuvered to have him released "so she would have the stage to herself." It was not the first time he had had an unpleasant encounter with Melba. April 1901 marked the twenty-fifth anniversary of his début in opera. The company was singing in Boston, and some of Edouard's friends planned to make an occasion of a certain performance of F a u s t. Melba heard about the proposed festivities and let it be known that if any wreaths or bouquets came across the footlights it would be to her and to no one else. "But what will my friends think?" asked Edouard. "They want to do this for me." That made no difference; if the demonstration so much as began she would refuse to go on with the performance. Edouard, placing art above personal feelings, quietly gave instructions that any flowers or other tributes intended for him were to be taken to his dressing-room.

When Jean heard about the incident, he made only one comment: "Well, if *I* had been there——!" One can picture his indignation at the tone of Hammerstein's admonitions to his beloved brother. Yet he himself knew that Edouard was not singing in the old way. Several of his pupils attended one of Edouard's concerts, and the next day it was discussed. Jean asked for opinions, but the pupils hesitated to speak out. Finally one of them, realizing that this was a laboratory question and not a tacit request for praise, ventured: "Why—I—thought he sang flat several times." Jean flushed and lowered his eyes, and then said sadly: "It is true. He did."

Shortly after this Edouard opened a singing school in London, but he was temperamentally unsuited for teaching. The monetary phase of it he neglected entirely. A friend asked how he was getting along. "Oh, fine!" replied Edouard. "I have forty pupils. Four of them pay me." After two years he gave up his London school and started to teach in Warsaw. By the end of 1909 he had, according to letters of that date, more than a hundred pupils. He was teaching from ten o'clock in the morning until eight o'clock at night. From time to time he complained that the pupils had neither voices nor talent. "But at least," he observed, "I am in my element and I occupy my time.... My brother Jean ... at least has the great satisfaction of seeing his pupils succeed."

Edouard was ill frequently. Recurrent attacks of bronchitis, and a "dizziness" which he said began during his last stay in London, soon forced him to abandon teaching. He went back to Paris to assist Jean, but the war compelled his return to Poland. Soon Warsaw was threatened, and orders were given to flee. On a bitterly cold night the evacuation took place. The children were told to march out over the Alexandrian Bridge and to return over it on some future day. As they drew near it, they heard a voice singing with a sturdy cheerfulness that sounded very strange in the midnight horror and alarm. The voice grew stronger and the melody became clear—"Jeszcze Polska"—it was the Polish national anthem. The children fell to marching in rhythm, as that great voice rolled on. They waved their handkerchiefs at the man of kingly stature who stood there. He responded with a sweep of his arm, telling them in song not to forget that they were the hope of Poland. "Poland is not yet dead, while we live," kept ringing in their ears. The opera houses of two continents had thrilled to that voice with which Edouard de Reszke now strove to make those two thousand waifs who had suddenly become refugees feel the soul of Poland.

Edouard went to his home in the country. It was not long before he was completely shut off from all means of communication. The horrors of war increased. The Germans came from one side, the Russians from the other. Shrapnel whizzed through his house. He and his family, with their neighbors, Prince and Princess Lubomirski, took refuge in the cellar of his home. They suffered cold and hunger; foraging expeditions yielded little. In one of the very few letters which got through the lines to Jean, Edouard said that he had "no coal, oil, or coffee, and only a handful of grain left." When quiet seemed restored, they abandoned the cellar, and lived in comparative comfort for a little while. Then one evening at dinner word came that they had better flee. They mounted horses which they had managed to keep in hiding, and rode for hours through the night, finding shelter at last in a cave. Edouard took cold, and when he returned to his home fell ill with a fever. Crippling rheumatism followed, and for months he was unable to lie down. He could not move his head, and day after day he sat in his armchair almost motionless. Gradually the pain and stiffness left him, but he never regained full health. He was very thin now. In other days he and Jean had been so fat that crossing their knees became a difficult feat, and they used to chaff each other. Now Edouard would cross his knees and say regretfully, "If Jean could only see this." No longer would it have been necessary to ask a hostess which chair she preferred him to sit in.

He talked constantly of the happy days gone by, recalling many amusing incidents. He did not lose his gentle disposition or his sense of humor. When his rheumatism was so painful that he could hardly stir, he said, "Now Jean wouldn't have to tell me so often to sit down, as he had to that time in the third act of M e i s t e r s i n g e r. We were sitting there singing, and I started to get up. 'Sit down, Edouard, sit down,' Jean said anxiously. I knew there was a good reason for his saying that, but I didn't find out until the end of the scene that a pillow had stuck to my trousers. I was pretty furious at Jean for not managing to let me know what the trouble was. But that wasn't as bad as the time Jean was furious at me. It was during a F a u s t performance. The red light blinded me as I rose out of the ground, and I couldn't tell where Jean was. Then I heard his voice coming from quite another part of the stage. Of course Jean was upset, but it wasn't my fault."

He especially enjoyed telling about something that happened during his and Jean's last season in Paris. One morning while they were practicing at their hotel, they were annoyed by a loud hammering on the wall. Thinking that their neighbors must be hanging pictures, they tried to sing on. When, however, the racket had continued with unabated vigor for about ten minutes, it began to be too much. The brothers paused to consider procedure. Suddenly the noise stopped. Instantly they resumed their practice, encouraged to hope for peace. Simultaneously the sound of hammering began again, this time so furiously that singing was almost impossible. After persevering against the clamor for some moments longer, Jean descended to the office to ask if the repairs could not be made at some other time. At the desk he found an irate American who, in the meager French at his command, was astounding the clerk with a tirade which in English would have been something like this: "It's an outrage, these fellows bellowing next to us all day! If *you* don't stop it, *we will!* We've already used up the shovel and the tongs, and now we're beginning on the poker. We'll have a hole clear through the wall in a minute." Jean, standing by unobserved, enjoyed the expressions which flitted over the American's face as the clerk, having produced the register, revealed the identity of his neighbors. When the complainant finally understood, he made but one remark: "And to think," he moaned, "that over in America I've been willing to pay almost any price just to hear those fellows sing for part of an evening!"

Edouard's one wish was to see Jean again. When the full realization came that he would probably never have that joy, he said, "Then I must say again how much I love him," and he wrote a letter telling Jean that he had meant more to him than anything else in life, more than mother and father, more than his art, more than his children.

All the sadness and longing of these last years found expression in music. Hour after hour he played the piano, sitting there with a waiting, wondering, enduring look in his kind eyes, finding in the strange absoluteness of music the only possible peace. In the spring of 1917 he became ill again, and on the twenty-fifth of May he died; not, as reported in the press, in a cellar and in poverty, but in his own home, where he had been lovingly cared for by his wife and his children.

Edouard de Reszke dead! The news struck deep into the hearts of his friends and of those thousands of others who had experienced his friendliness across the footlights. It was difficult to believe that the majestic voice was forever stilled; it seemed impossible that all that vivacity and mountainous good humor should pass into nothingness, that that noble form should be lifeless.

Although it was ten years since he had retired, when Edouard de Reszke died it seemed that Grand Opera had lost something anew. A newspaper editorial[128] sounded the note of universal regret: "Fashions come and go in music and in singing and, as well, in opera, which is a little of both and *le 12 Juin 1917*

Mon cher ami

Je te remercie du fond de mon
cœur désolé d'avoir ressenti avec
tant d'affection ma profonde
douleur. Aux plus beaux souvenirs
de notre vie ton nom est attaché
et ta bonté pour nous était un
des attraits de nos voyages en Amérique.

Tout cela est loin; je suis désemparé
car Edouard était la moitié de
moi-même et je serai triste jusqu'à
la fin de ma vie. Tendres remerciements
à ta femme et Yvonne.

Je t'embrasse cordialement
ton vieux Jean de Reszke

Courtesy of M. Edouard Brandus, the recipient

"Edouard was half of myself and I shall be sad
to the end of my life."

much of other things besides. But a giant is always a giant, and it needs no critical yardstick to know that the days of giants are not upon us now. Other years are coming and we shall hope, optimistically, for a new birth of opera. For that day we can ask no greater fortune than to hear again the equal of Edouard de Reszke."

JEAN HAD GIVEN up teaching soon after the outbreak of the war. His son Jean, an only child who showed marked talent as a painter, had enlisted in the French Dragoons, although he was a Russian subject. His great-grandfather on his mother's side, the Marquis de Goulaine, had served as a general under Napoleon, and with the declaration of war the boy's ancestral fighting blood was aroused. Cut off from all means of communicating with Edouard, and with his son in active service, Jean de Reszke was under too great a mental strain to enjoy teaching. A pupil * who asked if she might resume her lessons received this reply:

21 November 1914

DEAR FRIEND:

Thank you for your sweet little note. I am happy to know that you are far from this horrible war, which tries us so cruelly. For three months my whole family in Poland has been blockaded by the Germans.... No news, and I tremble for them.... My son has enlisted as a volunteer in the 11th Cuirassiers. As he is a first-class horseman and a remarkable fencer, he was allowed, after four days in barracks, to join the battalion which went to the Marne. He fought throughout the battle and was wounded—he was promoted to the rank of brigadier, and eight days ago he departed for the north of Belgium with his regiment. Under these conditions and this anxiety, I know I cannot think of giving lessons. That I regret, for I love teaching, but one must have the brain clear. I hope that Dippel will appreciate your qualities. Give him a thousand greetings for me.

I embrace you paternally.

Your devoted master
J. DE RESZKE.

Jean took an active part in relief work, and assumed the presidency of a committee for the aid of wounded Poles in the French army. When he heard of the appeal for cigarettes for the wounded, he immediately arranged for fifty thousand "De Reszke" cigarettes to be distributed in the hospitals of the Allied Armies and the British Navy.

* Miss Barbara Maurel.

In October 1915 he resumed teaching, as that was the only
activity which could help him to bear the stress of war days.
At his son's urgent request he moved to Fontainebleau in
1916, and it was there that he received word of Edouard's
death. It was a grievous blow. To an old friend who sent
him a note of condolence, he wrote: "I am torn apart, for
Edouard was half of myself, and I shall be sad to the end of
my life." Not long after this his brother Viktor died, and in
June 1918 his son was killed. Young Jean had fought gallantly
in the battle of the Marne, and had been wounded. He refused
to rest, however, stopping only long enough to change cloth-
ing and horses before returning to the front at Ypres. After
this he found life with the cavalry too quiet, and joined the
"Chasseurs à pied," working his way to the rank of lieutenant.
His bearing under fire won him the Croix de Guerre, and he
had been recommended for the Croix de la Légion d'Honneur
when he was killed by a bullet. One of his brother officers
described him (in a letter to me) as "an unaffected young man,
very brave in battle. His death is a proof of that, for I knew
more than one officer who would have remained in his place,
whereas he, with a rare audacity, did not hesitate to lead his
company in an attempt to recapture territory which the Germans had taken from us."

His son's death brought a double burden of woe to Jean,
for with the news of this calamity, Madame de Reszke suffered
a breakdown from which she did not recover for years. Jean
himself longed to return to Poland. He had hoped to spend
his last years in the beloved homeland, but to this his wife
would not consent. Jean wanted to see Poland free. It was
good to read that the new conditions were invigorating his
country and its people; but actually to see Polish troops go
marching by, under Polish colors, to hear school children singing Polish songs, openly and unafraid—that, he felt, would
indeed be sight and sound to gladden the heart of a Polish
patriot! But when Minia, who had gone to her Uncle Jean
after her father's death, asked him, "Why don't you go home
to Poland, if only for one visit?" the answer was always, "My
poor Marie is so ill—how can I leave her?"

Nor could Madame de Reszke bear to live in the Paris
home where she had been happy with her idolized boy, and
in October 1919 she and Jean took up their residence in the
Villa Vergemère in Nice. Here Jean again threw all his ener-
gies into teaching. He had endured much, but outwardly he

was usually cheerful. In other days he had wept with the sorrows of Romeo and Tristan in private before he tried to communicate them to the audience, and in later years, the greater his private sorrows the more he strove to hide them from his pupils and his friends. Once Tade Styka, the son of his old friend, and a friend of his son's, called on him. They talked about young Jean for awhile, and then Mr. Styka inquired after the health of Madame de Reszke. "She is still the same," replied Jean, and, putting his hand on his young friend's shoulders, added, "We Poles, we know how to suffer."

And always the yearning for Poland. Minia watched an international parade with him at Nice. "When my uncle saw a row of Polish officers go by," she told me, "he trembled with joy, and sobbed." He loved the surroundings of the villa Vergemère, which stood on the top of a high hill, bathed in the serene atmosphere of the French Riviera. Purple clematis and yellow mimosa and many other flowers grew there in radiant profusion, and through the palm trees and the tremulous leaves of the poplars the blue waters of the Mediterranean gleamed. But Jean's heart turned to Skrzydlow, where, on a winter's day, the snow lay thick on field and forest, and soft grey clouds lingered in the twilight; Skrzydlow, where the friendly peasant folk adored him, and where he felt closer to Edouard.

Of Edouard he spoke but seldom. Late one afternoon Minia, coming into the darkening studio, thought she heard the sound of muffled sobs. It was Jean, sitting in a corner with bowed head, weeping. "My dear Uncle," she cried, "what has happened?" "I—I was thinking of Edouard," he faltered. "It just came over me that I would never see him again." With a wan smile he went on: "Do you remember that funny little habit he had of putting everything on his dressing-table back into its exact spot, no matter how often it was moved?"

What memories must have come rushing as he tried to teach a younger bass to sing the music of Mephisto or Frère Laurent! One morning two pupils waiting for a lesson heard the strains of "Le veau d'or" coming from the studio. "Aha," said one of them, "that's a fine new bass the Maître has. I wonder who he is." He stole to the door and discovered that it was not a new bass, but the Master himself singing. Increasing years seemed only to ripen his powers, and his reverence for his art grew constantly. This deep respect for the art of dramatic singing he tried to inculcate in his pupils. He had an almost uncanny ability to communicate to them his own feeling for delicate phrasing and the artistic union of word and tone, but, unfortunately, few of them were vocally or intellectually equipped to receive all that he had to give. Sometimes they could reproduce the desired effect in the master's presence, but away from the studio all was lost. Jean said himself that it was almost impossible to teach any one how to sing; one could only give guidance—"the rest must be inside."

Pupils continued to come in greater numbers than he could accept. Applicants were willing to wait months, in the hope that some pupil would drop out, or that they might be called when regular pupils had to miss a lesson. He was very proud of this tribute to his art, but, with characteristic modesty, he showed consideration for other teachers. Madame Charlotte Lund, one of his first pupils, wrote a series of newspaper articles addressed to students of singing, and naturally they contained references to her own master. In acknowledging their receipt, Jean expressed his satisfaction, and added: "Continue along these lines, only do not speak particularly of me or of my pupils. That will hurt other teachers, and it might make them think that you were trying to advertise me."

But although Jean guarded against wounding the feelings of others, he sometimes worked harm to himself. Many voices had, as he put it, been "martyrized." To rid pupils of old faults and show them better ways required more than a few weeks or a few months, but not many were able, or willing, to stay the necessary time. "Before I have placed their tongues, much less their voices," he complained, "they want to know how soon they will make their débuts. To many of them I have to say: 'My dear, get married. A career is not for you.'" Some went home and let it be known that they had worked with Jean, for to be "a pupil of de Reszke" lent glamour to any student of singing; but more than a few of those who sought to secure engagements, or to teach, on the strength of their brief association with Jean, could not rightly be considered his pupils. Occasionally some one would ask him for a note to give to a teacher in another city, certifying that he had studied with de Reszke, and later Jean learned that the note had been taken to an impresario, who had assumed that it was a recommendation for an engagement. As the possibility of such action did not occur to a man like Jean, he took no precautions against it, but it grieved him deeply.

In other ways he was a victim of his own kindness. Whereas he seldom gave praise during a lesson, a simple "Bien" representing a real compliment, letters to pupils were sometimes couched in more generous terms than their achievements warranted, and were likely to be used to the best advantage (just as he had sometimes written flattering letters to prima donnas, which they published in their books). Nor was he spared the blandishments of the social climber, who paid for expensive lessons because she hoped to mingle with royalty in Jean's home and thought a command performance might follow.

Jean did not always have his own way in matters concerning his pupils. When, for instance, four young men who had been singing quartets together asked for permission to call themselves "The de Reszke Quartet," he was against granting the request. They sang very well, he said, but the quality might deteriorate, and then the name would continue, even though it no longer represented his own standards. His wife, however, felt that the plan had a certain value, and at her insistence he agreed to the use of his name, on the condition that the vocal and artistic standard should be maintained; but he wept while giving his consent. The Quartet enjoyed several successful seasons, and then, for various reasons, disbanded.

It was not a selfish egotism which made Jean reluctant to permit the use of his name. He himself regretted that there was no way in which it would be perpetuated musically. "My brother is dead and almost forgotten," he said, "my son is dead and is also almost forgotten. Soon I shall be dead and I shall be forgotten." Then he pointed to a box of "De Reszke" cigarettes and added ruefully, "The only thing to carry on the name is this." Certainly he wanted his pupils to succeed; his last years were devoted to them utterly. The long teaching day over, he pondered over their difficulties at the dinner table. "I am troubled about M———," he would say. "How can I get that F right?" Then, after a few moments of general conversation, "What can I do with that W———? He has not a very big voice." Thus he thought aloud about every pupil who had had a lesson that day, until his wife cried out: "Laissez les bêtes d'élèves!" "But they are my *life!*" Jean replied. "My pupils are my life!"

He kept in touch with those who had left him. He never seemed too busy to send the little note of congratulation or to give advice. "Pour le *Meineid* de Erda; don't crush the breath, but make your ribs as large as possible and give the tone with ribs in their greatest expansion." * He wrote many letters to a former assistant, and always he gave detailed information about the progress of various pupils; incidentally making comments that might have astonished some of them who boasted of being his "favorite" or his "foremost exponent."

Jean always took a few pupils with him for the summer, which he usually spent at Vichy, Mont Dore, or Deauville. His association with them kept him young, he said. The lessons over, they played golf, which Jean enjoyed. Thursday afternoons he reserved for golf entirely. He would start out over the course singing lustily, but if his companion made a particularly good drive, the song diminished, and Jean paused between phrases, looking ahead a little anxiously. Those who played with him frequently, knew that he did not like to be excelled, and obligingly sent the ball into the rough. Then Jean would say: "You must keep your eye on the ball. Now you see, I'm pretty good, but if I could keep my eye on the ball, I'd be *very* good. But I have to guess. My belly is in the way."

He had indeed grown rather corpulent, and although he was amused at the size of his belly—it was a word he delighted in using—he was well aware that he no longer presented the romantic figure of days gone by. When, years after his retirement, he was again urged to go to America on a concert tour, he pointed to a statue of himself as the young Siegfried, and then to his stomach, and said: "No, people remember Jean de Reszke as Romeo, as Siegfried, as Tristan. I was an ideal. I can't change that." Sometimes he even refused to see people with whom he had been on friendly terms in other days, saying that he had grown "old and bald and fat," and was loath to have any one see him who had known him formerly.

In his old age Jean wanted to live simply. He disliked having his home conducted as though he were holding a Court. "I don't want to stand so much as I have to when the King and Queen of Portugal are my guests," he objected. But his royal visitors never guessed how weary he was. Occasionally they even served to illustrate a point in teaching. One day as a group of them were leaving after a protracted stay, he called a pupil who had entertained them by singing, and said: "Now you see? They will say I am a very gracious host. You know why? Because all the time I was bowing them out I was

* From a letter to Miss Frieda Klink.

THE MAÎTRE
Jean de Reszke at Villa Vergemère, Nice
(From a photograph by H.R.H. the Princess Victoria, by permission)

lifting my cheeks and smiling. Not a grimace, of course, but it gives the face a pleasant look. That's how you must raise the cheeks in singing. If you can't smile—restez chez vous au lit."

Then, that extra lesson given, he would say, "Now come, we'll have a game of billiards." He was very skillful at billiards, and could easily beat an opponent by playing with only one arm. Jean was one of those people who are winners in nearly everything they attempt. Luck was always with him. His peasants in Poland thought he had some sort of divine protection. During the war, estates bordering on his were devastated, but his remained untouched. He always won at cards. His horses always won the race. Jean used to tell with great glee the reason his peasants assigned for his luck in horse racing. He was the first to take an American jockey (Tod Sloan rode for him) to Europe, and the peasants were unaccustomed to seeing any one ride in a forward, crouching position. "No wonder he wins," they said. "Master tells him what to whisper in the horse's ear." His success at billiards was, of course, owing more to skill than to luck. He said that he used the same principles of rhythm here that he used in making gestures on the stage.

During the years at Nice he played billiards or bridge (never more than one table) almost every evening, and seldom went to bed before midnight; but he was up early all the same, although it was sometimes an effort to go through his regular morning exercises. Promptly at nine o'clock he came downstairs, Koko on his shoulder—Koko, the parrot that sat there quietly as long as the lesson was satisfactory, but protested shrilly, in a kind of jungle falsetto, when the singing was bad and he saw the Master looking over his glasses in disapproval. Koko was no respecter of persons. He made no difference in his response between beginners and artists of recognized standing, many of whom went to Jean for a few lessons whenever they could. Earlier pupils had had a less vocal observer in the cat Jean named "Vaccai," in honor of the singing master of that name.

If Jean had not seen a pupil for some years, he would say, "I hope you will think that I have made some progress," or, "I've learned a great deal since you were last here." That was not merely to make conversation; he really had been studying just as faithfully as his most conscientious pupil. "One morning when I came in for a lesson," one of them told me, "I found the Master in a very happy mood. He informed me at once, with great satisfaction, that he had been working on his own voice, and that at last he had succeeded in doing something with it that he had been trying for a lifetime to accomplish, without success."

When Henry Finck sent him a copy of his book, *Success in Music and How it is Won,* in which he paid tribute to the art of de Reszke, Jean acknowledged it thus:

                                            December 20 1909

MY DEAR FRIEND:

I have read your book, *Success in Music and How it is Won,* with deep emotion. All my life as an artist has passed before my eyes, and my thoughts have been carried back to my dear comrades and the battles won at the cost of so much labor, perseverance, and self-denial.

I should blush to accept the praise you lavish upon me so generously. I have done my best, striving ever to advance in the art I loved beyond all else, and for which I lived.

May the story of my efforts and of the efforts of my illustrious fellow-workers serve as a guide and an incentive for all young people who would enter the theatrical profession! Your book shows them the path to fame, and I wish them success with all my heart.

                    Very sincerely yours
                              JEAN DE RESZKE

That his own singing lost none of its sweetness or power is attested by every one who heard him during those last years. In his *Lebens Erinnerrungen.*[129] Felix Weingartner describes a visit to Jean's studio. "To be present during his teaching hours," he writes, "was a rare privilege. Glorious, when he himself sang a phrase with his still sweet-sounding voice. Quiet as a pillar he stood there, and became furious if a pupil tried to compensate for faulty singing by eloquent movements of the body. 'Sing with your throat, not with your hips,' I often heard him call out...."

"On the way back to Vienna, I stayed in Nice for a day. ...Seventy-three years old he was, a regular old lion, unbroken, and in spite of the grievous sorrows that had befallen him, he had an unquenchable humor. 'Would you like to hear my voice?' he asked me, and sang a scale, singing from the lowest to the highest note with a power and beauty of tone that was astonishing. 'And see here, what else I can do,' he laughed, and very gracefully he swung his leg over an arm-chair. A living reminder of the far-off days of my youth stood before me in the form of this cheerful, kindly man." [130]

Jean himself was sometimes saddened by reminders of the past. He drove to Monte Carlo one day, to attend a concert directed by Walter Damrosch, who had conducted at the Metropolitan during his last season there. Jean sat near the front of the theater, and as the orchestra came to the Prize Song in the M e i s t e r s i n g e r overture, Mr. Damrosch could not resist the impulse to turn round and look at the man who had sung it so often and with such ravishing beauty. Jean gave him an immediate answering smile, but the tears were streaming down his cheeks.

He was living much in the past, for, after long urging, he had begun to write his reminiscences; but although he greatly enjoyed talking about his experiences, writing did not appeal to him, and he had not carried the account beyond the years of his childhood and adolescence when he died. He preferred to help develop the artistic possibilities of others. In November 1924 he and M. Aquistapace, one of his assistants, founded the Academy of Arts and Letters of Nice, and he became its honorary president.

And now he was planning to give a whole opera with his students. At last his dream was being realized; he had a school of singing where pupils could receive training in every phase of vocal and operatic art, and could appear in a Théâtre des Débutants. On December 8 1924 Mozart's D o n G i o v a n n i was given in the Théâtre des Variétés at Nice. The cast was as follows:

Donna Anna	.. Mmes.	Rachel Morton
Donna Elvira	..	Cora Gina
Zerlina ..	..	M. Tannahill
Don Giovanni	.. MM.	A. Andrèze
Leporello ..	..	Gauld
Don Ottavio	..	Benton
Mazetto ..	..	Kellog
Il Commandatore	..	Goffi

Villageoises: Mmes. Scabero, Altmann, Durand,
Treelaven, Pettit.
Villageois: MM. Colcaire, Sorrele, Campbell,
Luechauer, Petrovic.
Chef d'Orchestre: M. Reynaldo Hahn

The performance was spoken of as "a lyrical representation of such a quality, such interest . . . as we are not accustomed to seeing at Nice." [131] The opera was given several times at Nice and at Cannes, and some of the pupil artists secured engagements.

In the meantime, Amherst Webber, who had assisted Jean in his teaching during all these years, had been training the pupils in the "Heil, Hans Sachs" chorus from D i e M e i s t e r - s i n g e r, as a surprise for Jean on his seventy-fifth birthday, which occurred on January 14 1925. That morning Jean came down the staircase at nine o'clock, as usual, with Koko on his shoulder. As he entered the studio, forty voices rang out in a mighty "Heil, heil!" He stopped short, caught at the door, and stood still. The song finished, he started toward the singers, one of whom came forward and held out the little silver loving-cup they had brought as a gift. "Beloved Master," she said, "may your years be many with us, and full of happiness and good health." Jean brushed her aside, knocking the cup out of her hand in his haste to leave the room before the rush of his emotions overcame him. No lessons were given that morning.*

In the spring there were rehearsals for a special performance of D o n G i o v a n n i at Cannes. Jean worked tirelessly with individual pupils and at general rehearsals. He overtaxed his strength, and caught a chill at the dress rehearsal. During dinner that night Madame de Reszke picked up a newspaper, and, seeing mention of the fact that she and her husband had sat in a box during the rehearsal, exclaimed indignantly: "All the world knows that I have been in retirement since the death of my son. How dare they display my name in a public place!"

Jean looked at her in amazement and asked sadly: "Have I a wife or have I none? Must I go to these functions as a widowed man and be spoken of as such?" Then he added, wearily: "Laisse-moi tranquille. I am very tired." The next day lessons were canceled. Jean's over-exertion had lowered his resistance, and the cold he had caught developed into pneumonia. He became delirious, and in his delirium he sang some of the music from T r i s t a n.

Specialists were called from Paris, and one of them suggested an injection, informing Madame de Reszke that this was the only hope, though he could not tell whether it would result in a cure or death. Finally Madame de Reszke ordered

* See the appreciation by Rachel Morton, printed in the Appendix.

the injection to be given. Jean rallied momentarily, and sang a chromatic scale, the last sound that came from his lips. His strength failed rapidly. His wife looked in on him one day, said, "Mais, c'est fini," and never saw him again. Three days later he died, on April 3 1925, surrounded by Louis Vachet, Amherst Webber, Walter Johnstone-Douglas, and Minia.

All Nice lay fair in the lavender and bronze glow of the sunset. In the shadows of the hills lights began to twinkle. Slowly darkness enveloped the city. Beacons flared from each side of the peaceful Baie des Anges, and through the air a message was flashed afar: Romeo lay dead. The white dove of the Grail had flown down, and had borne Lohengrin back to Monsalvat. Isolde must look upon the noblest Tristan and lament: "Closed is the eye, and stilled the heart, and there is not even the zephyr of a passing breath. She must stand before you weeping."

A simple funeral service was held at the Église Notre Dame in Nice, and then the body of Jean de Reszke was borne to Paris, to be buried in the Montparnasse Cemetery there. On the night of Jean's death G ö t t e r d ä m m e r u n g was performed at the Metropolitan House of New York. It seemed fitting that he should be speeded into the Valley of the Shadow to the strains of its funeral march.

FINALE

OLD VIOLINS, it is said, keep in them something of all the sounds that were ever made on them. If that is also true of old rooms, what beautiful music—though unheard—must be floating through the opera houses in which Jean de Reszke sang. What visions of grace and beauty glimmer through the memories of those who saw him act; what warm gratitude lives in the hearts of those who knew him as fellow artist, as teacher, and as friend.

A contemporary singer says: "Jean always appreciated the art of others, and to do even a small part and do it beautifully was a thing that he of all my fellow colleagues understood best and appreciated most." [132]

W. J. Henderson, the discriminating critic who had reviewed hundreds of Jean's performances and had dedicated his book, *The Art of the Singer*, "To Jean de Reszke—Mastersinger," wrote, after Jean's death:

"His voice was by no means incomparable, but his art was. There is nothing known to the younger opera-goer to which it can be likened. A recital of the rôles in which he excelled may give some faint hint of his greatness, but even that will not be completely illuminating. He was the greatest Romeo that ever walked upon the stage. He was the greatest Tristan since Niemann and he sang the music of the part better than any one probably since Schnorr von Carolsfeld.

"He was great as Faust, great as Siegfried. He was matchless as Lohengrin. He was the ideal Walther von Stolzing. He was the finest Chevalier des Grieux, the unequaled Raoul in Les Huguenots, and John of Leyden in Le Prophète. No one except Italo Campanini rivaled him as Don Jose, and perhaps only Caruso as Radames. As Vasco di Gama he has had no rival." [133]

Lord Wittenham, who had known Jean well, expressed his feeling in a letter to *The* (London) *Times:* [134]

"I have heard all the great operatic tenors since 1873. Three stand out preëminently in my mind, each so different from the others—Tamagno, Caruso, Jean de Reszke: Tamagno, a tremendous tenore robusto, who literally made you jump from your seat in O t e l l o; Caruso, a golden tenor, who comes only once or twice in a century; Jean, who did all the wonders that he did, without a great natural voice, by the illuminating magic of his genius, by his extraordinary magnetism, and by an artistic perfection, dramatic and vocal, which subdued all things unto him."

Felix Weingartner, the well-known conductor, writes of Jean the teacher: *

"I was present many a time while he was teaching. When, today, I hear of every possible method employed by teachers of singing, I must smile in memory at this great master. His art was unbelievably simple, free from dogma, and adapted to the individual needs of his pupils. The results he achieved were startling. Often a few lessons sufficed to 'place' a voice. Jean de Reszke was, however, not only a great artist and a great teacher, but, in the highest meaning of the word, a *noble* human being."

An English pupil says:

"He wished to equip his pupils with his own ever-increasing range of color and subtlety of tone, so that gradually technique began to mean to them no longer the power of accomplishing their own desires in interpretation, but rather the opening up of new worlds as yet undreamed of. Indeed, what made his teaching baffling to so many was the constant disappearance of the horizon the nearer one approached to it. . . .

"It may be true that among his pupils have appeared as yet no more de Reszkes, no more Pattis, none of the 'Blood Royal,' though most of the world's great singers at some time or other came to him for lessons or advice. But that is not the only test by which a teacher is judged. His pupils learned from him no easy standard, but one of unattainable perfection, ever sought but never found. The Best for the Highest. Other constellations may rise in the heavens, but they must steer by the memory of a star that has set."

Late in life Jean said that he remembered only five really good performances in which he had taken part, five occasions

* In a letter to me, here translated from the German and published only in part.

when everything had been perfectly satisfying, mentally and emotionally. "That is fairly good for one life," he mused. But how richly this modest estimate is multiplied in the memories of those whose emotions were kindled by the ravishing quality of his art, and who sensed what could not be defined—the artistic culture, the integrity of the man and the artist, the personal charm which gave a peculiar radiance to his singing and acting. Some one has said that every artist dies twice, and that the first death—the death of his activities—is the only real one. But Jean's activities ceased only when life itself ended. His was a whole life devoted to a single purpose. By heritage, by environment, by intellectual and emotional inclinations, he was driven towards achieving perfection as an operatic artist, and death overtook him while he was striving to impart the secrets of his art to others. In the history of Grand Opera the name of Jean de Reszke must stand as that of its noblest interpreter.

APPENDIX

LETTER FROM JULIUS KNIESE TO
JEAN DE RESZKE

Verehrter Herr de Reszke!
Herzlich danke ich Ihnen für Ihren lieben Brief aus Borowno.
Wie Sie es rieten, dass man sich von hier aus mit Herrn Harris in
Verbindung setzen möge, ist es geschehen, leider bis heut ohne Erfolg:
Harris hat nicht geantwortet.

Nun komme ich noch einmal zu Ihnen, um Ihnen wieder unsere
herzlichste und dringendste Bitte um Übernahme des Siegfried vorzulegen. Sie können nachfühlen, dass wir hier nicht loslassen dürfen,
sondern Alles versuchen müssen, um den Siegfried von Ihnen zu "ersie-
gen," um des herrlichen Kunstwerkes und um der vom Meister hinterlassenen Institution der Bayreuther Festspiele willen, die es gebieterisch
fordern, dass man den vorhandenen besten Vertreter einer Rolle
gewinnt. Mit Ihnen die Partie zu studieren, soll mir eine innige Freude
sein, und ich erwarte nur Ihren Brief, um mich Ihnen zur Verfügung
zu stellen, so dass wir für Ende September unsere Bitten und Hoffnungen auf Ihr "Ja" erfüllt sehen dürften?

Was das Arrangement mit Harris betrifft: darf ich Sie um die
Ermächtigung bitten, sagen zu können dass es in Ihrem Auftrage geschieht? Dann würde ja wohl die Antwort an unsere Verwaltung nicht
ausbleiben.

Mit sehr ergebenen Empfehlungen Frau Wagner's und herzlich-
stem [sic] Grüsse an Sie und Ihre verehrte Frau Gemahlin, sowie mit
schönstem Danke für Ihre freundliche Antwort bin ich,

Ihr
verehrungsvollst ergebener
Julius Kniese

Bayreuth
31 Juli 1895

CRITIQUE OF THE DE RESZKES' PERFORMANCE
IN "TRISTAN UND ISOLDE," FROM DAHEIM,
MAY 29 1896

Wir haben von den beiden Reszkes Hervorragendes erwartet,
hatten wohl auch das Recht dazu; aber auf so überwältigend Grossar-
tiges waren wir nicht gefasst. Erst vorgestern haben wir einen "Tristan" und einen "König Marke" zum ersten Male so gesehen und
gehört, wie Richard Wagner sie gezeichnet hat. Und da beschlich uns
ein wehmütiger Gedanke. Ist es nicht jammerschade, das zwei solche
Männer, durch den Zufall der Geburt und der daraus entspringenden
musikalischen Erziehung in das italienisch-französische statt in das
neudeutsche Fahrwasser geraten sind! Sind es ja zwei Wagner'sche
Heldengestalten, wie sie sich der Bayreuther Meister nicht vollkom-
mener träumen konnte! Jean Reszke z. B.—welch ein Sigmund, ein

307

Siegfried, ein Walther! Eduard Reszke—welch ein Wotan, ein Hagen, ein Hans Sachs!

Einen idealeren "Tristan" als Jean Reszke können wir uns nicht denken, den schlecht singenden und deklamierenden Alvary wie den unbeholfenen, papageienhaft rezitierenden Grüning überragt er so wie der Eiffelturm in Paris den hiesigen Wasserturm überragt. Bei Jean Reszke ist Alles vorhanden, um einen vollkommenen Tristan zu gestalten: Feuer, vornehmes und dramatisches Spiel und herrliche gesangliche Interpretierung. Dieser Tristan deklamiert nicht, er trägt die Wagner'schen Worte mit höchstem Verständniss vor: dieser Tristan winselt und schreit nicht, er singt die Wagner'schen herrlichen Töne stets edel und mit höchster Vollendung. Ja, ein solcher Tristan gestaltet Isolde's Selbstopferung begreiflich.

Auf gleicher künsterlischer Höhe steht der "König Marke" des Eduard Reszke. Erst vorgestern haben wir diese Wagner'sche Gestalt vollkommen erfassen können. Dieser "Marke" war kein Waschlappen, sondern er blieb immer der stolze, wenn auch in seinem Stolz tief verletzte, König! Und wie sang er! Jeder Ton erschütterte unser Inneres.

LETTER FROM JEAN DE RESZKE TO MADAME LILLI LEHMANN

THE GILSEY HOUSE
New York 4 February 1899

DEAR MADAM:
We have been very sorry, Edouard and I, to know that you are ill, but we hope that it is nothing serious and that you will come back to us as soon as possible with your admirable voice, and stronger than ever.

You are a thousand times too good, to write something concerning us, and I can really give you very few details of the kind you ask for.

I was born on the 14th of January 1850. In spite of the fact that I studied at the University to become a lawyer, in my heart I thought only of music and of singing. Being the "prima donna" in our college choirs, I made my public début at the age of 13 in the Church of the Visitation at Warsaw, where I sang the air from Stradella. It seems to me that today I have more experience, more style and personality, but fundamentally I sing the way I sang as a child, and Professors Ciaffei and Cotogni, to whom my parents sent me, did not have to put in much work with me.

I made my début, it is true, as a baritone at the Fenice Theatre at Venice in 1874, and with much success, but the critics persisted in finding mine a tenor voice, and I abandoned the bass clef after two seasons at Drury Lane Theatre in London.

Then I spent my best years, that is to say from 1876 to 1884, traveling with my sister and my brother, who had engagements at Madrid, Lisbon, Milan, Turin, London, etc. I helped them with my

Malgré que j'ai travaillé a l'université,
pour devenir avocat, je n'ai au fond
pensé qu'a la musique et au chant..
Étant la prima donna dans nos chœurs
de collège j'ai débuté publiquement
a l'age de 13 ans a l'Eglise des Visitandines
a Varsovie ou j'ai chanté l'air de Stradella
Il me semble qu'aujourd'hui j'ai plus
d'expérience plus de style et de personalité
mais au fond je chante comme je
chantais étant enfant et les professeurs
Gasser et Cotogni auquels m'avaient
confié mes parents n'ont pas eu
beaucoup de travail avec moi.

J'ai débuté il est vrai comme baryton
au théâtre de la Fenice a Venise en
1874 et avec beaucoup de succès, mais
les critiques s'obstinant a me trouver
une voix de tenor j'ai abandonné
la clef de fa, après deux saisons au
Drury Lane Theatre a Londres. --
Depuis j'ai passé mes plus belles années,
c'est a dire depuis 1876 jusqu'à 1884.

A page of the 5-page letter here translated
(See pages 308, 310)

counsel, I heard all the great singers of the period, I compared, I worked at home, without letting myself be seduced by the brilliant propositions which impresarios made me. I should perhaps have continued not to sing in the theater, if Massenet and Maurel had not taken me by force to create Hérodiade in Paris in 1884. There began my career as a tenor; engaged by Massenet also to create Le Cid at the Opera, I remained there five consecutive years. Then came engagements in Russia and America, with thirteen seasons at Covent Garden in London.

I have sung Hérodiade, Le Cid, Manon, Werther, Les Huguenots, Robert le Diable, Prophète, Africaine, Otello, Aïda, Ballo in Maschera, Faust, Romeo, Carmen, Esmeralda, Elaine, Tristan, Siegfried, Götterdämmerung, Meistersinger, Lohengrin. The operas which I have sung most often are R o m e o and L o h e n g r i n.

As a curiosity I send you the names of the sixteen [sic] Juliettes whom I have had for my Romeo: Patti, Darclée, Lureau, Escalais, Eames, Melba, Mravina, Klamrzynska, Nordica, Cerrère, Marsy, Bertet, Sembrich, Engle, Saville, Bolska, Adams.

I have written you somewhat at length, but you can take, dear Madame, what you judge suitable for your article. Edouard will write you a little later. He is so busy that he is losing his head.

Au revoir, soon, my dear and great comrade, and thanks for all your kindness and affection.

Your devoted
JEAN DE RESZKE

A thousand friendly greetings to your charming sister.

JEAN DE RESZKE'S PRINCIPLES OF SINGING

BY WALTER JOHNSTONE-DOUGLAS

IT IS a difficult matter to write down Jean de Reszke's principles of singing in set order. In the first place he never codified them himself, he regarded with suspicion "singing made easy," and distrusted teachers who professed to hold any single key that would open the many doors of singing. His ideas changed in focus and perspective very often, and the longer he taught the better he taught. One of his first pupils, May Petersen, came back to him a few years ago, and his first remark to her was: "I hope you will think that I have made some progress." Moreover, the questions of technique were always in his mind, and teaching was not just an occupation for retirement, it was a genuine passion. Old pupils coming back would find new things that had been thought of, new "places" found, new analogies, new metaphors, but always the same Master.

Perhaps the best way of stating his ideas—he himself always rejected the word "method"—would be to put down in order the various steps by which he would take a pupil, more or less a beginner, and to give some of his own expressions and analogies, remembering always that with him imitation played a larger part than explanation. He would say: "I can imitate you (this was very true, he had a peculiar gift of mimicry); why, can't you imitate me?" A further difficulty is that with him voice-production, diction and interpretation were inseparable: the very earliest lessons, after vowel sounds pure and simple, would be on phrases from operas in any language, to exemplify the technical point that was being studied.

The object of his whole teaching was primarily the operatic stage, but was by no means confined to that. He said himself of his way of training: "*Au commencement, les petits galops, puis le grand entraînement, et après ça les courses classiques, les Derbys.*" He knew that in the theater one wanted all kinds of resource and color in the voice, but primarily power, "*Au théâtre il faut gueuler mais il faut savoir gueuler,*" * and he was out to get more power from voices, both by increasing their size and by the proper use of what size they had got already. He had an uncanny power of building up a voice out of little or nothing, and under his hand ordinary voices were transformed into something rich and strange. But his power was never obtained by the sacrifice of beauty of tone: it was said of him by Reynaldo Hahn: "*Il est le seul ténor qui ait du charme dans la force.*" Nor did he ever encourage his pupils to sing beyond their powers, though he constantly expected them to develop those powers more and more. Singing was to him like any other form of athletics, a question of training and natural gifts combined: the amateur has the natural gifts but the professional must have both. In producing more power he never allowed pupils to strain their voices. He would have preferred that all work should be done under his supervision, a lesson every day but no practice. It is impossible to hear yourself sing, you can only judge by sensation, and it is some time before your analysis of sensations is a sufficient guide. If any damage was done to voices, though I have never heard first-hand of such damage, it was done while the pupil was practicing misguidedly at something he or she had misunderstood. Those of his pupils who stayed several years, and came back frequently for more lessons, felt the full truth of this, and benefited by his acute diagnosis of the faults into which they had unconsciously fallen.

He also taught by exaggeration—*il faut en avoir trop, pour en avoir assez* †—and in each point of his teaching insisted upon the supreme, cardinal importance of that particular point. Not for many lessons did things begin to become relative to each other; they were always absolute. In this way his teaching seemed to contradict itself at times, and the stresses on one side of technique seemed to be too heavy, but to those who had patience and faith the kaleidoscope settled down to a clear picture.

The first step would be to secure the foundation on which everything was to rise, namely the "breath support," and to obtain that connection between the voice and its support which is so essential for control and depth of tone. To get this he would make the pupil sit down in an attitude of complete relaxation, round-shouldered, elbows on knees, hands hanging down ("*asseyez-vous comme ça et puis*

---

* "In opera one *has* to shout, but one must *know how* to shout."
† "One must have too much, in order to have enough."

méditez" *) in order to relax all the muscles of the chest, and prevent the use of any others except those of the diaphragm. Then, in inhaling, the lower ribs were to be expanded without raising the chest:— "Imagine yourself to be a great church bell, where all the sonority is round the rim." But this was not to be confused with sticking the stomach out—abdominal breathing; the abdomen was to be kept up and in, to give greater support to the diaphragm. In singing, this expansion was to be kept as long as possible, and the lower ribs not allowed to collapse, in order that the breath might be kept under compression to the very last. This was, in fact, the first step towards the legato style of the true Bel Canto. Trouble sometimes arose from beginners becoming frightened at the muscular fatigue this caused, if they had been brought up to think singing should be "easy and natural and effortless." Also, he made one exaggerate this compression to develop the muscles, and produce temporarily a tone which was over-*écrasé,* squashed or compressed. The tone was to be produced by the vocal cords and the mouth only, with no deliberately added resonance of chest or head. A word such as the French *puis* would be taken, with a much exaggerated *p* and extremely thin *u* and *i.* Quick breathing was the rule and through the mouth.

Another way of establishing connection between the voice and its support was to breathe out, right from the bottom of the lungs, the pure sound of the Italian "ah" *on* the breath and not *in* it, with no head resonance at all, the breath coming straight up from the diaphragm without compression, over the vocal cords and out of the mouth, as if one was breathing out on the hand to warm it. This gives complete relaxation of all the muscles of throat and tongue.

Now all this was unattainable without a low position of the larynx, and this deep breathing of course materially assisted the descent of the larynx. He insisted upon the lowest possible position of the larynx for all heavy singing as the great protection against overstrain. The vocal cords were to do their work as if the singer was speaking; one of his demonstrations was how the speaker's voice gradually merges, imperceptibly, into the singing voice. If the cords did not do their work properly, the illusion of speaking whilst singing could not be maintained. The proper functioning of the cords means that they must be kept tense, not flabby, hard, not unsteady, and with their edges close together, kept straight, not ragged. He often used the phrase: "You should stroke your cords," meaning that you must not attack too violently so as to damage them. The *coupe de glotte* was only allowed when working at getting the cords to work properly, and then only under his supervision.

The soft palate and uvula were the factors which chiefly determined the quality of the voice by controlling the passage to the nose. To get that most difficult sound, a clear Italian "a" in the lower part of the voice (up to middle C for men or the octave above for women), the palate must be low. The difficulty here is to keep the larynx low without the palate rising. To obtain more *timbre* in this part of the voice the palate was drawn back but not raised, and kept rigid. This is important, for if the palate be too high for these notes it produces

---

* "Sit down like this and then meditate."

a heady tone which booms, and makes it impossible to "speak" on the voice and give the vowels their true sound (a fault particularly common with contraltos). As the pitch rises, above C, so the palate rises too, retaining its back position as in the lower medium, in order to retain the *timbre,* and to prevent the high notes hooting in the head. Those who sing too much in the head, besides producing a dead colorless tone, have generally a tendency to sing sharp. The education of the palate was arrived at by the following means:—"Draw back the palate till it feels as if it was on the level of your ears, hear the pitch of the note mentally, and then strike as if you were trying to focus your voice on to the two sides of the pharynx at once." An exercise such as

was given to exercise the palate, so that you could feel it change its position and draw still further back and up as the pitch rose, thus blocking the nasal passage.

I am not going into the rather complicated matter of the male "covered" or "closed" notes. To do so without practical demonstration is almost impossible. Sufficient to say that more head resonance is required, without losing the diaphragmatic "support." A bass or baritone should begin to "cover" his voice on E flat or E, a tenor on F or F sharp, though for an occasional effect he should be able to "open" his E and F sharp respectively.

The tongue must not rest against the lower front teeth, but must be slightly drawn back with the tip curled down against the tongue-string. The back of the tongue had to be absolutely loose. If the tongue is too far forward it tends to bring the soft palate forward with it, and put the voice into the nose. If the tongue is stiff at the back, and the muscles at the base allowed to tighten, the tone immediately sounds throaty, because it becomes then supported in the throat and not from the diaphragm. The chin must be kept still and absolutely loose, the lower jaw hanging from the ears as if dislocated.

Another way of preventing a booming or spreading tone was by "pinching the uvula with the tonsils." This was, above all, useful on *o* and *oo* sounds, but everywhere, and especially in the upper part of the voice, it gave an added edge to sounds that might otherwise be flabby. Such a phrase would be taken as

po - po - lo   li   pros - tra

where the forward position of the lips, in an oval shape, would be a further help to securing the resonance of the *o* sound. This "pinching" was very difficult to get right, and it ought never to be practiced without skilled supervision, as pupils are apt to stiffen the muscles at the root of the tongue in their endeavor to alter the shape of the arch, which requires little or no muscular effort. This practice sometimes resulted in a temporary stiffness in the voice and excessive tightness in the tone, a fault of excess which could be more easily remedied than a fault of defect. In all his teaching he demanded, as I have said, exaggeration in order to get enough. If any detail became too prominent it was easy to relax a little there. When things had fallen into their place there remained just enough to give the desired effect, and a reserve of power if more were wanted. An element of great importance was the "mask" tone, to get the maximum resonance and ring in the voice, second only in importance to the support. To obtain this the uvula was held poised (*i.e.,* in not so exaggerated a position as when working at the "education of the palate"), so as to give just room enough for the tone to be thrown up into the resonating spaces behind the nose, using the sound of the French *"-an-"* as in *"souf-france."* If the sound did not strike behind the uvula it would go into the nose and produce a very ugly quality of sound, almost invariably flat.   The difficulty was, as he said, that *"le nez est l'antichambre du masque,"* * and many people remained in the ante-chamber thinking they were in the presence.† This "mask" tone was of general use, but never in *piano* singing. Because of its numerous nasal syllables, a very effective sentence to obtain this resonance was *"Pendant que l'enfant mange son pain, le chien tremble dans le buisson,"* monotoned on each successive note of the scale. This mask quality he insisted on as an essential ingredient in women's chest voices, which he would rarely allow to be carried above E above middle C, never above F: if carried above F a "break" inevitably develops. In a course of purely mask singing *o* and *a* would become as French *on* and *an,* the open *ê* as in *être,* became *ain,* and the *i* as in *si* and the closed *é* as in *été* were hardly placed in the mask at all, but were supported on the diaphragm. To get the maximum amount of "forward" tone to the voice, which he deemed "essential," it was his plan to imagine that you were drinking in the tone, rather than pushing it out. This idea encouraged the palate to draw back and give *timbre* to the voice, while it helped the tone to find its way into the true mask, whereas an attempt to push the tone out often results merely in a nasal tone, though when the voice is in the right place the tone seems to be resonating right on the hard palate, by the front teeth. This apparent paradox was often misunderstood by those who criticized his teaching without knowing it.

After a certain amount of work at these different "places," the pupil would be told to sing something, and just sing naturally, allowing all the various elements to fall—more or less—into their places. The great idea was to keep the line from the diaphragm, through the vocal cords into the mask, to control—*maîtriser*—the voice and not allow it to *"faire le steeplechase"* from chest to head, and nose to throat. The

* "The nose is the ante-chamber of the mask."
† The confusion that arises over this point among singers is sadly common. They think they are "in the mask," but they are, frankly, "in the nose." The result is most unpleasant, and, especially after they have been practicing assiduously, it takes weeks or even months to get the voice out of the nose and then replace it in the true mask.

whole body was to be as though one was "settling down" on to the
diaphragm, relaxed but ready to spring, as in tennis, golf, boxing, etc.,
rather than braced up and stiff as if "on parade." The effort was to
come from the back as if the sound was following "a line drawn from
the small of the back to the bridge of the nose." This invariably added
a velvety quality to the voice as it had done to his own. Every grada-
tion of power had to be employed from pianissimo to fortissimo, not
forgetting that most difficult of all, the rarely heard mezzo-forte: all
must have the same depth— *la voix bien assise* *—and not a superficial
voice which seems to come from no deeper than the larynx, and has
no carrying power. The whole body must always be behind the voice.
Of course, each single part of the machine needed and received continuous supervision and training, and the more it could do the more
was required of it. The pupil was occasionally disappointed at not
making any apparent headway, but the truth was that the Master knew
that so much progress had been made that there was more where that
came from. However, in returning to some aria or song which had
not been sung for several weeks, it became obvious that notes which
used to be difficult were much easier, and phrases which frightened
the life out of you before appeared quite singable.

No article of this length could possibly be complete, nor could
it detail all the weapons in his armory. But one ought not to forget
his pianissimo and *mezza voce* singing. The pianissimos were obtained
in three ways: what he called *la voix étouffée* † (more often applied
to men's voices), sung with almost closed mouth and low palate, the
larynx being rather high, but the support as deep and strong as possible. He used to describe how he used this voice in Lohengrin's farewell to the swan, *"Nun sei bedankt mein lieber Schwan,"* and how
other tenors would stand in the wings to see if they could find out
what he did to produce this marvelous tone, so clear and yet so full
of pain—sung genuinely from the heart. Then there was the piano
tone in the head, the pianissimo tone most commonly used, obtained
with a very high palate and a certain breath support. And lastly, the
pianissimo, which seemed to come from the middle of the back, without any obvious muscular support, with the larynx low, the mouth
open, and no apparent resonances, thus differing from the *voix
étouffée*. This is a wonderfully carrying tone, but can only be obtained
by complete relaxation. This, with slight variations, was the basis
of his *mezza voce* singing.

Declamation was to be absolutely natural, beginning with a
simple everyday sentence, worked up until the consonants were taken
from the diaphragm as deep as possible with the larynx low, but with
the vowels remaining as in speech. Of course in everyday speech the
larynx is high, but in much public speaking or in acting big tragic
parts it would be impossible to stand the strain unless the larynx were
low. He had heard Salvini act *Otello,* and used to imitate him, using
the whole range of his singing voice from low C to top B flat.

The position of the head was important also; he always said,
"Sing to the gallery," with the head slightly back, but not stiff, except

* "The voice well seated."
† "The crushed voice."

when trying to get the full mask tone, when "you feel as if you were butting your way through." Cheeks and lips were all mobile, the raising of the cheeks as the voice rose in pitch being particularly helpful, indeed essential, for men's upper open notes and all women's high notes, in that it obtains the maximum stretch of the soft palate. He used to call this *"la grimace de la chanteuse"* ("the singer's grimace").

It would be impossible to write here any adequate account of his amazing resourcefulness in teaching. If one means failed to accomplish the end he wanted with a pupil, he would immediately substitute another. His diagnosis of faults was searching and immediate, and his ear for a note not quite properly placed was unfailingly acute. He would never correct faults of intonation in a pupil by saying: "Can't you hear that you are singing flat," but rather by saying, for example, to a tenor whose E and F were out of tune: "The cheeks are not raised enough and therefore the sound is flat." The cause of faulty intonation is nearly always faulty technique, rather than a defective ear, and you cannot always make people sing in tune by pointing out that they are out of tune. You must show them the reason, and help them to correct the defect.

His teaching has been much criticized by those who did not know what or how he taught, and by some of those pupils who came to be "finished" and were rather hurt that they were bidden to stay to be "begun"! He demanded the absolute confidence of his pupils, and those who gave it never regretted it. He demanded concentration, and the complete attention of pupils. No one could benefit to the full from his teaching who did not give himself time to absorb all he taught, or who did not intrust himself absolutely to the Master's directions, or who did not come in real humility prepared to learn.

He has been criticized also for not having produced great singers among his pupils. Even if that were true—and most of the great singers sought his advice at some time—that is not the standard by which he must be judged. His triumphs were rather the improvement out of all recognition of voices which were neither magnificent nor generous by nature. His absorption in teaching was such that he preferred a voice which he had to "make," rather than a voice to which he had only to add qualities not already there. But cultivated voices, like cultivated flowers, tend to revert to their wild state unless they are carefully tended. His pupils were also expected by their friends to be able to reproduce at once the characteristics of the great de Reszke, their friends forgetting that great singers are the combination of great voices and great brains and great instincts. How rare such a combination is!

During the twenty years he taught his pupils must have numbered hundreds, from all over the world, to whom he gave liberally and generously from his stores of knowledge and never-failing inspiration. If the fame of a Master be measured by the devotion and love of his pupils, his title is well and honorably secured.

JEAN DE RESZKE AS TEACHER

By Rachel Morton

"COME for your first lesson tomorrow, and you need not speak to me of money until you have made the success in opera that I predict for you."

That is what Jean de Reszke said to me after an audition at the Villa Vergemère early in October 1922. The words are characteristic of the heart of the man, and they gave birth to my singing career. Not that I had never sung before, but I never sang with knowledge until I learned from Jean de Reszke. Much had gone before. I had studied with eminent teachers in Berlin for a year, and later in New York, where I had given successful recitals. I had sung with the New York Symphony Orchestra on several occasions.

Mr. Walter Damrosch procured a scholarship for me for the summer session at Fontainebleau, where I won a first prize in the opera "concours." At the end of that summer, I sat in the Bois de Boulogne and took stock of my position. Fontainebleau had taught me that I had some talent, but much to learn. It seemed to me that I should need at least five years in Europe to acquire an operatic repertoire, learn three languages, take on a musical culture and perfect a vocal technique which was far from secure.

They had told me after hearing me sing at the Women's Club in Paris that I ought to study with Jean de Reszke. Without funds, and standing in great awe of such a celebrated man, I felt that the sharing of a throne with the King of England was just as likely a proposition. But an audition was arranged, and I traveled for eighteen hours from Paris to Nice in a second-class compartment, sitting up with seven others all the way. I had brought a pretty frock to wear, but at the station I was told that the Master would hear me at once. Never will I forget that audition! The drive along the palm-dotted Promenade des Anglais, the dancing blue waters of the Mediterranean, the roses and oranges in the green gardens, and then, the Villa Vergemère high up on the hill, with all of Nice and the sea at its feet.

The great hall of the Villa served as a waiting-room for the pupils and several were gathered there when we entered. I heard two tenor voices singing, one old and hollow, the other young and gorgeous, and I thought, "The Master is no more in his prime, vocally." But wonder of wonders! the young voice was de Reszke's, and the poor youth was struggling painfully to imitate its golden quality.

At last we were ushered in and presented by Louis Vachet, that faithful and loving valet-secretary. I entered an enormous room, beautiful in furnishings and beautiful in outlook over garden and sea. And as the room was enormous to me, so also was the figure tremendous that approached me. Jean de Reszke was not an unusually tall man, but he stood so erect, his carriage was so magnificent, his presence so majestic, that one felt cowed and small on first meeting. At least, so it was with me.

He strode toward me with outstretched hand, hoping I was well, and what had I brought to sing for him? I, remembering the grit of the long journey upon my hands and clothes, stammered something of apology and brought out, of all things, the "Ritorna Vincitor" from A ï d a. There probably has never been a worse performance. The Master heard the dust in my throat and the nerve-shattered breath, the faulty production, and being a great artist, it tortured him. "You are using only a third of the voice God gave you, and you know nothing whatever of breath-control," he cried out at me when I had finished. "Oui, mon ami," said a rich contralto voice from behind a screen, "mais elle a beaucoup d'autres choses." It was Madame de Reszke, still unseen.

"Sing something else," he said. So I sang d'Erlanger's "Morte," and that was a happier choice, being simpler and more within my powers.

"That is better. Now sing something in English." Ah—now I was on the home stretch, in my own tongue and easily within my reach, vocally. The song was cordially received.

"So," said the Master, "you have much to learn, but I can teach you. Come tomorrow for your first lesson."

"But, Mr. de Reszke," I faltered, "I came here to ask only your honest opinion of my voice. Shall I go on sacrificing my life to it? Or if mine is to be only a mediocre career, let me put my energy and ambition into something else. I want to pay you for your frank and honest opinion." Then he questioned me about my past work, my hopes, my finances. Learning that there were no "finances," he made that generous proposal which I have quoted.

And so began my lessons with Jean de Reszke. Does one tell of the years of striving; of the hopeful march up the hill and the despairing plodding down; of the musical phrases begun so many times and never, never finished; of the handkerchiefs torn to bits in an agony of trying to do what the Master wanted: of Koko's screeching when the lessons were bad—Koko, that green monster of a parrot who loved only the Master and the Master's art, who sat upon his shoulder as he came down the staircase every morning at nine, and went back up again when the long teaching day ended? No—one remembers only the miracles along the way; the days when a bit of blue showed through the darkness of unfolding understanding, the rapturous joy of the Master when the tone was right and the phrase artistically rendered; the rare "bravoes" and the smile of pleasure when he was satisfied. De Reszke sang like a god in those last three years of his life, when I knew him. He sang with the basses, with the contraltos, with the sopranos, and, of course, with the tenors. There was no phrase too difficult, no cadenza too florid for his limpid tone. He sang high C's all day long and could spin them from a fortissimo to a pianissimo in a way that was uncanny. He allowed no falsettos with the tenor, adhering strictly to a natural, manly head quality. His singing was so beautiful, so controlled, so refined, so effortless, that one did not dare to defile the air with a vocal attempt afterwards. Often, after listening to him, I could not sing; I could only weep. They had said to me, "You will worship the Master." But I had replied, "We Americans do not worship!" Ah, I had not known de Reszke! How many times I found myself kissing his beloved hand, and my tears must have told him what my tongue could not. Jean de Reszke did not like sentimentality—he did not like tears or fawnings. He liked work well done, difficulties overcome, souls aflame with inspiration.

The first Christmas in Nice promised to be a lonely one. Far from home and friends, living in a small room without heat or comforts, it had been a pleasant diversion to look at furnished apartments from time to time. One in particular, on the Promenade, looked out over the blue ocean, and its tiny kitchen, its balcony and the salon with piano, seemed a dream of happiness. I had told the Master of it at one of those precious tea-times at the Villa, when Madame de Reszke came down in all her fragile, cameo-like beauty; when Chou, her pet dachshund, lay curled on the sofa before the fire; when the Master sipped his tea and chuckled over some event of the day, or discussed topics dear to his heart. Then one came close to the lovable personality of de Reszke, and the singing-teacher was forgotten. The pupils who were privileged to have a lesson just before tea-time were often invited to stay, and a "comfy," happy time it was. French was generally spoken, but if there were some present who knew no French, then English was spoken, although the Master was disinclined to speak English.

So the Master knew of my longing for a little home, with cooking privileges. On the day before Christmas I was summoned for an extra lesson. I remember it well. It was from F a u s t, and I had made the Master laugh uproariously when I sang instead of "Le vent murmure," which means "the wind murmurs," "Le *ventre* murmure," which means "the stomach murmurs." At the end of the lesson, he pushed me to the door after wishing me "Joyeux Noël" and in my hand he left something. In the hall I opened my hand and found three one thousand franc notes. I rushed back into the studio exclaiming, "Master, what does this mean?"

"It is for your Christmas," he said.

"Cher Maître," I protested, "I have enough goodness at your hands without this."

"Allez-vous-en! Rent that apartment you liked so well." And he would hear no more from me, but went slowly back into the twilight, to the piano. I rushed to the apartment, praying it would still be "à louer." It was, and I moved in, and for many months it was my home, as it was the last place in which I saw my father alive.

There were gay and brilliant soirées at the Villa Vergemère, always with music by the pupils. These were attended by the élite. Frequently present were His Royal Highness the Duke of Connaught, ex-King Manoel of Portugal, Grand Duke André of Russia, Reynaldo Hahn, Edmond Clément, Mary Garden, and celebrities from all walks of life. These illustrious guests would sit in the front row, with Madame de Reszke, like a queen, in the center. But her husband was nowhere in sight. After the music he would reappear, to welcome his guests. How strange, for one so used to the plaudits of the world and the spotlight of the theater, to be so diffident of close, personal adulation! He shrank from it as if it embarrassed him unbearably. Had he found such demonstrations empty? or was he shy by nature? I never knew.

January 14 1925 was the Master's seventy-fifth birthday, and his last. Amherst Webber had prepared the pupils in the "Heil, Hans Sachs" chorus from D i e M e i s t e r s i n g e r. Also, we had bought a small silver loving-cup, a gift from the pupils. Promptly at nine o'clock, as was his wont, our beloved Master came down the grand staircase with Koko on his shoulder. He entered the studio, and forty voices sounded out a mighty "Heil, heil." Never has a Hans Sachs been greeted so overwhelmingly with love. He came towards us as we finished, and I brought him the cup, saying: "Beloved Master, may your years be many with us, and full of happiness and good health." He brushed me aside, knocking the cup from my hand, and strode hurriedly out of the room, and no one saw him more that morning. Ah me!—when later, after his death, I stood in his bedroom in the beautiful home in Paris, and saw the great vases inscribed "Our dear Jean," from Queen Victoria, the Tsar of Russia, from all the crowned heads of Europe, I blushed at our little cup and our big audacity. But the little cup remained on the piano, even after he was dead and gone.

In my third year, I went to Vichy with him. I had a lesson every day for three months, and at the end of that time the mist cleared away. I began to understand the teaching of the Great Master. What he asked me to do, I could do, and one day he cried, "Dieu soit béni, maintenant la voix est placée!" He began plans for an operatic performance with his pupils. He selected D o n G i o v a n n i, and me for the rôle of Donna Anna. All the autumn we worked, and in December we gave the first production. It was so successful that we were engaged for three performances in the Opera of Nice, and one under the direction of Reynaldo Hahn in the Opera of Cannes.

The Master was exceedingly anxious for a perfect performance at Cannes, both because of his friendship for Reynaldo Hahn and because Cannes is fashionable. He labored long and tirelessly with each and every member of the cast. Rehearsals went on all day for the Master. I remember sitting with him in a loge during the dress rehearsal in Cannes, when I had not to be on the stage. He sat with a little black shawl over his shoulders and seemed very tired. Later we went to dinner with him, and in the evening he wearily sat with his head in his hands, saying little. On Monday, lessons were canceled, an unheard-of thing. The Master had a little cold, it was said.

D o n G i o v a n n i went on in Cannes, but the Master was not there. It was a fine performance, and as I have listened to that opera in many countries since, I may say it was an extraordinarily fine performance. A week passed and there were no lessons. My heart was troubled, and although the gardens of the Villa Vergemère were filled with lovely roses, I could not resist buying a few and sending them with my love. The next day came a note which I believe to be the last writing of Jean de Reszke. It was his card, and on it was written: "Mille remercîments pour les magnifiques roses and thousand kisses. Bravo pour Donna Anna. Magnifique!"

The second week of anxiety was too much to bear; so I boldly asked to see the Master. His niece Minia told me that the doctor had ordered that no one should see him. "Only let me look in upon him, and I promise he shall not see me or be disturbed by me—my word of honor, Minia." So it was agreed. Minia tiptoed in, and I followed. There he sat, huddled in his chair, the little black shawl with its narrow green stripe over his shoulders. He seemed so alone, so disconsolate, so forsaken, sitting there. I stooped from behind and kissed his dear bald head, and a tear must have caressed him too, for he sat up suddenly, exclaiming, "Who kissed me then?"

"I did, dear Uncle," said Minia.

"No, it was not you. Who, then, kissed me?"

"Shall I get you some water?"

"No, no, laisse-moi tranquille."

His head sank again on his breast, and Minia closed the door. Alas, alas! that my word of honor kept me from a last tribute of love, for which he so hungered. O that I might have lifted up my face, that he might read the devotion, the anguish, the gratitude that was in my heart. O that I might have told him that, should nothing more come into my life, it was enough to have lived and known the nobility of Jean de Reszke.

On Good Friday afternoon, April 3 1925, he died, at a quarter to four. The young men students stood watch until he was taken to the Catholic Church in Nice on Monday, where an immense throng gathered for the simple service. Eight of his devoted ones, including Minia, whom he loved dearly, and myself, went with the body to Paris. At the grave only a few followed our beloved one. Strangely enough, although the magnificent flowers sent from many lands were wilted, the blanket of Parma violets—he loved Parma violets—which covered the casket, the last gift of the pupils to their master, was fresh. One violet fell at my feet as the casket was lowered, and I have it, a last token.

In the Montparnasse cemetery you may see the black granite monument inscribed "De Reszke." A palm wreath in bronze is inscribed: "A notre cher maître bien aimé—ses derniers élèves." There he rests, and each time I visit Paris I sit with him who lives in my heart, whose teachings are my vocal creed, whose memory is my undying inspiration.

BIBLIOGRAPHY

To LIST ALL the newspapers, magazines and books from which I have drawn materials for this volume seems unnecessary as well as impracticable. In general, I have scrutinized the leading newspapers in the important music centers of Europe and America, and practically all the musical magazines published in England, France, Poland and the United States, covering the period about which I have written. So far as I can trace the authorship of newspaper criticism of operatic performances, I find myself most indebted to the writings of Mr. George Bernard Shaw, Mr. W. J. Henderson, and the late Henry T. Finck.

Of the scores of books which relate to my subject, I list below only those to which a direct reference is made in the text by quotation or otherwise.

E. F. Benson *As We Were: A Victorian Peep-Show*. London: Longmans, Green and Co., 1930
David Bispham *A Quaker Singer's Recollections*. London and New York: Macmillan, 1921
Dorothy Caruso and Torrance Goddard *Wings of Song: The Story of Caruso*. New York: Minton, Balch and Company, 1928
Felix Clément and Pierre Larousse *Dictionnaire Lyrique*. Paris
Walter Damrosch *My Musical Life*. London: George Allen and Unwin, Ltd. New York: Charles Scribner's Sons, 1923
Emma Eames *Some Memories and Reflections*. New York: D. Appleton & Company, 1927
Henry T. Finck *Success in Music and How It Is Won*. New York: Charles Scribner's Sons, 1909
Wagner and His Works: The Story of His Life with Critical Comments. New York: Charles Scribner's Sons, 1901
Grove's Dictionary of Music and Musicians. New York: The Macmillan Company, 1928
Reynaldo Hahn *Du Chant*. Paris: Pierre Lafitte, 1920
Minnie Hauk *Memories of a Singer*. London: A. M. Philpot, Ltd., 1925
W. J. Henderson *Richard Wagner: His Life and His Dramas*. London and New York: G. P. Putnam's Sons, 1901
The Art of the Singer. New York: Charles Scribner's Sons, 1906
James G. Huneker *Steeplejack*. London: T. Werner Laurie, Ltd. New York: Charles Scribner's Sons.
Clara Louise Kellogg *Memories of an American Prima Donna*. New York and London: G. P. Putnam's Sons, 1913
Herman Klein *Great Women Singers of My Time*. London: George Routledge and Sons, Ltd., 1931
The Golden Age of Opera. London: George Routledge and Sons, Ltd., 1933
The Reign of Patti. London: T. Fisher Unwin. New York: The Century Company, 1920

Thirty Years of Musical Life in London: 1870-1900. London: William Heinemann. New York: The Century Company, 1903

Unmusical New York. London and New York: John Lane, 1910

H. E. Krehbiel *Chapters of Opera*. New York: Henry Holt and Company, 1911

Mary Lawton *Schumann-Heink: The Last of the Titans*. New York: The Macmillan Company, 1928

Jules Massenet *Mes Souvenirs: 1848-1912*. Paris: Pierre Lafitte et Cie, 1912

Nellie Melba *Melodies and Memories*. London: Thornton Butterworth and Co., Ltd. New York: George H. Doran Company

Helena Modjeska *Memories and Impressions*. New York: The Macmillan Company, 1910

Montrose J. Moses *The Life of Heinrich Conried*. New York: Thomas Y. Crowell and Company, 1916

Adolf Mühlmann *A Grobber Koll. Erinnerungen von Adolf Mühlmann*. Chicago: Gutenberg Press, 1932

Lillian Nordica *Hints to Singers*. New York: E. P. Dutton and Company, 1923

Francis Rogers *Some Famous Singers of the Nineteenth Century*. New York, 1914

Anton Seidl: A Memorial. By His Friends. New York: Charles Scribner's Sons, 1899

George Bernard Shaw *Music in London: 1890-1894*. London: Constable and Co., Ltd., 1932

Albert Sowinski *Les Musiciens Polonais et Slaves Anciens et Modernes: Dictionnaire Biographique*. Paris: Librairie Adrien Le Clerc et Cie, 1857

Ellen Terry and Bernard Shaw: A Correspondence. London: Constable and Co., Ltd. New York: G. P. Putnam's Sons, 1931

The Letters of Queen Victoria: Third Series. London: John Murray, 1931

Felix Weingartner: *Lebenserinnerungen*. Zürich: Urell Füssli Verlag, 1929

TEXTUAL REFERENCES

See Bibliography for Publishers and dates of publication of the books mentioned

[1] *Les Musiciens Polonais et Slaves Anciens et Modernes: Dictionnaire Biographique.* By Albert Sowinski, p. 477.

[2] Compiled by the same author. Reszke (Emilia), z domu Ufniarski, amatorka śpiewu w Warszawie. Posiadała głos silny i dramatyczny i wystepowała często na koncertach no cel dobroczynny. Znając dobrze opery wielkich mistrzów, wykonała raz rolę *Desdemony*, na koncercie danym przez Towarzystwo Dobroczynności, około roku 1855 z wielkiemi oklaskami, Później śpiewła na koncertach Moniuśki i J. Wieniawskiego, w roku 1858. P. 321.

[3] An Act of Christening of the Parish of St. John of Warsaw for the year 1850, No. 155. This certificate is in the vault of Baron Leopold de Kronenberg of Warsaw, husband of the late Josephine de Reszke.

[4] An Act of Christening, Parish of St. John of Warsaw, No. 80 for the year 1856, also in Baron de Kronenberg's possession, as is the certificate for Viktor. In order to secure these Certificates of Christening the birth certificates had, of course, to be presented.

[5] May 7 1876.

[6] May 2 1874.

[7] Illustrated Sporting and Dramatic News.

[8] Daily Telegraph, July 21 1874.

[9] December 23 1896.

[10] Globe, April 20 1881.

[11] Memories and Impressions of Helena Modjeska.

[12] Illustrated Sporting and Dramatic News, August 2 1884.

[13] Herman Klein: Thirty Years of Musical Life in London: 1870-1900. Footnote, p. 211.

[14] Minnie Hauk: Memories of a Singer. London, 1925.

[15] August 1 1887.

[16] Klein, ibid., p. 224.

[17] Klein, ibid., p. 227.

[18] New York Times, October 30 1887.

[19] June 18 1888.

[20] The American Musician, July 28 1888.

[21] Ibid., pp. 254-5.

[22] Klein, ibid., pp. 251-2.

[23] Felix Clément and Pierre Larousse: Dictionnaire Lyrique.

[24] Herman Klein: The Reign of Patti, p. 250.

[25] Klein, ibid., p. 250.

[26] Romeo et Juliette.

[27] Le Matin, November 29 1888.

[28] Truth, June 29 1889.

[29] Klein: Thirty Years, p. 277.

[30] Ibid., pp. 278-9.

[31] E. F. Benson: As We Were: A Victorian Peep-Show, p. 159.

[32] Ibid., pp. 155-6-7.

[33] Klein: Thirty Years, pp. 243-4.

[34] New Leader, June 6 1902.

[35] July 29 1890.

[36] July 31 1890.

[37] Klein: Thirty Years, pp. 289-90.

[38] George Bernard Shaw: Music in London, 1890-1894. Vol. I, pp. 172-3.

[39] Entr'Acte, June 6 1891.

[40] Shaw, ibid., pp. 249-50.

[41] The Speaker, July 18 1891.

[42] Shaw, ibid., pp. 235-6.

[43] Ibid., p. 198.

[44] H. E. Krehbiel: Chapters of Opera.

[45] Richard Grant White, quoted by Krehbiel, ibid., p. 20.

[46] Krehbiel, ibid., p. 211.

[47] Chicago Daily News, November 11 1891.

[48] November 28 1891.

[49] Klein: Thirty Years, pp. 359-60.

[50] New York Times, December 15 1891.

[51] December 19 1891.

[51a] New York Dramatic Mirror, December 19 1891.

[52] The Pilgrim, April 1902.

[53] Entr'Acte, July 4 1891.

[54] Shaw, ibid., Vol. II, p. 227.

[55] Klein, ibid., pp. 263-4.

[56] Shaw, ibid., III, p. 45.

[57] Chicago Evening Journal, March 13 1894.

[58] Klein: Thirty Years, p. 361.

[59] Musical America, June 4 1910.

[60] Herman Klein: The Golden Age of Opera.

[61] Shaw, ibid., Vol. III, p. 243.

[62] Ibid., p. 268.

[63] Krehbiel, ibid., p. 254.

[64] Ibid., p. 258.

[65] New York Times, January 1 1896.

[66] Quoted by Krehbiel, ibid., p. 265.

[67] The letter was published in the Münchner Neueste Nachrichten, December 16 1895.

[68] Quoted by W. J. Henderson in Richard Wagner, His Life and His Dramas.

[69] Excerpts from Anton Seidl's literary essays are quoted as they appear in Anton Seidl—A Memorial. By His Friends.

[70] Ibid., p. 232.

[71] Quoted by Henry T. Finck in *Wagner and His Works, The Story of His Life with Critical Comments.*

[72] November 28 1895.

[73] W. J. Henderson in the New York Times.

[74] W. J. Henderson: The Art of the Singer.

[75] W. J. Henderson.

[76] F. O. Schwab in *American Musician,* quoted in London Musical Times, September 1890.

[77] "Nym Crinkle" in New York Journal, January 24 1897.

[78] New York Times, January 21 1900.

[79] New York Times, February 13 1897.

[80] New York Spirit of the Times, February 20 1897.

[81] December 31 1896.

[82] Music and Letters, July 1925, p. 198.

[83] Melba: Melodies and Memories, p. 163.

[84] David Bispham: A Quaker Singer's Recollections, p. 192.

[85] Chicago Journal, March 13 1897.

[86] Quoted in The Looker-On, Vol. 4, 1897, p. 441.

[87] New York Times, April 18 1897.

[88] Francis Rogers: Some Famous Singers of the Nineteenth Century.

[89] Cable to the New York Sun. Quoted in the Musical Courier, June 9 1897.

[90] As recorded in Musical Courier, September 8 1897.

[91] Ellen Terry and Bernard Shaw: A Correspondence.

[92] Monthly Musical Record, July 1897.

[93] Lute, July 1 1897.

[94] The Times, June 23 1897.

[95] Musical Courier, January 6 and 20 1897.

[96] Ibid., March 10 1897.

[97] Herman Klein: Great Women Singers of My Time, pp. 144-145.

[98] Melba: Melodies and Memories, p. 53.

[99] February 7 1897.

[100] Klein: Thirty Years, p. 391.

[101] Anton Seidl: A Memorial, pp. 258-259.

[102] The Times, July 5 1898.

[103] Hillary Bell in the New York Press, December 27 1898.

[104] Ibid.

[105] New York Evening Post, January 25 1899.

[106] New York Times, February 4 1899.

[107] New York Times, December 30 1894.

[108] Truth, July 12 1900.

[109] The Times, July 5 1900.

[110] Musical Courier, July 7 1900.

[111] The Times, July 9 1900.

[112] The Concert-Goer, August 11 1900.

[113] New York Times, August 21 1900.

[114] New York Times, January 5 1901.

[115] New York Times, January 18 1901.

[116] The Concert-Goer, February 2 1901.

[117] New York Times, January 20 1901.

[117a] The Looker-On, February 1897.

[118] Statement by Robert Grau, brother of Maurice, in Musical America, August 17 1912.

[119] Klein: Golden Age, p. 237.

[120] This example of Jean's mimicry is taken, by permission, from My Musical Life, by Walter Damrosch, p. 131.

[121] Dorothy Caruso and Torrance Goddard: Wings of Song—The Story of Caruso, p. 161.

[122] Musical Courier, March 22 1899.

[123] A Grobber Koll. Erinnerungen von Adolf Mühlmann.

[124] A Quaker Singer's Recollections, p. 292.

[125] Henry T. Finck: Success in Music and How It is Won, p. 221.

[126] Montrose J. Moses: The Life of Heinrich Conried, p. 201.

[127] Herman Klein: Unmusical New York, p. 61.

[128] New York Tribune, May 27 1925.

[129] Felix Weingartner: Lebens Erinnerungen, p. 211.

[130] Ibid., p. 392.

[131] L'Éclaireur de Nice, December 9 1924.

[132] Schumann-Heink: The Last of the Titans.

[133] New York Sun, April 6 1925.

[134] April 6 1925.

INDEX

OPERAS AND RÔLES